COMPUTERS IN ELEMENTARY MATHEMATICS EDUCATION

DOUGLAS H. CLEMENTS

State University of New York at Buffalo

Prentice Hall, Englewood Cliffs, New Jersey 07632

Library of Congress Cataloging-in-Publication Data

Clements, Douglas H.
    Computers in elementary mathematics education.

  Bibliography: p. 406
  Includes index.
  1. Mathematics—Computer-assisted instruction.
  2. Mathematics—Study and teaching (Elementary)
  I. Title.
  QA20.C65C58   1989   372.7   88–15253
  ISBN 0-13-167008-5

Editorial/production supervision and
    interior design: Serena Hoffman
Cover design: Ben Santora
Manufacturing buyer: Peter Havens

© **1989 by Prentice-Hall, Inc.**
A Division of Simon & Schuster
Englewood Cliffs, New Jersey 07632

Printed in the United States of America

10 9 8 7 6 5 4 3 2 1

ISBN 0-13-167008-5

PRENTICE-HALL INTERNATIONAL (UK) LIMITED, *London*
PRENTICE-HALL OF AUSTRALIA PTY. LIMITED, *Sydney*
PRENTICE-HALL CANADA INC., *Toronto*
PRENTICE-HALL HISPANOAMERICANA, S.A., *Mexico*
PRENTICE-HALL OF INDIA PRIVATE LIMITED, *New Delhi*
PRENTICE-HALL OF JAPAN, INC., *Tokyo*
SIMON & SCHUSTER ASIA PTE. LTD., *Singapore*
EDITORA PRENTICE-HALL DO BRASIL, LTDA., *Rio de Janeiro*

*To teachers dedicated to a new vision
of mathematics education,*

*To Mike Battista, for untold hours
of arguments leading to insights,*

and especially,

*To Holly and Ryan, who kept me
from going too fast—
often in the wrong direction*

CONTENTS

POWERFUL TOOLS   59

COMPUTER PROGRAMMING   76

Part III: Computers and the Evolving Curriculum

Part IV: Focusing the Vision

PREFACE

This book is addressed to those concerned with teaching mathematics to elementary school students. Given that computers are increasingly available in the classroom, there is a need to consider how these tools *can* be used and how they *should* be used to help students develop sound mathematical understandings. This book provides guidelines for such use, as well as numerous illustrations and suggestions for specific programs and activities.

To begin with the "big picture," Part I, Foundations of a New Vision, poses three critical questions: What are the present problems of elementary mathematics education? How do students learn mathematics? How best might computers aid in overcoming the problems and helping students learn? The answers to these questions can be surprising.

Part II, The Computer as Tutor, Tool, Tutee, introduces three roles the computer can play in the classroom. It can act as a sophisticated *teaching machine,* instructing students and monitoring their progress. It can serve as a *tool* for graphing or calculating. It can be *programmed* by students as they solve problems and explore mathematical ideas. For each of these roles, strengths, weaknesses, general guidelines, and specific suggestions are provided.

Part III, Computers and the Evolving Curriculum, provides detailed suggestions for using computers to teach the major topics in elementary mathematics education. Sample computer applications are examined in depth, and practical ideas for teaching are developed. Extensive lists of available computer programs are provided at the end of each of these chapters.

Part IV, Focusing the Vision, addresses four important questions regarding the implementation of computers into the classroom: When should we use computers? How can we integrate computer use into classroom routines? How can we integrate computer-enhanced mathematics with other subjects? How can we use computers to contribute to the mathematics education of students with special needs?

Thus, the focus of this book is not on computers per se, but on teaching mathematics *with* computers. Appropriate use of computers can help both teachers and students. This successful use, however, is not easily achieved. The goal of this book is to provide information to teachers who are willing to accept this challenge for the sake of their students. Such informed, interested teachers will pave the way for others and will gather immeasurable benefits for their students—and for themselves—along the way.

Douglas H. Clements

1

CHILDREN, MATHEMATICS, AND COMPUTERS

You are undoubtedly familiar with computers, at least to some extent. You've seen computer games and computer programs that give children practice with arithmetic facts. Whether or not you've actually worked with computers, the basic picture seems clear. You also have had years of experience learning, and possibly teaching, mathematics, and have developed certain impressions. This book offers a glimpse of new views—possibly visions—of how children can experience mathematics with computers.

I'd like to share visions of computers in mathematics education that may take a different perspective from those you've already seen. These visions may help you use computers to teach better mathematics and to teach mathematics better. But why *do* we need a new view of teaching mathematics, with or without computers? Doesn't present-day teaching represent the "best teaching"?

PROBLEMS IN ELEMENTARY MATHEMATICS EDUCATION

Results of the second and third National Assessments of Educational Progress (NAEP) in mathematics indicate major deficiencies in students' learning of mathematics. According to Carpenter et al. (1980), "students' performance showed a lack of understanding of basic concepts and processes in many content areas," and "it appeared that most students had not learned basic problem-solving skills, and attempted instead to mechanically apply some mathematical calculation to whatever numbers were given in a problem" (p. 28). Thus, it appears that the dominant focus of school mathematics instruction in the last decade has been on computational skills (which students are learning fairly well), but that the development of problem-solving skills and conceptual understandings has been inadequate.

Indeed, the NAEP provides empirical support for the National Council of Teachers of Mathematics' (NCTM, 1980) recommendation that teachers of mathematics provide opportunities for their students to be actively involved in learning, experimenting with, exploring, and communicating about mathematics as part of an environment that encourages problem solving.

This sounds grandly impressive. But what does this have to do with the "basics"? Let's ask a more *basic* question: How do children learn mathematics?

THEORIES OF LEARNING MATHEMATICS

Why Theories?

Many teachers seem to believe that the only reason that "theory" appears in books and courses is to satisfy some incomprehensible whim of the professor. It is true that theories in mathematics education are far from complete and that drawing direct implications for classroom practice is not always easy. It is equally true, however, that every "fact" gets its importance from being described from within the framework of some theory.

Let's look at a nonmathematical example. You have undoubtedly heard parents espouse the modern equivalent of "spare the rod and spoil the child." What theory lies behind this belief? Something like the following: Children share a certain natural tendency such that, without punishment (preferably physical punishment), their inherent selfishness and desire to break rules would grow without bounds. You have also undoubtedly heard a different opinion (usually from the parent of some young visitor who is tearing apart large portions of your house): "I don't want to stifle his curiosity and creativity, and besides, boys will be boys." Two theories are probably operative here: first, a misinterpretation of Freud's ideas about repressions; second, an impression that there is a natural tendency for males to misbehave vigorously, and that there is not much anyone can do about it. Understanding a bit about the theories that underlie their prescriptions would help these parents apply the theories more consistently and effectively. It also would help them apply them more correctly! One of these notions is invalid, the other (Freudian psychology) woefully misapplied.

In the preceding section we referred to two different approaches to mathematics education. One stated that learning is primarily a constructive process in which students take responsibility for building their knowledge; the other, that children have to be taught basic skills. Both are based on beliefs about mathematics and theories about how children learn. What are these theories? Is one more valid than the other? Are they incompatible? In this section we begin to answer these questions. The rest of the book will build on this beginning, based on the premise that:

> Without practice, theory is a flower not smelled or seen, a library whose dust-covered books are not read.

> Without theory, practice is a mere bag of tricks, a trivial compendium that, in mathematics education especially, may hurt more than it helps.

The Two Voices of Piaget

Piaget did not directly study teaching or classroom learning. Nevertheless, his investigations of the process of learning and the nature of knowing have profound implications for education. He stated two major ideas.

The first voice: The child actively constructs knowledge. Piaget believed that knowledge is not a state children are in, but rather a process in which they are engaged. Children know about balls and bouncing because they have played with balls and other objects that bounce. Thus, children construct their own knowledge. They learn by inventing.

But what of mathematics? Maybe we can accept that children learn about bouncing balls on their own, but can children really invent *mathematics* on their own? One interesting research study provides an answer. Groen and Resnick (1977) measured how long preschoolers took to solve simple addition problems. They found, as they expected, that it took longer for these children to solve 5 + 3 than it took them to solve 4 + 2, because the children would count 4 fingers (or other objects), then count 2 fingers, and then count all 6. Naturally, counting 5, then 3, then all 8 took more time. As they measured the children's responses over time, however, an amazing and unexpected thing happened. The times no longer fit the same pattern. Children began solving 2 + 8 faster than 4 + 5. The researchers examined the response times and discovered what was happening: The children were now starting with the larger of the two addends (e.g., 8) and counting up (or "counting on") from that number (e.g., "eight . . . nine, ten"). This took less time (even less time than did "five . . . six, seven, eight, nine"). *During the research study, these 4-year-old children had invented, on their own, a new and sophisticated method of solving addition problems—a method they had never been taught!*

This study is not the only one showing such results. We now know that students of all ages invent their own solutions for solving mathematical problems. Unfortunately, they are not usually rewarded for such inventions (most of which are never even recognized by the teacher). They are often told to "do it the right way."

Piaget believed that children must be engaged in direct action with the content of the curriculum. He also believed that this occurred too infrequently in school.

> If the aim of intellectual training is to form the intelligence rather than to stock the memory, and to produce intellectual explorers rather than mere erudition, then traditional education is manifestly guilty of a grave deficiency. (Piaget, 1970, p. 51)

Piaget suggested that educators provide children with things and ideas to manipulate that will make them conscious of problems and will encourage them to find answers for themselves. Because real comprehension involves reinvention by the child, the teacher should be less the giver of lessons and more the organizer of engaging, problematic situations.

Is the need for this type of education as urgent today as when Piaget wrote? The NAEP results indicated that students "perceive their role in the mathematics classroom to be primarily passive. . . . They feel they have little opportunity to interact with their classmates about the mathematics being studied, to work on exploratory activities, or to work with manipulatives" (Carpenter et al., 1980, p. 36). Remember, too, that problem solving was their weakest area. It is no wonder that the National Council of Teachers of Mathematics recommends that students be actively involved in learning, experimenting with, exploring, and communicating about mathematics.

The second voice: Development proceeds through stages.   A stage is a period of time in which a child's thinking reflects a particular mental structure. Piaget's periods follow an invariant sequence, with each period building on and incorporating the previous one. The *sensorimotor period* starts at birth and ends at about 2 years of age. Infants' learn through sensory and motor activity. They begin with reflex actions and gradually integrate them into exploratory and experimental actions.

The second period, from approximately age 2 to 7, is the *preoperational stage*. Children learn to use images and language. These symbol systems begin to free thought from concrete action. However, there are limitations to thought during this period. The symbols cannot be manipulated to produce completely logical thought sequences. Preoperational children's thought is:

> *Centered.* They find it difficult to take another's point of view. They also "center on," or consider, only one aspect of a situation and ignore other aspects.
>
> *Irreversible.* They cannot move back and forth between situations, relating before to after.

For example, you might show a child two rows of blocks, matched one to one:

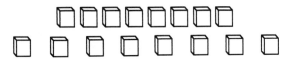

While he or she is looking, spread out one row and ask: Do the rows have the same number of blocks, or does one row have more?

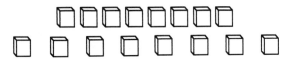

The child probably will center on the length of the row, ignoring the density (how close the blocks are to one another), and state that the second row contains a greater number of blocks. The child does not see that one could reverse the action by moving the second row back into one-to-one correspondence with the first. Children do not conserve number; they do not believe that the number of objects in a group remains the same (is conserved) when the spatial arrangement of the objects is changed.

From about age 7 to 12, during most of the elementary school years, the child is in the period of *concrete operations*. Children can think logically, applying such operations as classification, ordering, reversibility, and conservation (of number, and also of length and area). They can decenter, taking others' perspectives and taking into consideration several aspects of a situation. They can reverse their thinking; for example, they might understand that any addition can be "undone" by a subtraction operation.

But these students have not yet achieved the final period of *formal operational thought*. When they do, they will be able to deal with abstractions and hypotheses that have no direct connection to the real world. They will be able to think about ideas, about thoughts themselves. They will grasp such abstract notions as proportion. They will address problems systematically, scientifically.

Many theorists and teachers believe with Piaget that students actively learn mathematics. They manipulate objects and ideas in a continuous process of building up their own understandings. Not everyone, as we shall see in Chapter 4, believes that students' thought is absolutely "bound" by a given developmental period (actually, Piaget would have agreed to an extent). However, knowledge of these stages of cognitive growth is invaluable to teachers for understanding the thinking processes (and "errors") of their students.

Richard Skemp: One Name (Mathematics), Two Subjects

In the words of Richard Skemp, there are "two effectively different subjects being taught under the same name, 'mathematics'" (1976, p. 22). One subject, *instrumental mathematics,* consists of a limited number of "rules without reasons." The other, *relational mathematics,* is "knowing both what to do and why." It involves building up conceptual structures from which a learner can produce an unlimited number of rules to fit an unlimited set of situations. As Skemp continues, "what constitutes mathematics is not the subject matter, but a particular kind of knowledge about it" (p. 26). From this perspective, the current elementary mathematics curriculum is deficient because it neglects relational understanding. There is too much emphasis on instrumental understanding—formal symbolism and naming—and not enough on analysis, synthesis, and problem solving—on *meaning*.

To Skemp, mathematics is a system of concepts that becomes organized at increasingly higher levels of abstractions. To learn these concepts, students need examples, such as meaningful applications of arithmetic operations (e.g., subtraction). Such concepts, once learned, serve as meaningful examples for higher-level concepts. Rote or instrumental learning actually blocks later learning, because students do not build the necessary mental structures that support higher-level concepts.

Two Kinds of Worthwhile Mathematical Thinking

Skemp's arguments seem plausible; children should develop thinking processes. But don't they need practice for mastery? An answer to this question has come from research in psychology. There are two different types of worthwhile mathematical thinking. One, *automatic thinking*, involves fast, effortless performance. If certain skills and facts are not learned well, too much of children's thinking (cognitive processing capacity) is used up, and there is not enough left for higher-level problem solving. For example, children ultimately have to be able to count forward and backward from any number, without having to "think about it" too much.

The other kind of thinking is *reflective thinking*. Here, children are consciously aware of the problem and the solution processes they use to solve it. Although it is still true that children need lower-level skills and knowledge to become "experts," they also need to develop reflective thinking at each stage of their development of mathematical knowledge. Therefore, from the earliest years they need to be challenged to solve problems based on the skills and knowledge they currently possess. This helps them organize all their knowledge into strong, useful frameworks upon which future learning can be built.

Wait. Why is "automatic" thinking good, but "rote" or "instrumental" mathematics bad? Aren't these really two names for the same thing? No. Automatic thinking is necessary, but it can be distinguished from rote recitation of facts or mechanical processing of numbers. Students who have automatized a process they have learned with understanding can—at any point—pause and explain what they are doing and why. Students who have learned by rote cannot; they are on a meaningless treadmill of mechanical manipulations.

In somewhat simplified terms, then, we actually want students to act

FIGURE 1-1 Jon Secaur contemplates a problem-solving program with his students. (Photo by Gary Harwood.)

unconsciously in some situations and consciously in others. Both types of mathematical thinking are needed to develop micro-mathematicians. Understanding, however, must be the foundation in all cases. Automaticity is developed after reflective thought. Practice follows meaning.

Robert Davis and the Idea of Frames

Like Skemp, Robert Davis (1984) believes that different types of learning are possible. He makes an analogy with a German song, which can be learned with or without meaning. You can mimic the sounds without understanding what they mean, or you can understand both the tune and the words and thus enjoy the full meaning of the song. Similarly, one way of learning mathematics builds meaning; the other does not.

Frames.   What is "relational understanding"? Davis explains that children who understand mathematics have built up a large number of ideas that serve as a foundation for learning. These ideas are structured in frames. As a first nonmathematical example, read this passage:

On Saturday, John told his date that he was hungry and walked into the building on the right. They sat for a while. Then John left money on the table, paid the cashier, and left. They barely made it in time for the first feature.

What's interesting about this? Not the story itself (obviously), but what people can do after they read the story. The average person can answer the following questions: Did John and his date go to a restaurant? Did John order food? Did he eat it? Did he mistakenly lose the money he left on the table? Did he go to a movie that night?

What's so amazing? *None* of the answers are provided in the passage (check this carefully yourself). Why would most people know the answers? If asked about the story an hour later, why would they swear the passage had *said* that John went to a restaurant? On the slightly more ridiculous side, how do they know that John's "date" was not a dried fruit? (Be nice, now!)

What people do is use mental *frames* in understanding the story and answering the questions. A frame is a large knowledge representation structure that includes a considerable body of information. Most of us have quite specific frames for "dates" and "restaurants." We know that a Saturday night date is a person, and that two people on a date often eat at a restaurant and go to "features" at a movie house. We know that when people are hungry, they often go into restaurants and buy food. At the restaurant they usually order food; the food is brought by a waiter (male or female, do you think?); they leave a tip in addition to paying for their food; and so on. These frames provide us with the hooks upon which we hang what we read, hear, or see.

Frames even ask us mental questions. For instance, they tell us to look for certain information: Where did John and his date go? What was the date's name? What did they do afterward? At what kind of restaurant did they eat? More than this, if they are able, readers even answer these questions whenever the story doesn't: They went to a restaurant first, then a movie. Yes, they ate. It's not certain what kind of restaurant they ate at, but John left a tip, so it probably wasn't a fast-food restaurant. And so on.

Let's try one more experiment with frames. Read the following passage (adapted from Shuell and Lee, 1976). Try to remember and understand it.

> With hocked gems financing him our hero bravely defied all scornful laughter that tried to prevent his scheme. Your eyes deceive, he had said, an egg not a table correctly typifies this unexplored planet. Now three sturdy sisters sought proof forging along sometimes through calm vastness yet more often over turbulent peaks and valleys. Days became weeks as many doubters spread fearful rumors about the edge. At last from nowhere welcome winged creatures appeared signifying momentous success.

Test yourself. Try to retell the passage. Done? Now I'm going to provide you with two words to help you activate a relevant frame in your mind that provides a context and connections for the story, and that automatically answers questions (fills in the gaps) implicit in the story. Please read the two words, then reread the passage and try to retell it again. The two words are given at the end of this chapter.

How much more of the passage could you remember after reading the two words? How would you compare your first and second readings in terms of "meaningfulness"? Also compare how you *felt* during the two readings. If you're like most people, during the second reading you remembered more words, could "make sense" of the story, and felt comfortable and in control rather than "lost."

When we teach mathematics without meaning, we deprive our students of such frames. We force them to memorize numerous unconnected bits of information. We lead them to believe that mathematics doesn't make sense. We undermine their self-confidence and motivation to learn by creating feelings of confusion and helplessness.

Before we discuss their importance in mathematics, let's summarize some characteristics of frames that have implications for education:

> Frames are the foundation for understanding. We understand something by "retrieving," or "bringing forth from our memory," relevant frames (as we did when we read the "date" passage). Using these frames helps us answer questions and "fill in the gaps."
>
> Frames are never "erased." New frames are built, but old ones are never deleted. (Teachers know that even after seemingly successful instruction, children revert back to earlier ways; this is actually a strong original frame reasserting itself.)
>
> Often, frames that have their roots in "correct" early learning cause errors when they are misapplied in later situations. (Examples of this important characteristic are provided in the next section.)
>
> Similar frames are usually shared by most people (e.g., the restaurant frame and many mathematics frames).
>
> Frames are built on ideas and actions that we first learn in our earliest years. This important notion deserves elaboration.

Number, inequalities, and addition can be traced back to our initial childhood encounters with "'nother" (as in "I want 'nother cookie"). This is the notion of *more* and *one-more,* or $+1$. An infant's fascination with taking things out (e.g., clothes from a dresser) and putting things inside other things (not always the things adults would like) is a precursor of such geometric ideas as inside and outside, closed figures, volume, and many more. As teachers, we must continue to build up and build upon these basic frames, and help children not to overgeneralize. What we are doing is no less than helping children create the building blocks for the rest of their life's learning!

As an example, consider Davis's story of Alex, a 5-year-old girl whose brother, Paul, was age 3.

Alex: When Paul is 6, I'll be 8; when Paul is 9, I'll be 11; when Paul is 12, I'll be 14 (she continues until Paul is 18 and she is 20).

Interviewer: My word! How on earth did you figure all that out?

Alex: It's easy. You just go "three-FOUR-five" (saying the "four" very loudly, and clapping hands at the same time, so that the result was very strongly rhythmical, and had a soft-LOUD-soft pattern), you go "six-SEVEN [clap]-eight," you go "nine-TEN [clap!]-eleven." (Davis, 1984, p. 154)

Alex had learned to count at home and school. But she had never learned how to add, and certainly hadn't learned addition facts such as 12 + 2 = 14. How had she accomplished such remarkable mathematical thinking? Because she had experienced addition in her life. Through gathering stones and blocks, she had built her own intuitive addition frame. She also had frames for counting and for rhythmic patterns (from games, rhymes, songs, etc.). What she did was put these frames together in a way she had never done before—*and in a way no one had ever taught her to do*—to solve a mathematical problem. This is the way frames are built. This illustrates, too, that frames are built through the creative actions of children—Piaget's "re-invention of knowledge."

More arithmetic frames.   What do you think the most common erroneous answer is to the following?

$$4 \times 4 = \underline{}$$

One of the most common answers is "8." Why? Probably because students seldom had to look carefully at the arithmetic operation sign (the "×"). In the past they completed great numbers of addition exercises and had thus created a strong frame. But no discrimination was ever required for the *plus* sign! They never had to look at it. Old frames are never deleted, so a strong addition frame was activated.

What should teachers do? Ask the question the student actually answered!

Teacher: How about this? (Shows 4 × 4 = ___.)
Student: 8.
Teacher: What's 4 *plus* 4?
Student: Oh, I mean 16!

What has happened? The student retrieved the wrong frame. When the second question was asked, the contrast between the two helped to sort things out. An instant replay turned on a warning light and the student saw the error on the first question, which was reanswered by retrieving and applying the correct frame.

The addition frame is necessary, of course. What is harmful is that students have completed masses of exercises without enough variety and challenge, without enough thought and discussion.

Let's look at another example. Without variety, the students' addition frame "runs" only on two inputs (i.e., all exercises have been like 3 + 5 = ___ or its vertical form). No wonder that this frame leads students to the following answer:

$$
\begin{array}{r}
463 \\
+\ 29 \\
\hline
692
\end{array}
$$

Why? Because they (their addition frames) believe that "you must add two numbers together." The 4 must be added to some number, and the 2 is the closest!

The same teaching and learning methods affect all operations and all mathematics. To make our last example more vivid, please write a number sentence that will solve the following problem *before* reading on. Don't perform the computation.

What is the cost of 0.31 gallon of gas if 1 gallon costs $1.10?

Did you answer like most students: 1.10 ÷ 0.31? Now give the number sentence for this one, which has "easy numbers":

What is the cost of 3 gallons of gas if 1 gallon costs $1.00?

Was your answer 3 × 1? Most students (and adults) see plainly that multiplication is the correct operation for the second problem. Why, then, do they divide in the first problem, which is the same situation with only the numbers changed? The reason lies in their frames for multiplication and division. Multiplication is seen only as repeated addition. When you multiply, "you get bigger numbers." Division is seen as repeated subtraction, yielding "smaller numbers." In answering the first problem, students' frames were working against them in several ways:

They may have noticed that 0.31 gallon would be smaller than the cost of 1 gallon. Because their division frame included the notion that division "makes smaller numbers," they divided.

Because multiplication is based on a frame that is linked only to repeated addition (e.g., 3 × 4 = 4 + 4 + 4), they resisted multiplying by a fraction (i.e., how can you add 1.10 less than once?).

This does not imply that teachers should, for example, avoid introducing multiplication as repeated addition. They should, however, understand that once firmly established, such frames never disappear. Even when abstract, formal mathematics has been acquired by the student, the early frames influence mental behavior. Thus, teachers should help students build frames that are as meaningful, powerful, and free of incorrect generalizations as possible.

Mathematical Thinking: To Put It Simply

Mathematics is not just counting and naming numerals. It involves a combination of *conceptual knowledge*—the ability to understand things, and *procedural knowledge*—the ability to do things. Children should come to understand mathematical concepts such as number and space, and how concepts are related. They should also learn to do mathematics by solving problems; mathematics is a way of thinking. Students who think mathematically have a tendency to see mathematical structures in real situations, use mathematics to represent those situations, and find, solve, and explain the mathematical problems inherent in the situations.

COMPUTERS AND MATHEMATICAL THINKING

Computers and Mathematics Education

Enter the computer. As an all-purpose device, it is ideally suited to provide the different types of experiences necessary to develop different types of meaningful mathematical thinking. As a highly interactive device, it is ideally suited to engage energetic students with opportunities for active learning: thought-provoking experiences to develop reflective thinking, and well-designed practice to develop automaticity. It can help manage and individualize instruction. It can teach concepts dynamically. It can invite exploration of topics previously left for the high school or university because they involved tedious calculations or motion. It can challenge students to solve realistic problems and explore mathematical ideas. It can weave together problems from mathematics and other disciplines into integrated wholes.

But if teachers use it without a full understanding of mathematics education, the computer can also be used incorrectly to teach rote, instrumental mathematics. *Quality teaching of mathematics involves helping students learn the meaning of mathematical ideas and the power of mathematical processes.*

Seymour Papert: "Teaching Children To Be Mathematicians"

Papert (in Taylor, 1980) objects to the view of "technology and education" as

> inventing new gadgets to teach the same old stuff in a thinly disguised version of the same old way. Moreover, if the gadgets are computers, the same old

teaching becomes incredibly more expensive and biased towards its dullest parts, namely the kind of rote learning in which measurable results can be obtained by treating the children like pigeons in a Skinner box. (p. 161)

Papert argues for a grander vision of the education process in which children are not processed by a machine, but rather use technology themselves to manipulate, to extend, to apply to projects. Through such activity, children gain a greater and more articulate mastery of the world, a sense of the power of applied knowledge, and a self-confidently realistic image of themselves as intellectual agents.

Stated more simply, I believe with Dewey, Montessori, and Piaget that children learn by doing and by thinking about what they do. And so the fundamental ingredients of educational innovation must be better things to do and better ways to think about oneself doing these things. I claim that computation is by far the richest known source of these ingredients. We can give children unprecedented power to invent and carry out exciting projects by providing them with access to computers.... (p. 161)

Computers can make previously abstract and subtle mathematical concepts concrete and clear. Much of what seemed to children to be "distant from the real world turns into concrete instruments familiarly employed to achieve personal goals" (p. 162).

Would we teach English by drilling students on grammar and spelling, but never asking them to read or write a story? According to Papert, that is what we do in mathematics. We teach children the rules of the game, but we never let them play. People have some idea of what reading and writing are all about, but they believe mathematics is something you "know." Being a mathematician, however, means doing, not just knowing, mathematics. Children should work creatively in mathematics. Papert believes that, properly used, a computer can provide ways of "teaching children to be mathematicians vs. teaching about mathematics" (p. 177). We can teach a mathematical way of thinking. (Papert's own major contribution to this endeavor is discussed in Chapter 4.)

Thus, we do not need widespread "computer literacy," as usually defined—that is, knowledge of bits, bytes, RAM, and ROM, or awareness of social uses of computers, although these are valuable to some students in some contexts. We do need to find ways to use computers to encourage a new mathematical way of thinking.

INITIAL GUIDELINES

Listen to both voices of Piaget.

Constructivism

Approach mathematics as a problem-solving activity. Encourage children to find answers for themselves.

Encourage children to develop skill in asking questions.

Use high-level (conscious, reflective) questioning, and encourage high-level peer interaction.

Assist children, but only enough to get them going again.

Maintain a balance between teacher-directed activities and student-initiated projects.

Developmental Considerations

Know what lies behind children's errors and why particular processes are difficult for them.

Use child development as a guideline for choosing computer applications. Findings of developmental psychology can help you determine what to expect of children at each age level as they are engaged with computer (and noncomputer) activities, and they help you view these activities critically. However, you should also recognize that certain computer applications may enable accomplishments that exceed traditional expectations.

Use computer activities as a bridge. Computers should not replace all concrete activities. Many computer programs are best used as a bridge between initial real-world, movement-oriented experiences and abstract mathematical representations. However, let us not uncritically accept such overly simplistic models as "concrete to pictorial to abstract." We must remember that—from the beginning—mathematics happens in children's minds. They do not abstract mathematics from concrete things, but from their *actions* on these things. As we shall explore in more detail in later chapters, mathematical ideas like number are not "out there." As Piaget has shown us, they are constructions—reinventions—of each human mind. "Fourness" is no more "in" four blocks as it is "in" a picture of four blocks. It is created by the child who can build up a representation of number and connect it with either real or pictured blocks. Computers can often provide representations that are just as personally meaningful (i.e., concrete) as real objects, but also are more manageable, "clean," flexible, and extensible. "Concrete" is, quite literally, in the mind of the beholder. *Good concrete activity is good **mental** activity.*

Teach relational, rather than instrumental (rote), mathematics. Students should learn concepts from examples and strive to understand how concepts are connected. Emphasize analysis, synthesis, and problem solving. Evaluate students' understanding—the way they tackle new, although related, mathematical problems—rather than mechanical calculations.

Develop both reflective and automatic thinking, as appropriate. The development of meaningful concepts is the first step. Then those processes that must be automatic should be practiced, but not too much. *The ideal amount of practice is the **least** amount necessary to master a skill.* Teachers often misuse drill and practice, applying it too soon and in situations for which conceptual approaches would be more appropriate. Note also that students practice such skills while applying them to the solution of problems. *As much practice as possible should occur in the context of higher-level experiences. Finally, given the usual limited availability of computer resources, give priority to the development of reflective thinking.*

Develop powerful and appropriate frames.

Teach mathematics meaningfully, providing experiential frames so that students can make sense of mathematical ideas.

Reinforce definitions with informal, intuitive language (which helps form and reinforce useful frames). Of course, students' informal language can be inaccurate and misleading. The teacher's responsibility is to lead them to root out inaccuracies and develop more powerful informal representations and language.

Help students learn by metaphor.

Help students make connections between real-world and more formal representations of mathematical ideas.

Strive to understand the frames your students possess. Interpret errors in terms of these frames rather than as "sloppiness" or "laziness."

Develop every new mathematical idea of technique as a tool for accomplishing some sensible goal.

Teach mathematics not as facts and techniques but as creative, reflective constructions of relationships between ideas.

Don't miss the forest for the trees. Students should build and do and talk mathematics!

Recognize that teaching mathematics meaningfully is not easy.   It is easier to teach "the facts" than to help students build meaningful frames. But at least students will appreciate our efforts, right? Not necessarily. First, we've helped them exercise the all-too-human tendency to enjoy and expect having things "handed to us." They often respond to requests to do some real thinking with complaints unconsciously designed to wear teachers down: "You don't help us." "It's too hard." "No one else ever made us do this before." Second, appreciate what you are asking students to do. Imagine a fifth-grade boy whose teacher has asked him to stop applying mechanical procedures and begin making sense of mathematics. It is as if he were hanging over a cliff, clutching a single branch (mechanical procedures learned by rote). The teacher is leaning over the edge of the cliff, asking him to let go of that branch, offering a hand that will enable him to climb onto firm ground (meaningful learning). But the boy has never experienced the support of that hand before, and if he lets go of the branch, the possibility of falling (failing) is all too great. Besides, with his low confidence, he's usually looking down, out of fear, rather than up. It is hard to give such students a hand, but don't stop trying. They have nowhere else to go.

Begin with a decision: What should be learned?   Determine what should be learned. Not what *is* learned, not what *could be* learned (even with computer), but what *should be* learned because it is of the greatest benefit for students. Then ask if and how computers may contribute to students' learning of mathematics. In other words, revise the curriculum only if the "new" ideas have a higher priority than those they would replace. Doing something on the computer because it *can* be done makes the computer the goal, not the means.

A better goal is to develop the ten truly "basic" skill areas identified by the National Council of Supervisors of mathematics:

1. Problem solving
2. Applying mathematics to everyday situations
3. Alertness to the reasonableness of results
4. Estimation and approximation
5. Appropriate computational skill
6. Geometry
7. Measurement
8. Reading, interpreting, and constructing tables, charts, and graphs
9. Using mathematics to predict
10. Computer literacy

Ensure that computer uses are consonant with the principles and goals of the mathematics program. The role of the computer is not to replace teachers. The goal is to extend what students and teachers can do with mathematics, thereby changing what and how mathematics is done.

Focus on computers as tools students can use to construct knowledge of mathematics.

SUGGESTED READINGS

Davis (1984) provides a fascinating and fruitful description of the way people learn mathematics. Don't be afraid to "skim" sections that involve mathematics with which you are unfamiliar. Instead, read for the "big ideas." Interview several students and interpret their mathematical understandings from Davis's perspective.

Skemp (1976) describes his ideas about "relational understanding and instrumental understanding." Which best describes the manner that *you* understand mathematics? Which best describes your students' understanding?

Note for p. 8: Christopher Columbus.

2

COMPUTER-ASSISTED INSTRUCTION AND COMPUTER MANAGEMENT

Taylor (1980) introduced a framework for classifying educational computing: use of the computer as a tutor, tool, or tutee. As a *tutor,* the computer functions as a sophisticated teaching machine, teacher's aide, or audiovisual device. The purpose is to teach students skills, facts, or concepts. Usually, the computer presents information, the student responds, and the computer evaluates the response to determine what to present next. Elementary schools use computers in this way—typically termed Computer-Assisted Instruction (CAI)—more than any other. The purpose of another tutorial function, Computer-Managed Instruction (CMI), is to assign students to lessons, monitor and record their progress, and in other ways help the teacher plan and manage the instructional program. CAI and CMI may coexist in the same computer program.

As a *tool,* the computer must have a program entered into it that performs a specific function, such as graphing or calculating. Students can use this tool to solve problems, experiment with or search for information (data), or explore some mathematical phenomenon. Using the computer as a *tutee* is a fanciful way of saying that the student is programming the computer—"teaching" the computer by specifying a set of instructions that will solve a particular problem. Properly structured, such experiences can help students learn about mathematics, logic, computers, and their own thinking processes. In Chapters 3 and 4 we discuss the tool and tutee uses, respectively. In this chapter we describe the role of the computer as tutor.

COMPUTER-ASSISTED INSTRUCTION

Drill and Practice

Several programs provide simple practice in counting for young children. One places from 0 to 9 objects on the screen and waits for the child to type in the number (*Primary Math/Prereading* from MECC; see Fig. 2–1). If the answer is correct, a smiling face and the numeral appear; if not, the numeral is crossed off the list. Most drill and practice programs share certain characteristics with this one.

Purpose

To provide practice on skills and knowledge to help students remember and use that which they have been taught.

Methodology

1. Linear (progresses in a "straight-ahead" fashion, usually without branching to explanations if a student's responses are incorrect).
2. Repetitious.
3. Format: computer presents exercise; student types in response; computer informs student if answer is correct. If it is, computer goes on to next exercise; if not, computer asks the student to try again at least once before supplying the answer.

Strengths

1. Can efficiently build skills, due to individualization and feedback.
2. Can provide types of feedback that are not normally available in classrooms: for example, speed of response or comparisons of today's performance to that of yesterday or last week.
3. Is interactive (the student must actively respond to the program; the program responds to the student); sustained attention to the student.
4. Ensures that student is practicing correct response.
5. Can motivate student to perform what otherwise could be boring activity or repetitious practice.
6. Is easy to use.
7. May handle recordkeeping and other aspects of instructional management.

Weaknesses

1. Usually addresses discrete sets of lower-level skills only.
2. May use narrow range of teaching strategies.

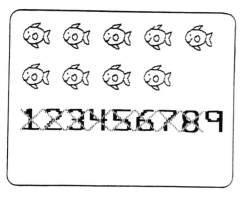

FIGURE 2-1
Counting practice. (From *Primary Math/ Prereading*, Minnesota Educational Computing Consortium)

3. May be boring if not well constructed.

4. May not correct erroneous concepts.

5. Necessitates considerable access to computer facilities (one or more computers available for periods of time that are long enough to provide sufficient hands-on experience for each student).

Drill and practice programs vary widely within this general framework. Some provide feedback in the form of elaborate sound effects and graphics, to the extent of mimicking arcade games. For instance, *Math Blaster!* (Davidson & Associates) is a fast-action game that reinforces basic facts in the four arithmetic operations and skills with fractions and decimals. There are five levels of difficulty for each skill. In addition, teachers (or students) may create their own lists of problems and save them on the disk. Whichever list is chosen, the object of the game is to compute the answer and launch the corresponding rocket. The problem appears at the top of the screen (see Fig. 2-2). The game can be played at five speeds.

This program encourages students to recall facts quickly and therefore constitutes an acceptable drill. Programs with elaborate graphics and sound, however, do not *necessarily* promote higher achievement. They may distract students from the task.

Other drill programs automatically advance the skill level minute by minute as the student's mastery increases. Some keep elaborate records concerning when material should be presented again, when to introduce new

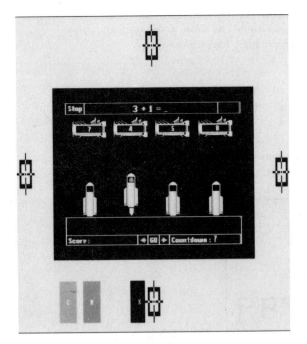

FIGURE 2-2 *Math Blaster Plus.* (Courtesy of Davidson & Associates, Inc.)

material, and even individual student's learning styles. Psychological research provides some guidelines for deciding among the many variations.

Implications from Research and Theory

Is the sole rationale for drill that "students need more practice"? From the perspective of cognitive psychology, complex tasks such as mathematical problem solving demand that many of the subskills reach the level of automaticity—fast, effortless performance (recall "automatic thinking" from Chapter 1). That is, the student has to be able to perform these skills without thinking about them consciously. This frees space, or capacity, in the student's conscious mind ("working memory") so that attention can be devoted to the more complicated aspects of the task.

Drill and practice might have a place in the instructional application of computers. But its use must be planned. The subskills practiced should be those necessary for the performance of higher-level skills. They should receive enough attention so that they achieve the status of automaticity—not only accurate, but effortless and rapid performance. Students should practice *only* essential subskills that they already understand but have not yet mastered. They should receive practice in situations where both correctness and speed are necessary. CAI is ideally suited to provide just this type of practice—if it is constructed on sound principles.

Research on interference in learning implies that computer drills should present only a few items at once. When these items have been learned, a new, small subset should be introduced as items already learned are systematically reviewed. Drill sessions should be short and spaced, rather than long and concentrated. Students should be able to resume drills with the same items on which they were working the preceding session. Review of incorrect items should be automatically scheduled by the computer (more on this "adaptive instruction" in the CMI section of this chapter).

In initial learning, students should receive positive reinforcement following each correct response. Once a basic level of responding has been achieved, reinforcement should be administered on an intermittent schedule (i.e., not every correct response should be reinforced; see Shuell & Lee, 1976).

Programs designed to increase automaticity in essential skills should emphasize accuracy and speed to provide drill in areas in which students fully understand the meaning of the concept or procedure, such as *Math Blaster!* is designed to do. Careful readers may have noted an apparent contradiction: One strength of drill was that students practiced correct responses; a weakness was that they may not correct flawed concepts. Both are true. Students in self-paced, individualized programs have been shown to attain the ability to supply correct answers without having developed an understanding of the underlying concepts. Like any drill, CAI drill should complement teaching for meaning.

When drill is appropriate, it should be planned and structured carefully, according to the guidelines presented here. For example, it makes little sense to use an expensive machine to provide workbook-type drill without utilizing its capabilities for providing the proper number of new items, individualized review, and full record keeping. Unfortunately, *not many currently available programs have these features.* Following are suggestions for the use of worthwhile drill and practice programs.

Appropriate Use

For situations in which there exists a set of essential skills that are already understood, but necessitate intensive practice with immediate feedback.

Suggestions for Use

1. Use drill after an understanding of the concepts has been developed.
2. Ensure that children have the intent to memorize and respond automatically.
3. Use short, frequent sessions in conjunction with regular conceptual review.
4. Introduce only a few new facts/skills at a time.
5. Vary drill activities and ensure that enthusiasm remains high.
6. Praise students and keep visible records (e.g., simple charts). Make sure that students develop a strong self-concept as they develop skills.
7. Make sure that students practice only those skills on which they need practice. Use the minimum amount of drill needed to achieve the objective(s).
8. Practice those skills that require immediate feedback.
9. If computer resources are limited, have students take turns. (Two might share a computer, depending on the program.)
10. Use programs that follow research guidelines. Optimally, they should:
    Emphasize the skill, not irrelevant graphics.
    Be carefully sequenced and well organized.
    Present only a few items at once and provide systematic, spaced practice.
    Emphasize differences between similar items at first, then deemphasize these differences.
    Provide discrimination practice where appropriate.
    Gradually increase the size of the "chunks" of information presented.
    Resume each session with the items from the preceding session.
    Provide adaptive instruction.
    Maximize students' time on task.
11. Make sure that *you,* not the machine, determine how much and what kind of drill is needed. Also, encourage students to take some control over their use of the program. They need to begin to "learn how to learn." For example, many students do not know how to improve their scores on drill-type tasks. One teacher helped students understand that the process they were using (e.g., counting) inhibited their performance, and that they could use the computer to identify which facts they knew least well so that these could be practiced at home. This dramatically improved the students' performance (Bransford, Sherwood, & Hasselbring, 1986).
12. *Consider omitting this application of computers if scarce computer resources force a choice between drill and more important problem-solving-oriented applications.*

Tutorial

Tutorial CAI teaches new subject-matter content. It attempts to interact with a student in much the same way as a human teacher would in a one-to-one situation. Some of the better programs use a Socratic questioning approach. In this technique, the student is asked leading questions. The computer then accepts his or her response, gives appropriate feedback, and either provides more information or asks additional questions.

The following is a brief excerpt from a simple tutorial, *Adding Fractions* by Don Ross (Microcomputer Workshops). Step-by-step instructions are presented. For instance, for $\frac{1}{3} + \frac{5}{6}$, the program prints:

```
1) Change to least common denominator.
2) Add.
3) Reduce.

Press 1 to begin to change the denominators.
```

When "1" is pressed, the screen displays, "The least common denominator (1cd) of 6 and 3 is 6! Type 6." The student is walked through the entire process, with the computer telling her what to type and providing explanations for each step.

For subsequent problems, the student takes a more active role. For example, for $\frac{5}{9} + \frac{3}{7}$, the student must:

```
Choose one:
    1) Change to least common denominator.
    2) Add.
    3) Reduce.
```

If the student erroneously chooses "2," the program responds, "To add fractions, you must have common denominators." After choosing "1," the student reads, "Enter least common denominator." If her response is incorrect, she is prompted to try again. If incorrect again, she reads, "I'm going to show you how to find the least common denominator (1cd). Pick one of the following methods: 1) Multiples of the denominators; 2) Prime factors; 3) Both. If the student chooses "1," the screen reads:

```
List the multiples of each denominator
up to the product of the denominators.

        9           7
       18          14
       27          21
       36          28
       45          35
       54          42
       63          49
                   56
                   63

The lcd is the smallest number that is a multiple
of both denominators, 63.
```

The student then enters "63" and reads "9 times ____ = lcd." The program continues, providing corrective feedback as needed (e.g., "Numerator and denominator must both be multiplied by 7, which is the same as multiplying $\frac{5}{9}$ by 1. $\frac{7}{7}$ = 1"). Finally, the screen appears as follows:

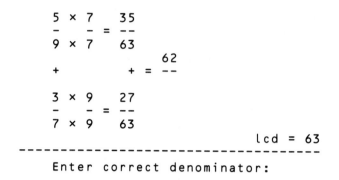

```
Enter correct denominator:
```

If the student enters "126," the program responds, "Do not add the denominators. The correct value is the least common denominator." If the correct answer is provided, a report is given on the student's performance in the following areas: procedural, computation, and least common denominator. Notice the branching that occurred when the student could not determine the lcd—only students who need this section are exposed to it. Similarly, the computer was programmed to respond to common errors, such as adding the denominators.

Tutorials differ widely in the amount of "intelligence" they display; however, many share the following characteristics:

Purpose

To teach the student about a particular well-defined topic.

Methodology

1. Linear progression with various amounts of branching.
2. Progression through a series of lessons.
3. Format: Didactic presentation and Socratic dialogue—presentation of information, questioning, and feedback dependent on the student's response; branching to explanations or review if student's responses indicate misconceptions.

Strengths

1. Can effectively bring forth the student's active involvement and understanding of knowledge.
2. Can provide individualized, self-paced instruction.
3. Ensures that student is participating in dialogue and responding correctly.
4. Although may be limited in certain ways, is more interactive than a lecture or textbook.
5. Can provide students with review of concepts or help students who have been absent to catch up.
6. Is easy to use.
7. May handle recordkeeping. May diagnose, prescribe, automatically present correct lesson/level of difficulty, and store information about student's performance, strengths, and weaknesses.

Weaknesses

1. Often uses a narrow range of teaching strategies.
2. Most possess severely limited "intelligence," especially compared to a teacher, who has considerable knowledge and intuition on which to rely. Therefore, the program's ability to respond to the student in a maximally helpful manner is also limited.
3. Similarly, most cannot participate in a rich, meaningful dialogue; instead, they follow a restricted multiple-choice format.
4. Overused, can become a game of "find out what the teacher wants." It can also promote a shallow and narrow understanding of concepts.
5. Necessitates considerable access to computer facilities.

Implications from Research and Theory

Most present-day tutorials make several crucial assumptions: for example, that mathematical concepts and abilities are best learned by mastering their fractionalized parts (reductionism), that these parts are best learned by practice, and that students will learn most effectively when rewarded for correct responses. In some situations, these assumptions are acceptable and this approach useful. However, full understanding of mathematics necessitates more than this, and where the assumptions are not feasible, such tutorials should not be used.

Gagne has applied research findings from cognitive psychology to the design of CAI. He has designed nine events of instruction corresponding to internal learning processes. The basic outline is shown in Table 2–1 (Gagne, Wager, & Rojas, 1981; see that reference for examples applied to different types of learning outcomes). Many presently available tutorials leave out one or more of these events. (Note that drill materials usually provide extensive experience with two events, 6 and 7; tutorials typically include all the events but relatively less practice.)

Greater memory and programming will make sophisticated tutorial programs available for microcomputers, such as those developed by Alfred

TABLE 2–1   Internal Processes of Learning and External Instructional Events That May Be Used To Support Them

Internal Learning Process	External Instructional Event
1. Alertness	1. Gaining attention
2. Expectancy	2. Informing learner of lesson objective
3. Retrieval to working memory	3. Stimulating recall of prior learning
4. Selective perception	4. Presenting stimuli with distinctive features
5. Semantic encoding	5. Guiding learning
6. Retrieval and responding	6. Eliciting performance
7. Reinforcement	7. Providing informative feedback
8. Cueing retrieval	8. Assessing performance
9. Generalizing	9. Enhancing retention and learning transfer

SOURCE: R. M. Gagne, W. Wager, and A. Rojas, "Planning and Authoring Computer-Assisted Instruction Lessons," *Educational Technology* (September, 1981), pp. 17–26.

Bork at the Educational Technology Center at the University of California at Irvine. Bork has demonstrated that certain characteristics are essential to effective tutorials—intelligent branching; carefully designed screens integrating text, graphics, and animation; and "natural language interfaces." Although there is much to criticize in many tutorials—they are certainly not as effective as human tutors—research indicates that in conjunction with regular school lessons, as little as ten minutes per day working with CAI tutorials can significantly increase students' achievement (see Box 2-1).

Following are suggestions for the use of tutorials:

Appropriate Use

For situations in which a well-defined set of information must be acquired.

Suggestions For Use

1. Choose topics that lend themselves to a focused, Socratic questioning approach.
2. Use tutorials alongside other instruction and for review.
3. Avoid overuse.
4. Discuss the content of the program with students, or otherwise ensure that the concepts they are acquiring are complete and accurate.
5. If appropriate, let students work in pairs on the computer. Consider social and emotional goals—ensure cooperation and success.
6. Consider programs that employ other media, such as tape cassettes, speech synthesizers, and videodisks.
7. Be very critical of the programs you select.
   If they are based on reductionist assumptions, this should be appropriate for the task.
   They should contain the nine events of instruction outlined in Table 2-1.
   They should help students organize the material.
   They should present directed and open-ended activities at appropriate stages.
   They should display appropriate intelligence in responding to students.
   They should branch to appropriate material if a common error is made.

Demonstration

Used for demonstrations, the computer is an audiovisual aid, helping the teacher to illustrate mathematical concepts for the whole class. It has the added advantage over overheads and concrete materials in that certain aspects of the program can be changed almost instantly. For example, at higher grade levels it could be used for graphing (or plotting) equations. By changing $y = 2x + 2$ to $y = 4x + 2$, and then to $y = 2x + 4$, the teacher can clearly and quickly demonstrate both the relationship between each equation and its graphic representation and the relationships among the equations. The focus is on these relationships rather than on point-by-point plotting.

Purpose

Serves as a flexible audiovisual aid for illustrating ideas and an enhancer of the teacher's presentation to students.

BOX 2-1:   Research on Computers and Mathematics Education

Extensive reviews and meta-analyses of the research concerning the effectiveness of computer-assisted instruction have been conducted (Atkinson, 1984; Burns & Bozeman, 1981; Edwards, Norton, Taylor, Weiss, & Dusseldorp, 1975; Fletcher, Suppes, & Jamison, 1972; D. Forman, 1982; Hartley, 1978; Kearsley, Hunter, & Seidel, 1983; Kulik et al., 1984; Niemiec & Walberg, 1984; Visonhaler & Bass, 1972). Most of them combine results from all grade levels; however, they may provide directions for elementary education. There is general agreement on the following points:

1. Use of CAI either improves performance or shows no difference when compared to traditional classroom approaches; it can be approximately as effective as individual tutoring.
2. Specifically, mathematics programs supplemented with CAI are significantly more effective in fostering student achievement.
3. CAI usually yields these results in less time.
4. Computers can make the learning experience more exciting, satisfying, and rewarding for learner and teacher; students have a positive attitude toward CAI, frequently accompanied by increased motivation, attention span, and attendance.
5. It is not clear whether students given CAI lessons can be expected to retain as much information. Some early studies indicated that CAI-trained students did not retain as much of what they had learned; however, others have favored CAI. Undoubtedly, additional variables are affecting these results.
6. The lower the grade level (from college to elementary), the greater the effects. Effects are particularly strong for primary children.
7. CAI drill and practice is more effective at all levels with disadvantaged students. Certain studies show that high achievers gain more, others that low achievers are the greatest beneficiaries.
8. Results are often strongest for *mathematics,* and good results have been reported for mathematics problem solving, as well as factual material.
9. Drill is most effective when used for 10 to 20 minutes each day.

The implications of two studies are important to teachers. McConnell (1983) found that CAI positively influenced total mathematics and computational skills more than other treatments, whereas concept application skills were improved more by the regular mathematics curriculum. Although this finding is restricted to the type of computer programs used, it does warn teachers that many of the available programs are not designed to teach higher-level abilities. In another project, children exposed to a drill and practice CAI program in mathematics outperformed control group children; however, a close look revealed that the former made the same type of errors. They merely omitted fewer items (Alderman, Swinton, & Braswell, 1979). Thus they were more adept and efficient at answering questions without necessarily having a stronger grasp of the concepts. This suggests that teachers using drill and practice computer programs need to integrate closely use of these programs and classroom work on conceptual understandings. They need to make sure that their students possess the prerequisite understandings necessary to work with the program correctly—practicing, in other words, procedures that are both correct and meaningful to them.

Methodology

1. Presentation of information, possibly including user input, calculations, graphing, and so on.
2. Format: Demonstration of one or more concepts; use of computer as a tool for presentations; may be menu driven to allow access to various sections of program.

Strengths

1. Capitalizes on the computer's ability to provide fast computations, sound and graphics, feedback, and records of information, thus freeing the teacher from these tasks.
2. Provides a clean, organized presentation.
3. Can be efficient if it combines the advantages of learning from a teacher and from computers.
4. Allows interactive demonstrations in which the illustration of concepts is drawn from experimentation on data provided by the user, not from previously set up calculations.
5. Can be dramatic, including dynamic graphics and animation, randomness, and input from various measuring devices (e.g., measuring heat, light, etc.)
7. Maintains teacher control over the content and rate of presentation; "orchestrates" the lesson.
8. Allows one computer to serve the needs of an entire class.
9. Reflects real-world use of computers.

Weaknesses

1. Use may be inconvenient. Large or multiple screens are needed. Setup is not always simple.
2. Often does not actually extend the characteristics of the chalkboard or other audiovisual device.

Often, computer demonstrations are valuable to the exent that they utilize graphics and animation to illustrate mathematical concepts. Well-designed displays that are constructed one step at a time, or that show mathematical processes in action, can effectively illustrate ideas and uncover relationships. Number sentences may be enacted under the class's control, or shapes might be altered, segmented, and rearranged. These examples bring us to the essential requirement: *Computer demonstrations should be interactive demonstrations.* Otherwise, other media would do the job better and less expensively.

A more complex type of software is computer-guided teaching, wherein the computer guides the teacher through the steps of the presentation (Hativa, 1984). In addition to providing computations, animations, and sound, the software sequences and connects the topics, summarizes main points, and provides questions and problems for class discussion.

Implications from Theory and Research

Research on educational media has shown that children can learn from a wide variety of delivery devices, and that there appears to be little difference among these devices (Clements, 1985b). This indicates that computer demonstrations that are planned within a valid instructional design format will be effective. It also implies a caveat: Other devices—easier to manage and less expensive—may be just as effective. Computer demonstrations should be used when they significantly enhance the quality of a presentation.

Appropriate Use

To provide demonstrations or illustrations of mathematical concepts that benefit from the use of sequentially constructed graphics, animation, rapid computations, change, and/or interaction.

Suggestions for Use

1. Integrate the demonstration into the lesson as a whole, using it only at appropriate times.
2. Work through the program several times before using it in class, testing a variety of inputs (e.g., can it handle very large or negative numbers, or special cases such as zero?).
3. Maximize the benefit of the demonstration by encouraging individuals or small groups of students to use it following the whole-class presentation.
4. Evaluate demonstrations critically.

   Demonstrations should match the objectives of and enhance the lesson. They should be constructed to fit appropriately into one or more of the nine events of instruction outlined in Table 2–1.

   They should help the teacher and students organize the material.

   The computer should significantly enhance the presentation through its special capabilities. Even if graphics are used, an overhead, television, or movie might as well be used if the demonstration is not interactive.

   The material should be suitable for presentation to a whole class. Text type should be large and kept to a minimum. The teacher should be able to control the program easily, preferably from a distance. It should run quickly.

   For computer-guided teaching software, all elements of good instructional design should be present and the teaching strategies should be consistent with those of the teacher.

   Every demonstration should be flexible, allowing use by teachers with a variety of teaching styles, objectives, and levels of students. It should allow the teacher to move forward and backward to any section of the program.

Simulation

Simulations are models of some part of the world. They are imitations patterned after real-world environments, containing a series of problems. Popular games such as "Life" and "Monopoly" are simulations. Computer simulations are mathematical models that can be programmed to respond in realistic ways based on real-world information. Therefore, they can be motivating and may enhance transfer as students actually perform activities replicating those in the real world.

"Foreman's Assistant" is the most difficult of four simulations in the package *Survival Math* (Sunburst). It is appropriate for older students (with approximately a sixth-grade reading level). Following is an example of two students' interaction with this simulation. As you read, keep a record of the mathematical skills and concepts they would develop working with the simulation.

FOREMAN'S ASSISTANT

```
     YOU'VE  BEEN  HIRED  AS  A  CONSTRUCTION  FOREMAN'S
ASSISTANT.  YOUR  JOB  IS  TO  ESTIMATE  THE  AMOUNT  OF
MATERIAL NEEDED TO FINISH SIX DIFFERENT JOBS.

     YOUR  JOB  INCLUDES  MEETING  A  STRICT  TIME  SCHEDULE
AND  BUDGET  LIMIT.  YOU  MUST  COMPLETE  YOUR  JOB  WITHIN
30  WORKING  DAYS.  YOU  MUST  NOT  SPEND  MORE  THAN  $50
FOR MATERIALS YOU WILL NOT USE.

     TOTAL SPENT ON EXTRA MATERIAL $0.00
     WORKING DAYS LEFT: 30

     YOU  MUST  BUILD  FOUR  WALLS  OF  A  PLAYROOM.  ALONG
EACH  WALL  YOU  MUST  PLACE  VERTICAL  SUPPORTS  NO  MORE
THAN  16  INCHES  APART.  CORNERS  WILL  HAVE  TWO  SUP-
PORTS. ROOM DIMENSIONS ARE 15 FEET BY 20 FEET.

     HOW  MANY  VERTICAL  SUPPORTS  ARE  NEEDED  FOR  ALL
     FOUR WALLS? 58
          THAT'S RIGHT.

     YOU MUST PAY $1.59 FOR EACH OF
     THE 58 SUPPORTS.
          TOTAL COST IS? 92.22
          YOU GOT IT.

     TOTAL SPENT ON EXTRA MATERIAL $0.00
     WORKING DAYS LEFT: 26

     YOU  MUST  PURCHASE  WALL  PANELS  FOR  THE  PLAYROOM.
EACH  PANEL  IS  4  FEET  WIDE  AND  8  FEET  TALL.  THE
PLAYROOM  CEILING  IS  EXACTLY  8  FEET  ABOVE  THE  FLOOR.
REMEMBER  THE  DIMENSIONS  OF  THE  PLAYROOM  ARE  15  FEET
BY 20 FEET.
```

As students continue through the simulation, determining how many bricks are needed to face one wall and how many gallons of paint to purchase to cover the remaining three walls and the ceiling, the number of working days remaining is reduced. If students overestimate any material, they must pay for the extra material (without exceeding the $50 limit).

"Foreman's Assistant" involves students actively in developing several mathematical skills and abilities within the context of meaningful problems. Other simulations—actually the more traditional type—allow children to explore the effect of a number of variables. For instance, in "Sell Lemonade" they determine what combination of three variables—number of cups made, price of each cup, and number of signs made—maximizes their lemonade stand's profit (see Chapter 10 for a detailed description).

Another program simulates a swinging pendulum. Children type in the specifics: weight, length of the string, height of the weight before release, and so on. They are to find out which variable changes the period (the length of time for each swing). What do you think of the program? Despite its interesting appearance, such a simulation should be used with caution. It may replace a valuable hands-on activity with an unnecessarily vicarious and abstract one. Students should swing the pendulum. They benefit from the motor activity—from the sensory input of feeling and manipulating real objects. In some cases, careful comparison of a simulation and a real-world event is beneficial; this is indeed recommended whenever possible. Thus, a pendulum simulation might be useful *if* it is used alongside experimentation with real pendulums, and *if* it allows children to form and test hypotheses about the physical world in a thoughtful and purposeful way. Such a simulation might allow children to stop the action of the pendulum at any point during the swing to examine the distance between the pendulum and the object. They could quickly, easily, and systematically vary relevant parameters (e.g., mass of object, length of string, length of swing). Playback capabilities would permit children to compare one swing to another. The trail of different swings could be recorded and compared. Children might construct an actual pendulum to gather ideas for more controlled, reflective problem posing on the computer. They could test the results of the simulation against the actual pendulum.

Simulations share most of the following characteristics:

Purpose

To promote problem solving, develop an intuition or sense about a particular situation (build a mental model of part of the world), facilitate the acquisition of skills and knowledge, and motivate interest in the subject and in learning.

Methodology

1. Often nonlinear.
2. Exploratory, discovery oriented.
3. Format: Provides a model of some part of the world through which children can learn by pretending, exploring, and manipulating.

Strengths

1. Allows interaction with and study of events that would otherwise be unaccessible due to expense, danger, or time constraints.
2. Can be motivating and highly interactive—permits learning by doing.
3. Is realistic; promotes transfer to out-of-school settings.
4. Can be efficient in the sense that it may remove distractions of real-world setting or allow student to control the rate of a process.
5. Promotes social interaction and discovery learning.
6. Lends itself to individualization in terms of a project approach.
7. Permits a wide range of teaching strategies (however, these are not always built in).
8. May allow one computer to serve the needs of an entire class.
9. Reflects real-world use of computers.

Weaknesses

1. Does not ensure that students are responding correctly (because they are designed to allow children to explore "wrong" paths; this could be seen as a strength if properly managed by the teacher).
2. Is relatively more difficult to use effectively; is an unfamiliar approach to education for many teachers.
3. If use is not well planned, can degenerate into an educationally trivial "beat the computer" game.
4. Often does not handle recordkeeping.
5. Is a copy of only some aspects of reality; may promote a misguided conception of real-world situations and problems.
6. Similarly, does not include other important aspects of the real world, such as physical action and sensory impressions.

Simulations can be categorized as continuous or interval. In continuous simulations, students must interact with the program steadily, completing the program in one sitting. Interval simulations allow students to interact with the program for a short period, leave to make decisions away from the computer, and return later, picking up where they left off. They allow more flexibility in planning.

Implications from Theory and Research

Properly used, simulations can make mathematics learning a "person-centered, constructive process" in which "students build and modify their knowledge" (recall Chapter 1). Their purpose is to provide representations of familiar situations—meaningful examples of mathematic ideas—with which students can experiment. The goal is to encourage reflective thinking as a way to develop more elaborate mathematical frames.

Simulations facilitate learning by simplifying the phenomenon. To promote transfer, they should add detail to imitate reality more closely as the student gains competence. Similarly, simulations might first provide tutorial-type assistance to students immediately, and gradually withdraw prompts and other types of assistance, letting more experienced students learn from the consequences of their actions.

Chambers and Sprecher (1983) have applied Bandura's social learning theory to the design of simulations—specifically, the four component processes that govern observational learning: attention, retention, conversion of symbolic representations into appropriate actions, and motivation. Thus, instructions for the simulation should gain attention, provide information concerning goals, and inform the student of the benefits of adopting the modeled behaviors. Simulations should enhance retention and the use of feedback in improving the modeling by including as much interaction as possible. Using a model that is as humanlike as possible will maximize motivation. In addition, high-status models should be used, and the subject matter should be made relevant to the student.

One dictionary definition for a simulation is a "sham." Although no simulation should trick a student, the caveat is real. Used unwisely, simulations can oversimplify or misrepresent real-world situations. Understanding of the complex and nonmathematical aspects of these situations must be developed by the teacher. Students should learn to critically evaluate simulations on these bases. Suggestions on using simulations follow.

Appropriate Use

To explore and develop intuition about events and situations that are too dangerous, expensive, complex, or time consuming to experience directly. To promote decision-making and problem-solving abilities.

Suggestions for Use

1. Do not use simulations as simple games.
2. Try out the simulation first yourself, then with a small group of students so that you can anticipate questions and problems.
3. Introduce the simulation with another trial run with the whole class so that everyone understands the procedures and general purpose of the program (not just what is to be done, but also what is to be learned).
4. Have students work in small groups for discussing the issues involved and making decisions.
5. Make management decisions:
   If time is short and only one computer is available, use whole-class presentations.
   If more time and/or computers are available, use small-group work. For continuous simulations, the completion time must be reasonable (5 to 15 minutes); consider the total time that must be scheduled.
   If all students are not using the simulation at the same time (especially necessary for continuous simulations), have other assignments for those not working with the computer which students can complete independently.
6. Have each group of students divide responsibilities in working with the program. Discuss what these might be and how they might be assigned. Simulations should develop social skills as well as academic skills.
7. As the unit develops, use guided questioning to lead students to develop concepts and strategies which help them succeed with the simulations. (This is more easily done with interval simulations.) One useful strategy is to change only one factor or variable at a time to observe its effects.
8. Have whole-class discussions comparing the strategies of different groups along with the results of those strategies and the assumptions that lie behind the simulations.
9. Have students read more about the subject of the simulation and report on their readings. The simulation could then be checked for accuracy.
10. Evaluate simulations critically.
    Objectives and directions for simulations should be especially clear.
    Both the goals of the simulation and the benefits of adopting certain behaviors should be presented to students.
    Simulations should simplify the phenomenon at first, gradually adding realistic details.
    Other techniques to facilitate transfer and retention should be used, such as maximizing interaction and making subject matter relevant.
    Tutorial assistance should be provided at first and then should gradually be withdrawn, increasingly being replaced by learning from natural consequences.
    Simulations should include documentation specifying the variables and as-

sumptions of the program, background information, and other support material.

Instructional Games and Exploratory Programs

These programs, like simulations, differ from the traditional modes of instruction with which most adults are familiar. "Games" here does not mean drill and practice exercises transplanted to outer space. In true instructional games, the concepts to be learned are intrinsic to the structure and content of the game. These programs provide new miniature worlds for children to explore, and therefore share certain characteristics of simulations.

Bumble Games (TLC) is a collection of six programs that teaches number lines, number pairs, and graph plotting to children from kindergarten to third grade. The first program, "Find Your Number," teaches the number line from 0 to 4, as well as concepts of greater and less, by having the child guess a mystery number. The choice is highlighted on the screen and an arrow appears if the mystery number is greater (→) or less (←) than that guess. "Find the Bumble" extends children's skill with a number line to include a two-dimensional grid. The grid consists of four rows labeled A, B, C, and D, and four columns labeled 0, 1, 2, and 3. The child is to choose one letter and one number from the grid. He is then shown that this number pair corresponds to one square which is highlighted on the grid. The object of the game is to find the Bumble's secret hiding place. Clues are given ("It's down and to the right"); arrows are also provided. "Tic Tac Toc," a version of the tic-tac-toe game, reinforces these plotting skills and expands the grid to 25 points (see Fig. 2–3).

These are educational games. The final program, "Bumble Dots," is an example of an exploratory program. Here children are asked to enter dots on a grid by typing in number pairs. As each new dot is entered, lines are drawn to connect them. In this way, children create a picture, which is named by the child and displayed with an electronic fanfare (see Fig. 2–4). Ability to use computers, knowledge of numbers, plotting, spatial visualization, and creativity are developed simultaneously in this exploratory program. Other examples of exploratory programs are provided in succeeding chapters.

The game/exploratory category is quite diverse in its characteristics. However, many examples share the following features:

Purpose

1. To facilitate the acquisition of skills and knowledge, including principles and processes.
2. To motivate interest in learning.
3. To develop problem solving and divergent thinking.

Methodology

1. Nonlinear.
2. Exploratory, discovery oriented.

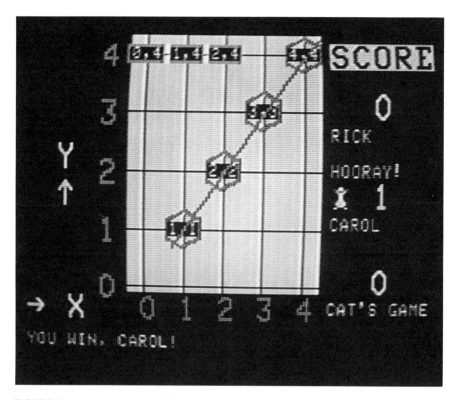

FIGURE 2-3 Tic Tac Toc, from *Bumble Games*. (The Learning Company)

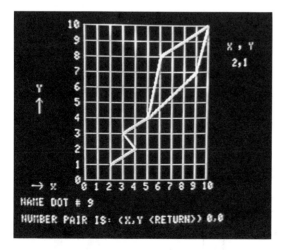

FIGURE 2-4
Bumble Dots, from *Bumble Games*. (The Learning Company)

3. Format: Provides a set of tools or a miniature (often fantasy) world which children use for explorations and productive play.
4. Games have clear goals, a set of (artificial) rules, elements of competition, and "entertainment" characteristics. In exploratory programs the student creates the goals, rules are less structured, competition is deemphasized, and the motivation is often in the student's creation or expression of an idea.

Strengths

1. Utilizes and develops convergent and divergent abilities.
2. Can be motivating and highly interactive.
3. Promotes social interaction and true discovery learning; children solve an actual problem that they pose themselves.
4. Can be individualized in terms of self-directed learning.
5. Can employ a wide range of teaching strategies.
6. Can be used again and again.

Weaknesses

1. Educational goals and objectives are not always clear.
2. Does not ensure that students are responding correctly.
3. Is relatively more difficult to use effectively.
4. If use is not well planned, can degenerate into little more than "playing with the computer."
5. Usually does not handle recordkeeping.
6. Is variable regarding requirements for computer access.

The most important question that teachers should ask themselves—about all computer programs, but especially about game/exploratory programs—is: "Why am I buying (or using) this program?" Not all interesting-looking games help children achieve important educational objectives. The program should not be the goal but a means of reaching an important educational goal.

However, well-designed games can have multiple goals. For instance, they might combine work on arithmetical facts with experience in problem-solving strategies. *How the West Was One + Three × Four* depicts a race between a stagecoach and a railroad engine. As a player, you must combine the numbers spun on three spinners using the basic operations (+, −, ×, /). The spinners in Fig. 2–5 have been combined as $2 \times 3 + 1 = 7$. After entering the equation, you must evaluate it. If you are correct, your marker advances that many units; otherwise, you lose your turn. If your marker lands on a city, you proceed to the next city. If you land on a shortcut (e.g., on 5) you take that shortcut (e.g., to 13). If you land on an opponent's space, he or she must go back two towns. (In Fig. 2–5b, the locomotive has sent the stagecoach back to the starting point by choosing an equation, $2 - 1 + 6$, that also yields the number 7.) Therefore, smart players can optimize their chances of winning by carefully selecting the best equation possible for their situation.

Implications from Theory and Research

Most theories of learning now consider motivation an essential component of learning. It is widely believed that CAI programs of all types, but games especially, "motivate" students to learn. Why? Although definitive answers are not yet available, several conjectures have been advanced.

Malone (1981) investigated the characteristics of computer games in an effort to ascertain what makes them intrinsically motivating. He found that three elements were especially important: *challenge, fantasy,* and *curiosity.* Each has several subelements. Challenge depends, first, on having a goal, an "object of the game." Good goals are personally meaningful and obvious.

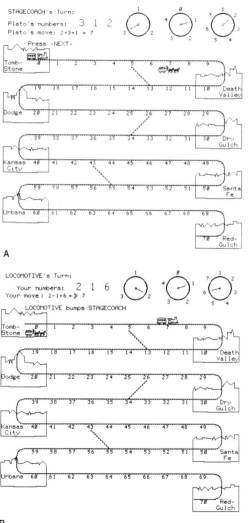

A

B

FIGURE 2-5
*How the West Was One + Three ×
Four* (Courtesy of Computer-based
Education Research Laboratory, Uni-
versity of Illinois at Urbana-Cham-
paign)

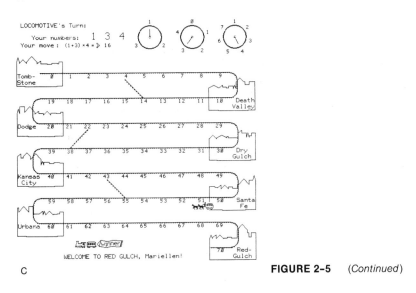

C

FIGURE 2-5   (Continued)

Students must receive some kind of performance feedback concerning their achievement of the goal. Challenge also depends on having an uncertain outcome. Computer programs might use variable difficulty levels (determined automatically or chosen by the student), multiple-level goals (environments that include scorekeeping or timed responses), hidden information, and randomness. Finally, challenge is motivating because it engages students' self-esteem. Continued motivation, of course, is dependent on success. Therefore, games should provide variable difficulty levels so that students can work at an appropriate level.

Fantasy should be intrinsic, that is, intimately related to the use of the skill. First, intrinsic fantasies may be more motivating. There is support for this notion from research on extrinsic versus intrinsic motivation in non-computer domains: If there is an integral relationship between the content of instruction and the content of the fantasy, students will be more interested in the subject matter in the future. Also, intrinsic fantasies may allow students to make analogies between what they know and what is to be learned, thus supporting that learning. Finally, the connected, vivid images may aid memory.

Curiosity can be both sensory and cognitive. Sensory curiosity involves attention-getting changes in graphics or sound. It can be used as decoration, to enhance the fantasy, as a reward, or, most important, as a representation system to enhance conceptual understanding. Cognitive curiosity can be aroused by showing students that their knowledge structures are incomplete, inconsistent, or unparsimonious.

Studies have shown that the use of noncomputer games raises achievement *if they are carefully selected to match curricular goals.* If games are not pertinent to mathematics skills to be learned and are not matched to students' age group and their individual needs, the more they are used, the *lower* students' achievement will be (Baker, Herman, & Yeh, 1981).

Another problem is that noncomputer games cannot simply be transferred to the computer without affecting their usefulness. For instance, a study by Bright (1984b) that used computerized versions of games designed to teach probability and geometry concepts to preservice teachers showed inconsistent, moderately discouraging results. Bright's research indicates that such seemingly insignificant characteristics of the computer environ‑ment as the orientation or size of the screen may have a detrimental impact on the possible benefits of a game.

Nevertheless, computer games can be effective. Kraus (1981) found that students exposed to a computer game designed to reinforce skills in addition facts got two times as many items correct on a speed test as did control students. The caveat is that without a proper introduction and clear purpose, games may lose much or all of their instructional benefit, as stu‑dents will not focus on important concepts and skills.

Appropriate Use

To achieve goals related to the development of independence, self-direction in learning, creativity, problem solving, positive self-concept, and positive attitude toward learning.

Suggestions for Use

1. Know what your goals are in using a game/exploration program.
2. Integrate games and explorations into the curriculum. Match games with your educational objectives.
3. Play the game yourself first. Then demonstrate it to the entire class.
4. Establish "class experts" who can help others play the game.
5. Through questioning, lead students to develop strategies that help them suc‑ceed with the game. (Done correctly, this has the advantageous side effect that students view the teacher as an ally rather than as a judge of their perform‑ance.)
6. Have whole-class discussions comparing the strategies of different groups along with the results of those strategies.
7. Try out the new strategies as a class.
8. Discuss what was learned. Make sure that students understand what is to be learned.
9. To help the whole child develop, encourage children to play games together. Make the experience a positive one socially and emotionally, as well as intellec‑tually.
10. Be especially critical of a game or exploratory program.
    It should achieve a significant objective in the mathematics curriculum.
    Goals and rules should be clear. The rules should be simple (and not more difficult than the mathematics content itself).
    It should provide a mathematically correct model that can be explored by students of different abilities.
    The educational aspect should be more salient than the entertainment aspect.
    Success should be dependent on the application of mathematical skill or knowledge, with an element of chance.
    The knowledge to be learned should be intrinsic to the structure and content of the game.
    The motivational elements of challenge, fantasy, and curiosity should be present.

EVALUATING MATHEMATICS SOFTWARE

Evaluation according to specific criteria is even more necessary for software than for printed or manipulative materials because (a) the teacher and children have less control over sequencing, use, and modification; (b) it is difficult to ensure that all important aspects of a program have been evaluated; and (c) most teachers are less familiar with computer materials. For these reasons, the following sections describe a series of steps and a checklist to use in evaluating software that will help ensure that the process is deliberate and complete. However, certain basic questions should be kept in mind at all times:

1. Is there a need for this instruction?
2. Is the computer the appropriate delivery device?
3. Is the instructional strategy appropriate?
4. Is the software appropriate for the students?
5. Is the software consonant with the curriculum and the principles on which the educational program is based?
6. Is the software consonant with the conclusions from theory and research described in the appropriate section earlier in this chapter?

Steps for Evaluating Software

  I. Establish goals first. Make sure that you know exactly what you want the program to do, and insist that it does it.
 II. Become familiar with the organizations and journals listed in the Appendix, which are dedicated to helping teachers locate and evaluate software. There may be a computerized data base that will allow you to search quickly for the programs you want (see also EPIE Institute, 1985).
III. When locating software, ensure that service is available, including someone who will willingly answer questions.
 IV. Obtain the basic documentation and program.
   A. Go through the program as a successful student would. Test the "intelligence" of the program by making creative or different responses.
   B. Go through the program as a less successful student would. Respond incorrectly, not only by making mistakes but also by typing letters instead of words, hitting the RESET (or RESTORE, BREAK, RUN/STOP, etc.) key, not following directions, and so on. Repeat the same incorrect responses and try different kinds of incorrect responses. What happens?
   C. If possible, observe several students using the program. Are they interested? Do they understand the program? Do they have any difficulties?
   D. Read the documentation, running through other parts of the program as needed.
 IV. Ask yourself the six "basic questions" listed previously.
  V. Complete the evaluation checklist provided in the next section.
 VI. Make a decision. If you decide not to purchase the program, return it promptly to the producer with a copy of the evaluation—a valuable way for educators to influence the quality of software.

Criteria for Evaluating Software

In this section we present a checklist that includes important criteria on which to base software evaluation (see Table 2–2). Explanations of selected categories of the checklist follow.

Identification

This portion of the checklist enables teachers to find the program that they need. Most programs developed for one type of computer will not run on other types that are not compatible. Therefore, it is essential to know exactly what hardware is required to run the software. As an example, one package requires:

> *Brand:* Apple II series
> *Memory:* 128K
> *Operating system:* DOS 3.3
> *Special language:* none
> *Disk drive*
> *Color monitor*

A few producers of software allow teachers to make their own inexpensive backup copies of the disk. Most, however, still "copy protect" their software; that is, they make it difficult to make a copy by normal means. If this is the case, make sure that a backup copy is provided or that one can be purchased for a reasonable price. For software that will be used on several computers simultaneously, you must ensure that: (1) it can be copied legally (i.e., a "site license"); (b) it can be "multiply loaded" into several computers from one disk legally; or (c) it comes in a "lab pack".

Description

Initially, teachers' greatest need is for a complete and detailed description of the program, including the subject/topic, objectives, prerequisite skills, age/ability level, instructional strategies (i.e., drill and practice, tutorial, demonstration, simulation, game/exploratory), and the presence of a management system (explained more fully in the next section). In addition, is the program intended to be used by individuals, small groups, or the entire class? Used in that grouping pattern, what is the average time it would take a student or group of students to use the program each day? Finally and most important, the narrative description tells what the program looks like, what it does, and how it works.

Evaluation

Content. The content of the software should match that of your mathematics curriculum. It should be educationally and mathematically significant. Both the mathematics presented and the spelling, grammar, and the like, should be accurate. The values of the program, whether explicitly

TABLE 2-2   Mathematics Software Evaluation Checklist

Identification

Name _____

Producer _____
   Address _____
   _____

Hardware required
   Brand _____
   Memory required _____
   Operating system _____
   Special language required _____
   Disk/tape/cartridge _____
   Equipment required (peripherals, number of
      disk drives, color monitor, printer, speech
      synthesizer, paddles or joystick, etc.) _____

Backup policy _____

Cost _____

Description

Subject/topic _____

Objectives _____

Preprequisites _____

Age/ability level _____

Instructional strategy _____

Management system _____

Program structure _____

Grouping _____

Average time of student interaction _____

Narrative description _____

Evaluation

	Rating	Comment
I. *Content*		
A. Appropriateness of content		
1. Does it match your curriculum?	_____	_____
2. Is it educationally and mathematically significant?	_____	_____

	Rating	Comment

B. Is the content accurate?

C. Are the values explicitly or implicitly presented those of your program?

Specifically, are positive beliefs about mathematics engendered?

II. Instructional considerations

A. Is it consistent with the principles of your educational program?

B. Instructional design
1. Is there a need for this instruction?
2. Is the computer an appropriate delivery device?
3. Are the objectives and purpose well defined?
4. Are prerequisite skills listed?
5. Are the learning activities well designed?
6. Are the assessments feasible?

C. Can it be modified for individual students?

D. Appropriateness of characteristics
1. Is the teaching strategy appropriate?
2. Does it stimulate convergent or divergent thinking appropriately?
3. Does the child control the rate and sequence appropriately?
4. Is the feedback appropriate?
5. Does it employ graphics (color and animation) and sound appropriately?
6. Is the management appropriate?

E. Are field test data available?

III. Social/emotional

A. Will the program motivate and sustain interest?

B. Will it build self-concept?

C. Does it encourage cooperation?

D. Does it encourage social problem solving?

(continued)

TABLE 2-2 (Continued)

	Rating	Comment
IV. Performance/operation		
A. Ease of Use		
1. Can it be used with little effort?	_____	_____
2. Are instructions simple?	_____	_____
3. Is input appropriate?	_____	_____
4. Are directions, menus, and on-line help available?	_____	_____
5. Is the level of difficulty appropriate?	_____	_____
6. Is the presentation clear and consistent?	_____	_____
B. Error handling		
1. Is the program reliable (free of bugs)?	_____	_____
2. Are keys that are not used disabled?	_____	_____
3. Can children correct mistakes?	_____	_____
4. Does the program limit the number of errors it allows before offering help?	_____	_____
5. Can the program handle diverse input?	_____	_____
C. Is the operation (i.e., loading before and during operation) fast?	_____	_____
V. Is the documentation for teachers and students adequate?		
A. Are clear directions for loading the program included?	_____	_____
B. Is there a full description of the program, including objectives, background, prerequisite skills, etc.?	_____	_____
C. Are support materials supplied?	_____	_____
VI. Global evaluation		
VII. Comments (strengths, weaknesses, potential)		

Rating scale: 0–5
  0 Characteristic does not exist in program
  1 Very low
  5 Very high

stated or hidden, should reflect those of your educational program. For example, games that are based on or that reward violence, or games that emphasize competition rather than cooperation, may be inconsistent with the values of the community and the school. Materials containing racial, ethnic, or sexual stereotypes should be avoided. Finally, positive beliefs about mathematics should be presented. For instance, the following beliefs might be engendered (usually, implicitly) by high-quality software:

> Mathematics is a worthwhile, interesting endeavor.
>
> A mathematical way of thinking is a powerful tool with which to understand the world.
>
> More than merely computation, mathematics involves problem solving, identification of relationships, pattern searching, understanding space, and much more.
>
> There is an underlying structure to mathematics which is more important than surface details.
>
> Problem solving is more than finding a rule to apply so as to get the answer. It involves defining the problem, choosing an appropriate representation and helpful heuristics, monitoring the solution processes, and more.
>
> In general, mathematics is orderly, predictable, and above all, understandable and learnable. Mathematics makes sense.
>
> Mathematics is constructed by people.

Instructional considerations. The software should be consistent with the principles on which your educational program is based, and it should follow the rules of instructional design. As mentioned previously, there should be a need for the instruction, and the computer should be the appropriate delivery device. It should have an identified purpose. Prerequisite skills should be listed so that it can be determined what skills or knowledge the child must possess before using the materials.

The learning activities must be well designed, following the suggestions presented earlier in this chapter regarding the appropriateness of different instructional strategies. Assessments, if included in the program, should be expected to meet the same standards as any other tests. They should be reliable, yielding results that you can trust. They should be valid; that is, they should actually measure what they purport to measure.

Programs can be individualized for students in many ways. Some, discussed in the following section, involve computer management of the assignments given to students. However, individualization may also involve the provision of rich environments for learning that can be explored at many levels of complexity and difficulty. Many computer games and exploratory environments are designed to be individualized in this way.

Although all programs should follow the rules of instructional design, it is a mistake to believe that all good programs should be identical in every way. Some characteristics are appropriate for one type of program but not for another. Thus, software should be evaluated in terms of the implications of theory and research for the specific type of CAI (as discussed earlier in this chapter).

Every type of CAI requires high-quality feedback. Research shows that effective feedback does not *reward* students; rather, it helps them locate and correct their errors. Feedback should provide *information* more than reinforcement. If offered, however, reinforcement must be well planned. In one counting program, a train chugs onto the screen containing a different number of cars each time. The child counts them and types the number. If correct, a new train chugs on; if not, the train falls apart. Which do you think young children would rather see? What does that encourage? The best reinforcement is tied to content. For example, some programs reward good performance by allowing entry to an exploratory activity that extends the lesson.

Is immediate feedback best? In some situations, feedback that is delayed is more effective. Immediate feedback is most useful for younger students or those being introduced to the material, for teaching knowledge-level objectives, and for enhancing short-term retention. Delayed feedback is most useful for more knowledgeable students, for teaching comprehension and application-level objectives, and for enhancing long-term retention. In these situations, students may benefit from thinking about their responses before receiving the computer's feedback.

Similarly, graphics, color, animation, and sound are valuable components when they support learning. When they help illustrate concepts, especially dynamic concepts, they are important aids. However, research has not shown that elaborate color graphics increase learning in every situation. Color has potential disadvantages. Color monitors are more expensive, and some children are colorblind to certain shades. High-quality software has options for those without color monitors, such as different black-and-white shadings. In addition, peripheral enhancements may draw the attention of many young children away from that which is important. For prereading children, for drawing programs, for programs that illustrate vocabulary words and the like, graphics are, of course, essential. There should be an option to turn off sound which is not essential.

Social/emotional. The program should be interesting to children, possibly containing elements of challenge, fantasy, and curiosity. In addition, many children are motivated to use programs that address them in a personal style, have a friendly tone and employ simple humor, use graphics and other computer capabilities in creative and significant ways, allow for a variety of responses, include a high degree of active involvement and control, provide appropriate, helpful feedback, and illustrate the child's progress.

Another concern is that programs sustain children's interest. Programs that are more complex or open-ended often maintain attention more effectively. Recall that competence motivation is enhanced by programs that provide exercises at an optimum level of difficulty. Programs that motivate children and sustain their interest are more likely to build the child's self-concept. Whenever possible, programs should also encourage the child to invent his own ideas, and allow each child to express his own creativity and personality.

Programs can be designed and used in ways to encourage, rather than discourage, interaction among students. Competition may be used effectively on occasion, such as between groups involved in a simulation or between students and the computer. However, both these examples also involve cooperation among students. Simulations that necessitate cooperation among students in a group are especially valuable. Student team learning, in which students study material in four-member heterogeneous learning terms and are rewarded based on average team performance, has consistently been shown to raise achievement (Slavin & Karweit, 1984). There is no reason not to utilize and extend this technique within computer environments.

Performance/operation. The program should be easy to use for both students and teachers, including demands on input (typing), reading level, attention span, and level of reasoning. Menus and help should be offered and readily accessible. Obviously, programs should be free of programming errors. But they should also handle errors by users. If someone enters a word instead of a number, the program should not freeze or fail ("crash"). (For a more detailed description of performance/operation, see Clements, 1985a.)

Documentation. Documentation, the written materials accompanying a program, should list the objectives and prequisite skills. It should supply a basic description of the content and structure of the program, including all the information described under identification on the checklist. Clear directions for using the program should be included, such as directions for loading, special keys and commands, and information about program flow and on-screen menus. Sample "runs" are helpful. Support materials should offer suggestions for introducing, integrating, and following up on the program. Background information and resources are useful. When appropriate, the materials should be tied to specific chapters in widely used mathematics textbooks. Some programs include a student workbook. Possibilities for program modifications should be described in detail. Some teachers want lengthy, detailed documentation. However, this is not always necessary for simple programs. The best often combine an extended discussion with short summaries and charts to serve both needs.

Remember that no single software evaluation checklist fits every type of program, and no software evaluation is satisfactory for all teachers. Educators must decide what their needs are and use the information available to help them meet those needs.

Beyond Categorical Thinking About CAI

Each of the five categories of CAI presented in this chapter has a place in the classroom (research on its effectiveness, mostly regarding tutorials and drills, was summarized in Box 2-1). However, some of the most promising and interesting applications of computers to mathematics education combine, or go beyond, these categories. For example, programs that combine categories might provide tutorial-type assistance to students working with a simulation or game. Applications that go beyond these categories might incorporate features of the computer as tool or tutee, which will be discussed throughout the remainder of the book. The development of intelligent computer-assisted instruction (ICAI), which will have the capability to "understand" the subject and the learner and thus engage in less structured instructional dialogues, will also stretch the boundaries of CAI beyond the categories presented here.

COMPUTER MANAGED INSTRUCTION

Management of Instruction

Carmen strode into room 116 with a purpose. She booted the class disk and took attendance for Ms. Fitzgerald's third-grade class. Before the advent of the computer, Carmen had hardly ever done the attendance; it seemed that the more vocal students were always chosen. Now, the computer scheduled these chores, just as it scheduled its own use for the day. Carmen checked this schedule, which revealed that Miranda was to work on her arithmetic skills first. Carmen put away the disk, walked by Miranda and tapped her on the shoulder, and then unobtrusively took her seat. Miranda booted the *Microtutor Arithmetic Skills* diskette that Scott had worked with yesterday and began to work on subtraction problems with no regrouping. Carmen glanced at her teacher, who was already well into her lesson with a small group, and thought, "Ms. Fitzgerald sure teaches a lot more!"

Carmen's observation was accurate, but only because her teacher carefully planned how she would use the computer to help her manage specific aspects of her mathematical program. Let's "flash back" to the week before as she prepares the computer management system.

Ms. Fitzgerald presses two keys simultaneously to enter the management system. She is presented with the main menu.

```
MICROTUTOR II    MANAGEMENT SYSTEM
1 - DISPLAY ALL STUDENTS' RECORDS (SHIFT-1) ...
    TO PRINTER
2 - DISPLAY ONE STUDENT'S RECORD (SHIFT-2) ...
    TO PRINTER
3 - ERASE ALL STUDENTS' RECORDS
4 - ERASE ONE STUDENT'S RECORD
5 - ADD/ASSIGN STUDENT PRESCRIPTION (LESSON DISK
    ONLY)
6 - TRANSFER RECORD(S) FROM DISK TO DISK
7 - RETURN TO LEARNING/TEST SYSTEM
8 - MODIFY LEARNING/TEST SYSTEM
```

To enter a new student into the system, Ms. Fitzgerald types "5." She is asked for the student's full name. The system then queries her about two sequences that can be altered to individualize the system. First, she has to adjust the difficulty-level step size (here, "difficulty" reflects the number of digits in each number in the problem and the response time allowed).

```
NAME:   DONALD   HANK

------------------------------------
DIFFICULTY  LEVEL  SEQUENCE  NOW:    0

------------------------------------
AVAILABLE  DIFFICULTY  LEVEL  SEQUENCES:

0.   ALL  LEVELS
1.   MIN.,  THEN  MAX.  LEVEL
2.   MAX.  LEVEL  ONLY

SEQUENCE  (NUMBER)  DESIRED  FOR  STUDENT?
```

She selects 0, as the records from Donald's previous school indicate that he is a slow student. The next screen displays choices for the instruction-level step size.

```
NAME:   DONALD   HANK

------------------------------------
INSTRUCTION  LEVEL  SEQUENCE  NOW:    0

------------------------------------
AVAILABLE  INSTRUCTIONAL  LEVEL  SEQUENCES:

0.   ALL  LEVELS
1.   OMIT  LEVELS  1  AND  3
2.   OMIT  LEVELS  1,  2,  3  AND  6

SEQUENCE  (NUMBER)  DESIRED  FOR  STUDENT?
```

Again, she chooses "0." For faster students, she may have skipped some of the levels (recall the description of several of these levels earlier in this section). Next, she is asked to select a problem type.

```
NAME:   DONALD   HANK

------------------------------------
DIFFICULTY  LEVEL  SEQUENCE  NOW:

INSTRUCTION  LEVEL:
------------------------------------
AVAILABLE  SUBTRACTION  TYPES:

1.   SNGL  DIG
2.   10  TO  19
3.   NO  REGRP
4.   REGROUP
5.   MXD  RGRP
```

```
6.   REGRP-0
7.   MX RGP-0
     --OR--
0.   BYPASS REMAINDER OF LESSON DISK

WHICH ENTRY TYPE (NUMBER) IS DESIRED FOR THIS
STUDENT?
```

The terms are mnemonics for types explained in the manual. She selects the same type as Scott worked on, "6. REGRP-0," which are subtraction problems in which regrouping is always required and in which students must "borrow" across zero. Finally, the instruction level is selected.

```
NAME:   DONALD HANK

----------------------------------------
DIFFICULTY LEVEL SEQUENCE NOW:   6- REGRP-0

INSTRUCTION LEVEL:
----------------------------------------
INSTRUCTION LEVELS:

1.   MEANING
2.   MEANING/RULE RELATIONSHIP
3.   DIRECTIONS/RULE
4.   RULE/REMEDIAL
5.   DESCRIBING RULE PROCESSES
6.   SHORTCUT INSTRUCTION
7.   SHORTCUT (MENTAL) CALCULATION
8.   TIMED PRACTICE
9.   MASTERY TEST

WHICH INSTRUCTION LEVEL (NUMBER) IS DESIRED FOR THIS
STUDENT?
```

She chose "1" for Donald. She is then asked if she wishes to add another name with the same prescription or with another prescription.

Actually, although teachers can make these assignments in *Arithmetic Skills* themselves, they do not have to. It is a diagnostic/prescriptive system as well. Most teachers would have the students work with the pretest disk first, which determines which types of problems the student can solve and whether the student has mastered prerequisite skills such as the basic facts. The program uses this information to make students' assignments automatically.

In addition to assigning the type of problem, the system sets the two step sizes (difficulty- and instruction-level sequences) and automatically adjusts these during the year according to how efficiently the learner is progressing (e.g., a learner might move from difficulty-level step size 0 to 1 by missing fewer than 10% of the questions asked during instruction). At level 2, the student receives instruction only at the highest difficulty level (e.g., problems with many digits) and can progress quite rapidly (similarly for instruction-level step size). Students are automatically moved forward or backward in problem type and difficulty level according to their mastery of the material.

Any combination of options might be optimal for someone. For example, one teacher might want to assign all his students to the particular topic in which he is providing whole-class instruction but still allow the program to adjust step sizes automatically.

Regardless of a program's sophisticated self-management, teachers need to monitor students' progress themselves. For example, at the end of the week, Ms. Fitzgerald may wish to view Scott's record. From the original main menu she selects "2 · DISPLAY ONE STUDENT'S RECORD (SHIFT-2) ... TO PRINTER" (if she pressed shift-2, the records would be printed on paper). Selecting Scott, she would see

```
1.   JON
--LESSONS-- --------MASTERY-TESTS--    -----------
           NO. NO. -----% CORRECT-----   -----------
-TYPE-     P'S S'S  RVW   MNG   RUL   DES      MEN   TIM

SNGL DIG             TESTED OUT IN PRETEST
10 TO 19             TESTED OUT IN PRETEST
NO REGRP             TESTED OUT IN PRETEST
REGROUP              TESTED OUT IN PRETEST
MXD REGRP            TESTED OUT IN PRETEST
REGRP-0    35   75  100   100    92    90       90
MX RGP-0             IMPENDING
```

These records indicate that on the pretest, Scott exhibited satisfactory mastery of the first five problem types. In working with regrouping with zero, he needed to complete 35 problems to master all difficulty and instruction levels. To complete the mastery test Scott had to perform 75 detailed steps. He got 100% of the steps on review (RVW) problems correct, 100% on the meaning (MNG), 92% on the rule (RUL), and so on. When he works with the program next, he will be assigned to mixed regrouping with zero.

Option 8 on the main menu allows the teacher to modify the learning/testing system. For instance, if the sound is obtrusive, she might choose to eliminate it. Other modifications involve the mastery test criterion (percentage correct to progress to the next problem type), progress criterion, step-size increase and decrease criteria, various minimum time parameters, and so on.

Assisting the Teacher

The program just described provides one example of Computer-Managed Instruction (CMI), an educational approach in which a computer information-management system supports the teacher's functions of directing the educational program. Emphasizing the computer's ability to gather and interpret information, it actually helps the teacher help students, unlike CAI programs (or the CAI component of programs which also include a management component), which help students directly. CMI programs vary in how they perform this function. Several different programs will be described briefly.

Classroom Management System—Mathematics A (SRA) tests specific skills defined by objectives. It evaluates each student's performance by administering a wide-ranged "placement" test and, based on these results, probe tests to ascertain specific weaknesses. It then prescribes remedial work based on the objectives each student has not yet mastered. The prescriptions are keyed to six major basal math textbooks and several SRA programs. The teacher's own materials, games, activities, and texts can also be added to the list.

The Computer Curriculum Corporation (CCC) elementary software, *Mathematics Strands,* is based on a fine-tuned CMI system. Students usually begin their first sessions about one-half level below their present grade level. For example, a second grader might begin each of the strands (such as number concepts, addition, subtraction, measurement, etc.) at grade level 1.5. Then for the initial 10 sessions the system constantly adjusts the problems presented to be easier or harder, according to the student's performance. After a couple of weeks, the student might be at the 2.0 level in addition, the 1.6 level in subtraction, the 2.3 level in measurement, and so on. If a student is behind the average grade-level placement in a strand by 0.3 of a year (e.g., as this student was in subtraction), the number of exercises in that strand is increased. Exercises themselves are not generated randomly. Instead, the system generates each item by following rules designed to ensure the mastery of prerequisite skills and the provision of carefully tailored practice. Thus, the mixture of exercises from each strand, the sequence of levels within strands, and the number and type of exercises within levels are all selected individually for each student. Finally, individualized worksheets can be printed at any time, and reports for a whole course, for monthly gains of individuals, and for grouping (i.e., a list of all students 0.25 level or more below the average) can be generated. Research done with the CCC materials has been positive; if a school system is willing to follow the suggested time of 10 minutes per day 5 days per week for 150 school days per year on these drill and practice materials, it is not uncommon to almost double performance on the skills practiced.

Like CCC, the PLATO/WICAT school system runs on a minicomputer; extensive CMI such as that employed by these systems often requires more memory than most presently available microcomputers can offer. The PLATO/WICAT CMI features diagnosis and placement, individually sequenced and paced lessons, and automatic review. It can produce six class and individual reports, including such information as quartile ranking, number of lessons mastered, time on task, number of review lessons mastered, number of failed lessons within a unit, number of right and wrong answers in a lesson, number of times a student asked for help in a lesson, current lesson numbers, and a graph comparing student progress to the class average. Students can also choose to repeat a lesson or do additional practice until they believe they have mastered the material. Teachers can rearrange the order of the lessons to make them conform closely to their own sequence. They can move individual students backward or forward in the curriculum, or move the entire class back for review and retesting.

A list of some available mathematic programs that include management functions is provided in Table 2-3, which follows the end of this chapter. Remember that some merely keep simple records. Future management systems may possess all the features of the systems already described and more, providing detailed information and advice to teachers and students about students' strengths and weaknesses, and recommending special instruction based on this information.

COMPUTER MANAGEMENT TOOLS FOR THE TEACHER

Computer Testing and Utilities

Numerous computer packages provide services to teachers beyond the direct management of the instructional program. Table 2-4 lists some of the functions of these programs. One especially powerful use is in assessment.

Testing and diagnosis. Computer scoring of standardized achievement tests is familiar in most schools. In-house microcomputers can perform similar services, with additional advantages (e.g., *Quickscore,* PICA Foundation; for additional programs, see Clements, 1985a, and Riedesel & Clements, 1985; Nitko and Hsu, 1984, describe a comprehensive system for managing testing). They give teachers greater control over the process and provide quick "turnaround," which allows teachers to actually use the information in planning instruction. Many are capable of scoring teacher-made tests and providing basic statistics for the test such as item analyses and reliability estimates. Programs may also help teachers generate tests by storing items according to objects and creating tests according to the teacher's design specifications (e.g., *Super Quiz II,* Sterling Swift; *Test Master,* Micro Software). *Instructions and Management System: Mathematics* (Systems Impact) provides a broad screening test with detailed placement tests for each content area covered; all tests are paper and pencil, with results entered into the computer. Based on the diagnosis, individually prescribed worksheets are generated. The system also generates a mastery worksheet, determines the next objective(s), and prints reports as needed. *Elementary TestBanks* (Holt) includes a data base of professionally prepared test items keyed to learning objectives in Holt's mathematics tests (grades 3 through 8). Teachers can prepare tests according to their own teaching sequences—by learning objectives, chapters, or chapter groups. They can also add their own items and reword existing items. Used with their *Class II CMI* system, the program can automatically generate an individualized test for each student in the class.

Test generating programs go beyond the presentation of identical items to each student. They can generate a myriad of different quizzes on arithmetical skills, or they might select a specified number of items from an established pool of items. Problem generators can construct a wide range of different problems according to rules. For example, to assess students' ability to find a percent of a number using a decimal, the computer might randomly select one of several mathematically similar problem situations,

TABLE 2-4   Ways Computers Can Help Manage a Classroom

Managing Instruction
Supporting CAI programs with computer-managed instruction
Generate IEPs (individual educational plans)
Project planning
Scheduling

Managing Tests
Test scoring and analysis
Test generation and printing
Administering tests in an individualized, interactive situation

Aiding Communication
Grade contracting
Scheduling one-to-one time between teacher and student
Message handling

Organizing and Reporting Information About Students
Keeping attendance
Storing, analyzing, and reporting student records
Storing, sorting, and analyzing guidance records
Keeping class records (computerized grade books)
Generating reports to parents
Generating report cards
Detailed evaluation of instructional programs

Organizing and Reporting Information About the Classroom
Media reservations
Resource allocation
Purchase orders
Label or mailing list printing
Inventories
Information storage and retrieval
Library circulation

such as the grams of protein in a slice of bread or the number of students buying lunch. The numbers provided would also be chosen from a preestablished range. In this way, students always receive unique items, even if they take the test several times, as they might in mastery learning environments. They can even be encouraged to discuss the tests, adding the element of peer learning.

In addition, testing can be "tailored." During the testing, the computer selects items for the test which are appropriate for the student based on his or her previous responses (McKinley & Reckase, 1980). If the student's performance indicates that he or she will not be able to handle certain types of items, these are not presented. Computer testing also allows the efficient use of more open-ended items rather than the restricted multiple-choice format. Errors of measurement are minimized, testing time shortened, frustration reduced, reliability improved, and total test information gathered increased. Some programs also provide students with feedback while they are taking the test, so that it is a learning experience as well.

Research in the field of artificial intelligence has contributed to our understanding of errors that children make in procedural skills such as arithmetical algorithms. J. S. Brown, VanLehn, and others have created a computer program that can diagnose students' errors in multidigit subtraction. *Debuggy* can explain the reason for the underlying error in students' subtraction processes rather than simply identifying the procedural mistake. This type of program is discussed in detail in Chapter 7.

Research has supported the efficacy of computer diagnosis and remediation of arithmetical errors (see Travis, in Hansen & Zweng, 1984). A caveat is that we not lose sight of what is most important: students' understanding of arithmetic. Indeed, given the presence of errors, both procedural and conceptual remediation should be considered. Knowledge of bugs should also help teachers plan instruction that will prevent their development.

Utility Programs

Materials generation. Several types of classroom materials can be generated by the computer, such as tests (e.g., *Computer Generated Mathematics Materials,* MECC, generates exercises on problem solving), overhead transparencies, slides or transparencies, puzzles containing hidden words, or even reports to parents (*Parent Reporting,* Hartley). Several packages generate mathematics worksheets (e.g., *K-8 Math Worksheet Generator,* Radio Shack). Teachers using *Mathsheet* (Houghton Mifflin) choose an operation (addition, subtraction, multiplication, division) and then choose a specific skill (e.g., for division, from "1. Choose your own divisor," "2. Divisor 15, basic facts," to "10.3- or 4-digits/1-digit, 3-digit quotient, no remainder," to "18. 5-digits/3-digits, remainder"). It is correlated with the Houghton Mifflin mathematics textbook series, but its adaptability lends itself to use with any series. Other worksheet and test generators are listed at the end of this chapter in Table 2–5.

Better generators allow a variety of operations on one worksheet, printing in different sizes, easy but specific selection of difficulty level, printing of teacher and student answer keys, and viewing before printing. But we must ask whether better worksheets will address the most important educational problems.

Handling information. Clerical chores can often be handled by the computer. For instance, computerized grade books may assist in keeping track of absences, daily grades, and extra credit. They may provide test scores (weighted if desired), total grades, percentages, item analyses of tests, daily attendance and grade reports, notices of children who are failing, and individual cumulative records (see Clements, 1985a).

Word processing. A word processor is a program that allows the user to type in text; delete, insert, or move around portions of it; save it and retrieve it later; print it on paper; and manipulate it in numerous other ways. It allows teachers to construct handouts, tests, and lesson plans effortlessly, revising as needed. Students might write about topics in mathematics, an activity in which they are too seldom engaged.

Whether the computer is used to help manage instruction or other aspects of the classroom, this type of application must be examined critically to ascertain if the use is compatible with the rest of the educational program and is a high priority. The following sections address this issue from the perspectives of CMI research, misuse, and evaluation.

RESEARCH IMPLICATIONS FOR CMI

Effectiveness of computer management. Results comparing classrooms with CMI to those without it usually favor the former, both in terms of students' achievement and, more consistently, attitude toward the subject (Chanoine, 1977; Knight & Dunkleberger, 1977; Spuck & Bozeman, 1980). However, results have not been positive in every case, and positive results have not always been statistically significant (Bozeman, 1978; DeVault, 1981; Wilkins, 1975). In a meta-analysis, Kulik et al. (1984) found the effects of CMI to be trivial and nonsignificant. Thus, achievement under CMI may not always be better than under traditional systems. Also, if teachers do not bring in and control the system, their authority might be undermined.

Adaptive instructional systems. Some recent studies indicate that certain CMI techniques may be more effective. One of the more sophisticated and effective of the CMI approaches is that in which the computer adapts the instruction to the student's needs during the lesson. For example, a computer might provide adaptive feedback during a drill sequence on the names of shapes. If the student responds with an item that is not on the list being learned, the computer would provide the correct answer. However, if the incorrect item is on the list being learned, the computer would give discrimination feedback, telling the student the correct answer and providing the stimulus–response pair for the incorrect response as well. For example, if the student incorrectly responded "parallelogram," for another polygon on the list, the computer would say that the correct answer is trapezoid and show a parallelogram with its name and possibly its characteristics. In addition, the computer would immediately present each of these polygons, and the student would have to respond correctly to both stimuli to return to the drill. Research indicates that this adaptive feedback significantly reduces discrimination errors (Siegel & Misselt, 1984).

Another adaptive technique that is effective is increasing ratio review. In simple practice a missed item is placed at the end of the list for additional practice (this is true of both traditional computer drills and typical noncomputer flashcard drills). Unfortunately, if the list is long, the student forgets the answer; if the list is short, the student is not shaped in remembering the item over longer periods. Instead, in increasing ratio review, the computer inserts the missed item (trapezoid) into the list at several places, such as the 3rd, 7th, and 13th item to be presented to the student. Therefore, after responding incorrectly, the student will see the correct answer, work two other problems, repeat the missed item, work three other problems, repeat the missed item again, and so on. This technique has been shown to increase students' achievement without increasing the total time they work on the task (Siegel & Misselt, 1984).

Intelligently managed drills can teach generalizations as well. Subsequent items generated by the increasing ratio review can be altered by the computer to reflect the range of the concept. For example, the newly generated items might present trapezoids of different sizes, angles, orientations, and so on. This focuses attention on the concept rather than on the specific memorizable example.

Research has also substantiated the effectiveness of adaptive systems (e.g., Tennyson et al., 1984). These systems perform an initial diagnostic assessment of each student (or skip this time-consuming process if prior information indicates minimal existing knowledge). Then this assessment is continually updated and new prescriptions are made as a student works. The amount of instruction given is based on the student's progress toward the mastery of the objectives. This reduces off-task time. Ross (1984) compared instructional treatments that provided lots of practice time and numerous examples with this kind of adaptive instruction. Interestingly, more examples reduced achievement, whereas the adaptive instruction increased achievement. Once they mastered the material, students probably became bored and lost concentration when merely given more examples.

Adaptive systems may also provide continuous advisement to students on their learning progress and needs. Left on their own, good students often choose too many examples (wasting their time); poor students choose too few. However, with this advisement, students can gradually learn to control their own learning effectively. Finally, adaptive systems can even adapt the context of the lesson to the interests of students; for example, a lesson on graphing might appeal to certain students if it was of video game speeds and characteristics, to others if it was of food consumption trends.

MISUSES OF CMI

One teacher uses a program that helps her individualize specific, essential components of the mathematics curriculum. Students work at their own pace on tailor-made lessons gauged to their level of difficulty. They are allowed to achieve competence at each level before advancing to the next, and are given some measure of freedom and responsibility in their learning.

A second teacher uses a program in which students are tested constantly. If they fall below a prescribed level of mastery, they are required to work alone until they are ready to be retested. The curriculum is teacher centered and consists of thousands of minute behavioral objectives. The students have few choices about what and how to learn. Curiously, these two teachers use the same program. The difference is in the depth of understanding, and the resulting use, of a program built on certain principles.

Management systems in general are a result of the convergence of three themes of American education thought: individualization, behavioral objectives, and educational technology (Baker, 1978). They attempt to individualize instruction, provide immediate feedback, and ensure success. However, the skills management systems approach was borrowed from the business world and tends to be based on the particular view of education— the school as factory. Following this model, goals are specified as observable behaviors, students' initial capabilities are assessed and instruction prescribed, performance is continuously monitored, and so on.

This model can be abused. The second teacher overemphasized the assessment of observable, fractionalized behaviors. His "individualization" was restricted to students' rate of progress. Materials were confused with original purposes and became the ends instead of the means. Misused, the CMI model tends to emphasize the content rather than the process, the logical rather than the psychological, the mechanical rather than the meaningful, and organized structure rather than flexibility allowing the opportunity for incidental growth. If teachers trust the system rather than their own personalized diagnosis, they may lose control over their mathematics program.

However, the first teacher allowed herself and her students to retain control. She used it only for the management of a restricted set of necessary skills. Most important, she retained the "hidden strengths" of group instruction—the power of working in groups, the positive pacing effect of the traditional class, and the orchestration of skills by the teacher (Lipson, 1976).

Thus, teachers should use the system as a single tool, keeping the responsibility for professional decisions with themselves rather than with the system. In keeping with the principles stated in this book, one such decision should be to maintain the integrity and wholeness of every domain of the curriculum, emphasizing the higher-level, meaningful aspects. Doing mathematics is not the ability to complete isolated exercises. CMI can help children efficiently develop these abilities (which are, of course, important components of mathematics). It should not be allowed to let students, teachers, and parents mistake these abilities for true understanding.

SUGGESTED READINGS

Dugdale (1983) discusses computer games that are "intrinsic models." The game centers on the mathematics to be learned.

Hansen and Zweng (1984) edited a yearbook for the National Council of Teachers of Mathematics that presents a wide range of examples of worthwhile computer applications.

Malone (1981) discusses the features that make some games, including computer games, intrinsically motivating. How might some of the computer programs listed in this and other chapters be changed to be more motivating? Could noncomputer activities also be so adapted?

Spuck and Bozeman (1980) provide models for evaluating CMI systems.

Taylor (1980) provides a classic set of readings from leaders on using the computer as a tutor, tool, or tutee. After reading it, consider: Have the issues or practical ramifications changed since the book was published?

TABLE 2-3   Examples of Commercial CAI Mathematics Programs Possessing CMI Component

Title	Producer
Basic Math Facts	Houghton Mifflin
Basic Math Skills	Learning Systems
Basic Math System S	Mathware
C-AIM	Contact Dr. Thomas Bishop
	Department of Computer Science, Mathematics, and Physics
	P.O. Box 70
	State University, AR 72467
CADPP—Computer Assisted Diagnostic	Contact D. Glowinski
Prescriptive Program	Buckingham County Public Schools
	P.O. Box 292
	Dillwyn, VA 23936
Classroom Management System	SRA
Computerized Management System (CMS)	Skillcorp
Diagnostic Prescriptive System	Learn. Unlimited
Elementary and Pre-Algebra Mathematics	Montgomery Public Schools, MD
Elementary Mathematics Classroom Learning System	Sterling Swift
Fundamental Mathematics, Basic Math Facts Drill	Random House
General Mathematics Diagnostic	Educational Medial Assoc.
K-8 Math Program	Radio Shack
Mathfiles	Micro Learn.
Math 1	Prism Software
Math Machine	SouthWest
Math Power Program	I/CT
Math Sequences	Milliken
Math System and Mathematical Concepts	Opp. Learning
Mathematics Assessment/Prescriptive Edu-Disks	Reader's Digest
Mathematics Strands	CCC
Multiplication Facts Diagnostic Disk	Depot
Prescriptive Math Drill	Hartley
Trillium Basal Math-Ware	Trillium
Whole Numbers	Control Data

Publishers of Integrated Learning Systems
(minicomputer/hard disk configurations packaged with software)

CCC Microhost	CCC
Degem Integrated Learning System	Degem
Dolphin	Houghton Mifflin/TSC
Educational Systems Technology Corp.	ESTC
ICON Educational Micro	Cemcorp
Ideal Learning	Ideal Learning
PLATO/WICAT System 300	PLATO/WICAT
Wasatch Educational System	Wasatch

(*continued*)

TABLE 2-3 (Continued)

Title	Producer
Management Systems Only (mathematics content entered by teacher)	
Class II Management System	Holt
Curriculum Management System	Learning Tools
Customized Instructional Management System	Random House
Customized Prescriptions	Random House
Detroit 80 Diagnostics	Precision People
E-Z Learner	Silicon Valley System
Mastery Management System	Hopkins Public Schools

Tables 2–3 and 2–5 are the only ones in the book that do *not* include descriptions and evaluations of the software. This is merely to avoid redundancy. Most of the programs listed here, as well as other topic-specific programs with CMI components, will be listed in tables at the end of the appropriate chapters (see Chapters 5 through 11).

TABLE 2-5   Worksheet and Test Generators

Title	Producer
The East Quiz Maker	Compress
The EA Mathematics Worksheet Generator	Ed. Act.
Electronic Master I	Ed. Software
IMS	Grolier
Math Doctor M.D.	Modern Education Corp.
Mathematics: A Worksheet/Test Generator	Continental
Mathematics Worksheet Generator	DCH
Number Facts Sheet	Gamco
P.D.Q.	Micro Power
Skill Tester	Allyn and Bacon
Testmaster	Midwest
Trillium Basal Math-Ware	Trillium
Whole Number Test Series	Ed. Micro. Sys.
Worksheet Generator	Micro Learn.
Worksheet Wizard—Fractions	Edusoft.

3

POWERFUL TOOLS

Recall from Chapter 1 the importance of the student's role as an active learner of mathematics. Several categories of CAI described in Chapter 2, such as simulations and games, emphasized such a role. Another step toward active, independent learning is made when students use the computer as a tool for solving mathematical problems. Used as a tool, the computer is programmed to perform a specific function, such as calculating, graphing, or storing and retrieving information. Unlike the more traditional categories of CAI, however, students must identify the problem to be solved and how the program will function to help solve the problem.

Such an application of computers has several advantages. First, the problems students solve can become more complex as the computer assists in organizing information and performing calculations. Second, computer tools allow, even encourage, students to find different solution methods, which develops strategic problem-solving ability, divergent thinking ability, and a mathematical way of thinking. Third, students can work in groups, developing and sharing ideas. Fourth, students can use the computer in ways similar to those of adult problem solvers, therefore experiencing interesting and practical applications of mathematics as well as applications of the computer for solving real-world problems. As we shall see, these tools can also be used effectively in exploring mathematics itself.

ELECTRONIC SPREADSHEETS

An electronic spreadsheet, such as VisiCalc, is a program that transforms the computer into a large table of rows and columns. Like an addition or multiplication table, some numbers in the table are determined by operating on other numbers. For example, in an addition table, the number at the intersection of the "5 row" and the "3 column" is "8." Unlike an addition table, these computations are performed by the computer; values or operations can be changed at any time, with all computations immediately recalculated; and there are often many different types of computations (formulas) involved. For example, a spreadsheet might be used by a teacher to record and compute students' grades, including high and low marks and averages (both averages on a particular assignment for all students and a particular student's average for all assignments).

Rows in a spreadsheet are usually identified by numbers (positive integers), and columns are identified by letters. Each location, called a *cell*, is an intersection of a row and a column. Each cell can contain an alphabetic descriptive label (e.g., TEST 2), a number (e.g., 76), or an algebraic formula that may refer to other cells in the spreadsheet. Any such formula is the *definition* of the cell (and is displayed on the top line when the cursor is on the cell), but the spreadsheet displays the evaluated expression (i.e., the number that the formula yields) at the cell's location on the computer screen. For clarity's sake, examples in this book will occasionally show both the *screen display* (this illustrates how the speadsheet actually appears) and a figure called *spreadsheet definition*. In the latter, what is entered by the user for each cell is shown. That is, each cell which contains a formula that the user entered as a definition of that cell will show the formula instead of the number that would actually appear on the screen.

One teacher introduced the applications of electronic spreadsheets by having each student enter his or her name in the first column (column A); the first student's name appeared in cell A1, the second in cell A2, etc. She pointed out that the spreadsheet displayed the term LABEL at the top of the screen (any data that start with a letter are considered words). Moving the cursor to the next column (column B), at the first row (cell B1) they typed "1986." The term VALUE now appeared on the top line. Rather than retyping this number next to each student's name, the teacher showed them how to use the Replicate command to have the computer enter this information automatically. In the next column (column C), each student entered his or her year of birth. Finally, the teacher entered a formula in column D to subtract each student's date of birth from the present year: B4–C4, for Cheryl, who occupied the fourth row. This formula, too, was Replicated for all students. The teacher showed the groups how to specify that they wanted the formula to be relative for each row (student); that is, for the next student, the formula automatically became B5–C5. Column D showed each student's age.

Spreadsheet Definition (first five rows)

D5 (V) (B5-C5)

	A	B	C	D	E
1	NAME	PRESENT	BIRTH	AGE IN	
2		YEAR	YEAR	YEARS	
3					
4	CHERYL	1986	1975	(B4-C4)	
5	AMELIA	1986	1976	(B5-C5)	

Screen Display

```
D5  (V)  (B5-C5)

          A        B         C        D        E

    1 |  NAME   PRESENT   BIRTH   AGE IN
    2 |          YEAR      YEAR    YEARS
    3 |
    4 |  CHERYL   1986      1975     11
    5 |  AMELIA   1986      1976     10
```

To demonstrate the spreadsheet's power of recalculation, the teacher asked her students how they would show their ages in the year 2001. They altered column B to contain that number and saw that each number in column D changed automatically, displaying the new calculations.

One student protested that he was not yet 11, as originally shown, although he agreed that the calculations were correct. After discussing the problem and possible solutions, the group decided that months had to be added to the spreadsheet. The teacher explained that new columns or rows could be inserted anywhere, and that she would do so for the next lesson. The following day, she asked students to fill in the appropriate information on the modified spreadsheet template. (A *template* is a spreadsheet definition, complete with major labels and formulas, ready for specific information to be entered.) The first five rows of the template and the completed screen display can be seen below.

Spreadsheet Definition
(first five rows, without student information entered)

```
G4  (V)  F4/12

     A        B         C         D        E       F              G

 1 | NAME  PRESENT   PRESENT   BIRTH   BIRTH   AGE IN         AGE IN
 2 |       MONTH     YEAR      MONTH   YEAR    MONTHS         YEARS
 3 |
 4 -|        3        1986                     (B4+(C4*12))    F4/12
   |                                           -(D4+(E4*12))
 5 |
   |        3        1986                     (B5+(C5*12))    F5/12
   |                                           -(D5+(E5*12))
```

Note: Computers usually use an asterisk (∗) to denote multiplication rather than the typical multiplication sign (×), which could be confused with the letter X.

Screen Display (including student information)

F4 (V) (B4+(C4*12))-(D4+(E4*12)

	A	B	C	D	E	F	G	H
1	NAME	PRESENT	PRESENT	BIRTH	BIRTH	AGE IN	AGE IN	
2		MONTH	YEAR	MONTH	YEAR	MONTHS	YEARS	
3								
4	CHERYL	3	1986	11	1975	124	10.33	
5	AMELIA	3	1986	2	1976	121	10.08	
6	AIMEE	3	1986	7	1975	128	10.67	
7	JON	3	1986	7	1976	116	9.67	
8	SANDY	3	1986	2	1975	133	11.08	
9								

The teacher had the students work with this spreadsheet template by themselves, calculating the ages of friends and acquaintances and family members. The teachers also challenged a few talented students to display the present age in years and months instead of decimal fractions of years (as they are above).

As a second project, the teacher helped her students fill in another template for keeping track of their grades, with averages for each subject as well as an overall average. To begin, she reviewed how to:

1. Boot the spreadsheet program.
2. Remove this disk and insert the storage disk.
3. Load the appropriate template from the storage disk.
4. Move the cursor and identify what type of information (label or value) is in a particular cell.
5. Enter data, and edit them if necessary.
6. Predict what effect this entry will have on other cells.
7. Write a formula into a cell.
8. Use the built-in functions in writing formulas (e.g., SUM).

Asking "What if ... ?" questions was a valuable experience in this spreadsheet, as students were provided with a memorable illustration of the effects of low grades (especially a zero!) on averages. Students also asked such questions as: "What do I have to score on the next test to obtain a 90 average?"

Suggestions. Other teachers find it helpful to give students a work-sheet laid out in rows and columns for projects like the previous two. Students complete the entire worksheet (e.g., fill in the entire gradesheet) *without* the computer. Only then is the electronic spreadsheet introduced. This may make spreadsheet use more concrete and more attractive! Some teachers introduce a familiar table, such as the addition or multiplication table, implemented on the spreadsheet. They encourage students to explore the formulas that underlie such a template and to examine the ideas of naming cells and changing values (see Chapter 7). This helps students understand that cells are named in a specific way, that a change in any cell affects all other cells that depend on it, and that the screen display is a consequence of the spreadsheet definitions. This last point is extremely important, as what is usually *seen* (the screen display) is not as important as what underlies what is seen (the spreadsheet definitions). Some spreadsheets, such as *Apple-Works* (Apple), allow students to switch back and forth between these two. For most others, students can only see the definition of a single cell at a time by moving the cursor to it.

Using such teacher-prepared templates allows elementary school students to work successfully with spreadsheets without entering the formulas themselves. While the spreadsheet performs the calculations, students are learning to use a powerful tool, observe the effect of manipulating numbers on related values, discover patterns, and, perhaps most important, gain intuition about mathematical concepts such as variables and functions. With such experience, older students can set up their own spreadsheets (they should begin with simple formulas).

Spreadsheets can be useful for exploring numerical patterns. Using a simplified spreadsheet, *Kid Calc* (E. David), along with the suggested activities, one teacher set the numbers in column A to 1, 2, 3, 4, . . . and defined column B as A * 2 and column C as A * 3. Students recognized that column A incremented by one, B by two, and C by three. The teacher had a student change A to 1, 3, 5, 7, ... Students noticed that B now increased by four and C by six. The teacher challenged them to predict outcomes given other changes in column A, as well as changes in the definitions of B and C. (For example, if B is defined as A * 3 and C as B + 2, how does each increment? How about if B is defined as A * 3 and C as B * 2?)

If column B = A * 11 and C = 10 * A + A, how do the numbers in columns B and C compare? Is there a pattern to multiplying by 11? What pattern emerges with B = A * 10 and C = A + B? These explorations led into "guess my rule" games wherein students or groups of students specify rules for columns B and C and then their partners enter numbers in column A and attempt to determine the (hidden) rules.

Another beginning project for students might involve counting all the money in their possession. Spreadsheet definition and display spreadsheets for this project might appear as follows.

Spreadsheet Definition

D4   (V)   (B4*C4)

	A	B	C	D	E
1	COIN	VALUE	NUMBER	AMOUNT	
2	. . . .				
3					
4	PENNY	0.01		(B4*C4)	
5	NICKEL	0.05		(B5*C5)	
6	DIME	0.10		(B6*C6)	
7	QUARTER	0.25		(B7*C7)	

(continued)

8	$1	1.00	(B8*C8)
9	$5	5.00	(B9*C9)
10			
11		TOTAL	(D4+D5+D6+D7+D8+D9)†
12			

†In place of this formula, spreadsheets allow a summation command that would automatically add the proper cells: for example, @SUM(D4 . . . D9).

Screen Display

D4   (V)   (B4*C4)

	A	B	C	D	E
1	COIN	VALUE	NUMBER	AMOUNT	
2	. . . .				
3					
4	PENNY	0.01	7	0.07	
5	NICKEL	0.05	2	0.1	
6	DIME	0.10	0	0	
7	QUARTER	0.25	3	0.75	
8	$1	1.00	4	4	
9	$5	5.00	0	0	
10					
11			TOTAL	4.92	
12					

Students should experiment with simple sheets such as this, changing values and observing the effects on the totals, adding new coins or bills, and so on.

More practical calculations with money—budgeting—is a common application of spreadsheets. Students might use a teacher-constructed template to construct an annual budget, part of which might look like this:

Screen Display

E13   (V)   (D13+E3-E12)

	A	B	C	D	E
1	MONTH→	JAN.	FEB.	MARCH	APRIL
2					
3	INCOME	1500.00	1500.00	1500.00	1575.00
4	. . . .				
5	HOUSE	670.00	670.00	670.00	670.00
6	FOOD	175.00	175.00	175.00	175.00
7	INSUR.	125.00			250.00
8	CAR	140.00	140.00	140.00	140.00
9	UTIL.	200.00	200.00	200.00	200.00
10	ENTER.	50.00	50.00	50.00	50.00
11	OTHER	100.00	100.00	100.00	100.00
12	TOT. EXP.	1460.00	1335.00	1335.00	1585.00
13	SAVINGS	40.00	205.00	370.00	360.00

Note that income is predicted to increase by 5% in April. House payments are constant, but insurance expenses vary by month.

After setting up such a budget, students can be encouraged to ask questions. What if the initial income were only $1400.00? What if food expenses suddenly rose by 15%? What if a category, such as clothing, were added to the model? The ease with which students can answer and explore this type of "What if . . . ?" questions illustrates the power of an electronic spreadsheet.

More complex economics (and mathematics) can be added through the introduction of an inflation rate, which would affect month-by-month expenses in certain categories, such as food, entertainment, and "other" expenses:

Screen Display

C7   (V) (B7*B4)

	A	B	C	D	E
1	MONTH→	JAN.	FEB.	MARCH	APRIL
2					
3	INCOME	1600.00	1600.00	1600.00	1680.00
4	INFLA.	1.01			
5	. . . .				
6	HOUSE	670.00	670.00	670.00	670.00
7	FOOD	175.00	176.75	178.52	180.30
8	INSUR.	125.00			250.00
9	CAR	140.00	140.00	140.00	140.00
10	UTIL.	200.00	200.00	200.00	200.00
11	ENTER.	50.00	50.50	51.01	51.52
12	OTHER	200.00	202.00	204.02	206.06
13	TOT. EXP.	1560.00	1439.25	1443.54	1697.88
14	SAVINGS	40.00	200.75	357.21	339.33
15					

Spreadsheet Definition (to February)

C7   (V) (B7*B4)

	A	B	C
1	MONTH→	JAN.	FEB.
2			
3	INCOME	1600.00	(B3)
4	INFLA.	1.01	
5	. . . .		
6	HOUSE	670.00	(B6)
7	FOOD	175.00	(B7*B4)
8	INSUR.	125.00	
9	CAR	140.00	(B9)

(continued)

10	UTIL.	200.00	(B10)
11	ENTER.	50.00	(B11*B4)
12	OTHER	200.00	(B12*B4)
13	TOT. EXP.	@SUM(B6...B12)	@SUM(C6...C12)
14	SAVINGS	(B3-B13)	(C3-C13)
15			

Notice that income was raised in this model (why?). Other variables could still be entered into the model, such as interest on the savings account. Also notice that while some numbers are entered, most of the cells in the months after January will be defined by formulas that refer to other cells—often as simple as one term such as "B3," which means "copy B3's value into this cell." Finally, it should be pointed out that spreadsheets have a considerable amount of complicated functions and commands; however, it is not necessary, and usually not pertinent, to learn all of them. A small core of commands allows completion of most projects.

Other economic problems might be generated from students' interests. One teacher overheard his students complaining about their parents' demands that they turn off lights to save electricity. He had his students calculate how much electricity light bulbs of varying wattage wasted over standard time periods. Reading the rate for kilowatt hours (KWH) from electric bills, students constructed the spreadsheet displayed below. Students were impressed how much money even medium-wattage bulbs wasted over long periods; however, they were also struck by how (seemingly) little they cost for an hour or a day. (One student proclaimed that the next time her father yelled at her for leaving a 100-watt light bulb on for a day, she would "flip him a nickel and say, 'Keep the change.'" Wisely, the teacher dissuaded her.)

Screen Display

E4 (V) (C4*D4)

	A	B	C	D
1	WATTS	KILO-	KWH FOR	RATE:
2		WATTS	1 HOUR	$/KWH
3				
4	20	0.02	0.02	0.018
5	40	0.04	0.04	0.018
6	60	0.06	0.06	0.018
7	80	0.08	0.08	0.018
8	100	0.1	0.1	0.018
9	120	0.12	0.12	0.018
10	140	0.14	0.14	0.018
11	160	0.16	0.16	0.018
12	180	0.18	0.18	0.018
13	200	0.2	0.2	0.018
14				

(continued)

E	F	G	H	I
COST: 1 HOUR	COST: 1 DAY	COST: 1 WEEK	COST: 1 MONTH	COST: 1 YEAR
0.00036	0.00864	0.06	0.26	3.15
0.00072	0.01728	0.12	0.52	6.31
0.00108	0.02592	0.18	0.78	9.46
0.00144	0.03456	0.24	1.04	12.61
0.0018	0.0432	0.30	1.30	15.77
0.00216	0.05184	0.36	1.56	18.92
0.00252	0.06048	0.42	1.81	22.08
0.00288	0.06912	0.48	2.07	25.23
0.00324	0.07776	0.54	2.33	28.38
0.00036	0.0864	0.60	2.59	31.54

Electronic spreadsheets allow students to explore solutions for problems typically introduced in later years, such as: A woman purchased two
brands of house paint, one costing $11 per gallon, the other $8 per gallon.
If she paid $131 for 13 gallons of paint, how many gallons of each brand
did she buy? Students can be guided in setting up a spreadsheet that allows
them to experiment with possible solutions (see the following screen display
and spreadsheet definition). Students can specify a number of gallons of
$11 paint. The spreadsheet automatically computes the number of gallons
of $8 paint, the cost of each, and the resulting total cost. Students can try out
different values to determine the answer. More important, they are actively
manipulating one number and observing the effects of that manipulation.
In this way, even before students work with algebraic solutions, they can
learn about estimation, trial-and-error strategies, and effects of changes of
variables on other variables by using spreadsheets to solve mathematical
problems.

Screen display

B3 (V) 5

	A	B	C
1		$11	$8
2		PAINT	PAINT
3	GALLONS	5	8
4	$/GAL	11	8
5	COST	55	64
6			
7		TOTAL COST	119
8			

Spreadsheet Definition

```
B3 (V) 9

           A         B         C
         ┌──────────────────────────
    1     │                $11       $8
    2     │              PAINT    PAINT
    3     │ GALLONS          9    13-B3
    4     │ $/GAL           11         8
    5     │ COST        (B3*B4)(C3*C4)
    6     │
    7     │       TOTAL COST(B5+C5)
```

Screen Display

```
B3 (V) 9

           A         B         C
         ┌──────────────────────────
    1     │                $11       $8
    2     │              PAINT    PAINT
    3     │ GALLONS          9        4
    4     │ $/GAL           11        8
    5     │ COST            99       32
    6     │
    7     │       TOTAL COST       131
```

   As with most mathematics problems, there is more than one method of
solution. One student set up the spreadsheet a different way, systematically
altering the number of gallons. Advanced students might attempt to use the
spreadsheet's logical IF statement in determining the answer.

E13 (V) (B13+D13)

	A	B	C	D	E
1	$11 PAINT		$8 PAINT		TOTAL
2	. . . .		. . . .		. . . . .
3	GAL	COST	GAL	COST	
4	0	0	13	104	104
5	1	11	12	96	107
6	2	22	11	88	110
7	3	33	10	80	113
8	4	44	9	72	116
9	5	55	8	64	119
10	6	66	7	56	122
11	7	77	6	48	125
12	8	88	5	40	128
13	9	99	4	32	131
14	10	110	3	24	134
15	11	121	2	16	137
16	12	132	1	8	140
17	13	143	0	0	143
18					

Used in this way, spreadsheets can help students discover what a formula is, then test their hypotheses. As another example, consider the question: "How can you determine the number of diagonals in any regular polygon?" A spreadsheet might be set up to display the number of vertices in a regular polygon. Next to this, students could display the number of diagonals they counted after drawing the diagonals of the first few polygons. In the third column, they could enter a formula which they hypothesized would generate the correct number of diagonals. These columns (B and C) can be compared. The formula-defined column predicts what the next number of diagonals would be (27 for 9 vertices); students can then check this prediction. Students who achieved success at this task might explore number patterns further by defining another column as the difference between the number of diagonals in successive rows (column D).

Spreadsheet Definition (first six rows only)

D5 (V)

	A	B	C	D
1	VERTICES	COUNTED	PREDICTED	DIF-
2		DIAG.	DIAG.	FERENCE
3	. . . .
4	4	2	(A4-3)*A4/2	
5	5	5	(A5-3)*A5/2	(C5-C4)
6	6	9	(A6-3)*A6/2	(C6-C5)

Screen Display

D5 (V) (C5-C4)

	A	B	C	D
1	VERTICES	COUNTED	PREDICTED	DIF-
2		DIAG.	DIAG.	FERENCE
3	. . . .
4	4	2	2	
5	5	5	5	3
6	6	9	9	4
7	7	14	14	5
8	8	20	20	6
9	9		27	7
10	10		35	8
11	11		44	9
12	12		54	10
13				

Similarly, students could use the spreadsheet to list the integers from 1 to 100 and, in the next column, the sum of all the integers to that point (e.g., next to 4 would be 10—1 + 2 + 3 + 4; can you think of more than one way to do this?). In the next column, they could enter a formula that would specify the sum given only the row number [e.g., D1 * (D1 + 1))/2].

Spreadsheet possibilities are numerous. Students could investigate conversions, for instance, placing selected numbers representing a certain temperature in Fahrenheit in one column, then defining the next column as Celsius (⅝ of the first column minus 32). Or they might explore how changes in the dimensions of two- and three-dimensional shapes affect their areas, perimeters, and volumes. For example, one group chose a cube. In the first column (column A), they entered the length of the sides of different cubes. The other columns were defined as the perimeter (12 times A), the area (A times A times 6), and the volume (A times A times A). Entering different lengths for different sides in column A, they were able to explore the effects of changing that length on the other measures (e.g., for a side of 1, the other columns were 12, 6, and 1; for 2, they were 24, 24, and 8; for 4, they were 48, 96, and 64; for 8 they were 96, 384, and 512). They compared their observations to those of students who investigated similar effects on other shapes. Many formulas can be studied in the same way; for example, students learning about interest could vary the rate or time while keeping the principal constant to observe how this affects the interest

$$I = P \times R \times T.$$

Spreadsheets written specifically for students and adult novices are beginning to appear. For example, *Scholasticalc* (in the *Microzine* series by Scholastic) is an easy-to-use spreadsheet that comes with fantasy-based puzzles that must be solved with the spreadsheet. *EduCalc* (Grolier) contains a tutorial on electronic spreadsheets (appropriate for good readers), practice templates, and a full-featured spreadsheet program. *WhizCalc II* (World Book) combines practice in solving word problems with step-by-step guidance and the use of a simple spreadsheet. *Formula Vision* (Gentleware) is a small, 15-cell spreadsheet that emphasizes meaningful names for variables in formulas. A program related to spreadsheets, *SemCalc* (Sunburst), is discussed in Chapter 5.

The difficulty of using spreadsheets, however, should not be underestimated. If substantial time can be given to learning them (ideally, over the course of several years of education), they can be a powerful tool. But teachers should plan carefully for such use and ask if the investment yields a commensurate return (especially for students in grades below middle school).

Finally, the examples of spreadsheet use in this chapter emphasize problem solving. There is little reason to spend time familiarizing students with computer tools for their own sake or to perform routine tasks such as simple calculation. Work with spreadsheets should involve such high-level activities as making and testing hypotheses and predictions, investigating the effects of changing one value on other values in the spreadsheet, exploring number patterns, and modeling complex situations.

STATISTICS AND GRAPHING PROGRAMS

Children of all ages should be involved in collecting and displaying data. Several programs facilitate the creation of accurate graphs (*Exploring Tables and Graphs*, Xerox; *Easy Graph*, Grolier). Many provide statistics on information that is entered (*VisiPlot/VisiTrend*). Because data representation consti-

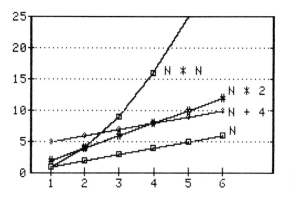

FIGURE 3-1
A graph of several number series
generated by a spreadsheet.

tutes an important topic in itself, these programs are discussed fully in Chapter 10. One example, however, illustrates that the combination of the spreadsheet and the graphing program can lead to many interesting investigations. For example, a class used the spreadsheet to create several series. Starting with the counting numbers in the first column, they defined each succeeding column based on a different transformation of the first column. The second column was defined as the first column plus 4, the third as the first multiplied by 2, the fourth as the first multiplied by itself, and so on. These series were then plotted, providing a visual representation of the concept of a function, and allowing the comparison of linear to nonlinear functions (see a section of such a graph in Fig. 3-1).

INFORMATION MANAGEMENT

One ability that is assuming ever-increasing importance in our world is the ability to find and manipulate information. Knowledge is becoming less a matter of memorizing and more a matter of knowing how to find information. Computers are an ideal tool for this purpose. Students can learn how to use simple computer-based information systems.

What is an information system? Educators everywhere have to be able to store and have access to large amounts of information about students—their names, addresses, dates of birth, parents' names and place(s) of work, medical history, test scores, and so on. All this information is usually kept on cards in filing drawers or in folders in a filing cabinet. Periodically, it has to be brought up to date. It also has to be referred to for writing reports on a student, charting progress of a group of students, assigning students to classes, determining how many students and also which students have scored above or below a certain level, locating all students who live in a specific area, and so on. The storage of this information, along with the method of organizing and using it in various ways, is an example of an information system.

To be useful, data must be structured in some way. If the students' files were not in order, it would take a considerable length of time to find a particular one. But they are in order, usually by grade, then by teacher, then alphabetically. A computer might use a similar data structure. A computerized data base management system (DBMS) consists of a "base" of information and computer programs that make it easy to make needed changes in this information or to answer certain questions about the information.

The most meaningful use of a DBMS often integrates mathematics with social studies and science units. For example, using a DBMS in a unit on mammals, students could answer such questions as: What is the smallest mammal? What mammals weigh more than 100 kilograms? Is it generally true that the larger the mammal, the faster its ground speed? To answer the last question, students could print a report that lists each mammal in order of weight, including only the following information: the mammal's name, weight, and ground speed. Because the mammals are ordered by weight, students could scan the list to ascertain the relationship between weight and speed. They could also plot speed against weight utilizing a graphing program, to check the relationship visually.

One class investigated a similar question with *Friendly Filer* (Grolier). After completing the tutorials that come with the program, they began exploring a file of 111 North American mammals, which can be purchased along with the *Filer*. They first sorted the mammals by head and body length, then printed out the mammals equal to or less than a foot in length. They used the computer to construct a graph comparing the animals' length and weights (Fig. 3–2). As expected, the trend was for longer mammals to be heavier, but the dips in the line graph provoked discussion. They were amazed when they later extended the graph; the graph they had constructed to that point completely changed shape when such mammals as the 246,000-pound blue whale were included!

As with spreadsheets, work with a DBMS should emphasize problem solving rather than such simple tasks as entering or retrieving information. Students should determine what information is relevant to a solution, reorganize information to test hypotheses, and draw conclusions and generalizations. They might begin by constructing and using a noncomputer data base (e.g., organized sets of index cards) so that they understand the relationships among fields, records, and files. Next, they could solve significant problems (such as finding relationships) using professionally constructed data bases (such as *Friendly Filer* or one of several available from Scholastic). Finally, they should construct their own data base—still with teacher guidance. Without such a sequence, students' construction and use of data bases is often trivial, limited to simple searches and listings.

Work with a DBMS can also be used to sharpen logical thinking skills. For example, generating reports actually involves the construction of sets with logical connectives (e.g., "and" and "or")—albeit in a meaningful situation. For example, to find all the mammals that live in North America and weigh more than 100 kilograms is to locate a subset of the universal set of mammals that is the intersection of two other subsets, mammals weighing more than 100 kilograms and those living in North America. The complement of the subset of all mammals weighing more than 100 kilograms would be the subset of all mammals weighing 100 kilograms or less. When and how would a data base be searched to find the union of two subsets? Although this terminology need not be used, teachers aware of these logical

Common name	Bat, little brown
Scientific name	*Myotis lucifuous*
Order	Chiroptera
Family	Vespertilionidae
Survival status	Common
Head and body length	0.16 ft
Weight	0.019 lb

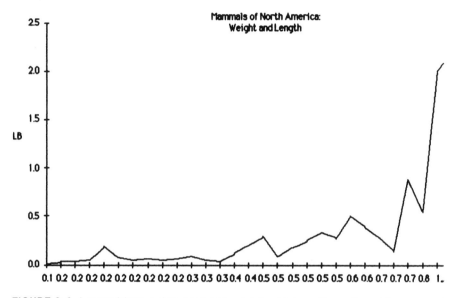

FIGURE 3-2 A record from a data base and a graph of information gathered from several such records.

foundations can enhance their students' understanding and application of the basic ideas.

Similarly, generating reports involves equivalence and order relations (e.g., "equal to North America" and "greater than 100," respectively). Data base systems utilize order relations and algorithms as well. To help students understand a computer algorithm, teachers might have them dramatize a simple sorting technique (Hedges, 1980–81). For purpose of discussion, let the numbers 1 through 5 represent five students of varying heights. The students stand in front of the room in random order: 5 3 1 2 4. The first child is then compared to the second; because he is taller, they switch places: 3 5 1 2 4. The first child now is next compared to the third. Again, they switch: 1 5 3 2 4. The first child (1) is then compared with the fourth and fifth, but because he is shorter, no switch is made. Next, the second child is compared to the third, and they switch: 1 3 5 2 4. The second, now (3), is compared to the fourth and switched: 1 2 5 3 4. The second is compared to the fifth, but no switch is made. The third is compared to the fourth and switched: 1 2 3 5 4. The third is compared to the fifth (not switched), then the fourth to the fifth (switched): 1 2 3 4 5. The students are properly sorted. Students could compare this method with their own.

Describing data quantitatively is the domain of statistics. Therefore, additional discussion of information management is presented in Chapter 10.

On-line data bases.   Soon, students will be communicating with data bases in school using computers equipped with a *modem,* a device that allows communication between computers over phone lines. These data bases will be the encyclopedias, card catalogs, and libraries of the technological society. Again, the ability to understand the use and structure of these data bases will be important life and study skills. Furthermore, the challenge of using the computer to find the information they need, and the motivating and positive feeling of satisfying their curiosity quickly and easily, may help students become independent learners.

Large general data base services include CompuServe, the Source, and Dow Jones. Many specialized data bases exist. They provide rapid key-word searches through numerous sources of information, including encyclopedias, government publications, newspapers, and so on. Therefore, they are a useful tool for gathering and analyzing information. As a simple example, one student wanted to know if there were metric prefixes "larger and smaller" than those her teacher knew about. She impressed her classmates by showing them a printout listing such prefixes as exa = 1,000,000,000,000,000,000 and atto = 0.000 000 000 000 000 001.

SOME GUIDELINES FOR USING COMPUTER TOOLS

1.   Emphasize use of the programs by students. When they actually have to decide how to use to the program, they gain deeper knowledge of the program, computer applications in the outside world, and mathematics.
2.   Focus on mathematics and mathematical problem solving, not computer functions.
3.   As applications arise, ask first: "What is the important structure of this information?"

   In electronic spreadsheets, the structure to be thought out involves (a) the content of the rows and columns and their relationships, and (b) the mathematical formulas to be employed.

   In information systems, the structure includes the content and relationships of the file, the records, and the fields, as described above.

   In statistical/graphing programs, the relationships between the data sets, and between the data sets and the format of the graph(s), need to be considered.

Just providing instruction on how to use such tools will do little to develop high-level cognitive processes. Teachers must guide students on using the tools to solve problems. Some ideas in mathematics, computational science, and problem solving might better be approached by taking yet another step toward putting students into an active learning role, asking them to program the computer with a child-appropriate computer language, a subject to which we turn next.

SUGGESTED READINGS

Arganbright's (1985) *Mathematical application of electronic spreadsheets* will challenge those advanced in mathematics with topics such as Fibonacci numbers, factorials, Euclid's GCD algorithm, and differentiation.

J. M. Brown (1986–87) provides a command reference sheet that you can duplicate and provide to your students.

Kelman and others (1983) provide several vignettes of spreadsheet use.

Luehrmann (1986) provides additional introductory activities for spreadsheets, such as recipe-doubling and maintaining players' and teams' scores for sporting events. Construct several others that would be of interest and benefit to your students.

COMPUTER PROGRAMMING

Two first graders, Christine and Elizabeth, are writing a Logo program to produce a birthday card for their friend. They want it to say "HAPPY BIRTHDAY" and to have a picture. They have constructed separate procedures (series of instructions) for each letter and shape of their program. They began by specifying instructions to tell the "turtle"—a pointer whose movements they direct to create drawings—how to make the letter "H." They had finished the left vertical line and the middle bar and are now using concepts of equivalence and symmetry to determine their next step.

"Now go forward 20, just like on the other side."

"OK, then we'll come back ... umm ... 40 to end up at the bottom."

Later in the session, the girls recognized that once they "taught" the computer a procedure for making the "H" for "happy," they could use the same procedure for the fifth letter in "birthday" (notice the identical H's, A's, P's, and Y's in Fig. 4–1). As they began working on the sole "R," Christine had an insight: "We can break that down, too. Use our 'P' and add a slanted line." And thus, the P procedure was used to create a new procedure, R.

As a final creative touch, the girls used the turtle as a part of their picture. There it was, a tortoise metamorphosed into a proboscis, between the eyes of the smiling face (adapted from Clements, 1986b).

Unfortunately, their friend was 6 years, 1 month old by the time they finished. But the present was appreciated anyway, and both the product and the process were worth waiting for. As a third grader put it, Logo is "very hard ... but it had to be done. I liked doing it" (Carmichael et al., 1985, p. 90).

These children were engaged in sophisticated thinking involving such problem-solving strategies as problem determination, subgoaling, construction of procedures, and persistence; and such mathematical concepts as equality, symmetry, part–whole relationships, and arithmetic operations.

FIGURE 4-1
Two first graders' birthday
greeting, programmed in Logo.

The computer programming language they are learning and using—Logo—
was designed to facilitate just such thinking. Therefore, we will focus on
Logo first, and later discuss other computer languages. We will begin to
answer the following questions:

> Why use Logo, or any computer programming language?
>
> What is Logo?
>
> What does research tell us about using computer programming to teach math-
> ematics?
>
> How might computer programming be used in the classroom?
>
> What about other computer programming languages?

Most specific applications will be discussed in the following topical
chapters. To benefit the most from all these discussions, it is strongly recommended that you engage in hands-on experience with Logo yourself.

WHY USE LOGO?

Origins of Logo

Seymour Papert, one of the creators of Logo, studied with Piaget for
several years. Of the two major voices of Piaget (recall Chapter 1), Papert
listened to and followed the first one to a profound degree; he heard, but
did not completely follow, the second.

The first voice: The child actively constructs knowledge. Recall that Piaget
believed that knowledge is not a state children are in, but rather a process
in which they are engaged. Children learn by doing and by thinking about
what they are doing. According to Papert, what they are doing and thinking
in Logo is far richer than in most other environments. Students may create
a procedure, try it out, find the errors or limitations, fix or enhance it, try
it out again, and possibly extend it to become a more generalized proce-

dure. They use Logo as an *idea expresser.* Therefore, Logo is not just a computer programming language to learn. It is a language with which to learn and to express learnings.

The second voice: Development proceeds through stages. Also recall that Piaget said that children develop through stages, and their thought at each stage is qualitatively different from their thought at any other stage. Criticisms of Logo are often spoken from this voice. It has been argued that preoperational or concrete-operational children either cannot deal with computer programming, or that using Logo may force formal operational thinking too soon, damaging children's development. It is true that developmental characteristics of children should be carefully considered when designing educational experiences for them. However, it is Papert's position that the reason many ideas are not developed until adolescence is not due to inevitable age/stage limitations, but to the lack of rich environments that embody these ideas. The goal of Logo is to "concretize" the formal, making it accessible to younger children. Papert looks to ideas that *could* develop, not to those that at present *do* develop.

Is this overly optimistic? Piaget himself stated that the notion of inflexible stages characterized by invariable chronological age limits and by fixed thought content should be rejected—that sound teaching methods can increase children's intellectual development. Children develop due to interactions with their environment. According to Papert, our present cultural environment provides few "building blocks" for mathematical ideas; Logo may enhance this environment.

Thus, Papert was most profoundly influenced by Piaget's idea that children construct their own knowledge. Papert argues that the most beneficial learning is "Piagetian learning," or "learning without being taught." Papert recounts his own early involvement—intellectual and emotional—with gears and the way they meshed and worked together. He learned to understand many mathematical concepts by asking: "How is this like gears?" Gears, for him, became tools for thinking and learning. He believed that computers could provide such a tool—albeit a more powerful one—for children.

Papert, along with Harold Abelson, Andrea diSessa, Wallace Feurzeig, Marvin Minsky, and others at MIT and at Bolt Beranek and Newman, Inc., designed Logo as a framework for learning mathematics and problem solving. But do children really need to learn to program computers? What unique contribution will this make to their learning of mathematics?

Logo and Mathematics

You may have read criticisms of computer programming in the schools. For example, "In the future, most people who work with computers will not have to program them." Unfortunately, this observation completely misses the point. Wise teachers do not help students learn Logo mainly to develop their "computer literacy" or "occupational skills." Their students learn Logo so that they can do more with mathematics, and they learn more mathematics so that they can do more with Logo. Used in this way, Logo "provides an operational universe within which students can define a mathematical process and then see its effects unfold. It is accessible to very young children for simple tasks, yet its operations can be systematically extended to express problems of considerable complexity" (Feurzeig & Lukas, 1972, p. 39).

For example, children can create geometric figures by typing sets of instructions into the computer that direct the movement of a cybernetic "turtle" on the computer screen. (These commands can be relative, such as FORWARD and RIGHT; they can utilize a set of coordinate axes; and they can include a full range of arithmetic functions.) Once students decide on or are assigned a figure to draw, they must devise a set of instructions that will make the turtle draw the figure. They must analyze the figure and break it into smaller parts that are more easily constructed. They must determine angle measures and lengths of line segments. Thus, they are constantly involved in mathematical problem solving. Through such activity, Logo emphasizes verbalizing goals and strategies before making overt moves toward a problem solution, creating efficient problem representations, making executive decisions, and debugging (finding and fixing the errors in) algorithms—problem-solving skills that are too seldom explicitly taught in schools.

In addition, a student who is asked to construct a set of commands to draw a square, for example, must make her concept of square explicit. Entering the commands into the computer allows the student to test the validity of her conceptualization. In this way, her concept of "square" is expressed as an active object which she can manipulate, modify, and study. Through such activity, students build a conceptual representation, or frame, that is an understandable, powerful "isomorphic image" for dealing with problematic situations of similar types (Davis, 1984). Or, as one intermediate-grade Logo programmer said, "I've thought about circles in ways I've never considered before" (Carmichael et al., 1985, p. 285).

WHAT IS LOGO?

A Language for Learning

Let's begin by summarizing and expanding on what we have discussed so far. First, Logo is a computer language, a program that translates commands and instructions people understand into electronic signals that the computer can "understand," in other words, into instructions that the computer can follow. In this way, Logo is like a translator in a foreign country who helps you say what you want to say but never tells you what to say.

Second, Logo is a language for learning that can be used by preschoolers and college graduates; that allows a person to create interesting programs almost immediately, but provides for explorations of unlimited depth; that can serve as a conceptual framework for teaching mathematics and problem-solving skills, helping students gain an explicit awareness of themselves as thinkers and learners.

Turtle Graphics

Next let's take a closer look at that part of Logo which often serves as an introduction to the language: "turtle graphics." The figure in the middle of Christine and Elizabeth's screen is called the turtle. (In some versions of Logo it looks like a turtle; in others, it is a triangular pointer.) The first turtle was a dome-shaped, computer-controlled robot, called a tortoise or turtle by its inventor, that scurried around on large sheets of paper, drawing shapes.

The turtle responds to instructions. If you type FORWARD 50, the turtle moves forward 50 "turtle steps" in whatever direction it is pointing (see Fig. 4–2a). FORWARD is a command; 50 is its "input" (i.e., this command needs a number "put into" it to determine how far the turtle goes forward). RIGHT or LEFT rotates the turtle a given number of degrees— the turtle turns "in place." RIGHT 90 commands the turtle to make a "quarter turn" to the right (i.e., clockwise; see Fig. 4–2b). PENUP and PENDOWN tell the turtle to stop and start leaving a trace of its path on the screen. (Notice that these commands do not "take inputs"; that is, they do their jobs without being given a number.)

Interesting drawings can be created just using these commands (Fig. 4–2c). But one can also "teach" the computer new words. For instance, one second grader taught the computer how TO make a square:

```
TO SQUARE
  FORWARD 50
  RIGHT 90
  FORWARD 50
  RIGHT 90
  FORWARD 50
  RIGHT 90
  FORWARD 50
  RIGHT 90
END
```

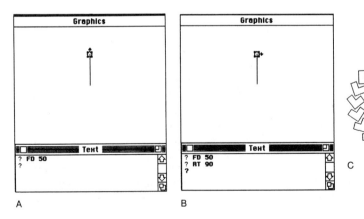

FIGURE 4-2 Logo commands and their effects.

SQUARE is now a new Logo procedure. The first, or title, line specifies the name (which didn't have to be SQUARE—it could have just as well been called BOX or MYSHAPE.) The "TO" reinforces the metaphor of teaching—the girl taught Logo *how to* draw a square. The last line, the word END, indicates that this is the end of the definition of the procedure. In between, the body tells the computer how to carry out the procedure. The body is a list of instructions. SQUARE tells the turtle to go forward 50 steps, turn right 90°, go forward 50 steps, turn right 90° again, and so on. But this SQUARE can only be one size, unlike the more versatile FORWARD, which takes an input that determines how far the turtle should move. What if we wanted our SQUARE procedure to draw squares of any size? We would need to change the procedure to have inputs—a name for the length of the sides. Then when we instructed the turtle to draw a SQUARE, we could tell it—right then—what this length would be. For example, SQUARE might be written this way:

```
TO SQUARE  :LENGTH.SIDE
  FORWARD    :LENGTH.SIDE
  RIGHT 90
  FORWARD    :LENGTH.SIDE
  RIGHT 90
  FORWARD    :LENGTH.SIDE
  RIGHT 90
  FORWARD    :LENGTH.SIDE
  RIGHT 90
END
```

Note that the title line now includes the name of the input, preceded by a colon (called "dots" in Logo). Now if we type SQUARE, we must specify a certain length for the sides (see Fig. 4–3).* If we forget we've changed the

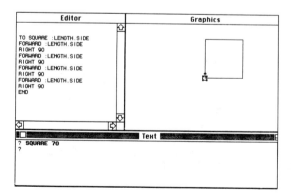

FIGURE 4-3
The SQUARE procedure and its input.

*Sometimes, the figures shown will only be the *graphics screen* on which the turtle draws, or a combination of the graphics screen and the *text screen*, the area where we type instructions (e.g., Fig. 4–2). One other type of screen is the *editor*, where new procedures we are "teaching the turtle" are typed in and changed (e.g., Fig. 4–3). In fact, most versions of Logo do not show the editor alongside the other two screens. Instead, one switches back and forth between them. Because this mode of presentation may help you connect the three, it will be used here.

procedure to take inputs, Logo "complains" (the word shown in *ITALICS* is typed by the student):

```
SQUARE
NOT ENOUGH INPUTS TO SQUARE
```

LENGTH.SIDE is a variable.** A *variable* is a bit of information with a name. The name is LENGTH.SIDE. The colon in front of :LENGTH.SIDE means "the bit of information whose name is LENGTH.SIDE." The information stored under that name will depend on what the user types. SQUARE will draw a SQUARE, and the length of the sides will be that number. The information stored can easily be changed or varied each time we draw a square; that is one reason for the name variable.

Incidentally, you might have noticed that we seemed to repeat ourselves a bit. Couldn't Logo do some of that work? Yes, the procedure might have been written as

```
TO SQUARE :LENGTH.SIDE
 REPEAT 4 [FORWARD :LENGTH.SIDE RIGHT 90]
END
```

REPEAT is a command that takes two inputs. The first must be a number that specifies how many times we want to repeat something. The

FIGURE 4-4 Elementary students illustrate the concept of variables through function machines designed to build rectangles.

**The period in LENGTH.SIDE is for readability's sake only. All variable names must be a single word, without spaces. Thus, we might have just called this variable LENGTHSIDE. To ease reading for children, we can insert a period: LENGTH.SIDE.

"something" we repeat is the second input. This is a list of instructions that we want Logo to repeat. For SQUARE, the turtle should go forward the amount given in LENGTH.SIDE, then turn right 90°. It should do this four times.†

Finally, we can now use either of our new square procedures to make many interesting pictures and designs (Fig. 4–5). Each contains simple but meaningful mathematics (what mathematical ideas can you identify?). For Fig. 4–5c, a new procedure was written:

```
TO DESIGN
  REPEAT 8 [SQUARE 30 RIGHT 45]
END
```

Because SQUARE is used as a part of those procedures, we call SQUARE a subprocedure of these new procedures. Another important idea is demonstrated in the program that produced Fig. 4–5e:

```
TO TOWER
  SQUARE 20 SEAM1 20 SQUARE 20 SEAM1 20 SQUARE 20
  SEAM2   20 30
  SQUARE 20 SEAM1 20 SQUARE 20
  SEAM2   20 10
  SQUARE 20
END

TO SEAM1 :LENGTH
  RT 90
  FD :LENGTH
  LT 90
END
```

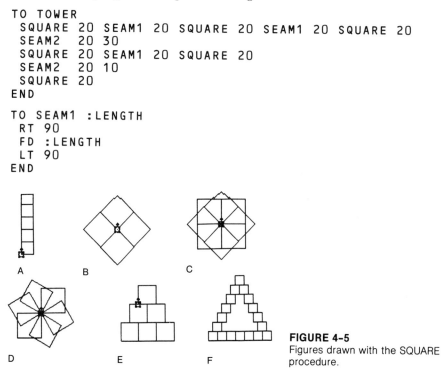

FIGURE 4-5
Figures drawn with the SQUARE procedure.

A   B   C

D   E   F

†Are you starting to feel a bit lost? Do not worry. You cannot learn computer programming solely by reading a book. In addition, space limitations here prohibit anything but the briefest discussion of Logo as a language. You have at least two choices. The best choice is to find a computer, the Logo language for that computer, and a tutorial (the one that comes with Logo or one mentioned toward the end of this chapter). Then sit down and try programming yourself. The second choice is to read this chapter slowly, following the examples step by step, to gain an intuitive notion of Logo programming. Don't concentrate on details, but attempt to get a holistic view. That is, don't worry about mastering commands until you can get some hands-on experience. Instead, concentrate on the possible ways Logo could be used in your classroom.

```
TO SEAM2 :LENGTH1 :LENGTH2
  FD :LENGTH1
  LT 90
  FD :LENGTH2
  RT 90
END
```

Notice that we introduce the use of common abbreviations here, such as RT for RIGHT, FD for FORWARD, and LT for LEFT. The procedures that draw parts of the picture (each one is SQUARE in this example) are separated from the procedures that "sew" these together (called SEAM1, SEAM2, etc.). Teachers often neglect to stress the importance of these procedures, which move the turtle from one part of the drawing to another. Students often include the "seam" commands inside the procedures they write to draw basic shapes. This leads to confusion and mistakes. Can you see how putting a "SEAM" in with the SQUARE procedure would make it almost impossible to use SQUARE in so many different programs? Because these seams are not *seen* in a picture, they are difficult for students to understand (Leron, 1985).

Note that Logo is procedural. Logo programs consist of small, understandable procedures (such as SQUARE or the letters in HAPPY BIRTHDAY), each of which has a specific job to do. This allows students to look at the "big picture," first, planning what they want to do, and then breaking this large plan down into what one student described as "mind-sized bites" (Papert, 1980). For example, three first-grade boys started by writing the following procedure:

```
TO E.T.
  THROAT
  HADE
  EYE
  EYE
  EYEBROWS
END
```

They then taught the computer how to draw each part, defining the throat, "hade" (head), eye, and eyebrows separately. This produced Fig. 4-6. In this way, students can "divide and conquer" problems as they begin to see, in concrete fashion, how tasks may be broken down into procedures, how procedures may be combined to form "superprocedures" like E.T. and TOWER, and how procedures interact.

Beyond (and Behind) the Turtle

The turtle may be Logo's best friend, but paradoxically, it also tends to limit people's perception of Logo's potential. The attention given to turtle geometry leaves many believing that Logo is "just a drawing program for kids." Unfortunately, they have missed two essential points. First, as discussed above, Logo is structured to aid learning in a profound sense. That is, Logo is based on a theory of learning. Second, although Logo is an interesting and useful language for explorations of graphics and geometry, its

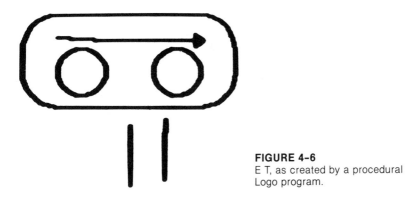

FIGURE 4-6
E T, as created by a procedural
Logo program.

power does not stop there. *Behind* the turtle—that is, the foundations under-lying Logo programming—are powerful geometric and numerical ideas. As a simple example, two first-grade boys were writing a program to make a drawing of a clock tower in their town (Fig. 4-7). Starting on the left side, they made three horizontal lines across the top. They used ideas of symme-try and equality in planning for the third line (FORWARD 20) to be equal to the first (FORWARD 20). Then at the bottom they used the mathematical concept of composition and skills in mental computation to combine the three inputs—20 + 35 + 20, and typed FORWARD 75.

Beyond the turtle, Logo can deal directly with numbers, numerical op-erations, and words. As a simple example, children might use the PRINT statement to label their pictures. Extending the SQUARE program would yield

```
TO SQUARE :LENGTH.SIDE
  REPEAT 4 [FORWARD :LENGTH.SIDE RIGHT 90]
  PRINT SENTENCE [THIS SQUARE'S SIDES ARE] :LENGTH. SIDE
END
```

Another example of simple nonturtle mathematics comes from two fifth graders, Michelle and Jonathan, who were challenged by their teacher to write an arithmetic practice program for their classmates. They benefited

FIGURE 4-7
CLOCK.TOWER, a program that
elicited arithmetical thinking
from its first grader authors.

from simultaneous experience with programming, problem solving, and practice (see Clements, 1983).

Other turtle and nonturtle challenges will be presented throughout the following chapters. Most are more mathematically sophisticated than the fifth graders' practice program; however, most are less complicated in terms of programming! This combination—high math, low programming— holds much promise for integrating Logo into elementary mathematics.

Microworlds

A *microworld* is a small playground for the mind. More specifically, it is a computer program that allows students to explore a concept from an initial, intuitive level to a formal, deductive level. A boy showed some understanding of this sequence when he stated that "with Logo I am doing things in math before we ever learn it" (Carmichael et al., 1985, p. 288). It is not a tutorial or drill; rather, it provides interesting ("neat") phenomena that invite experimentation. Scientists experiment with a system—a certain set of materials (airplane wings in a wind tunnel, chemicals, etc.)—to determine how it "works"; that is, what rules govern its behavior. Similarly, students experiment with a computer microworld to form and test hypotheses to determine the underlying rules of some mathematical system. These experiments are guided by the teacher.

Papert states that each microworld involves just a piece of reality, simple enough to "get ahold of" but rich enough to encourage exploration. Thus, the microworld, as a part of a more complex system and as a method for learning, is not unlike a construction kit. Turtle geometry itself might be seen as one general microworld. We will meet others in the following chapters.

RESEARCH ON LOGO

There are reasons to believe that—properly done—Logo programming may increase children's achievement and thinking skills. Is there any evidence testing this belief? We know one thing: programming is not an easy task. It is problem-solving intensive and precision intensive. Research also demonstrates that young Logo programmers *do* use notions such as number, approximation, arithmetic operations, and geometric concepts. Do they transfer this knowledge to non-Logo tasks? The evidence is mixed, with most studies showing little transfer to performance on typical achievement tests. It is possible that, without guidance, many students do not see the connection between these concepts and other mathematical tasks.

For example, an interview from a longitudinal study by the author illustrates how one third grader's work in Logo remained unconnected with other aspects of his mathematical knowledge. John had previously responded incorrectly to an item from a commercial mathematics achievement test: "How many angles are in a triangle?" When the same question was posed in the follow-up interview, John asked: "What do you mean 'angle' ... corners?" Later in the interview, John was asked how he drew a triangle with the turtle when he was in first grade.

John: We started and then I put 'LEFT' and I made it turn so it would be like that (rotating hand). Then I made it go forward so it would go like that and then I made it turn on an angle. An angle (shouting and laughing)! A turn! A turn ... the same thing. (Pause)

Interviewer: That's neat, huh? That's the same thing! So how many angles would the turtle have to make to do it?

Thus, in his experience with Logo, John had developed the useful notion of an angle as a turn. Probably because his Logo experience was not so designed, John failed to see connections between the Logo concept of "turn" and the notion of angle he was encountering in his classroom mathematics work.

His performance suggests that the standard treatment of the angle concept that he was receiving in his classroom was inadequate in two respects. First, using classroom-based knowledge of angle, he was unable to answer the achievement test item and felt the need to ask for a definition during the interview. Second, it can be hypothesized that John's classroom experiences with angle were so infrequent and static that it was not until the interview that he made the connection. However, John's response also revealed that children do not relate their Logo experience to other experiences in mathematics. For example, had the interview never occurred, it is highly unlikely that John would have made a connection between the Logo concept of "turn" and the notion of angle he was encountering in his classroom mathematics work.

To promote students' construction of such connections, teachers must take great care to create explicit "mappings" or links between Logo and other mathematical activities. Such mappings between Logo explorations and classroom work will enrich students' knowledge structure of particular mathematics topics, allowing them to build new semantic connections within those topics (Davis, 1984) and new mental representations, or frames, for mathematical situations. Furthermore, by highlighting how geometric concepts manifest themselves in different environments (Logo and non-Logo), the mappings will facilitate transfer. Thus, through proper teacher guidance, students may construct elaborative schemata, or frames (rather than mechanical chains of rules and terms) for specific mathematical topics such as angles and variables. Evidence from intensive interview studies indicates that this is the case (Clements, 1986–87). If such mappings are used, gains in problem solving and creativity are also achieveable (Clements, 1986a; Clements & Merriman, in press).

The following section provides teaching suggestions designed to give more concrete meaning to the phrase "proper teacher guidance." The suggestions are limited, however, to introductory activities and to general guidelines for teaching any topic with Logo. As stated previously, ideas for teaching specific mathematical topics with Logo are included in the following chapters as appropriate (for example, several ideas for teaching geometry with Logo are included in Chapter 9).

TEACHING AND LEARNING WITH LOGO

Off-computer Introductory Activities

Readiness for programming.   Several activities help develop skills that are involved in computer programming. Note, however, that these skills are also important in their own right, and their development can impact significantly on students' educational progress in several areas. It would not be justifiable to spend limited class time merely "preparing students for programming."

Procedural thinking.   Procedures are step-by-step instructions on how to do a specific task. People follow procedures all the time without being aware that they are doing so, but computers need exact instructions in order to operate; these instructions are procedures. Considered as such, they are similar to directions, such as those already discussed. However, they are more than simple directions in two ways: (1) they describe a specific and limited set of directions that accomplish a specific task (mathematicians refer to "algorithms" in much the same way); (b) they can be combined in various ways to perform quite complex tasks. The first characteristic can be introduced to children by having them describe a familiar activity in procedural form. Children should be led to see that:

> Procedures are instructions for doing a job.
> Procedures need to be described exactly.
> Procedures can be acted out.
> Procedures can be modified as necessary.

Guiding children to describe these procedures in detail will help them both understand procedural thinking and perform the task. A kindergarten teacher often had her classes place wooden rods in order from smallest to largest as a mathematics readiness activity. To extend the activity and develop procedural thinking and problem-solving abilities, she decided to ask children how they solved the problem. Here are some of their solutions, which also illustrate young children's real ability to solve problems.

> "You pick up any one and if it's not right (if it breaks the uniform increase of the 'stairs'), then you put it back and get another one."
> "See you get one and then you try to see where it goes. If it doesn't go at this end or this end, you have to move some of the others over."
> "You choose any one and then you've got to find just the right place for it. Like this, see, it has to be bigger than all these, and, uh, like not as big as any of these."
> "Easy. Find the smallest one, then the very next smallest one, and keep going like that."

All of these students had found a solution. Some were more sophisticated than others; however, they all gained from describing their own method in terms of procedures and from comparing their procedure to those of others. Note that this process of ordering actually has many similarities to computer programming. First, it is accomplished by carefully following a logical series of actions or steps. Second, it involves repetitive use of these steps. Third, at certain points it involves making decisions. Fourth, different procedures are equally successful at solving the problem. This teacher also enriched her pupils' understanding by having a puppet, "Mr. Mixup," order the rods incorrectly. She had the puppet ask the children to find the "bugs" (errors) in his procedures and—with words—tell him how to fix, or "debug," his method.

A first-grade teacher guided her students in developing a procedure to compare the capacities of pairs of containers, labeled with letters. Her students suggested: (a) put sand in one of the containers; (b) pour it in the other container; (c) if it overflows, write down the letter on the first one in the "more" column (of a chart they had developed); (d) if it doesn't fill up the second container, write down the letter on the second one in the "more" column. This was a good start, and the teacher encouraged several students to try it out. It seemed to work well until one child neglected to fill the first container completely. First graders might not yet fully understand measurement, but they understand what's fair. "That's not fair! You didn't fill it up." Step "a" was quickly amended so that the container was filled "level." Another bug was found: "Hey, these are the same." "So write down that they're the same." "That's not on the chart or in the procedure." Step "e" was added. And so it went, with children developing abilities in measurement, pouring, letter reading and writing, procedural thinking, and problem solving. Teachers of older students might conduct a similar lesson dealing with "how to subtract two multidigit numbers."

Conditional thinking. All computer languages have a way of expressing conditionals—"*if* something, *then* do something." Children need to express and hear many examples of this type of thinking. They might brainstorm to fill in the blank: "If it is raining, then _____." Point out to children whenever conditionals are used in the classroom: "That's an *if/then* statement. *If* I put two more pencils in the can, *then* there will be just enough for each person."

Additional activities are more specific to turtle geometry.

Turtle walks. Classroom turtle walks are an effective way to introduce Logo programming. Have one person be the turtle while one or more others give directions. It is a good idea if you are the first "turtle," so you can model following directions exactly without interpreting them, even if they have bugs. Children also enjoy "ordering around" the teacher. Then let a child be the turtle. At first the goal might be to get the child-turtle from one place to another in the room, avoiding obstacles. Then the child-turtle could be blindfolded and given directions—with all due provisions for safety, of course. Lead the children to discover that the most useful directions involve telling the turtle to walk forward or turn right or left. Some children like to pretend they are the "control tower" and the child-turtle is an airplane on a foggy day.

It is not too soon to informally introduce significant geometric ideas. That is, the turtle walks a path—a record of movement. Using only the forward and back commands creates a path that is straight (a line segment).

The right and back commands specify turns (rotations) that, together with segments, construct an angle. Paths constructed may be closed (those whose starting and ending points are the same) or not closed, simple (i.e., do not intersect themselves) or not simple.

After a couple of gamelike practice sessions, have the computer available. While one child acts out the commands, have the Logo turtle do likewise on the screen. Let the activity itself emphasize that the turtle does exactly what the programmer(s) tell it to do. By using their own movement, show them that direction is *relative* to position. Have them imagine that they are the turtle. This will take advantage of their own knowledge of their bodies in space and encourage them to use this knowledge in their explorations of geometric ideas.

Grid games. Give each pair of children two grids, such as centimeter squared paper, small pictures of a turtle that fit in the squares, pencils, and a screen. Each child sits on one side of the screen. They both start their turtles at the upper left-hand square of the paper, facing down. One child draws a path while describing it to his partner in "turtle talk." The partner tries to follow the instructions. At the end, papers are compared.

Turtle clocks. Using masking tape, draw a large clockface on the floor. Have one child stand at the center, another at 12:00, and another at 9:00. Have them stretch a piece of yarn between them. Talk about what shape they have constructed. Have the child at 12:00 move to 11:00 and the child at 9:00 move to 8:00. What happened? Recreate these shapes on the screen, asking children to specify each step. Then provide a board with 12 nails placed in a circle and one in the center. Children use rubber bands to make shapes and figure out angles. A regular geoboard with a 5 by 5 rectangular arrangement of nails can also be used to construct new designs. These materials are just as useful to supplement and aid on-computer activities.

Off-computer activities ensure continuity between concrete and kinesthetic activity and the more abstract activity of Logo programming. They also provide a concrete model for children to use in tackling more difficult programming challenges and finding elusive bugs in their procedures.

On-computer Introductory Activities

Introducing Logo to young children. Three levels of procedures can be used to support young children's initial programming efforts. These programs give children what good teachers often give—just enough, but not too much, support. They provide the "scaffolding" that allows children to reach what would have been beyond their grasp. As children's abilities develop, parts of this scaffolding can gradually be removed. Level 1 removes many of the mechanical obstacles, such as typing, spelling, and estimating distances as well as the obstacles of planning a sequence of instructions. It permits children to use single keystrokes in moving the turtle, defining procedures, and combining these procedures. Level 2 removes only the difficult demands of abstract planning and ordering instructions. It allows children to write and define new programs in the full Logo language while the turtle simultaneously carries out each command. Level 3 provides only a set of procedures that children could use as "black boxes" in their programming.

Level 1: Singlekey. This is a single-keystroke program, which permits children to move the turtle, define procedures ("teach the turtle new words"), and combine these procedures by pressing only one key for each major command. These commands include the following (the regular Logo command which each key duplicated is in parentheses): F (FORWARD 10), B (BACK 10), 1–9 (REPEAT the next command typed that number of times), R (RIGHT 30), L (LEFT 30), U (PENUP), D (PENDOWN), C (CLEAR-SCREEN), T (teach the turtle a new procedure), P (asks what procedure you want the turtle to draw), and E (erases last command). Certain commands (e.g., R or F) are erased immediately; that is, the turtle merely "backs up" and erases an unwanted line, or turns right to erase an L command. A child who has drawn a triangle and a SQUARE (square) with the F and R commands, and taught the turtle each with the T keystroke, might combine them into a house. Typing P, she would be asked

```
WHAT PICTURE DO YOU WANT TO SHOW?
YOU HAVE TRI SQUARE
```

She might type SQUARE and, after the turtle drew this, move to the top of the square, press R, then P(icture), and then TRI. The house would be drawn. She could then T(each) the turtle the house, and possibly use it to draw several houses in a row. Ideas for using SINGLEKEY in the learning of specific mathematical topics are offered in later chapters. Versions of such programs are available from several sources (e.g., many versions of Logo come with such a program, often called INSTANT; see also Clements & Battista, 1988; Clements, 1983–84).

Level 2. Here children type the usual Logo commands, but in addition use several procedures provided by the teacher. Typing TEACH allows children to define a procedure. However, as in level 1, the turtle carries out the commands one by one as the children enter them, permitting them to use their intuitive visual strengths in creating their procedure. If the children type E, the turtle erases the last command entered. If an instruction is entered that is unknown to the turtle, the program informs the children of this and does not enter it into the program being defined. For instance, if they type FORWARD50, the program responds: DID YOU FORGET A SPACE? THERE IS NO PROCEDURE NAMED FORWARD50. Typing END instructs the computer to define the procedure. A listing of this TEACH program, which you can type in, can be found in Clements (1983–84).

Some teachers make one additional modification at this level. In the SINGLEKEY program, the turns are executed slowly, on purpose, so children see exactly "what is happening." Even so, when moved to regular Logo command, children often cannot visualize the rotations. They also find it hard to understand why RIGHT 360 doesn't seem to do anything, why RIGHT 300 looks like a left turn, or why FORWARD 1000 moves the turtle only a little more than FORWARD 230 (because the turtle has "wrapped

FIGURE 4-8
Young children work with the
SINGLEKEY program and a floor
turtle to trace paths and explore
directionality.

around" the screen several times). Thus, the teachers type in procedures for
each of the four basic commands such as

```
TO F :NUMBER
 REPEAT :NUMBER [FORWARD 1]
END
```

The turtle will move slowly, giving children an opportunity to see exactly how it moves. Children need only type in R 300 instead of RIGHT 300
or RT 300. With many versions of Logo, it is just as easy for the teacher
actually to redefine the FD, BK, RT, and LT commands to be these "slow"
versions.

Level 3.   At this level, children use the traditional Logo editor along
with special procedures supplied to them. These include CIRCLE.RT (draws
a circle curving to the right; the child must specify a radius), POLY (draws
a polygon; the child must specify the number of sides and the length of
each side), and so on. In fact, they should include any procedure students
can use with understanding, although they might not yet be able to define
it on their own.

Game/Activities for Skill Development

Feed the turtle.   This activity actually begins as an off-computer game, and thus constitutes a good transition between off- and on-computer activities (adapted from Kull & Cohen, n.d.). In this game, a number line from 0 to 100 is laid on the floor. Five cards, all of which have arrows on the top side, and one of which has a picture of a fish on the bottom, are placed at random on the line (the arrow indicates the precise location of the card on the number line). One student is the turtle. He or she begins by placing a cutout triangle at zero. The other students then take turns instructing the turtle with FORWARD and BACK commands in an attempt to "land on" the same number as one of the cards. For example, if the turtle had landed on 74 and a card was located at 68, a child might command the turtle to move BACK 6. If the turtle lands on a card, he or she turns the card over. If it is blank, the game continues (Fig. 4–9). If the card has the fish, the turtle is "fed" and the student who directed the turtle to that number is the new turtle. One teacher limited the placement of the cards to multiples of 10 at first, then multiples of 5, then any whole number.

After a couple of days of play, the teacher introduced an on-computer version of this game. She helped students load a prewritten computer program (see FEED.TURTLE in the Appendix*) that drew a vertical axis (where

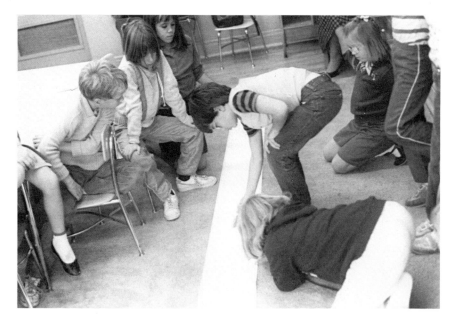

FIGURE 4–9 Playing Feed the Turtle.

*Logo programs are listed in the Appendix in the order in which they are referred to in the book.

each mark stood for 10 steps) and "cards" (lines) and waited for students to type commands. She pointed out that the program always printed the old and new position of the turtle at the bottom of the screen. As before, they typed FORWARD or BACK commands in attempt to match the position of a card. If they did, the program informed them that they were successful, and if the fish were found, drew a picture of the fish. Different strategies were emphasized (including the obvious, but often neglected, use of paper and pencil for more difficult addition or subtraction).

How far?   Challenge students to determine the exact length and width of the screen in turtle steps. Also explore turtle turns. What input to RIGHT makes the turtle turn "half-way around," pointing in the opposite direction (i.e., 180°)?, and so on. Stress such notions as perpendicularity ("right angles"). For both challenges, ask students to explain how they determined their answer. Many, for example, use successive approximation: guessing, then—on the basis of the turtle's movements—guessing more or less, all the while keeping a running total. For example, one pair guessed FD 50 for the distance from the turtle's HOME (the center of the screen) to the top of the screen. They saw that was not sufficient. They also saw that it was more than 50 additional turtle steps. So they typed FD 55 and wrote 50 + 55. Only a bit more was needed. They typed, in succession, FD 10, FD 10 BK 7, FD 2, and were finally satisfied with their overall total, 50 + 55 + 10 + 10 − 7 + 2, or 120 turtle steps. Their teacher then asked them to name other situations, in and out of school, in which a successive approximation strategy would be useful. She also challenged them to create as many ways as they could to get to, say, the bottom of the screen.

Hit the spot.   Children work in pairs, taking turns. One places a finger or small sticker anywhere on the screen. The other types in as few Logo commands as possible in order to place the turtle directly beneath the other's finger. A related game involves having one child create a list of commands off the computer. His partner puts a sticker at the place on the screen that he believes the turtle will stop. The prediction is checked by typing in the commands.

Mazes.   Draw a maze on acetate and tape it over the screen. Children direct the turtle through it. Or write Logo procedures that draw the mazes.

Shoot.   A variety of games, written in Logo, are available which are similar to those above; that is, children are challenged to hit a target drawn by the turtle. The turtle is placed in a random location and a random heading on the screen. Children receive a limited number of turns (RT or LT) and a limited number of moves (FD or BK) in an attempt to direct the turtle into the circular target (e.g., Watt, 1983).

Helpful tools.   One useful tool is a protractor. Although many are commercially available, one class was understandably proud of the one they constructed themselves with Logo (see Fig. 4–10). Their teacher duplicated the turtle's drawing on transparencies. This protractor is placed directly on the screen, so that it is facing in the same direction as the screen turtle. Then the turn is read off the protractor.

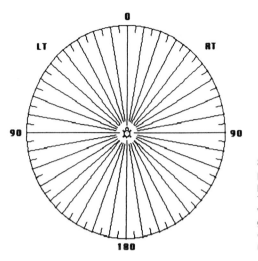

FIGURE 4-10
Students constructed their own protractor by writing a Logo program. The teacher made transparencies for each student, which were placed over geometric figures on and off the computer whenever the measure of turn was needed.

Another helpful tool is a ruler. Students might again determine how to have the turtle draw one; note, however, that a printed copy will not necessarily match the screen dimensions (students could trace from the screen). Some teachers have children measure their drawings in millimeters, which approximate turtle steps on some monitors.

Learning and Teaching Logo Relationally

Organizing knowledge of turtle commands.   Students tend to view Logo procedures as isolated words. Teachers should help them see the connections among the commands. One way of looking at the turtle's "world" is shown in Fig. 4-11. Turtle commands can be seen as affecting either of two large areas, the turtle or the screen (the large upper and bottom boxes). Commands directly related to the turtle can be further subdivided. Those that affect the turtle's state answer "Which?" and therefore are qualitative commands (the left top box). They address the visibility of the turtle and the turtle's trail and the color of the trail. Those that affect the turtle's position answer "How much?" and therefore are quantitative commands (the right top box). They address the turtle's heading, or orientation, and its position in space.

Such an organization helps students understand the logical nature of turtle commands and their relationships. In addition, it is an aid to programming. For example, students often write a procedure, a WINDOW for example, *assuming* certain states (e.g., the pen down and the trail color white). As they use WINDOW as part of a larger HOUSE program, however, they often put the pen up to move to the window's location. Then they are confused that the WINDOW is not drawn (i.e., the turtle follows the path, but does not leave a trail). The organization of commands in Fig. 4-11 may help emphasize that, for each procedure, the state commands should be considered first (Is the pen up or down? Is the pen color set correctly?),

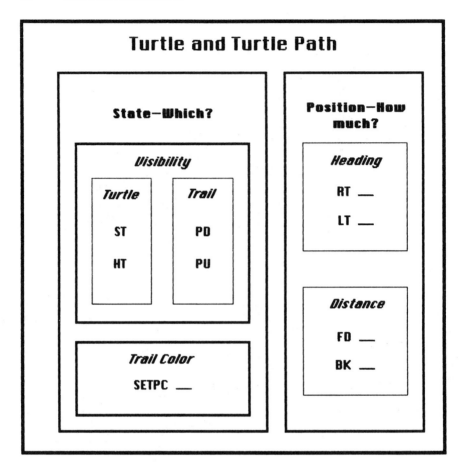

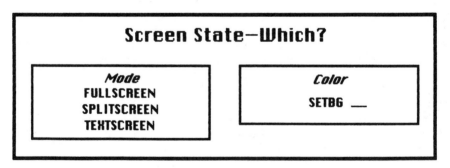

FIGURE 4-11 One way to organize thinking about turtle commands.

followed by the position commands (Is the turtle oriented correctly? How far should it move?). Similar organizational schemes could be created and illustrated for other Logo procedures.

Learning commands completely. In addition, students often learn only the bare minimum about each procedure. For example, many learn about a command, such as PRINT, only as "a way to get one thing done," in this case, as a way to print a word, number, or the like. They then cannot see all the ways the command might be used. For instance, if they are not guided to understand that PRINT also prints a carriage return (it moves the cursor down one line to the left margin), they will often not perceive PRINT (with an empty sentence or word as its input) as a way of double spacing or creating a blank line. Thus, commands, procedures, and the like should be examined and discussed fully to be understood and applied effectively.

For the teacher, and ultimately for students, a worthwhile format for describing procedures fully has been suggested by Harvey (1985). Modified slightly, it is:

Name the procedure.
State its purpose.
Tell whether it is a command or operation (reporter).
Tell about its inputs.
Tell what it does (if a command, what its effect is; if an operation, what it outputs).

For example, let's try it for FORWARD.

Name the procedure.	FORWARD
State its purpose.	is used to move the turtle forward, either to draw (with the pen down) or to change its position without drawing (with the pen up).
Tell whether it is a command or operation (reporter).	It is a command,
Tell about its inputs.	that takes one input, a number,
Tell what it does (if a command, what its effect is; if an operation, what it outputs).	and moves the turtle in the direction it is heading, that number of turtle steps.

And for QUOTIENT:

Name the procedure.	QUOTIENT
State its purpose.	is used to divide two numbers.
Tell whether it is a command operation (reporter).	It is an operation,
Tell about its inputs.	that takes two inputs, both numbers,
Tell what it does (if a command, what its effect is; if an operation, what it outputs).	and outputs the results of dividing the first by the second.

Of course, having students memorize these definitions would probably yield mere instrumental learning. Teachers should, however, find this format helpful for organizing essential information for themselves as well as for organizing meaningful learning experiences. Whether or not students can repeat this information, they should understand it relationally to obtain full benefit from programming. It can serve them as internal prompts, guiding them through programming problems.

Planning and Procedures

Planning. Help students plan and program their own projects by "breaking the problem down" into manageable pieces from the beginning. One class developed the following general planning strategy:

1. Make a "creative drawing," a freehand picture of your project. Remember to keep it simple and label its parts.
2. Then make a planning drawing.
   Use the planning form (basically, paper turned to side with the turtle at HOME).
   Draw the turtle where it starts the procedure.
   Have the turtle end in the same location and same heading at which it started ("state transparent"; see below).
   Label each line, turn, or PROCEDURE.
   Use the ruler and protractor to measure line segments and angles.
   Show the "moves" with the pen up (or seams) as dotted lines.
   For each new procedure that needs to be written, make a whole new planning form (i.e., start at the beginning of step 2 for each new procedure).
3. Have one partner read the instructions in order as the other records them at the right-hand side of the planning sheet.
4. Type them into the computer.
5. Debug each procedure separately, then the program as a whole (specific ideas for debugging are described in Chapter 5).

For example, in a research study by the author, two third-grade boys were writing a plan (off the computer) to make a spaceship. They first analyzed their "creative" drawing, ascertaining that they needed only two basic drawing procedures, a rectangle and an equilateral triangle. They wrote procedures for both of these, then constructed their planning drawing. Using these procedures, they traced through the drawing step by step, recording each command in the Procedures space. They first measured the rectangle on their planning drawing and found that the body of the ship was 30 mm by 55 mm. Therefore, the first step was RECT 30 55. They measured again and moved FD 5. Using their protractors, they determined that the correct turn was LT 120. Then a call to TRI 25 completed one rocket. "O.K., now just RT 120, to get back straight up . . . umm . . . then how far forward?" We want to go . . . how much? F-D 5, so 5 from the top. The rectangle is 30 tall, so forward 20." They continued around the perimeter of the rectangle, planning the appropriately sized triangles for the fins and the head of the ship. They used arithmetic again on the lower side. They needed to know the distance from the lower right-hand corner to the start of the fin. They added 18 (the distance they had gone forward from the upper right-hand corner near the tail to the "back" of the top fin) to 25 (the side of the "fin") and subtracted the sum from 55 (the side of the rectangle). Thus, they knew to go FD 12 to reach the bottom fin. This type of meaningful application of mathematics (measurement, arithmetic, etc.) is common in well-designed Logo environments. (The boys' actual procedure and plan is shown in Fig. 4–12.)

Students, especially younger ones, find it difficult to break down a picture into manageable parts and define the pieces as separate procedures. They might be guided to trace each part onto a separate piece of tracing paper, labeling each part. Each of these parts is written as a separate procedure. Each should be *state transparent*. This means that the turtle should end heading in the same direction (orientation) and in the same location as it was when it began the procedure. (*Mathematics note:* Ending in the same location usually means that the turtle has drawn a closed path.) This is an extremely useful technique. No matter where or when one uses the procedure, one knows the heading and location of the turtle when it completes the procedure.

Just deciding on a good way to break the problem down into pieces is often difficult. For instance, in planning to draw Fig. 4–5e, many students plan to go around the outside (perimeter) of the figure. One teacher discussed how to examine the drawing to find the most basic shapes. Students determined that if you *saw* the drawing as composed of squares, that was the only basic procedure you needed!

This kind of planning and group work encourages not only social interaction, but also planning ahead. It helps students become better problem solvers and it allows more students to get more programming experience on limited computer resources.

Chalk it, walk it, talk it.   If children are having difficulty writing the commands for one of their procedures, encourage them to return to "acting it out." They might go outside on a large concrete surface and draw the desired design with chalk (inside, use masking tape on the floor). Then they walk the design and simultaneously "talk it out" (describe exactly what they are doing in turtle commands) and write it down (record the steps so that they can type them into the computer.) On paper, children can use small pictures of turtles.

Dramatization.   Dramatizing the programs is a powerful teaching strategy, one that should never be abandoned because students are "too old." Dramatization in some form can take place in groups or individually. Group dramatizations, however, are especially helpful for understanding how procedures combine to make a program. The three boys who wrote "E.T." were asked to dramatize it for the class. Each procedure was anthropomorphized as a child who held a sign with the procedure's name and a list of the procedure's instructions. In this way, each procedure had one job to do. One boy pretended that he was the procedure E.T. He stood up, looked at his list of instructions, and called THROAT. This request caused another boy, who was playing the part of THROAT, to stand up. He looked

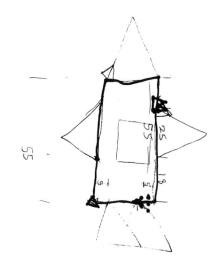
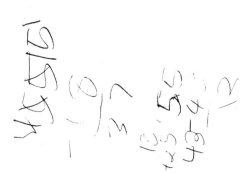

FIGURE 4–12 Two third graders' Logo plan.

at the commands that made up his procedure. The first thing he was to do was to call FORWARD and tell her to push the turtle forward 40 steps. FORWARD walked over to the turtle (another girl) and pushed her forward. The turtle left a trail with tape. FORWARD told THROAT she was done and sat down. THROAT then asked PENUP to do his job. PENUP walked over to the turtle and broke off the tape, placing it in the turtle's hands. PENUP told THROAT he was done and sat down. THROAT called RIGHT and said her input was 90. RIGHT stood up, walked over to the turtle, turned her 90° to the right, told THROAT she was done, and sat down. THROAT continued to call other commands until he was done, then informed E.T. of this and sat down. E.T. then called HADE. HADE stood up and looked at his instructions. The dramatization continued in this way. After being called by THROAT, HADE called CUR.LT, who in turn called REPEAT, and so on.

It is especially helpful to dramatize recursive procedures. Recursion is a powerful Logo programming technique. In recursion, part of a procedure's definition can be the procedure itself (unlike a dictionary). For example, examine the following procedure:

```
TO SQUARE
  FORWARD 30
  RIGHT 90
  SQUARE
END
```

Let's walk (or trace) it through. SQUARE begins by drawing a line segment 30 turtle steps in length. It then turns the turtle right 90°. Finally, it "calls itself"; that is, it generates another copy of itself. This copy draws a line segment, turns the turtle, and generates a copy of *it*self which . . . and so on and so on.

The most accurate way to dramatize such a recursive procedure is to have one child be SQUARE. As before, he calls on FORWARD and RIGHT. Then he calls SQUARE. This is not actually calling himself, but another copy of himself. In other words, SQUARE calls another child who is also SQUARE, who stands up and calls FORWARD and RIGHT,. who sit down after doing their job. She then calls another SQUARE. Notice, neither SQUARE has yet been told that everyone they called is done, so they cannot sit down. This continues as long as desired, or until the class runs out of children!

Of course, this is merely an illustrative example. First, SQUARE would more likely be written in a straightforward manner, as we did before. Second, this SQUARE would never stop! In actual recursive programs, we would write a "stop" rule. For example, let's play with the SQUARE procedure, first adding the variable we used previously:

```
TO SQUARE :LENGTH.SIDE
  FD :LENGTH.SIDE
  RT 90
  SQUARE :LENGTH.SIDE
END
```

This gives us a recursive square with any length side. Each SQUARE would create a copy of itself and "hand over" to this copy the same value of LENGTH.SIDE—the same number—it was given. Now let's change (vary) that variable, *inside* the procedure, to produce a NEW.SQUARE

```
TO NEW.SQUARE :LENGTH.SIDE
  FD :LENGTH.SIDE
  RT 90
  NEW.SQUARE ( :LENGTH.SIDE + 3 )
END
```

What will this NEW.SQUARE procedure do? If we typed NEW.SQUARE 10, the instructions would be FD 10 (that's what LENGTH.SIDE's value is for this NEW.SQUARE), RT 90, and then ... ? NEW.SQUARE would generate a copy of itself. But instead of handing over 10, it would first add 10 + 3, and hand over 13. Therefore, the instructions for the next copy of NEW.SQUARE would be FD 13 (the value of LENGTH.SIDE is for *this* copy of NEW.SQUARE), RT 90, and (tell it to yourself first!) then, this NEW.SQUARE would generate a copy of itself, handing over the value of 16. Read this paragraph again, tracing the steps, to be sure you "get the picture" (the Logo picture you get—partially completed—is shown in Fig. 4-13). If you believe you have, explain exactly how a group of children would dramatize this new procedure. (Note that NEW.SQUARE does *not* draw a geometric square, but a spiral with 90° turns.)

We see that recursion generates actions that can be quite interesting, if somewhat confusing at first. We have but one step to go—NEW.SQUARE still does not have a stop rule; it continues forever. We want it to stop when the length of the side is getting almost as long as the screen; that is, we need a conditional (IF/THEN) instruction.

```
TO NEW.SQUARE :LENGTH.SIDE
  IF :LENGTH.SIDE > 100 [STOP]
  FD :LENGTH.SIDE
  RT 90
  NEW.SQUARE ( :LENGTH.SIDE + 3 )
END
```

FIGURE 4-13
A figure produced by
NEW.SQUARE.

For Terrapin Logo:*

```
TO NEW.SQUARE :LENGTH.SIDE
  IF :LENGTH.SIDE > 100 THEN STOP
  FD :LENGTH.SIDE
  RT 90
  NEW.SQUARE ( :LENGTH.SIDE + 3 )
END
```

This new command tells each copy of NEW.SQUARE first to check if the value it was given for LENGTH.SIDE is greater than 100. If so, that copy should stop running immediately *after* it informs the copy that called *it* that it's done. Then *that* copy can tell the copy that called *it* that it too is done, and so on and so on.

To return to the dramatization: Each copy of NEW.SQUARE would first check if the value of its LENGTH.SIDE were greater than 100. (Actually, a teacher without a lot of students and a lot of time would wisely change the procedure to stop at a much lower number!) Say that after several sides were drawn, a boy was the first to be given such a value. He would have told the NEW.SQUARE that called him (say a girl) that he was done and then sat down. She would have told the NEW.SQUARE that called her that she was done and sat down, and this domino-like process would have continued until everyone was sitting.

Such dramatizations can help students build dynamic mental models of computer programs. Even young children can make sense of Logo in ways that are meaningful and natural to them (perhaps taken to the extreme by the kindergartner who, when instructing a girl-turtle, yelled "C" for Clearscreen and demanded that she "drop dead"!).

Analogies. One potent problem-solving strategy is to "make it your own by making it familiar." We have already discussed how to make the FORWARD, BACK, RIGHT, and LEFT commands real to childen by acting them out. This strategy can also involve making analogies between Logo commands and children's real-life situations. For instance, the PRINT command instructs the computer to act like a typewriter and print a list of words on the screen.

Understanding of another difficult concept, variables, can be aided through analogies. We use the idea of variables every day. "Who's the leader in line today?" "Jackie." "LEADER is the variable name—the people who are the leader vary day by day. This is just like "LENGTH.SIDE, which is the variable name; the value it takes varies each time you use the procedure SQUARE. One teacher used several similar situations to help her students relate to variables. For instance, they always sing a song, but the song they sing differs; it's as if their procedure was SING :SONG. In "May I"-type

---

*There are many different "dialects" of the Logo computer language. Many of the procedures we will use run unaltered in most of them. However, when there is a difference, the main procedure will be written in the most common LCSI dialect (this is the basis for Apple Logo, LCSI Logo II, IBM Logo, LogoWriter, etc.). For short programs, versions for Terrapin and other similar dialects of Logo will be provided directly following the LCSI version. Terrapin versions of longer programs are listed in the Appendix.

games, they use procedures such as WALK.BABY.STEPS :NUMBER.STEPS. In arithmetic, they used procedures such as SUBTRACT :NUMBER1 :NUMBER2. The subtraction procedures were always the same, but the numbers they subtracted varied.

Sometimes in Logo you have a specific command that sets a variable, such as MAKE "LENGTH.SIDE 50. The classroom analogy would be MAKE "LEADER "JACKIE (another day, MAKE "LEADER "JOHN).

The REQUEST (READLIST in some versions) command can be thought of as a person who asks "What do you think (or want)?" and waits for an answer. It instructs the computer to print a "?" on the screen, wait for a response to be typed in at the keyboard, and give that response to whatever procedure called REQUEST. Similar analogies can help children make meaningful models for other commands.

Prediction practice. When students are about to try something new, ask them to predict what it will look like. Structured prediction activities can also be beneficial. Write a simple program on the board in the morning. Challenge children to draw what they think the picture will be. Have one student enter and run the program to check. If appropriate, feature programs that children have written.

Logo and creativity. Encourage divergent thinking as children generate, elaborate, modify, and name procedures. Ask them: What else could you make, or do, or name it, and so on? How could you change that? What else could you make with that? Students should be allowed to experiment and explore the language, as well as meet challenges set by the teacher. Such exploration is of little benefit, however, if students are not guided to reflect on its meaning, or if they do not have the tools to figure out why something happened (e.g., tracing the program by hand; see Chapter 5).

Especially for younger students, encourage creativity and fantasy. Children might pretend that the turtle is going on a trip; they might make up stories about their drawings, and so on. In one class we provided a challenge to our students' geometric creativity while strengthening notions of procedurality and seams. Students were given four figures. They were asked to do the following:

> Write procedures for each figure (each one being state transparent, as described previously).
> Design as many programs/pictures as they could:
> that use all four figures.
> that use one figure as many times as possible.

Students could also add other figures as needed. Figure 4–14 shows some of our third graders' creations. (Make sure that you isolate the four basic figures as you examine them.)

GENERAL GUIDELINES

Use developmentally appropriate versions of Logo. Use versions of Logo that are developmentally appropriate for young children, for example, the "levels" described previously.

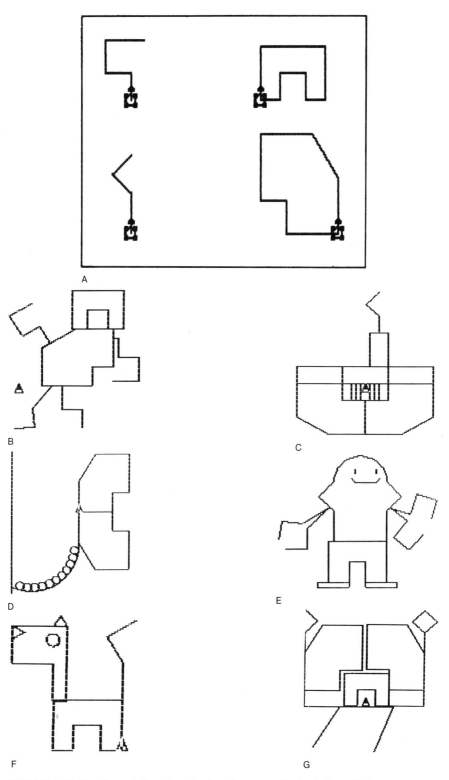

FIGURE 4-14 Creative solutions to using four figures as the basis for a design.

Help students learn Logo relationally. Ideas for organizing students' knowledge of turtle commands and for describing procedures completely were provided previously. Both help students learn Logo relationally rather than instrumentally. Also recommended is helping students recognize and utilize larger units of programming code, such as several procedures or lines of code that work together to achieve a purpose. Often called programming templates, they can be thought of as reusable *patterns* of code. We shall see examples of such patterns in later chapters.

Balance your lessons. Maintain a balance among teacher-directed lessons, teacher-posed challenges, and student-planned and student-executed projects (which can, ideally, utilize the mathematical ideas learned from the challenges). Unstructured activities alone are not sufficient. Didactic presentations also have a place. Many mathematical ideas can be presented through Logo, as the following chapters illustrate; however, without careful structuring by the teacher, it is not likely that these ideas will be learned by the majority of students.

Accept different learning styles. As much as you encourage planning and "top-down" thinking, children will differ in the styles of learning and programming. Some children will delight in planning, copying down procedures, and thinking ahead (the E.T. group). Others will use "bottom-up" thinking. Like block builders who start putting blocks together until they "recognize" something, these children tend to draw quite a bit before they combine procedures into a larger picture or other program. Each style should be accepted, even if you also plan to encourage children to adopt other styles when appropriate.

Also, some children use analytic thinking, such as evidenced in the OUTSIDE program (Fig. 4–15a). Here two girls figured out how much larger each half-circle in the rainbow had to be based on the distance between the vertical lines. Others use intuitive thinking, like the boys used in designing the FLOWER (Fig. 4–15b). They used visual approximation and some good guessing: "I think it will take about 15 half-circles to get around . . . No, how about 20?" All children should be gradually encouraged to see the strengths and weaknesses in both, so they can use them effectively.

Teach for transfer. Use questions such as: What else could be made from Rebecca's procedures? Susan, would that help you with your program? What are you planning to do now to extend your work? Who has a suggestion on how she might do that? How is this similar to other procedures you have written? Different? How is that procedure similar to the process we used yesterday to solve the mathematics problem?

The goal is students' conscious, deliberate efforts to transfer their knowledge, to recognize the need to recruit past experience to solve current problems, to genuinely understand the abstraction (relationally rather than instrumentally), to articulate the plan or principle being applied. What is necessary to engender such transfer? Socratic interaction with learners, calculated provocation of abstraction, and great sensitivity on the part of the teacher for the ebb and flow of enthusiasm and understanding in the individual student.

A   B

FIGURE 4-15 (a) OUTSIDE, a Logo procedure designed with analytic thinking; (b) first graders used visual estimation in making this flower.

Emphasize mathematics and problem solving. If Logo is to be used to teach mathematics, focus on the mathematics, and on mathematical problem solving, not on "programming" issues. Specific suggestions are given in the following chapters.

Develop Logo as a tool across topics and across grades. If Logo's potential is to be fully realized, it will be necessary for students to learn to use it as a tool for exploration across several topics and several grades. An isolated experience may have some value, but no tool will have wide-ranging effects used in that fashion. (Note that virtually all research studies of Logo have been limited to such experiences.) Students who learn to use Logo as they

FIGURE 4-16
Christine and Elizabeth discuss their Logo program.

do pencils or rulers—fully, naturally, and flexibly—will reap the full benefits of a powerful mathematical tool.

A Final Word on Projects

We suggested that some time be found in which students can work to
complete their projects—long-term enterprises that are personally meaningful to them. Why? Projects can represent powerful educational experiences in which children have the time and the commitment to develop an
understanding of mathematics as a process. Perhaps more important is the
child's sense of engagement—the burning desire to accomplish, to create,
to build.

Join me in a bit of reminiscing. What do you remember as the potent
educational experiences of your life? Most that I recall were projects of one
form or another. One was building a robot that welcomed people (not too
intelligently!) to a school science fair. Another was constructing an induction coil capable of generating enough voltage to shock my sister (the first
version of this project had an extremely short life). Both projects took more
than half a year to complete.

Sometimes, writing a Logo program takes a substantial amount of
time. So do other projects, such as building a Lego construction (a vehicle,
Ferris wheel, or city) that is controlled through Logo (see Chapter 11). This
may take time away from the traditional curriculum, as traditionally taught.
And teachers should certainly not dedicate only, or all of, their mathematics
periods to such projects. In other words, not all (or even most) mathematics
could or should be taught in such a fashion, and time for projects should
not come solely from mathematics. (In fact, given the time now spent on
mathematics, all the time might best come from other areas.) Something is
given up. But what is gained?

How might such projects influence children's

integration of mathematics topics, and of mathematics with other subject-
matter areas?

beliefs about mathematics and the process of "doing mathematics"?

attitudes toward and engagement with mathematics and learning?

self-concept?

I did not continue my interest in mathematics and science because my
teachers "covered" the year's content. I do not remember all of that content.
But I remember that robot, and I remember the concepts that I used to
build it. And those electric sparks burn as brightly for me now as ever.

What about you? What about your students?

OTHER PROGRAMMING LANGUAGES

BASIC

BASIC, Beginners' All-Purpose Symbolic Instruction Code, was developed by Professors Kemeny and Kurtz in 1963 to help college students write
programs. In recent years there has been much debate concerning the ap-

FIGURE 4-17
A shared project.

propriateness of teaching BASIC to elementary students. There are advantages to BASIC:

> If any programming language is "built into" a computer, and thus available when the computer is turned on, it is usually BASIC.
> It is interactive.
> It is relatively easy to learn to write simple programs (e.g., compared to Pascal).

What are the problems? Languages such as BASIC were written for computers from the 1960s which had small memories. Therefore, the primitives, the words the computer understands, were kept to a minimum. Often, the small number of basic words was taken as an advantage. Wouldn't that make the language easy to learn? To answer that question, answer another: Could you express yourself more easily with a language limited to a 100-word vocabulary? BASIC's origins have left it with several other disadvantages.

> Most versions are not procedural. Each of these BASIC programs is a single list of instructions. Children cannot "teach the computer new words" and teachers cannot supply younger children with "black box" procedures.
> It is not a well-structured language. It is difficult to start with the general and work toward the specific, in a top-down planning style.
> It is often difficult to debug and to change BASIC programs.
> Most important, BASIC was not designed for elementary grade students. It lacks the feature of turtle geometry. Its error messages are short and cryptic.

It is important to note that there *are* versions of this language that ameliorate many of these problems. For example, True BASIC (True BASIC, Inc.) and QuickBASIC (Microsoft) are more structured and have better editing and debugging features. However, because they have to be purchased, one of the main advantages—that BASIC is often "built in"—is lost, and other languages such as Logo might still be preferred. Therefore, much more space in this book is dedicated to languages such as Logo than to BASIC. It is important to note, however, that it has not been proven that any one language is superior. Although Logo is probably a better language for most purposes, if it is not yet available, good mathematics can still be done with well-planned BASIC activities. Luehrmann (1982) has argued that the important thing is not using any particular computer language, but teaching children to think carefully and write clearly in whatever language is available.

How can this be done? Simply by using the techniques that were described previously. For example, analogies for computer statements should be made. Programming should be introduced in the context of writing graphics programs. This is true even though BASIC pictures are created by plotting numerous points on a coordinate grid, rather than by directing the movements of a turtle. Computer programs should be dramatized. For example, one class dramatized a FOR-NEXT loop in a student's program.

```
10 REM BOBBY'S ADDING PROGRAM    REM allows a REMark that is ignored
20 FOR N = 1 TO 10               FOR begins a "counter loop"
30 PRINT N " + " N " = " N+N     The middle of the loop
40 NEXT N                        The end of the loop
50 END
```

When RUN by its author, it produced

```
 1 +  1 =  2
 2 +  2 =  4
 3 +  3 =  6
 4 +  4 =  8
 5 +  5 = 10
 6 +  6 = 12
 7 +  7 = 14
 8 +  8 = 16
 9 +  9 = 18
10 + 10 = 20
```

Challenged by the class to make it "run higher," he changed one line.

```
20 FOR N = 1 TO 100
```

The class was delighted as the program proceeded to add every number from 1 to 100 to itself. To help children understand the program, the teacher asked several children to pull their oval rug to the middle of the room. She placed the box on which the class had written "memory" for a previous computer dramatization near the edge of the rug. Several children drew a picture of the monitor on the chalkboard. Others, under Bobby's directions, wrote each statement (with the line number) on a separate strip of tagboard. An ordered deck of cards (1 through 10) were placed near the rug. The arrangement looked like Fig. 4–18.

Children took turns taking the role of the computer. Ignoring line 10 ("That's just a remark, it doesn't do anything") the students would go to line 20, pick up the next card off the pile, deposit it in the memory box, and

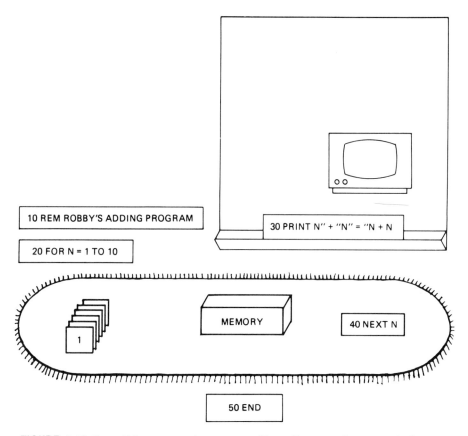

FIGURE 4-18 Dramatizing a computer program. (From Clements, *Computers in Early and Primary Education,* p. 179. Reprinted by permission of Prentice-Hall, Inc.)

print the correct number sentence on the board. Then, passing line 40, they would have to check if they had reached the last number. If not, they headed back to line 20. When card 10 had been processed, the loop was finished. They then went on to line 50, which told them to END. Everyone had a chance to participate, especially as the class experimented with changing lines in Bobby's program. Such active, understandable models are aids to learning programming and problem-solving skills.

While Logo and other child-appropriate languages are more desirable than BASIC, creative teachers use the tools they have to construct challenging and enjoyable experiences for their students. The educational emphasis for teaching any programming language should be on teaching mathematics and mathematical problem solving.

Micro-Dynamo and Modeling

Certain programming languages permit students to model problem situations and test their solutions against information from the real world.

With Micro-Dynamo, students and teachers can write their own simulations. What they simulate is change. Based on the notion that change is central to all fields of study, the materials* attempt to teach the process of complex change. The approach used is system dynamics, a method for understanding and solving complex, interdependent problems. A system is a collection of interacting parts that work together for some purpose. For example, the circulatory system includes the heart, bloodstream, and lungs. A "systems dynamics approach" examines the connections among the parts of a system.

For example, Fig. 4–19 presents a graph of the actual population of the snowshoe rabbit in northern Canada (estimated from records of pelts). What causes such an oscillation? Could it be natural disasters, such as droughts or epidemics? Although possible, it does not appear likely that either of these would explain the regular cycles that appears to characterize Fig. 4–19. Another explanation adds an additional part to the system—a predator. The lynx has a large appetite for rabbits and is well suited for hunting them. Rabbits, of course, are famous for reproducing as much as possible within natural constraints. For years, their numbers increase rapidly. This might create a good environment for the lynx; as their food supply expands, so might their population. Of course, now the lynx would be killing more and more rabbits, until the number of rabbits declines. Could this explain the oscillation?

Students might begin exploring this question by analyzing the factors that influence the number of lynx (simply, how many are born and how many die; the number that die depends on the availability of food). This would be summarized in a feedback diagram illustrating the causal links. Similarly, they would analyze and diagram the factors affecting the rabbit's

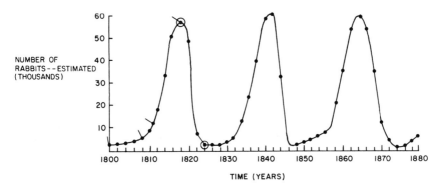

FIGURE 4-19 A graph of the population of the snowshoe rabbit. (From Roberts et al., *Introduction to Computer Simulation*, p. 119. Used with permission of Addison Wesley, Publishers)

*The materials include computer software, manuals, and a textbook (Roberts et al., 1983) with an answer key and instructor's manual. Significant parts of these can be used by fifth graders and above. The advanced chapters and software materials are more appropriate for enrichment for elementary school students; however, teachers could do the Micro-Dynamo programming for a model set up by the class.

population. Again, the total number of rabbits depends on the number that are born and that die. The number that die depend mainly on the number of lynx. Food and disease are in turn affected by the concentration of rabbits. Linking the two diagrams together creates the feedback diagram of the rabbit–lynx system (Fig. 4–20).

The students then move from this type of representation to a computer simulation, which is a more precise tool. They set up formulas that show the relationships between these variables. For example, the population of the lynx at time 2 might equal their population at time 1 (i.e., some previous time) plus the number of births (determined by the birth rate times the population at time 1) minus the number of deaths (the death rate times the population at time 1). They have to specify an equation for each such relationship and give initial values (e.g., the initial populations and the rates). From there on, however, the Micro-Dynamo language determines how to combine the equations and it runs a simulation based on this information, creating both tables and graphs. Figure 4–21 shows a graph created by running one model of the rabbit–lynx system. Note that it takes some time before the rabbit population reacts to the changes in the number of lynx and before the lynx population reacts to the changes in the number of rabbits. The two populations are thus out of phase. Importantly, this simulation closely matches the graph of the actual rabbit population. In addition, the graph of the lynx population also matches data from actual lynx sighted in the area. Thus, there is support for the validity of the simulation.

Students might also collect the real-world information themselves. Consider the example of a cup of hot coffee or water. The hotter it is, the faster it tends to cool. In fact, a scientific law states that the rate of cooling is proportional to the difference between the temperature of the coffee and the temperature of the surrounding air (i.e., there is some number, called a cooling constant, that this difference must be divided by to determine the decrease in temperature). Students might collect actual temperatures from a cooling cup and the room, set a computer model with Micro-Dynamo, and try out various cooling constants until they found one that made a close fit between the temperatures they measured and their simulation. They might

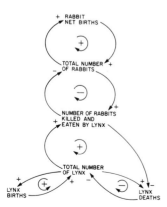

FIGURE 4-20
A partial rabbit-lynx feedback diagram. (From Roberts et al., *Introduction to Computer Simulation*, p. 126.)

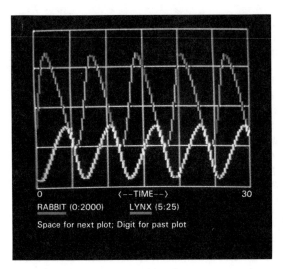

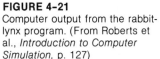

FIGURE 4-21
Computer output from the rabbit-lynx program. (From Roberts et al., *Introduction to Computer Simulation*, p. 127)

also see if the cooling constant was the same for all conditions (e.g., does it matter what type of material the cup is made of?).

Recall that it is not necessary for students to complete every part of this process alone. Classes might solve many of the problems working together. Students could work on small parts of the project in groups. The teacher would then write the simulation based on the students' conjectures regarding important variables and processes. Then the class could run the teacher-written simulation, discuss its strengths and weaknesses, suggest improvements, and explore how changes in the model affect its behavior. In each case, students are engaged in considerable problem solving and creative thinking.

Authoring Languages and Systems

Most teachers do not write their own mathematics textbooks. Most will not write a significant number of their own CAI programs. Developing good software is time consuming. When you want a particular program for a particular job, it is advisable to search for an available program first. If you do have a unique need not met by commercial software, you could learn an authoring language or system with which to write your own CAI program. But you would need to use it a considerable amount to justify the effort.

An authoring *language* such as PILOT is a special computer language that attempts to help a person who is not familiar with the intricacies of programming write software for use in the classroom. Using statements of only one or two letters, you can present information, ask questions, accept and store responses, and branch to different parts of the lessons depending on those responses. A particularly useful feature of many authoring languages is their ability to provide special methods of drawing graphics, special characters, and music, and integrate these into the lesson.

An authoring *system* provides more of a structure than an authoring language. It asks you a series of questions, what information you want to present, what questions you want to ask, what the correct answers are, what feedback to give, and so on. The system then creates the lesson for you. An authoring system takes advantage of the fact that many lessons follow the same format: Information is presented, questions are asked, and feedback is given based on the student's responses. For example, *The Game Show* (Computer Advanced Ideas) is a takeoff on the TV show "Password." Given a set of clues, each player attempts to guess a word or phrase. A number of possible subjects to choose from is already provided; however, teachers and students can insert their own subject area, words, and clues. The program asks you for the name of the subject, the "target" word or correct answer, and a set of clues. You type these in, and a new game is ready to be played. (Clements, 1985a, contains a list of authoring languages and systems.)

While the idea of writing instructional programs using a language designed specifically for this purpose is appealing, criticisms can be made. Most languages, including Logo, BASIC, and Pascal, have very similar commands. Although they usually consist of more than one letter, they may not be that much more difficult to learn to use if the programmer wants to become proficient in a language. Additionally, learning such a high-level language might be more useful to the teacher in a variety of settings and applications than learning a more limited-application authoring language. Much of the simplicity of use of an authoring language is achieved through the reduction of the number of commands of a computer language. This makes the program easy to use but restricts the range of possibilities. In addition, commands are included that are designed specifically for instructional applications. Although this can be helpful, it can also encourage users to adopt and utilize only one instructions strategy—presenting content, questioning, checking answers, giving feedback, go to the next section, and so on. If programs end up as technological page turners, or as endless sequences of the same pedagogical approach, they will not lead to increased student achievement or attitude. Ask yourself: Will the software I would write make a contribution to learning that could not be more easily accomplished in some other manner? You may find that the answer to this question is "no."

PROGRAMMING IN THE FUTURE

Which language will be used in the future? Will everyone program computers? Answers to these questions can be speculative only, but it would seem that, just as today, people will program at varying levels. Some will, of course, still design and program computers at a technical, "machine language" level. At the other extreme, some may only employ "user-friendly" programs which ask them what they want done. In the end, it does not matter how much a programming language could do for a student. What matters is what a student could do with the language and what that engagement could mean for the student's development of mathematical ideas.

SUGGESTED READINGS

Billstein, Libeskind, and Lott (1986) provide numerous projects in Logo, with an emphasis on the underlying mathematics.

Bork (1982) and Luehrmann (1982) present pro and con views about teaching BASIC.

Harvey (1985) provides anyone beyond the "beginning stage" with an excellent discussion of intermediate computer science concepts and programming projects using Logo as a framework.

Kelman and others (1983) discuss the use of several programming languages in education, including BASIC, Logo, and Micro-Dynamo.

Leron (1985) discusses "bugs" in the *way* Logo is often taught and offers suggestions about how to fix them.

Martin and Bearden (1985) show how many mathematical ideas can be explored with Logo.

Moore (1984) provides sequenced lessons on learning geometry with Logo, on black-line masters that can be duplicated for students.

Papert (1980) speaks about Logo and the learning of mathematics. "Practical" classroom teaching ideas should not be expected, but serious reading of this book is strongly suggested for anyone interested in the use of computers in mathematics education.

Riordon (1982) provides suggestions for creating a Logo environment in the classroom. Make an outline of his questioning techniques.

C. S. Thompson and Van de Walle (1985) provide ideas for lessons with patterns and geometry with Logo.

Thornburg's (1983) introduction to Logo emphasizes the beauty and mathematics in nature.

Watt (1983) highlights "powerful ideas" and "helper's hints"—suggestions for teaching Logo to others. Recommended as an initial tutorial to Logo and a source of teaching ideas.

PROBLEM SOLVING

Chapter 1 emphasized the development of problem-solving abilities as a critical goal of mathematics education. It is not difficult to find teachers who will agree with this—the goals of most educational programs include problem solving. When observing their programs in action, however, it is more difficult to find activities that are designed to develop problem-solving ability. In fact, many teachers have difficulty even describing what problem solving is, or how its development can be facilitated. Often, verbal arithmetic problems—or exercises—are offered as the solitary example. Teachers are not alone. Most people, including curriculum designers, professors of education, and psychologists, struggle to grasp the essence of this elusive ability. We do not yet fully understand what human problem solving is or how it can be taught, especially using computers.

As always, however, teachers cannot wait for educational psychology to provide clear answers. They must teach children today. And we do understand many things about problem solving that we often do not use. In this chapter we suggest how children's ability to solve problems might be developed, on and off the computer.

The chapter is divided into two main sections: understanding and teaching problem solving, and computers and problem solving. Problem solving—with or without computers—is discussed separately for several reasons. The first is that it *is* difficult to understand and to teach. Discussing it apart from computer applications allows us to tackle one problem at a time. Second, it is especially important to integrate and connect computer and noncomputer experiences. Therefore, a unified framework is necessary for understanding and teaching problem solving with and without computers.

UNDERSTANDING AND TEACHING PROBLEM SOLVING

The Nature of the Problem-Solving Process

What is a problem?   Is "What is 3 times 4?" a problem? Or is this merely practice? What if it were couched in a verbal format such as: "Three friends each have 4 toy cars. How many toy cars do they have in all?" If the student can simply multiply and say 12, has he or she solved a problem? In one sense, yes, of course. In another sense, however, there was no problem, only an application. Can this example ever be a "true" problem? Yes; give a set of toy cars to a group of kindergartners and ask them the same questions. Let them figure out the answer among themselves in any way they can. Some may act out the situation. Some may count on their fingers or out loud without objects. Even if they make a counting mistake they have engaged in problem solving.

Solving a problem that we "already know how to solve"—an application—is an important part of mathematical ability, as we shall see. But we also want to emphasize "true" problems. These are situations in which a person wants to reach a goal but does not know immediately what actions to take to achieve it. In other words, this type of problem solving is the ability to "know what to do when you don't know what to do." Finally, note that 3 × 4 can never be a problem for students unless they want to know the answer (i.e., they accept the problem). Let's see what cognitive psychology has to tell us about understanding and teaching children how to solve problems; to know what to do, even when they don't (immediately) know what to do.

How do people solve problems?   Sternberg (1985) hypothesizes that different types of processes are carried out by separate components of people's information-processing systems. Each component has a special function or job which it performs. It is as if each played a role in a drama or business company. Tasks are completed through cooperation within the company. For example, in solving the transitive inference problem (or syllogism), "Mark is taller than Pete; Bob is shorter than Pete; who is tallest?" one component needs to encode, or take in, the information by reading. Another might represent the first two statements as spatial arrays (i.e., a mental "picture" showing Mark as taller than Pete, etc.). In this way, the mind is seen as a company in which a group of separate members—components—work with each other. The metacomponents—the "executives" of this "mental company"—plan and evaluate all the information processing. Thus, they are critical to successful problem solving. Their "jobs" include:

Deciding on the nature of the problem (understanding that the problem is to order the three people and find the tallest)

Selecting a representation for the problem (deciding to draw lines representing each person or to visualize them mentally)

Selecting a strategy for combining performance components relevant to the solution of the problem (deciding to order the first two people, place the third within that ordering, and determine which is the tallest)

Monitoring solution processes (Keep track. Am I answering the right question? Can I visualize everything without getting mixed up, or had I better switch tactics and write it on paper?).

It is helpful to examine some of these metacomponents in more detail.

Deciding on the Nature of the Problem

What exactly does it mean to "understand the problem"? Features of the problem must be connected with what is already known. In words from Chapter 1, a relevant frame must be found, or activated. Key words or phrases may activate such a frame. (If accepted without further thought, this can lead to errors, as when students add the numbers in a problem only because they saw the word "and.") The student often has to analyze relationships between parts of the problem or search for patterns among these relationships to build up a useful mental representation of the problem. Then this partially formed representation must be compared to existing frames, because the student must locate a frame relevant to solving the problem (e.g., "That's just like the 'How many outfits can you make from 3 shirts and 4 skirts'? problem"). Once found, such a frame contains information about the typical problem goal and helpful solution strategies. If not, this process is repeated, as often as necessary.

Deciding on a Strategy and on a Representation

Extending one's understanding of the problem. The student is almost simultaneously exercising two additional metacomponents: selecting a mental representation and selecting a solution strategy for the problem. If the frame contains specific information, this is often easy—the solution is already known (e.g., you "just know" how to solve "One toy costs $4; how much does a carton of 12 cost?"). If this information is not available, a mental search begins. Usually unconsciously, students are searching for answers to questions such as: Is this problem like other problems about whose solution I know more? Might I plan a solution by breaking it down into parts, or subproblems, that I can solve in order? What representations have I used successfully (e.g., drawings or tables) that might help with this problem as well? Could I gather more information somehow?

Good strategy users. What one is searching for is a useful *strategy*. Good problem solvers know numerous strategies (the following is adapted from Pressley, 1986). Strategies include routine procedures such as counting or arithmetic operations (addition or division) and problem-solving procedures such as drawing a diagram. The latter processes are often called heuristics, which means "serving to guide, discover, or reveal," because they may (or may not!) help in solving a problem.

Thus, teachers should teach strategies (this teaching often must be more explicit for younger children). For example, in beginning arithmetic, such strategies as counting on and back, and doubles + 1 are useful (see Chapter 7). This is a goal-specific strategy, applicable to one type of goal only. Other strategies, such as the heuristic of pattern searching, are more general. They can be used in many situations and can be tried when problem solving becomes "what we do when we don't know what to do." With this generality comes the disadvantage that it may be more difficult to ascertain which one to choose and how exactly to use it to get an answer. Box 5–1 is a list of some of the more important general strategies, including an example problem to which that strategy might be applied.

Good strategy users also know when (in what type of situation), why (what does the strategy accomplish), and how to use each different strategy. Students also know how to modify a strategy to fit a certain situation and how to combine strategies. For example, a student might recognize that a problem involving solving the perimeter of a rectangle might be efficiently

BOX 5–1: Problem-Solving Strategies with Example Problems

Draw a diagram or picture.

A woman was standing on the middle rung of a ladder. She stepped up 8 rungs. Then she stepped down 5 rungs. Finally, she climbed up the remaining 12 rungs to the roof. How many rungs does the ladder have?

This strategy and the next are effective means of building a representation and suggesting other solution strategies.

Act it out.

A man buys a horse for $70, sells it for $80, buys it back again for $90, and sells it for $100. How much money did he make or lose?

Look for a pattern.

What is the 21st number in the series 1, 5, 9, . . . ?

Pattern search can be used in a variety of problems beyond those such as this one, in which the use of patterns is palpable.

Make an organized list or table.

If you had a penny, a nickel, and a dime, what different amounts could you spend without getting any change?

Systematic guess and test.

The sum of two numbers is 33. Their difference is 17. What are the two numbers?

What three whole numbers yield the same number whether they are summed or multiplied?

Break a problem into parts.

Apple juice costs 90 cents for one 32-ounce bottle. At the school fair, Sarah sold cups holding 4 ounces for 25 cents each. How much money or profit did Sarah make on the apple juice in each bottle?

This is useful for multistep problems, which are often more complex than difficult (although without enough experience with these problems, students find them difficult!)

Write a number sentence.

Many arithmetic problems can be solved by applying this strategy (such as the preceding example). Note, however, that it is often not appreciated how difficult this strategy is for students. Its use should not be "forced" too soon.

Working backwards.

Joe went shopping. He spent three-fourths of his money on clothes and $5 for lunch. He had $1 left. How much did he have at the start?

solved with a formula. A slightly more complex problem, however (the perimeter of a 4-meter walkway bordering a pool 20 by 10 meters) might best be first approached by drawing and labeling a diagram as an aid to visualization (building a representation) as well as an aid to problem definition. This type of knowledge is used by the metacomponent of selecting a strategy. To help students gain this knowledge, teachers should provide practice in strategy use in a variety of situations, always striving to help students become explicitly aware of where, when, and how to apply the strategies.

Finally, good strategy users possess knowledge about the domain or topic at hand. In some cases, this obviates the need to use a strategy at all—the answer, or an algorithm that yields an answer—is "just known." (This is fine from the perspective of solving that problem, as it effectively "reduces" the problem to an application. Teachers should make sure that both applications and problems are presented to all students.) In other cases, knowledge allows the use of many strategies. For instance, general problem-solving strategies (e.g., break a problem into parts) can be used only when the student has a lot of information that can be "plugged into" the problem (what are meaningful "parts" of a certain problem?).

Solution Monitoring: A Neglected Metacomponent

Students often do not monitor their own problem solving. They believe that ideas just "come to them" or not, without any willfulness on their part. Once they start working on an idea, they rarely pause to see if it will help them solve the problem, or if it makes any sense at all. They do not generally examine their ideas and work for errors. They believe that they fail because they are "stupid," and that errors are absolute; that little can be learned from them. There are ways—with and without computers—to help them develop these abilities. These will be described throughout this and the following chapters.

Implications for the Classroom

How can we translate these understandings into classroom practice? In general, we should discuss, model, and suggest these problem-solving processes. These are not "steps" to follow in a lockstep manner; people jump from one process to another during all phases of problem solving. However, for planning instruction it is useful to employ four broad phases. Table 5–1 (loosely adapted from Charles & Lester, 1984) shows these phases and describes what both students and teacher should be doing in each. For typical mathematical problems, these phases might all take place during a single lesson. For others, and for many computer-based problems, the first phase might occur with the whole class on a Monday and the third or fourth at the end of the week when all students have had a chance to work on the problem.

Research has supported the effectiveness of such an approach (Charles & Lester, 1984). Several conclusions in a review of research on

TABLE 5-1   Phases of Problem Solving: Student Processes and Teaching Techniques

Students	*Teachers*
1. *Understand the problem.*	*Help students understand the problem.*
Read the problem again.	Present the problem to the class.
Write what you know.	Answer questions about the problem.
Tell it in your own words.	
Look for key phrases.	Lead a discussion concerning the nature of the problem.
Find the important or missing information.	Focus on the questions and the given information.
Ask questions for clarification if necessary.	Discuss implicit as well as explicit information.
Tell what you are trying to find.	Ask: What is the problem?
	Ask questions that can be answered mentally.
	Discuss possible solution strategies (but avoid evaluating them at this time).
	Organize students to begin work (small groups seems best).
2. *Solve the problem.*	*Help students solve the problem.*
Use an appropriate representation and strategy.	Encourage students to share ideas.
	Analyze difficulties.
Draw a diagram or picture.	Observe and question students to identify "where they are" in the problem-solving process.
Act it out.	
"Make it your own."	Provide prompts and hints.
Look for a pattern.	When students get "stuck," what do you say first? What next? A useful sequence of questions was successfully used by Perkins and Martin (1986). There are three types of questions that are asked in order, starting with the most general:
Make an organized list or table.	
Guess and test (systematically).	
Solve part of the problem.	1. *Prompts:* Prompts are general strategy questions that one might ask oneself, such as "What's the first thing you need to do?" "What do you need to do next?" "How would you describe the problem to yourself?" "Are there any other ways to . . . ?"
Write a number sentence.	
Solve a simpler, but similar, problem.	
Work backward from the solution.	2. *Hints:* If a couple of prompts are not enough, try hints. Hints are leading questions or tiny bits of information that suggest a strategy. "Doesn't that remind you of a problem we did yesterday?" "Do you think making a drawing would help?" "What does the problem mean, the difference in the numbers is 17? The difference of which numbers?" "The woman started on a MIDDLE rung. If there's a middle rung, would the total number of rungs be even or odd?"
Monitor the solution process.	
	3. *Giveaways:* If several hints are not successful, try a "giveway": Here you provide a specific solution idea. "Let's try listing all the possible combinations of coins there could be. One penny, one nickel, one dime, one penny, and

Students	Teachers

Teachers:

one nickel . . . what next?'' ''Find two numbers that sum to 33. Is their difference 17? How could we keep the sum the same, but increase the difference?''

Pose questions (from Shoenfeld, 1985). There is a special class of prompts that one should ask all students, even if they're not stuck! They encourage monitoring and reflection. Consistently ask the following three questions to groups or individuals.

1. What exactly are you doing? (Can you describe it?)
2. Why are you doing it? (How does it fit into the solution?)
3. How does it help you? (What will you do with it when you're done?)

They may not be able to answer you well, especially at first, but each question will serve as a powerful prompt for them to monitor their progress. They should be challenged to critique their own strategies. Eventually, they will internalize the questions and begin to query themselves.

Students:

3. *Check and answer*
   (final monitoring):
   Check if the right question was answered.
   Check if all relevant information has been used.
   Check computations.
   Check if the answer makes sense.
   Write the answer in a complete sentence.

Teachers:

Help students check and answer.

Ask students if they have checked their solution.

Was the right question answered?

Was all relevant information used?

Are computations correct?

Does the answer make sense?

Students:

4. *Extend knowledge of problem solving.*
   Discuss solutions (your own and others').
   Analyze what worked and why.
   Solve the problem in another way.
   Make up and solve a similar problem.
   Identify generalizations.

Teachers:

Help students extend their abilities.

Allow three to five students to demonstrate their solutions.

Name the solution strategies used.

Encourage analysis.

Facilitate transfer.

Have students make up similar problems and identify possible generalizations.

Help children to make connections between these problems and others. They should identify other problems (and other software programs) that can be solved with similar strategies. In addition, demon-

(continued)

TABLE 5-1   (Continued)

Students	Teachers
	strate how problem-solving strategies and concepts developed on the computer can be used in other situations—in solving problems in and out of school.
	Have children apply what they have learned to a variety of contexts.
	Even if students are taught a strategy . . . even if they *use* it, they might not use it the next time. To encourage this transfer, ask them (and as soon as possible have them ask themselves) Pressley's three questions:
	1. Which strategy worked for me?
	2. Why was it best (i.e., in this situation)?
	3. What will I do the next time?

problem solving by Suydam (1982) support, and serve as a partial summary of, what we have said:

> Strategies can be taught and they help students achieve correct solutions.
>
> There is no single optimal strategy for solving problems. Students need a wide repertory of strategies.
>
> Problem solving is best improved by integrating it into the curriculum.

Teachers should:

> Include a variety of problems so that students develop creative approaches to problem solving.
>
> Encourage multiple solution strategies and emphasize that mathematics is more than facts and algorithms.
>
> Provide sufficient time for discussion, practice, and reflection.
>
> Provide wait time. *Whenever* you ask a question, wait at least 3 seconds before doing anything else (asking another question, asking another student, giving a hint, etc.)

In addition, I believe it is important to:

Be a good model of a problem solver.

Work out some problems in front of the students (see also Schoenfeld, 1985). *Do not* do them "perfectly." A reasonable "stream of consciousness" might be: "Let's see. We have to find out _____. We know _____ and _____. We could try _____, or _____, or _____. What do you think is worth a few minutes' try at first?" and so on.

At other times, serve as the "monitor" only, writing down students' ideas and raising general questions ("Do we all understand the problem before going on?", or, in the middle of a solution attempt, "Is this working? Are we getting somewhere?").

Encourage creative thinking.

Davis (1984) believes that math must be creative. Why?

It's impossible to teach rules for every problem, every situation. Students must be able to solve problems creatively.

Students *are* creative if they are allowed and encouraged to be. We shall see examples of kindergartners creating significant mathematics, on and off the computer.

Approaching mathematics as a creative activity substantially increases students' motivation.

Originality is a goal of all education, including mathematics education.

Mathematics in the real world is not rule based and routine.

The field of mathematics is not static. More new mathematics is created every month.

Certain types of questions stimulate creativity. For example: Can you think of a problem just like this one that you have solved before? Can you create and solve a similar problem? Can you solve the problem in a different way? Can you solve a more general problem? Each of these questions asks students to look carefully at problems and their features (encode), combine information and processes in new ways, and compare the present problems to other problems. Each of them asks students to "Keep thinking!"

Address students' belief systems.

What students believe about mathematics and mathematical problem solving strongly influences what they do. Most students believe the following (Shoenfeld, 1985):

1. Mathematics is facts and rules with one way to get one right answer. You find the rule and get the answer.
2. If you don't solve a problem in 5 minutes, you'll never solve it. Give up.
3. Only geniuses discover or create (or re-create) mathematics. So if you forget something, you'll never be able to figure it out on your own. Also, you can't really understand why things (e.g., algorithms) work the way they do.

Work to change these beliefs. Have students solve problems in a myriad of ways. Have them discuss—and argue about—their solutions and ideas. Work in groups on problems that take some time to solve. Respect students' ideas, regardless of whether they are "right" or "wrong."

One more suggestion: Do not (unconsciously) give in to common (unconscious!) student behaviors that dilute problem-solving activities. When such activities become challenging, students often complain that they do not understand, that no one else expects them to do such difficult work, that you aren't teaching them how to perform the activity (they often get their parents behind them, especially on this one), and so on. It is often easy to simplify, explain, or omit activities in the face of such negative reactions. Resist such temptations. Meet the resistance squarely. With some groups, you might even discuss it. After meeting your challenges successfully, after changing their beliefs about school, about mathematics, about learning, and about the satisfaction of solving problems, these negative reactions will taper off. And you will have effected a change with more powerful ramifications than any other.

Develop an accepting, trusting atmosphere.

Make most of your mathematics lessons into problem-solving lessons as well.

COMPUTERS AND PROBLEM SOLVING

The Role of Computers in Problem Solving

What, then, is the role of computers in developing students' problem-solving abilities? There are several options, from simulations or gamelike challenges, to traditional tutorials and practice in problem-solving processes. Some experimental programs even provide hints similar to those listed on the right side of Table 5–1, although teachers will be responsible for the vast majority of this type of assistance for a long time. Without such teacher intervention, the programs will have little effect.

To determine optimal roles for computers, we might begin by listing their advantages for the teaching of problem solving. At their best, computers can:

Allow students to explore problems, receiving feedback concerning their efforts.

Provide multisensory presentations (especially important is their potential to increase visualization of problematic situations).

Encourage creativity and divergency in solution paths.

Encourage engagement with realistic ("real-world") problems.

Encourage cooperative, team-oriented problem solving.

Increase motivation and engagement with (acceptance of) problems.

With these in mind, let's examine some different types of problem-solving software. First, however, one additional warning. In this book, as in pupils' texts, chapters or sections on problem solving tend to give the impression that this is a separate mathematical topic. A teacher might say: "That's it for the problem-solving unit; we should return to mathematics." Nothing could be further from the truth or more harmful to students. It is true that teachers should be aware of problem-solving processes as described in the first section of this chapter. It is also helpful to engage students in activities and discussions focusing on problem solving. It is not, however, beneficial to keep problem solving isolated from the study of other topics. It is essential to keep the following points in mind.

Students don't solve mathematical problems without using knowledge from other mathematical topics (such as geometry, arithmetic, or graphing). When they learn problem solving, they should be learning these topics simultaneously.

Students shouldn't learn such topics apart from solving problems. As we have discussed, students should not first learn, say, subtraction, and then learn to apply it or solve problems with it. They should initially learn subtraction by solving a problem that demands subtraction. Such applications lend purpose, meaning, and motivation to the study of mathematical topics. They also develop problem-solving skills.

Some strategies are unique to a particular topic (e.g., fractions) or skill (e.g., memory). But most of those in Box 5–1 are general, applicable to solving problems involving many different topics.

So some illustrations of problem solving with computers are offered in the remainder of this chapter. However, these are just examples for the sake of discussion. Most are described in Chapters 6–11 (indeed, many listed in Table 5–2 are described in those chapters).

Tutorials and Practice

Traditional tutorials.   Some programs take a traditional approach of presenting the steps of problem solving didactically. For example, *Read and Solve Math Problems* is a series of tutorial-and-practice programs designed to teach students how to solve one- and two-step arithmetic problems. The basic approach is to convert written problems to number problems:

"Kim played 18 minutes in the first half and 20 minutes in the second half of the game. If Bob played only 22 minutes in the entire game, how may minutes less did Bob play than Kim? STEP ONE: Type the left side of the equation. _____ = N."

If students type incorrect numbers, they are told, "Look again at the problem. Kim played 18 minutes in the first half and 20 minutes in the second half of the game. Try typing the equation again." On the other hand, if they type, say, 18 ∗ 20, they read, "First you must find how many minutes Kim played altogether. To do this, you ADD." Then they must perform the operation and give the answer with its label (i.e., 38 minutes) and finally complete the second step.

Often, this type of tutorial demonstrates how to solve several different types of problems. *Wordmath* is an individualized, diagnostic-prescriptive tutorial and drill program. There are seven modules, each of which includes simple and complex problems, with such titles as basic (or routine) word problems, extraneous number problems, key word identification, and mixed problems. The general strategy of the program is to (a) read the problem, (b) find all the numbers, (c) choose the operation, (d) choose the number you need, and (e) solve the problem (in light of what we discussed in the first section of this chapter, what are the advantages and disadvantages of this approach?). For an "extra numbers" module, the overview includes: "What are extra numbers? Extra numbers are numbers that are not needed to solve the problem. Extra numbers are unnecessary pieces of information." An example is provided.

The student then chooses a theme. Problems in the program are divided among 15 themes, from sports to monsters. Students are presented problems within the theme they choose. They are to read the problem and choose an arithmetic operation and the relevant numerals. If the correct operation and numerals are chosen, they complete the computation on the screen. If they err, the program presents them with appropriate hints (e.g., "Since this is a lesson on hidden numbers, keep in mind that each problem might contain one or more numbers written as words"). If more errors are made, they are led through the problem in a step-by-step manner. While this approach offers immediate feedback and may provide remediation in step-by-step problem solving for some children, other approaches to CAI problem solving are available.

Strategic approaches.   *Problem-Solving Strategies* is designed to help children generate and apply the strategies of trial and error, searching for a pattern, drawing a diagram, collecting and listing data systematically, and simplifying a problem. The first two programs are tutorials in which students learn about the strategies and how to use them. In "Diagonals" all the strategies are applied to one problem: finding the total number of diagonals in a dodecagon. This allows students to concentrate on the strategies and their differences rather than on the peculiarities of specific problems. They first are asked to attempt a trial-and-error solution (interpreted here as almost random guessing, an ineffective strategy for this problem!). They are then led to write down or draw in all the diagonals in an orderly manner (systematic collection and listing). Finally, they examine simplified cases such as triangles and pentagons to find a pattern that can be extended to answer the original problem.

Following these tutorials, students apply the same strategies to two opened-ended problems. In "Thinking with Ink," students compete for the lowest cost in coloring a pattern of rectangles. In "Pooling Around," they discover rules to predict the behavior of a ball—that is, the number of bounces and the pocket into which the ball falls—on a pool table through analysis of data they collect. They observe the number of bounces and the final pocket and record this information on a data sheet. The program displays the data. The students then search these data for patterns on which to base predictions. The computer is then used to test these predictions. The handouts that accompany the program help students form hypotheses and lead them to more systematic explorations (e.g., by holding the number of bounces and the final pocket constant in their investigations of the data).

Of course, the teacher should continue this good example by (a) forming small groups to encourage the sharing of ideas; (b) leading discussions regarding the use of these strategies (during students' engagement with the activities); and (c) challenging students with additional problems to which the strategies apply.

Other programs do not include computer tutorials, but do provide practice using various problem-solving strategies. They are often interesting and worthwhile *if* teachers enhance the programs by placing them in the framework discussed in the first section of this chapter.

The ESC program addresses problem solving in two ways. First, it asks children to analyze and solve routine problems, ferreting out correct information, identifying the action and operation, and so on. Second, it provides a wealth of nonroutine experiences (e.g., logic, clues, facts with variables, tiling, guess the number, simulations) and six selected strategies to help address such situations (e.g., Fig. 5-1).

The Factory is a problem-solving program designed to promote the strategy of working backwards and breaking a problem into parts, as well as skills such as spatial visualization and sequencing. The problem is discussed in more detail in Chapter 9. For now, it is sufficient to know that the factory includes punch, rotate, and stripe machines which students combine in various "assembly line" sequences to make products. The important point for this chapter is that good teachers coordinate, and often introduce, these types of computer experiences with concrete noncomputer experiences. For example, one class built facsimiles of the Factory's machines, set up an in-class assembly line, and dramatized the sequencing of machine operations that created a product. They discussed the problem-solving strategies involved for this concrete version and for the computer version. They also discussed other problems that might be solved using similar strategies.

B

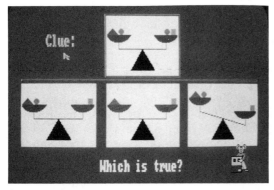

A

FIGURE 5-1
Two problem-solving programs from the ESC materials. In A, students know that the top "clue" is true, so which of the bottom three is true? Part B is a game in which random digits must be placed by the students in the first four boxes. Then they determine the answer, which they have tried to make as big as they can. (Courtesy of Education Systems Corporation)

Gertrude's Secrets is a set of classification activities. The program encourages students to develop logical thinking skills through forming and testing theories. For example, say that two 8-year-olds are working with the "Two Loop Puzzle," in which two frames overlap. The children first observe the example, in which one frame is labeled "Blue" and contains blue pieces differing in shape. The other is labeled "Squares" and contains squares of different colors. In the overlapping section are blue squares. The children then move to the empty loops into which they are to classify a group of shapes. They pick up a square and drop it inside one of the boxes. It falls out of the box and comes to rest beneath it. Hey! They thought squares went in this one! They have just created a theory, or idea, and had it contradicted. Maybe it's not just squares; it could be any shape (second theory). How about hexagons (third theory)? They pick up a blue hexagon and place it in the box. It stays. Elated, they assume the second box will hold a certain color (fourth theory). They choose red (fifth theory). Picking up a red hexagon, they place it in the second box. It falls out. Yellow (sixth theory)? Nope. Blue (seventh)? No. Wait a minute! There is no other color, but . . . oh! The red hexagon! It should have gone in the middle, where the boxes overlap (eighth theory and major insight). It works.

Even young children, then, can use quite sophisticated logical concepts if they are presented in an appropriate format. But a good teacher will help students benefit fully from such a program by preparing them for it and extending their problem-solving experiences.

As an example of an extension, a teacher might take the opportunity to illustrate the differences between the union of nondisjoint sets (those that share members in common, such as the red hexagons in the preceding example) or logical addition, and the union of disjoint sets or numerical addition. In the former, you may have five red pieces and three hexagons but have only seven pieces in all (i.e., if one is a red hexagon). In numerical addition, no members are shared, so $5 + 3$ always equals 8.

Also, teachers should encourage children to play similar games off the computer. Playing in pairs with attribute pieces and two drawings of the two intersecting loops, one player would think of a secret rule for solving the puzzle. He or she would record this rule by secretly coloring the appropriate pieces into one of the drawings of loops. The other player would then try to guess the rule by placing attribute pieces into the empty loops. The first player responds to each placement by saying, "Yes, that fits" or "No, that doesn't fit" (in this case, the piece is removed). When the rule is guessed correctly, they exchange roles.

Puzzle Tanks is a computerized version of the old problem, "You have two containers, one holds 8 quarts (or liters), the other holds 1 liter. If the containers are not calibrated, how could you get exactly 7 liters of liquid?" (How?) Students have to solve the problem by filling and emptying the containers, or tanks, or by pouring liquid from one to the other. The simplest solution is to fill the 8-liter tank and pour enough from this tank to fill the 1-liter tank. Thus, 7 liters are left in the first tank. This problem is from the easiest of four levels. An example of a "Champion" challenge is: Given a 5- and a 6-liter tank, fill each one with 3 liters (How?) There are also some problems that are impossible to solve; students must determine this and choose the response "It can't be done."

Valuable discussions, arguments, and thinking occur as students work together on such a program. Teachers can substantially enhance learning by asking students to reflect on their discoveries. One teacher introduced her class to the problematic situation using actual containers. Then small groups worked on the computer, eventually reaching several challenging problems. Following this work, she asked: "Let's say you have tanks holding 2 and 4. How could you get 3?" (Readers are advised to solve this and the next few problems themselves.) Students, working in groups away from the computer, came to agree that it was not possible. The teacher repeated the challenge for: using tanks of 3 and 6 to get 5; using 3 and 9 to get 10; using 4 and 8 to get 1; and so on. She then asked students to discover what these pairs of tanks had in common. Why couldn't you get 5 using 3 and 6? One student offered, "No matter how you add or subtract 3 and 6, you'll never get 5."

Teacher: Why?
Student 1:   You only get numbers like 3, 6, 9, 12 . . .
Student 2:   It skips around the other numbers.
Student 3:   Yeah, it's multiples of 3. That's all you can get.

The teacher turned their attention back to the other "impossible" examples. After further discussion and exploration of these and other problems, the class concluded that you could only "get" numbers that were multiples of the lowest common divisor of the two numbers (tanks).

These students learned far more mathematics than they would have in an undirected situation. Gifted students might explore these notions further, possibly hypothesizing that two numbers that are relatively prime (i.e., that have no common divisor other than 1) can produce any number (given adequate storage for the liquid).

Students' search for the "best way" might reveal that in efficient solutions one tank is always filled, whereas the other is always emptied. For example, given tanks of 7 and 3 with a goal of 5, one efficient solution would be:

Move	Seven tank	Three tank
Fill seven	7	0
Seven → three	4	3
Empty three	4	0
Seven → three	1	3
Empty three	1	0
Seven → three	0	1
Fill seven	7	1
Seven → three	5	3
Empty three	5	0

There's the 5! Can you see that we always filled the 7 and emptied the 3? Mathematically, the problem can be seen as an equation with two variables: $7X + 3Y = 5$; where the X represents how many times we should fill (or empty) the 7 tank and the Y represents the number of times we should fill (or empty) the 3 tank. The 5 is, of course, the goal.

We can summarize our solution by saying that we filled the 7 tank two times (pouring it into the 3 tank whenever possible) and emptied the 3 tank 3 times. Thus the X becomes 2 and the Y becomes –3 (the negative number meaning "emptied"). Thus, our solution is equivalent to the equation

$$7(2) + 3(-3) = 14 - 9 = 5$$

Because there are two variables, there is more than one solution. In fact, there is another solution to this problem that is just as efficient. Can you find it? (Hint: Try only filling the 3 tank and only emptying the 7 tank.)

You might say that we have wandered over your students' heads and out of the elementary school. Possibly. There are several good reasons for this trip, however. For if teachers do not see the mathematics inherent in problem-solving activities such as *Puzzle Tanks:*

They will be unable to guide their talented students in deeper explorations.

They will also be unable to help average students fully! To teach at any level well, teachers need to understand higher (and lower) levels. In other words, they should know more content than they are teaching directly. They should also know where their teaching is heading.

They will tend to view all such activities as merely recreational "teasers," to be solved in most part by random trial and error.

In general, valuable opportunities to learn more about mathematics and problem solving will be lost.

Although space limitations prevent discussion of teacher enhancements for each program, no software package should be used without considering the role of the teacher in providing a complete educational experience.

Several programs provide practice in induction, deduction, and logic concepts. In the *Enchanted Forest* a witch has changed all the animals into geometric figures and placed them in ponds. Students must find each pond, then describe and "record" it by indicating the color, shape, and size of each figure. Students proceed to either the witch's school or witch's computer. In the school, they learn about logical concepts. For negation they might see a screen filled with negation statements and all the attribute shapes. If they choose "not large," only the small figures remain displayed. In the computer, they can free the animals from the ponds by using these logical concepts. To do this, they must find a logical connective that describes the set of figures in each pond that they previously "recorded."

To master *Code Quest,* students use such strategies as looking for patterns, classification, trial and error, and sequencing. The program chooses a mystery object and presents coded clues which students must unravel to reveal the object's identity. It can be adapted to fit any topic in mathematics because teachers and students can enter their own clues and mystery objects (e.g., students could write clues about "mystery objects" such as a certain number, or a concept such as primes or trapezoids). Students could also invent codes based on mathematical transformations. Finally, discussion of substitution codes might lead to statistics/graphing lesson dealing with frequency of letters in written works (see Chapter 10).

Discrimination, Attributes, and Rules includes several computer and noncomputer activities in these three areas: visual discrimination, conceptualization via classification by attributes, and induction of rules (relationships between two or more concepts). For example, there are two computer activities that provide practice with the induction of rules. Students in grades K through 2 might play "Iggy's Gnees" ("Gnee" means "examples of a concept"). Students examine colored shapes arranged in sets. Some are Gnees, some are not. They must use these examples and nonexamples to discover Iggy's secret rule. They then use this rule to construct a new Gnee. Try to finish the Gnee in Fig. 5-2 yourself. Students in grades 3 to 6 might tackle "Gnee or Not Gnee." They are given a set of figures that fit a rule and a set that do not. They must induce the rule and apply it to select other figures that fit the rule. The early ones are fairly easy (what is the rule in Fig. 5-3a and b?) Later ones are increasingly challenging (try Fig. 5-3c).* If students are incorrect, they see another set of examples and nonexamples. Teachers should encourage students to verbalize and record both their hypotheses regarding each rule and the information they receive as feedback. Unfortunately, the software permits a "keep guessing until you recognize all the examples" strategy, which should, of course, be discouraged.

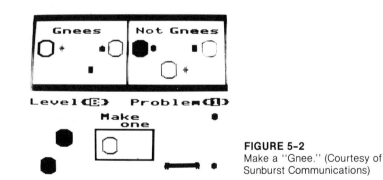

FIGURE 5-2
Make a "Gnee." (Courtesy of Sunburst Communications)

*A confession: I was quite proud of my ability to discover these rules, when I happened to remark to a pair of fourth graders I was helping that I had no idea where the producers got the crazy names for the figures for each rule. Giving me a quizzical look, one of the pair said, "Dr. Clements, that's the easiest rule. Each harder challenge starts with the next letter of the alphabet." I mumbled something incoherent and left quickly, properly humbled. This footnote allows me to hide the answers: the Abips and Blips are closed figures; the Xibies have one line of symmetry.

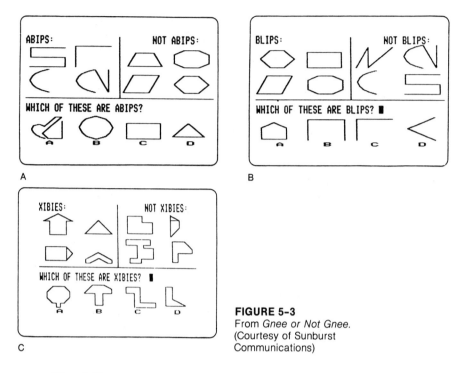

FIGURE 5-3
From *Gnee or Not Gnee.*
(Courtesy of Sunburst
Communications)

Simulations

Some simulations deal directly with traditional mathematics content. In *Math Shop* students act as salesclerks in a variety of shops in a simulated mall. They serve customers by solving a problem using a specific curriculum concept such as proportions, fractions, decimals, measurement, or arithmetic operations. They make change, measure goods, and pack purchases efficiently. In doing so, they must use such skills as arithmetic operations, fractions, estimation, and problem solving. For example, in the lumber shop, students might be asked to cut a piece of lumber (e.g., 9 feet) into two pieces so that one piece is a given amount (e.g., 1 foot) longer than the other. If they make the common error of subtracting (9 − 1), the program graphically represents the two pieces, lists the difference and the total, and provides a sentence of feedback at the bottom (Fig 5–4a). In the repair shop, students are presented with some working computers (function machines) (Fig. 5–4b on the left) and some that are broken. They have to determine what number sentence relates the inputs to the outputs (in this case, the "rule" was "input × 6 + 4 = output"). Other examples of the problems posed by the shops—some answered, some not—are shown in Fig. 5–4c and d. True to life, students can be put under some pressure for efficient performance. If they serve customers too slowly, other potential customers may leave. If 50 leave, the game ends.

In a similar vein, the comprehensive series *Mathematics Unlimited Problem Solving* provides real-life applications or minisimulations for each grade, 1 through 8. For example, in grade 5 students are "Troubleshooters," travel-

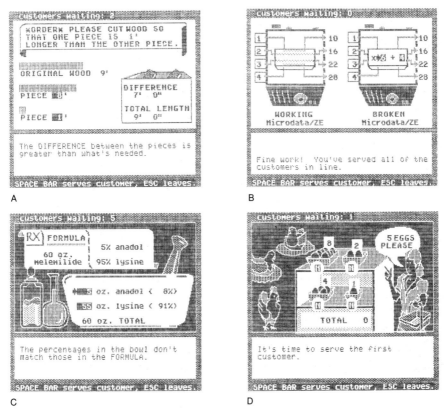

FIGURE 5-4 Challenges from *Math Shop*. (Scholastic, Inc.)

ing over the world to solve problems, each of which is presented in a story format. For instance, they may plan a route for warning people of an impending flood. Feedback emphasizes logical consequences; if a poor route is planned, homes are damaged. Grade 6 students manage their own music band. They might fill in missing sections of a score by using patterning and the fractional relationships among notes (e.g., quarter, eight, and sixteenth notes) or create a two-part song program which satisfies constraints about the length of the sets and the distribution of solos among the players. Young children learn about problem solving in simpler settings, of course. Second graders are "hired" as newspaper reporters who are given stories with the job of identifying the sentence that asks the question, deleting all the sentences that contain extra information, and selecting a headline that answers the problem. Each problem addresses at least one significant skill/content area, such as estimation, number, arithmetic, fractions, measurement, statistics, and so on, as well as one or more problem-solving strategies.

Mathematics Problem Solving Courseware also places students in simulated "real-world" situations in which they must solve problems. For example, children working with the level 5 materials are hired by a hotel owner as undercover detectives. They must solve many problems in that role, each having mathematical aspects. A "Notepad" tool is available to set up equations and do computations. It also offers three levels of help, each providing a greater degree of assistance.

Other worthwhile simulations cross traditional subject-matter lines. For example, in *Discover: A Science Experiment,* students take charge of a laboratory and have the responsibility of discovering the conditions necessary for the survival of several alien organisms. All they know so far is that there are eight creatures which behave differently and that there are four types of food. Students can observe a creature's movements over time as they alter such variables as availability of the different food types and the proximity of other creatures (some creatures are attracted to others or hostile to others, etc.). The program is designed to develop such strategies as close observation and information gathering, analysis of data, and construction and testing of hypotheses (while controlling irrelevant variables). While formulated from the "scientific method" perspective, these are also relevant to the development of general problem-solving processes.

Less realistic, but more suitable for younger students is *The Incredible Laboratory.* Students choose and mix 15 "crazy chemicals" which produce various features of a monster. Each chemical determines a variation of one of the monster's five key body parts—head, arms, body, legs, or feet. At higher skills levels, chemicals have changing properties and may be combined to create new variations. The students' job is to discover each chemical's effect using the strategies of trial and error (including systematic alteration of one variable, or chemical, at a time) and making organized lists. Remember, unless you discuss such strategies with your students, and encourage them to use them in the solution of other problems, the program cannot be expected to be of much benefit. Chapter 11 discusses other programs that integrate mathematics with other subject-matter areas.

Problem Solving and Basic Skills

The HOTS (Higher Order Thinking Skills) program is designed to develop problem-solving skills *and,* simultaneously, improve basic skills and social confidence. In fact, the program replaces part of a school's traditional drill program with involvement with intellectually challenging software. Substantial gains in basic skills—up to three times the gains produced by conventional approaches—have been reported using this approach (Pogrow, 1986).

The HOTS program does not attempt to match software with a single subject-area topic. Instead of providing direct practice, software is used to develop higher-order thinking skills. Teacher-directed lessons in the program are limited to 12 minutes, to maximize time for students' independent work. Teachers coach students engaged with the computer programs to work independently.

1. Teachers should respond to student questions about "what to do" by:
    Determining if the clues are already on the screen. If so, they simply tell the students that they are smart enough to figure that out on their own.
    If the clues are not on the screen, they simply tell them what to do.

If the information is on the screen but one or more words are too difficult, those words (only) are read and explained.

2. Teachers should respond to students who do not know what choice to make on a menu by:

Telling students that they are not sure and that they should try what they think is the right choice.

If the choice in incorrect, ask the students if what they obtained is what they wanted. Make sure that they return to the main menu, read the choices, and determine their next move.

3. Teachers should use cruising techniques.

Watch for students making good progress or having difficulties. Praise the former, asking for explanations about their strategies. For the latter, use questions (e.g., prompts and hints).

4. Teachers should respond to students' questions about the quality of their solutions by:

Refusing to evaluate or judge.

Asking students to compare their results to those of others or to their own expectations.

Problem-Solving Tools

Computer tools. In Chapter 3 we discussed computer tools relevant to mathematics. Obviously, the primary purpose of these tools is to solve problems. Properly used, they have the potential to make a dramatic positive impact on student's abilities and beliefs related to solving problems. Additional ideas regarding their use will be left to the topical chapters. Here it is pertinent to emphasize that the use of these tools should be embedded in the problem-solving framework summarized in Table 5–1. Such a framework will substantially increase the depth of use of the tools, and thus, the benefits students will accrue from such use.

CAI plus tools. A series of programs that represents a strong integration of CAI and computer tools is *Strategies in Problem Solving*. A brief introduction to the "Dinosaurs and Squids" program informs students that two children have found a "prehistoric island" on which they observe *Brontosaurus* and *Tyrannosaurus rex* dinosaurs. They are presented with the following problem: "Chiang climbs to the top of a cliff and looks down. She counts 12 dinosaur heads. From the boat, Calvin counts 40 dinosaur feet. How many of the dinosaurs are *Tyrannosaurus rex?*" They are then shown a "strategy menu," which offers a variety of options for working on the problem. For example, option 3 provides information about the two types of dinosaurs, including relevant (number of legs) and irrelevant (weight) data. Option 4 provides a series of hints (after one hint has been read, that hint plus another are offered the next time option 4 is chosen). Hints remind the student that (a) the number of heads tells you the number of dinosaurs; (b) the types of dinosaurs do not have the same number of feet; (c) they could find the number of feet if all the dinosaurs were the same kind; and (d) making a table would be a good way to keep track of the number of heads and feet.

Whether they read all the hints or decide on their own to use the strategy of making a table, students might choose option 5. They are presented with a table and a visual representation of the 12 dinosaurs in the problem. Students can change a type of dinosaur to another. With every such change, a new row of numbers is created in the table to reflect this change (e.g., in Fig. 5–5a, the student just changed a tyrannosaur to a brontosaur). Thus, the table is under the students' control, and strong connections between a pictorial representation and the numerically based table are maintained. Students can change the dinosaurs and table until they see the combination that yields the correct total number of feet.

Options 7 and 8 allow students to use a calculator and computer (for writing a BASIC program) as tools for solving the problem. Finally, students are allowed to see a solution (or stop working!) if they are overly frustrated. They must have tried at least five choices on the strategy menu before they can see a solution, however.

Successful problem solvers are automatically advanced to a review problem which is mathematically similar to the main problem but embedded in a different context. If they are successful, they can "create a problem." Here they choose from the same problem settings, but the problem is displayed without any numbers (Fig. 5–5b). The students enter numbers of their own choosing in the blank spaces. They also provide four possible answers for a multiple-choice question that the computer must answer. The computer then solves their problem.* Teachers might then have students make up problems for their friends to solve that are mathematically similar to those in the program but are embedded in a different context as well as some with the same context but a different mathematical structure. One characteristic of good problem solvers is that they readily understand and remember the structure of problems, rather than the surface details.

Although not perfect and somewhat limited in scope (each package in the series only deals with one type of problem), this series illustrates how CAI and "tool" approaches can be integrated to provide students with significant problem-solving experiences. Graphics and feedback are combined

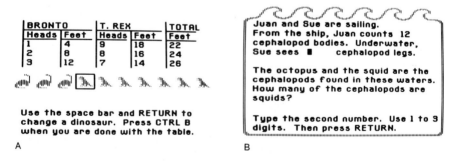

A

B

FIGURE 5-5 "Dinosaurs and Squids" from the series *Strategies in Problem Solving.* Copyright © 1985 by Scott, Foresman and Company. Reprinted by permission.

*Acting, perhaps, like a student, I first constructed a problem that had no answer (there were 12 sails but 14 hulls). The program informed me that it was not possible to solve the problem I had posed!

effectively. Hints and strategy options encourage students to use the meta-components of deciding on the nature of the problem, selecting a representation, and selecting a strategy. Appropriate problem-solving strategies are prompted and supported with the computer's capabilities. Students are allowed to choose the strategy(ies) that make sense to them. Finally, it allows students to enjoy (and learn from) "turning the tables" on the computer by creating problems for it to solve.

Homework Helper: Math Word Problems is targeted toward older students. It, too, combines traditional CAI techniques and computer "tools" in one comprehensive package. Briefly, the three-part program addresses algebraic word problems such as those involving number, age, mixture, and distance. It begins with tutorials that demonstrate how each type of problem is solved (i.e., how to translate them into equations.) In the second part, students use these methods to solve problems supplied by the program. Students are allowed to set up these problems the way they wish; the program guides them from there as necessary. In the third part, they can type in word problems from their own homework assignments and use the tools to solve them. The program does not solve the problems, but will try to guide them to solve it for themselves. Tools include a table or "work grid" for organizing information, an algebraic calculator, and help files. The calculator will show a step-by-step method of solving algebraic equations.

SemCalc (for "Semantic Calculator") is designed to help students solve arithmetic word problems. It provides an electronic scratch pad set up in rows and columns. The student fills in the numbers and corresponding units of measurement, as well as the mathematical operation to be used. For example, a problem might be: "A family averages 55 miles per hour driving a car that gets 28 miles per gallon. How many gallons per hour will they burn?" Students might enter the following:

```
                HOW MANY?      WHAT?
A)                 55          MILES/HOUR
B)                 28          MILES/GAL
OPERATION          A/B
```

The computer would then print:

```
EVALUATING
   55 MILES/HOUR
DIVIDED BY
   28 MILES/GAL
THE UNITS TO THE ANSWER ARE  GAL
                             ----
                             HOUR
55 MILES/HOUR / 28 MILES/GAL = 1.964285714 GAL/HOUR
```

The final quantity is added to the scratch pad for possible future use. If the students had chosen a different operation, say A times B, the computer would have responded that the units would be MILES * MILES/HOUR * GAL (would that make sense?) If they tried B/A, the units would have been HOUR/GAL (does that make sense? Yes, *if* you wanted to know how much time it took you to use a gallon of gasoline).

How might students using *SemCalc* address the classic problem of "adding apples and oranges"? The computer would ask: "Can APPLES be converted to ORANGES or can ORANGES be converted to APPLES?" If the student types N, the computer asks: "APPLES and ORANGES are both what?" If the student types FRUIT, the program displays 7 FRUIT + 12 FRUIT = 19 FRUIT, and the quantity 19 FRUIT is added to the scratch pad. Could the student have answered PIZZAS instead of FRUIT? Of course. SemCalc is merely a tool; it is not designed to tell students the answers. In other cases, of course, conversion is possible. If the student had attempted to subtract grams from kilograms, and then responded that one unit could be converted to the other, SEMCALC would ask: "How many KILOGRAMS in one GRAM or how many GRAMS in one KILOGRAM?"

Logo. Recall Sternberg's "mental company" from earlier in this chapter—the metacomponents responsible for directing one's problem solving. Let's imagine a child attempting to create a Logo procedure. She must first decide exactly what to draw (deciding on the nature of the problem), say, a triangle. She might then decide on a representation. She may physically draw a triangle and represent it as a visual image, or she may represent it mentally as a process ("go up, over to here, and then back to the beginning"). She would choose performance-level processes ("It would be three FORWARDs and three RIGHTS. I could use a REPEAT 3 command"). She might decide she had spent enough time planning and should try out her ideas (allocating resources). Typing in REPEAT 3 [FORWARD 40 RIGHT 90], she would observe a figure that was not the triangle for which she had hoped. Being sensitive to the screen's feedback, and monitoring her solution process, she might conclude, "Oh, I can't go RIGHT 90—that's like a square. It will have to turn . . . more." Her knowledge-acquisition components may have stored new knowledge (e.g., "turtle turns in triangles cannot all be 90, because that would be like a 'box'").

So children engaged in Logo projects may tackle significant, complex problems of their own design. They may use each metacomponent at each phase of completing their projects. To help them do this, the framework for teaching problem solving described previously can be applied directly to many Logo lessons. As one specific example, the notion of prompts, hints, and giveaways came directly from research on teaching programming. The following are Logo programming examples of these question types:

Prompts

What's the first thing you need to tell the computer to do?
What does this command (e.g., RT 90) do?
Are there any other ways to make the turtle . . . ?
What instruction (or procedure) should go next?
What will this procedure really do?
Why did my procedure do this instead of what I intended?

Hints

Can you think of a command to get the turtle to move without drawing a line?
Your problem is to repeat something 12 times. Do you know a command for that?
Could you use a variable in the procedure somehow?

Giveaways

Try PENUP, then FD some amount.
Type REPEAT 12 [FD 10 RT 30].

One valuable way to present information as giveaways to students (in the context of their own work) is as a "good trick" or "good advice." For example, the use of variables, REPEAT, or recursion might be seen as "good tricks," writing only state transparent drawing procedures as "good advice." Note that the problem-solving framework should be used appropriately; there are also many times when lecture/discussions are the best teaching strategy. In addition, monitoring is essential in computer programming. (The last two prompts are monitoring prompts.) We turn to this next.

Promote a "learn from debugging" atmosphere (emphasizing the solution monitoring metacomponent). Bugs in procedures should be welcomed, not avoided at all costs. They lead children to reflect on their own thinking processes and reveal valuable misconceptions. Children need special tools to monitor their progress. In programming (as in many other mathematical activities), an essential tool is tracing (or hand tracing). Here, students pretend they are the computer, tracing the program line by line, executing each instruction that they read exactly as the computer would do. (This is difficult; it's so easy to do what you *meant* to tell the computer to do! The child-turtle games described earlier help students fight this tendency and instead do precisely what was instructed. In all situations, guard against kids believing the computer has intelligent interpretive powers—that it "knows what they mean.")

Students who know how to trace programs can exercise the important problem-solving skills of predicting or "looking ahead" on one hand, and debugging errors on the other. For debugging, Carver and Klahr (1986) provide a well-developed model. Simplified, it is:

1. *Check for bugs.* Run the program. See if there are bugs.
2. *Identify the bug.*
   A. Describe the discrepancy between your goal picture and the turtle's drawing.
   B. Based on this, propose a specific type of bug that might be responsible. For example, if the orientation is off ("This is going over here instead of down"), an angle/rotation is probably buggy.
   C. If more than one possibility exists (e.g., "These are spread apart too far" could mean a distance bug or an angle/rotation bug), describe the discrepancy more precisely.
   D. When only one possibility remains, go to the next step.

3. *Locate the specific bug.*
   A. Represent the structure of the program to investigate the probable location of the bug. For example, can the problem be identified as occurring within a REPEAT instruction? Is it in a certain subprocedure? For example, is the problem that a SQUARE procedure is not producing that shape? At worst, trace the entire program.
   B. Check the location for the bug (e.g., for angle/rotation bugs, look for the faulty RT or LT).
4. *Correct the bug.* Examine the goal picture to determine the appropriate correction. Replace the buggy instruction with the correct one. Then go back to step 1 and try again.

   Students might record the discrepancies they have found and the type of bugs that caused them for future reference.

Some versions of Logo offer debugging procedures that are useful in tracing. Most, for instance, offer PAUSE and CONTINUE commands that are placed in a program at strategic points. When the program reaches the point of a PAUSE command, it is suspended. Students can examine the output (graphics or not), type in other Logo instructions to "see what happens at that point," print the value of variable, and so on. They can then type CONTINUE, and the program will continue running from where it left off.

TRACE (or STEP in some versions) allows students to run a program one line at a time. After each instruction is executed (and shown on the screen), the program halts until a key is pressed. Such tools make tracing easier, but students still must be taught when, why, and how to perform such monitoring actions.

Creative expression. As discussed, creativity should be encouraged and rewarded in all problem-solving activity. In addition, other activities, such as Logo programming, combine creative and logical thought (see Chapter 4). In *Patternmaker* and *Creativity Unlimited,* children design and explore patterns and symmetry. They view patterns artistically and mathematically. They take a pattern and perform transform and move it in certain ways to produce a larger pattern. Applications such as these involve divergent thinking in the solution of problems of creative expression.

Reminders

1. *Use the problem-solving framework* (Table 5–1). When introducing a program, remember to discuss the nature of the problem. Help students establish goals and strategies (make sure they include strategies that use paper and pencil!). Include a closing discussion and extensions.
2. *Focus on strategy use.* As we discussed, it's important to discuss students' strategies. For instance, students might divide into groups based on their choice of strategy. Then, by playing the game repeatedly, they could determine which strategies were most effective.
3. *Present systematic problem-solving instruction.* Remember, to develop good problem solvers, you must understand that:
   Students must solve problems to develop problem-solving ability (rather than only learning subskills such as presented by some textbooks, computer programs, and teachers).
   They develop this ability over a long period of time.

They benefit from a consistent, planned approach. Many guidelines have already been offered. In addition, it is often useful to move from open-ended, exploratory use of programs to challenges concerned with finding and using the most efficient strategies.

They need to solve a variety of problems.

They respond best to a warm, anxiety-free environment

Everyone, students and teachers, should enjoy problem solving.

SUGGESTED READINGS

Charles and Lester (1984) described the problem-solving phases they used in their teaching/research "success story" with problem solving.

Pogrow (1986) has published a program that uses existing software embedded in a problem-solving framework to develop "higher-order thinking skills" as well as basic skills. Which of the suggestions provided has the most merit? What could be done to integrate the programs better into the ongoing mathematics curriculum?

Pressley (1986) describes what a good strategy user needs to know and provides numerous examples from mathematics.

Suydam (1982) provides a succinct summary of research on problem solving and its implications for teaching mathematics.

TABLE 5-2 Software: Problem Solving

Title	Producer	Notes
Alpine Tram Ride	Learn. Tech.	Deductive reasoning in determining identity and placement of four animals by process of elimination. 4–6.
Amusement Park	SVE	Students run a simulated amusement park. 2+.
Arrow Dynamics	Sunburst	Preprogramming and problem solving. 4+.
Balancing Act	JA-MOR	Determine the unknown weight on a balance scale. 2–4.
Building Perspective	Sunburst	Spatial perception. 1987 CCL Award Winner. 4+.
Calculated Risk!	Woodbury	Math skills used in graphic adventure. 2+.
Cause and Effect	Marshware	Induction and deduction with moving shapes. 5–8.
Clowning Around	Learn. Tech.	Remembering which objects appeared in which of several numbered boxes. 2–6.
Color Keys	Sunburst	Analysis and synthesis; pattern searching at 43 levels. 4–12.
Computer Generated Mathematics Materials: Vol. 2—Problem Solving	MECC	Five components each make worksheets or tests for individuals or an entire class. Select from 236 different objectives. 3–8.

(continued)

TABLE 5-2   (Continued)

Title	Producer	Notes
Country Combo	Micro Power	Puzzle of congruence of shape, pattern, and color. 1–6.
Creative Play: Problem-Solving Activities with Computers	MCEP	25 programs emphasizing problem solving, designed to introduce children to computers. Some old "classics" (Hurkle, Nim) and some new games. A decent deal, especially considering the price. 3+.
Creativity Unlimited	Sunburst	Create unlimited patterns with iterations and movements of simple shapes. Interesting program. 2+.
Data Hurdles	World Book	Data manipulations problems, including ordering, rounding, sets, totals, fast math, time, money, percentages, measuring, comparing. 5–12.
De-Bug	Electronic Arts	Students play a strategy game. Without warning, the "D-Bug" computer freezes up. Students must "crawl inside," to find broken parts to repair or replace. A tutorial describes the computer's components and explains how they work together. They can also view an expert fix a problem (for a fee). Errors might include defective video chips, loose chips, or improperly connected cables. Several levels of difficulty.
Deduction	Micro-Ed	Students use clues they request to figure out how variables are related. 5–12.
Discrimination, Attributes, and Rules	Sunburst	A sequel to "Memory." See text. K–6.
Dolphin Math	Houghton Miff.	Problem solving, including CMI with diagnosis. 1–8.
The Enchanted Forest	Sunburst	Logic; concepts of conjunction, disjunction, and negation. Identifying attributes in a fairytale situation. 4+.
ESC Mathematics	ESC	Problem-solving activities ask students to identify the question, cite the important information, choose the action required, and find the missing or irrelevant information. Students use visualization, logic, and judgments. A comprehensive program with CMI for grades 1–6.

Title	Producer	Notes
Extended Instuction Courseware	Laidlaw	Drill and practice and problem-solving strategies correlated with the publisher's textbook. Includes some lessons on Logo and BASIC. Some CMI.
Facemaker	Spinnaker	Includes a memory game based on a chaining strategy. P–3.
The Factory	Sunburst	Visualization, analysis, and sequencing. Students create geometric "products" by sequencing machines in a simulated factory. 4–12.
The First Men in the Moon	Fisher-Price	Practice with arithmetic operations, both unadorned algorithms and applications in word problems, set in an adventure-game format. 4–7.
Freddy's Puzzling Adventures	DLM	A series of games designed to stimulate logical thinking skills, including spatial relations, strategy use, and sequencing. 2+.
Fun House Maze	Sunburst	Visualization of three-dimensional maze. 4–12.
Gamepac I	Pers. Comp. Art	Several activities for logical thinking. 1–12.
Gears	Sunburst	Select the number of gears to line up and number of teeth for each gear. Given the number of rotations of the first gear, predict the direction and number of rotations for the last gear. 4+.
Gertrude's Puzzles	TLC	Logic puzzles using shapes (can be user defined). 1–6.
Hexaplex	Berta-Max	Object of the game is to get the numbers on facing sides of each hexagon to match. 3–8.
High Wire Logic	Sunburst	A game based on Boolean logic. A set of shapes is balanced initially on a wire; one set remains, another falls into the net. Students must write as many rules as possible that fit the shapes on the high wire but not those in the net (see Fig. 5–6 on p. 146). The rules involve the use of logic types, AND, OR, AND-OR, OR-OR, and EXCLUSIVE OR (e.g., a rule might be "green or hexagons"). 5–12.

(continued)

TABLE 5-2 (Continued)

Title	Producer	Notes

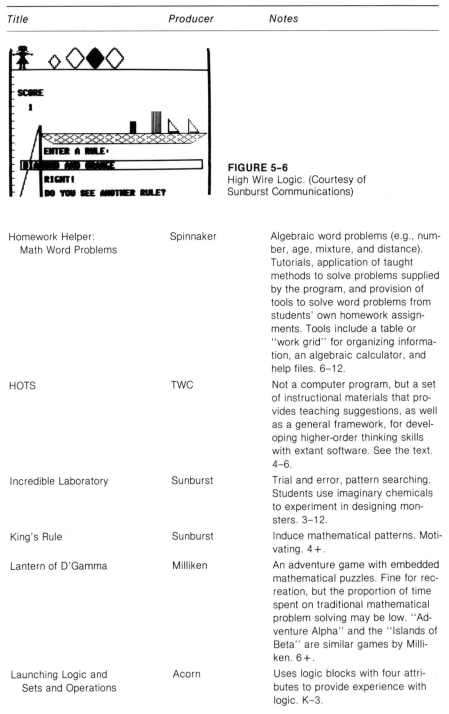

FIGURE 5-6
High Wire Logic. (Courtesy of
Sunburst Communications)

Title	Producer	Notes
Homework Helper: Math Word Problems	Spinnaker	Algebraic word problems (e.g., number, age, mixture, and distance). Tutorials, application of taught methods to solve problems supplied by the program, and provision of tools to solve word problems from students' own homework assignments. Tools include a table or "work grid" for organizing information, an algebraic calculator, and help files. 6–12.
HOTS	TWC	Not a computer program, but a set of instructional materials that provides teaching suggestions, as well as a general framework, for developing higher-order thinking skills with extant software. See the text. 4–6.
Incredible Laboratory	Sunburst	Trial and error, pattern searching. Students use imaginary chemicals to experiment in designing monsters. 3–12.
King's Rule	Sunburst	Induce mathematical patterns. Motivating. 4 + .
Lantern of D'Gamma	Milliken	An adventure game with embedded mathematical puzzles. Fine for recreation, but the proportion of time spent on traditional mathematical problem solving may be low. "Adventure Alpha" and the "Islands of Beta" are similar games by Milliken. 6 + .
Launching Logic and Sets and Operations	Acorn	Uses logic blocks with four attributes to provide experience with logic. K–3.

Title	Producer	Notes
Linear Search/Grid Search Games	Creative Pub.	Search for a member of an ordered set. 5+.
Logic and Deduction	Ed. Micro. Sys.	Deduction of numerical code. Modification of "Mastermind" game. 4–12.
Logic Builders	Scholastic	Building, matching, and creating "spiders' webs" to develop visual discrimination, pattern matching, and problem-solving abilities. 2–6.
Math #1: The Mechanics of Word Problems	Ellen Nelson	Teaches a six-step method for solving arithmetic word problems. Uses "key word" approach. 3–6.
Math Efficiency System	Comp. Assisted	Reinforces problem-solving skills. Some CMI, including pre- and posttests. Several disks at each level; five levels available.
Math Power: Creative Problem Solving	JWW	Order-of-operations game. Presents the answer, and students must make up the problem. They arrange a series of digits, operations, and functions to equal the target answer. 4–12.
Math Shop	Scholastic	Students help in various stores in a mall by solving problems, each using a specific curriculum concept such as proportions, fractions, measurement, or arithmetic operations. See the text. 6–9.
Math Story Solvers	Learn. Cons.	Arithmetic word problems at four levels. Two beginning levels—in the first, students identify key words associated with arithmetic operations; the second associates visual information with verbal information. The third level involves two-step problems. The fourth combines all previous levels and includes fractions. Students analyze problems by answering three questions: What do I know? What do I want to know? What operations do I need to use? Students can enter their own names and other information to personalize the problems. Some CMI. 4–8.
Math Strategies: Problem Solving	SRA	Solving multiple-step problems using four strategies: simplifying a problem, breaking a problem into parts, identifying needed informa-

(continued)

TABLE 5-2 **(Continued)**

Title	Producer	Notes
		tion, and making a model of the program. 6+.
Math Word Games	McGraw-Hill	Word problems in six games. 4–6.
Math Word Problems	Creative Tech.	Word problem generator, including weights and measure, trips, money, and time. 6+.
Math Word Problems	Intellectual	Guides students through problems one step at a time. 2–6.
Math Word Problems	Weekly Reader/ Optimum	Hundreds of problems in numerous variations. Similar to the Stickybear series. On-screen calculator. Automatic adjustment of difficulty with limited CMI. 8+.
Math Worlds	Sterling Swift	Seven units, including input–output (functions), strategies (design strategies for the computer to use in playing Nim), sampling, data analysis, and turtle geometry. 6–9.
Mathematics Activity Courseware	Houghton Miff.	A package of activites for each grade level designed to provide experiences in problem solving, estimation, computation, and concept development. Tied to series fairly closely. 3–8.
Mathematics Problem Solving Courseware	McGraw-Hill	Simulation/adventure game in which students play a role. They meet characters who present realistic math problems for them to solve. Some CMI. Recommended. K–8.
Mathematics Problem Solving Software	Addison-Wesley	Series of grade-level programs accompanying Addison-Wesley's math text. CMI. 1–8.
Mathematics Today Practice Diskettes	Harcourt Brace	Making and using tables to create graphs and choosing the correct operation. Drill correlated with the publisher's text series. Embedded in gamelike activities; provide "clues" when students make errors. 1–8.
Mathematics Unlimited: Problem Solving	Holt	Comprehensive series including problem-solving strategies and mini-simulations. Applied mathematics to real-life situations, many of which are motivating to students. Features realistic problems, help files, opportunities to "try out" full or partial solutions (with graphic representations), opportunities to retry prob-

Title	Producer	Notes
		lems, on-screen calculator, and some CMI. 1–8.
Mathematics Word Problems	Intellectual	Tutorial. Several individual packages; problems for each grade level. Students often asked to estimate as one step of problem-solving process. K–6.
Memory Building Blocks	Sunburst	Students build visual and auditory memory skills. K+.
Mind Castle I	MCE	Solve logic puzzles to go from room to room in a castle. Part of a series of programs designed to teach reasoning. Challenging problems, if somewhat removed from reality. 4–12.
Mind Puzzles	MECC	Activites on logical thinking; mazes and patterns. 4–7.
MindPower I	SRA	Four categories of thinking skills: ordering, classifying, understanding spatial and temporal relations, and using deduction and inference. Designed to help students become aware of problem-solving strategies and develop problem-solving abilities. 1–6.
Mindstretcher Series	Island	A series of games and activities which are based on fairly sophisticated mathematics such as number theory (but can be played on an intuitive level). 3–9.
Mission Control	Academic Ther.	Solve word problems to launch a shuttle. 3–12.
Monkey Business	Learn. Tech.	Stack monkeys in a "Tower of Hanoi" type of situation. 4–6.
Moptown Parade	TLC	Pattern recognition and logic. A series of games with attribute characters. 1–5.
Number Quest	Sunburst	Binary search strategies must be used to locate hidden numbers, including fractions and decimals. 3–9.
Odd One Out	Sunburst	Discriminate and classify objects. P+.
Odin	Odesta	A strategy game. Students can get hints as to strategy, best move, or countermoves. 4–12.
Patternmaker	Scarborough	Fundamentals of symmetry, balance, color, and design in an ex-

(continued)

TABLE 5-2 (Continued)

Title	Producer	Notes
		ploratory program in which students create and combine patterns with simple commands. 5+.
PAVE	I/CT	Includes memory practice. The same company publishes similar memory programs. 1+.
The Pond	Sunburst	Patterning, generalizing, thinking logically. Game in which students guide a frog through a pattern of lily pads across a pond. Levels of difficulty. 2–12.
Problem Solving	CCC	Teaches techniques of solving problems through specific comments, hints, and error messages. Seven strands: How Many; Money; Mystery Numbers and Age; Measure; Number Systems; Time, Rate, and Distance; and Geometry. 3–6.
Problem-Solving Computer Tutor	RG	Tutorial and practice. 4–8.
Problem Solving in Everyday Math	MCE	Tutorial with simulations teaches step-by-step approach to solving common problems. 3–6.
Problem Solving in Math	Berta-Max	Tutorials. 3–6.
Problem Solving Software	Riverside	Randomly generated word problems completed with yes/no answers. No graphics. 3–8.
Problem-Solving Strategies	MECC	Two activities teach strategies of trial and error, exhaustive listing, and simplifying the problem. Two others ask students to apply these strategies to more complex problems. See the text. 5–9.
Problem-Solving Strategies	Reader's Digest	Allows students to use the computer as a tool for solving problems with any of six strategies. For example, they might instruct the computer to draw and label Venn diagrams. If they answer incorrectly, the program leads them through a solution. They begin by highlighting the goal sentence and all the relevant facts. Then they see the program draw, label, and use a Venn diagram. 5+.
Problems and Solutions Series	Media Materials	Using a strategy to solve word problems. 5–12.

Title	Producer	Notes
PSST—Problem Solving Strategy Training	Porter	Leads students through steps necessary to solve typical verbal problems. First focuses on the question being asked, then to an analysis of the facts contained in the problem, and finally to selection of the appropriate mathematical procedure to use in its solution. For example, on one problem the student might identify the line that contains the question; decide if the problem has just enough, too much, or not enough information; choose an operation; and answer; 45 problem sets, each having different characteristics. 4–12.
PSST: Problem Solving Strategy Training	Winners Circle	Strategies for solving word problems. Illustrates steps such as paying attention to detail, identifying parts of a problem, and reaching conclusions through reasoning. 2–6.
Puzzle Tanks	Sunburst	Using two tanks of given capacities, try to fill, empty, and transfer to produce a given amount (e.g., variation on the standard "two buckets problem"). 3+.
Quintominoes	Dynacomp	Object of geometry game is to lay down shapes on a grid so that they connect correctly. 1–6.
Read and Solve Math Problems	Ed. Act.	Sequenced tutorial and drill on the important elements of word problems and translation to number sentences. 4–6.
Rocky's Boots	TLC	Logic. Students design their own logic machines using simulated computer circuits. 2+.
Safari Search	Sunburst	In a safari trip though a gridlike environment, students must decipher clues to reveal the hiding place of a mystery animal. They collect and organize information and make inferences. 3+.
Scrambled Eggs	Learning Tech.	Formulate hypotheses about numerical sequences to discover which chicken is in which egg. 4–6.
SemCalc	Sunburst	See the body of the text. 6–12.
Series M: Macmillan Mathematics CAI	Macmillan	Exercises for series M texts. Optional CMI. 1–8.

(*continued*)

TABLE 5-2   (Continued)

Title	Producer	Notes
Simon Says	Sunburst	Sequencing. Operates with keyboard, Muppet Learning Keys, or Touch Window.
Sliding Block	Learning Tech.	Jigsaw puzzle. 5–8.
Snooper Troops	Spinnaker	Gather and utilize information as a detective. A series of programs. 3–12.
Solving Story Problems	Houghton Miff.	Real-world story problems in a tutorial series that teaches 412 skills and strategies in a step-by-step manner. Tutorial help for incorrect answers. 3–8.
Solving Word Problems	Aquarius	Remedial programs. Students are asked to apply problem-solving steps by computing a series of statements. 4–10.
Solving Word Problems in Math	Orange Cherry	Reading and understanding word problems involving fractions, ratios, perimeter, and area. Isolation of key words and translation of solution into verbal form. 3–8.
Space Mission Problem	Orange Cherry	Problems involving weight, volume, rate, time, and distance in a setting of space exploration (e.g., low fuel, cosmic dust storms). 4–7.
Sports Problems	Intellectual	Word problems in sports settings. 2–8.
Spotlight	Apple	Four games on reflection of spotlight, guessing a three-digit number given clues, and capturing squares on grid. 4–8.
Story Problem Practice	Micrograms	4–8.
Story Problems	Amidon	Five sections, one on each arithmetic operation and one mixed. 3–7.
Story Problems in Addition and Subtraction	Micro Ed.	Drill on word problems.
Storybook Addition and Subtraction	Edupro	Students work together to solve problems involving number searches, mazes, etc. K–4.
Storybook Number Relationships	Edupro	Students work together to solve problems involving relationships. K–4
Strategies for Problem Solving I and II	Silver Burdett & Ginn	Lessons and simulations. Students apply strategies to solve problems in microworlds. 3–6.
The Super Factory	Sunburst	Problem-solving strategies and spatial visualization are developed in a

Title	Producer	Notes
		three-dimensional version of "Factory." Students rotate cube in three dimensions, placing pictures on its faces. They can create their own designs, or be challenged to construct a given design at four levels of difficulty. Good documentation, including classroom lesson plans; 5–adult.
SuperMath	Sunburst	Games and puzzles for gifted students, including magic squares, math codes, and binary numbers. 5+.
Tangrams	Home Computer	Classic geometry game. 3–12.
Teasers By Tobbs: Puzzles and Problem Solving	Sunburst	Two programs designed to teach logical thinking. Determine which number can't be, might be, or must be the missing number in grid problems. 4+.
Teddy & Iggy	Sunburst	Sequencing. Operates with keyboard, Muppet Learning Keys, or Touch Window. 1–3.
Think Tank Mathematics	Opp. Learning	High interest/low reading skill word problems. Math skills in each section range from 2 through 6.
Trading Post	Sunburst	Students must make strategic decisions within the context of a given set of exchange rules. Players are given a set of shapes. They either add to their set or exchange shapes (by selecting an exchange rule) in an attempt to match a different goal set. 3–7.
Treasure Islands	Intellectual	Maps, plotting coordinates, bearings (degrees). Simulations for two groups, in the role of the crew of a treasure ship and a pirate ship. "Adventure Island" is similar. 5–9.
Tutorial Problem Solving in Math	Random House	Multiple lessons on seeking clues to the arithmetic operation required and to test the logic of one's answers. 3–4.
Vennman/Vennkids/Gates	Acorn	Logic, Venn diagrams, and prediction activities. 2–7.
What's My Logic	Midwest	Analytical thinking skills, trial-and-error strategies, and rules of logic (negation, conjunction, inclusive or, and exclusive or) are practiced in a

(*continued*)

TABLE 5-2 (Continued)

Title	Producer	Notes
		"Mastermind" format. Students move on a checkerboard according to rules they must induce. 3–12.
What's That Weight	JA-MOR	Determine the value of an unknown weight on a balance scale. 1–3.
WhizCalc II	World Book	Word problems with step-by-step guidance. 5–12.
Weird Problems	Opp. Learn.	Word problems involving "cops and robbers," space, etc. 6–8.
Word Problems	Gamco	Drill in word problems. The first disk at each of three levels develops prerequisite skills, the second gives practice in solving actual word problems. Reward game for motivation and some CMI. 3–8.
Word Problems	Intellectual	Drill and practice word problems with "hints." Some CMI. Series sold separately by grade level. 1–8.
Word Problems Project	ETC	Allows students to display information from a problem in several representations simultaneously (e.g., pictures, tables, and graphs). Students manipulate the information in one representation, and immediately see the consequences in the others. They use the program to solve problems such as missing-value and proportional reasoning. 3–9.
WordMath	Milliken	Tutorial and practice in four types of word problems (see the text). Some CMI. 4–8.
Zandar 3	SVE	Solving a mystery using clues and conjunctive rule of logic. Tutorial and practice. 3–6.
Zany Zoo	Opp. Learn.	Word problems involving whimsical creatures. 1–3.

This and all other tables that list software contain Notes that briefly describe the programs, evaluate them in some cases, and list the grade-level placement suggested by the publishers. P–3 indicates that a program is recommended for students from preschool to grade 3; 3+ Indicates grade 3 and above. Readers are cautioned that publishers often "stretch" this range.

LOGICAL FOUNDATIONS AND NUMBER

LOGICAL FOUNDATIONS OF MATHEMATICS

Number can be viewed as a property of a set (a group of objects, called elements or members of the set). Therefore, it is logical to assume that children need to study sets before studying number concepts. In fact, Piaget's early theory of number development postulated that a combination, or synthesis, of classifying and seriating (ordering) was necessary to construct the concept of number. On this basis, the logical operations of classification and seriation are often called prenumber concepts. However, recent research does not substantiate the claim that these so-called prerequisites must be mastered before number can be understood. In fact, experience with counting and other number skills may lead to improved performance in both number skills *and* logical operations (Clements, 1984). Therefore, it is probably most helpful to view these logical abilities as developing concurrently with numerical concepts and skills, with the two domains becoming increasingly integrated.

This does not actually decrease the importance of classification and seriation skills—they help lay the groundwork for hierarchical classification, abstract relationships, and formal reasoning and logic. It merely views them from a slightly different perspective—as basic abilities that should be taught simultaneously with number concepts, as mutually reinforcing sets of abilities that share a structural similarity. Or, in other words, as separate but partially connected frames that can grow in tandem, enriching their connections with each other and with other frames.

Classification

Classification activities should be a part of the mathematics curriculum at every grade level. Several illustrative classification programs, from relatively easy to more challenging, will be discussed.

Initially, classification activities might develop simple discrimination ability. Several programs that provide young children practice in these skills are listed in Table 6-1. For example, the inhabitants of *Moptown,* "Moppets," have four attributes: tall or short, fat or thin, red or blue, Bibbit (big feet and big nose) or gribbit (tails). In one of the beginning activities, children see four Moppets and must choose the one that is different. In another, four Moppets are seen in a house. The child must identify the one thing that is the same about all of them. Other activities involve analogies and "guess my attribute" and "guess my rule" games, such as guessing the rule for inclusion in a clubhouse. Such activities are best taught within the problem-solving framework described in Chapter 5.

These programs, along with others, such as *Gertrude's Secrets* and *Gnee or Not Gnee,* do have limitations. For example, correct classifications are mostly predetermined. Children should have the experience of discovering that categories are the creation of people's minds. Therefore, teachers should also provide children with open-ended classificatory experiences, such as classifying "junk" materials like buttons in as many different ways as they can. Classification should also be done for a *purpose.* For example, young children might classify materials into "attracted to magnets" or not, and then try to determine the critical difference between these groups. Classification activities on and off the computer demand not only that students categorize, but also that they determine the nature of the problem, represent the problem in a meaningful way, induce relationships, construct hypotheses, test these hypotheses, monitor their solution processes, and utilize mathematical (e.g., geometric) concepts.

Seriation

In a seriation, or ordering, activity from *Kinder Koncepts,* children are presented with five bars of varying length displayed against a measuring grid. They must press the key from 1 to 5 that corresponds to the longest or shortest bar. A caveat is that such computer-screen ordering does not involve active manipulation, which may limit its impact on young children. Having children seriate many different kinds of materials in different ways (by length, weight, roughness—sandpaper, shades of color, tone, etc.) will help ensure learning of more breadth. Somewhat more control is offered children in "Fence" from *Early Childhood Learning Program.* Children create graphics by selecting any of nine bars of varying length that correspond to the numbers 1 to 9. The bars can be moved forward or back, rotated, and so on so as to construct letters, shapes, and pictures.

Relationships

Several programs introduce young children to number relationships. The *IBM Elementary Mathematics Conceptual Series* asks young children to place "more," "less," or "the same" number of blocks on one side of a balance than have been placed on the other (see Fig. 6-1). Older students might

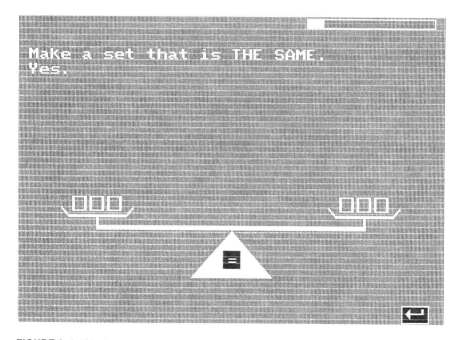

FIGURE 6-1 *IBM Elementary Mathematics Conceptual Series.* (Used with permission of IBM Corporation/WICAT Systems Inc.)

write simple Logo procedures that test whether a number is equal to, greater than, or less than another number. This provides experience not only with relationships, but also with logic and the important concept of *conditional* (IF/THEN). It is probably most interesting to embed such tests in a game such as "guess the number." A typical interaction with such a program might be

```
GUESS THE MYSTERY NUMBER. IT IS BETWEEN 0 AND 100.
WHAT IS YOUR GUESS? >50
50 IS GREATER THAN THE NUMBER.
WHAT IS YOUR GUESS? >20
20 IS LESS THAN THE NUMBER . . .
```

And so on, until the number is guessed. Possibly the most important benefit students accrue from *playing* this game is the acquisition of the binary search strategy. Other significant learning might occur as students extend the procedures in several ways, such as adding informational feedback (e.g., stating whether the guesses are getting closer to the target), adding error trapping, or teaching the turtle to indicate a range on a number line (see GUESS.NUMBER.TURTLE in the Appendix for one model). The program might state whether a binary search strategy is being used; it might even model such a strategy! Teachers should, of course, encourage students to use similar relationships and conditionals in their own programming.

Patterning

Mathematics has been *defined* as the study of patterns. In arithmetic and algebra, we study number patterns. In geometry, we study visual/spatial patterns. Piaget has stated that intelligence is a structuring that imposes patterns on the interaction between people and objects.

In one of the *Moptown* activities, students see four Moppets arranged in a pattern. They must discover the pattern and identify which Moppet comes next (see also *Size and Logic*). These one-dimensional patterns are extended to two dimensions in *The Pond*. Here, students must recognize and articulate patterns, generalize from data, and think logically to determine the pattern of moves across lily pads that will get a green frog across the pond to a magic lily pad. They see only a part of the pond at any one time and discover the pattern by moving the frog one pad at a time. However, to reach the magic lily pad, they must induce the pattern of moves and type them in (e.g., in Fig 6–2a the student would have to specify down three, over four, down one, over three; the pattern of the whole pond is illustrated in Fig. 6–2b). Patterns can be complicated by distractor pads, such as the four-step pattern in Fig. 6–2c. Discussions can be concerned not only with pat-

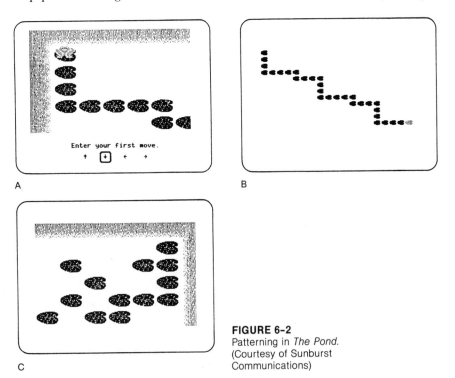

A

B

C

FIGURE 6-2
Patterning in *The Pond*.
(Courtesy of Sunburst
Communications)

terning and its extension beyond the program (e.g., "Hey this pattern, 1, 4, 6, 9, 11 ... is like the three pads up, two pads left pattern in *Pond"*), but also with effective problem-solving strategies, such as finding regularity in complex situations and separating the relevant from the irrelevant.

Complementing such on-computer activities, students might use tiles or cutout lily pads to create their own "pond patterns" with which to challenge each other. Students, especially younger ones, should also move in patterns (e.g., wink, slap, slap, clap; wink, slap, slap, clap, ...), construct patterns out of materials (e.g., Unifix cubes: red, green, green, blue; red, green, green, blue, ...), and translate patterns from one form to another (e.g., the first example into the second). They should plan, name, and construct patterned beds and paper chains for holiday decorations. All students should observe patterns in their environment (from those on shirts to those in the construction of buildings) and their mathematics (e.g., the patterns inherent in counting by fives).

Numerical sequences and patterns. Several programs provide practice "filling in the missing numeral." The *IBM Elementary Mathematics Series* contain simple dot-to-dot activities in which young children sequence either numerals or sets of squares to reveal pictures. Even preschool children can connect the dots using the "mouse" (on the Macintosh computer) in *Kids-Time.* Similarly, connecting dots in order (1, 2, 3, ...) creates a picture in "Connect the Dots" on the *Preschool Disk.* Before you get feeling too superior, try it with the binary option (Fig. 6–3)! Octal and hexadecimal bases are also available, in addition to the traditional decimal. Both programs have the capability to allow teachers to change existing puzzles or create their own.

The *King's Rule* is a challenging program. Students must discover the numerical rules that allow them to work their way through a king's castle. At each of six levels of difficulty, players are given three numbers related by a secret rule. They are then invited to try three numbers of their own. The program tells them whether or not their numbers fit the rule. They continue generating and testing hypotheses in this manner as long as they wish (Fig. 6–4). When they feel confident that they have figured out the rule, they take a "test" in which they determine whether a sequence given by the program fits the rule (the rule in Fig. 6–4 is "numbers multiplied by 4").

Besides developing the ability to recognize numerical relationships, working with this program develops appreciation for the need to test hypotheses rigorously. When first given the sequence "2 4 6," students may test "6 8 10" and "14 16 18," conclude that they "have the rule" (i.e., consecutive even numbers), and opt for a test. Given "13 14 15," they respond that it does not fit the rule and are quite surprised to have the computer respond that they did not pass the test! Without guidance, some even persist trying out sequences such as "10 12 14" that provide no new information. More helpful would be "5 7 9," "10 15 20," "9 8 7," or "10 14 6"—because the rule could be "numbers separated by a constant" (either "2" or any constant), "numbers in ascending order," or "even numbers" (in no

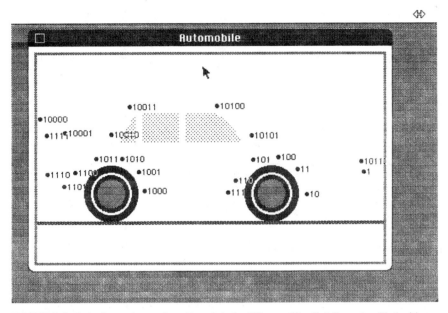

FIGURE 6-3 A challenge for readers: Complete the "Connect the Dots" puzzle with the binary number system option selected.

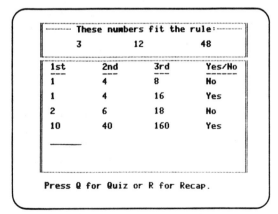

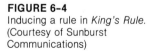

FIGURE 6-4
Inducing a rule in *King's Rule.*
(Courtesy of Sunburst
Communications)

particular order). Rules at the first levels are quite straightforward, but those at the later levels are challenging to anyone (e.g., "2 10 6," "7 7 7," and "15 25 20" all fit what rule? Try it before reading on, and check your answer at the end of this chapter.) Looking for patterns is a powerful problem-solving heuristic. Students should apply the skills learned with programs such as *King's Rule* to other situations.

Logo procedures can easily print arithmetic or geometric sequences. This recursive procedure for arithmetic sequences takes three inputs: a starting number or term, a number to add to each term to continue the sequence, and the number of terms desired.

```
TO ARITH.SEQ. :TERM :ADDEND :NUM.TERMS
  IF :NUM.TERMS < 1 [STOP]
  TYPE :TERM SPACES 1
  ARITH.SEQ (:TERM +  :ADDEND) :ADDEND (:NUM.TERMS - 1)
END

TO SPACES :NUMBER
  REPEAT :NUMBER [TYPE CHAR 32]
END
```

In Terrapin Logo:

```
TO ARITH.SEQ :TERM :ADDEND :NUM.TERMS
  IF :NUM.TERMS < 1 THEN STOP
  PRINT1 :TERM SPACES 1
  ARITH.SEQ (:TERM + :ADDEND) :ADDEND (:NUM.TERMS - 1)
END

TO SPACES :NUMBER
  REPEAT :NUMBER [PRINT1 CHAR 32]
END

ARITH.SEQ 1 2 5
1 3  5  7  9
```

It is easy to add graphics to this procedure, with the help of two procedures (not given here): SETUP, which positions the turtle, and DRAW.LINE, which draws a line whose height is the current value of :TERM and then moves the turtle over (Fig. 6–5a). Notice that the increase in an arithmetic sequence is a constant. We change the "slant" or slope of that line by changing the value of :ADDEND (Fig. 6–5b and c). In contrast, a geometric sequence is produced by successively multiplying each term by a given number. This type of sequence produces a "curve" (Fig. 6–5d). The increase from one term to the next is not constant; it increases. The sequence increases so quickly that only a limited number of terms can be graphed on our screen (Fig. 6–5e).

Similarly, exponential growth can be explored with simple Logo programs. If you fold a large sheet of newspaper once, how many thicknesses are there (2; have children try it each time to check their reasoning). Twice (4)? Three times? How about six times?—Before you try it, guess: How many times do you think you can fold it before it becomes too thick to continue?

FIGURE 6-5
Using the ARITH.SEQ procedure
with different inputs.

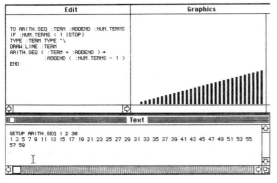

A

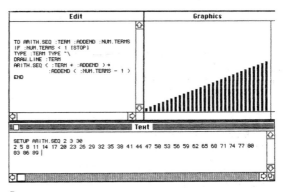

B

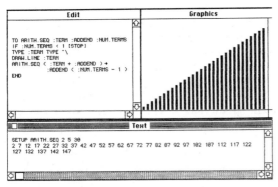

C

FIGURE 6-5 (*Continued*)

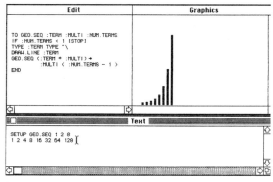

D

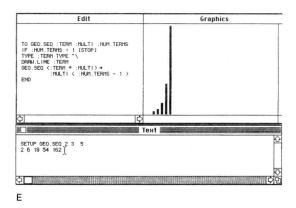

E

How many thicknesses will there be after, say, ten folds? At this point, it might help to have a computer program print out the pattern.

```
TO DOUBLE
TYPE [TIMES DOUBLED] SPACES 2 PRINT [THICKNESSES]
DOUBLE.IT 0 1
END

TO DOUBLE.IT  :TIMES :THICKNESSES
  TYPE :TIMES   SPACES 15 PRINT :THICKNESSES
  DOUBLE.IT ( :TIMES + 1 ) ( :THICKNESSES * 2 )
END
```

In Terrapin Logo:

```
TO DOUBLE
 PRINT1 [TIMES DOUBLED] SPACES 2 PRINT [THICKNESSES]
 DOUBLE.IT 0 1
END
```

```
TO DOUBLE.IT  :TIMES  :THICKNESSES
  PRINT1 :TIMES   SPACES 15   PRINT :THICKNESSES
  DOUBLE.IT ( :TIMES + 1 ) ( :THICKNESSES * 2)
END
```

Until these procedures are stopped, they will continue to print out the number of times a paper was folded and the number of thicknesses:

DOUBLE TIMES DOUBLED	THICKNESSES
0	1
1	2
2	4
3	8
4	16
5	32
6	64
7	128
8	256
9	512
10	1024 ...

Estimate how many folds you now think are possible, then check this by actually folding newspaper. After nine folds, there are 512 thicknesses. About how many centimeters would this measure (could you use an approximation, such as that a package of 500 sheets of duplication paper is about 5.5 cm thick)? After 24 folds? (Amazingly, these 16,777,216 thicknesses measure over 1.8 *kilo*meters, or more than a mile.) Could you alter the program to print out this measure after the number of thicknesses?

If you let the procedure run farther, the number of thicknesses would begin to be reported in scientific notation, providing an introduction to that notation. At 31 folds, one computer printed 2.14748E9, which means $2.14748 * 10^9$ or 2,147,480,000 thicknesses. Students would also discover that computer programs are usually limited in the size of the numbers that they can handle: one computer quit doubling after printing the 126th fold (thicknesses: 8.50708E37, or 85,070,800,000,000,000,000,000,000,000,000,000,000. It then printed a NUMBER TOO BIG message.

How could the program be modified to solve different variants of the "doubling" problem? For example, should Linda accept $500 for a month's pay, or a penny on the first day, double that on the second day, double that on the third, ... ? Meeting such challenges helps children to transfer their computer work to their classroom mathematics work and to transfer all this work to problems they will encounter throughout their lives.

WHOLE NUMBERS AND COUNTING

The concept of number is often oversimplified and misunderstood. As mentioned at the beginning of this chapter, Piaget postulated that number is constructed by the child as a synthesis of classifying and ordering. Children have to order objects to be counted mentally to ensure that each one is counted once and only once. Young children often skip objects or count some twice. In addition, children must, at each count, mentally include all the previous objects. After counting five objects, young children may respond to the question, "Show me five," by indicating only the *fifth* object. Children who have mastered hierarchical class inclusion in number understand that "two" *includes* "one," "three" *includes* "two" (as well as "one"), and so on.

Complete, logical development of the number concept probably does require relatively advanced understanding of classification and ordering. However, more recent research has shown that children do develop considerable knowledge about number through counting, even before these logical structures are fully in place. These researchers do agree with Piaget about one important point: Number is *not* "out there," embedded in objects. It is a construction of the human mind. Each child must reinvent his or her own understanding of number. Therefore, while the counting word sequence ("one, two, three, four . . .") is arbitrary and thus can and should be directly "taught to" children, the *concept* of number, and numerical abilities such as counting, should be constructed by these young learners. They should do this by acting on objects and then reflecting on their actions. Mentally, they put things into relationships. For example, Piaget tells of one mathematician who remembered how, as a boy, he counted a group of stones. Playing with the stones, he happened to rearrange them. He counted them again. The number was the same. But, of course, he had neither added nor subtracted stones from the group, and could always place them back in their initial arrangement! To him, this was an exciting result. He repeatedly rearranged and counted the stones, intoxicated with the joy of this logic: No matter how a group of things is arranged, its number remains the same. He had reinvented number conservation. Any worthwhile computer program will encourage, or at least allow, such active learning.

There are more programs that teach counting and number–numeral correspondence than you can count. One example, *Number Farm*, contains six programs in which young children count horseshoes, barnyard sounds, and vegetables; estimate and count eggs laid by hens; and count farm animals to complete the song "Old MacDonald."

Many programs, unfortunately, treat counting as a routine activity. Children count a set of objects and type in the number. However, counting is a complex ability. Children's counting reveals deep cognitive functioning. Also, it is easy for children to harbor misunderstanding about it. It is always advisable to talk to them about their counting. One child, when asked to count, stood straight up and counted to ten. Praised and asked to count backward, he turned around and counted "one, two, three, . . ."! A kindergarten girl also counted to ten. She was asked if she could count higher. She took a deep breath and counted to ten in a squeaky voice two octaves higher.

Help young children develop sound counting concepts in these ways:

1. Select programs that let the child control the movement of objects.
2. Talk to children about their counting. Help them discuss and master basic counting rules:

A. Say the number words in order.
B. Count each object once and only once.
C. Keep a one-to-one correspondence between each number word and each thing.
D. The final number word you say represents the number of items in the set.
E. It does not matter what order you count the objects (Gelman and Gallistel, 1978).

3. Select programs that encourage children to count on from numbers other than one and to count backward as well as forward.
4. Help children organize their counting of objects by organizing a "plan" for counting (e.g., going left to right and top to bottom through a set), or better, by moving them if possible.
5. Help children develop ability in counting *and* instant recognition of the number of a small group of objects (0 through 6).
6. Encourage children to use strategies of counting on and back from known sets ("How many in all? We can see this is four. So, four. . . . five, six, seven!").
7. Make sure that children do most of their counting in meaningful situations, such as getting enough scissors for their group.

One program based on recent research on counting is *Counters.* Children work on five levels. At the first level, a row of objects such as train engines move onto the top of the screen. Each is accompanied by a beep and the appearance of the appropriate numeral. A horizontal line is drawn to separate the top of the screen from the bottom. One by one, engines move onto the bottom, stopping directly underneath the corresponding engines on the top. The child must press any key when the number on the bottom is the same as the number on the top. If the child is correct, the engines move together on the screen. If a key is pressed too soon, the program places the correct number of engines on the bottom, then highlights the engines that were omitted by the child, and finally demonstrates the correct correspondence by changing the color of pairs of engines—one from the top and the matching one from the bottom—one pair at a time. If a key is pressed too late, a similar sequence is followed, except that the extra objects are first crossed out.

The second level is similar, except that the objects on the bottom are not placed directly under the matching object on the top. At the third level, objects move onto the top, but are then erased and replaced by a numeral. At the fourth level, objects move onto the top, and the child must press any key when a written numeral incrementing at the bottom matches that number (Fig. 6–6). If the child is incorrect, the answer is crossed out and the numeral increments in color to show a correspondence to the count of objects on the top. The fifth level is similar, except that the objects on the top are randomly arranged. This program is not perfect, either; it would be better if some activities allowed the child to create a number such as five by pressing a key five times—to feel the action of creating "five." For example, programs in the *IBM Elementary Mathematics Series* ask the child to press a "right arrow" key the correct number of times to construct a set equal to a given numeral.

Most of children's counting experience should involve real objects. However, one of the benefits of counting on the computer is the feedback children receive on their performance. In "Dog Count" (on *Learning with*

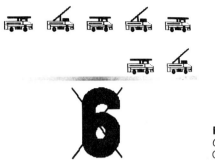

FIGURE 6-6
Counters. (Courtesy of Sunburst Communications)

Leeper) young children see a group of dogs (e.g., 3) and a column of groups of bones (e.g., from 1 to 6). They select the group whose number corresponds to the number of dogs. If they select a group with too few bones (e.g., 2), two dogs walk over and eat a bone from the group selected; however, the dog without a bone sits up, begs, and whines.

Counting skills should be extended far past the traditional "count the number in a group" to include counting subsets, counting backward, and counting on and back from a given number. For example, in "Wuzzle" (on *Prereading/Counting,* see also *Introduction to Counting),* children count objects in a group of mixed shapes (see Fig. 6-7). The skill of counting on, an im-

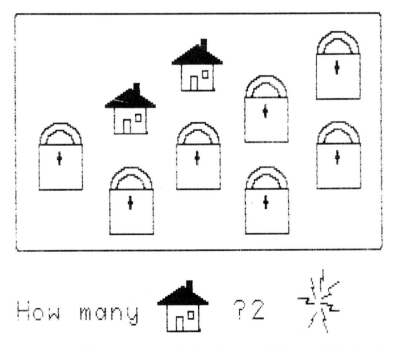

FIGURE 6-7 "Wuzzle." (*Prereading/Counting* from Minnesota Educational Computing Consortium. This MECC program has recently been supplanted by products in their Early Learning Series.)

portant precursor to addition, is practiced in "Balloons" (from *Numbers*). The computer pops some balloons on the screen and then asks the child to continue popping balloons until a specified total of balloons has been popped.

PLACE VALUE

Our entire number system is based on place value. The position of a digit represents its value. With it, any number can be represented using only ten digits; without it, we would have to remember a separate symbol for every number. However, like many powerful, abstract ideas, it is not mastered quickly or easily. Often, difficulties in understanding arithmetical operations (especially those involving renaming) and concepts such as decimal and percent can be attributed to a lack of understanding of place value.

As with concrete manipulatives, computer representations (models) of place value can be proportional or nonproportional. In proportional models such as bundled sticks or Dienes (also known as multibase) blocks, the material for 10 is ten times the size of 1. In nonproportional models such as money or an abacus, such size relationships do not hold. Both are useful. However, both off and on the computer, *proportional* models should be used until children have a firm grasp of place-value concepts. Not all programs follow this guideline. For example, *Hodge Podge* contains an activity wherein a number, represented both by a numeral and by a stack of blocks, is increased by one with each press of a key. This is fine; unfortunately, the numbers larger than 10 are represented via a new stack to the left of the first; that is, 13 is represented nonproportionally as

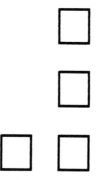

Concrete proportional models can themselves be subclassified. With collectable models (e.g., sticks), ten 1's can be physically bundled to created one 10. Noncollectable models (e.g., multibase blocks or bean sticks) are exchanged, for example, ten units for one "long" (10). Collectable aids should be used initially. One advantage of computer models is that even traditionally noncollectable models such as multibase blocks can be collected rather than exchanged on the screen.

For example, in a module of place-value lessons, students can command the computer to group ten 1's (unit cubes) together to create one 10 (Champagne & Rogalska, in Hansen & Zweng, 1984). In the first lesson, students must write the number symbol that tells how many cubes are in a bag (Fig. 6–8). They do this by grouping cubes into tens and hundreds. They are then shown how to generate the number symbol that corresponds to

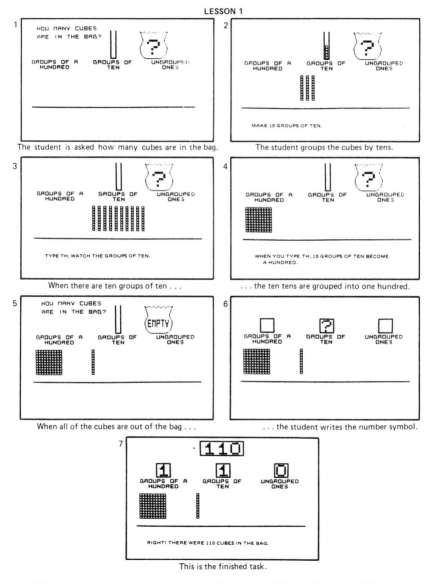

FIGURE 6-8 The first place value lesson. (Courtesy of National Council of Teachers of Mathematics)

the pictorial display. Importantly, these lessons create explicit *mappings*, or connections, between the physical representation and the symbols. Such mappings have been shown to be essential to learning. As an example of these mappings in the computer module, the sixth lesson teaches the correspondence between a regrouped display and the number symbol (Fig. 6–9). The operations performed on the Dienes blocks are performed simultane-

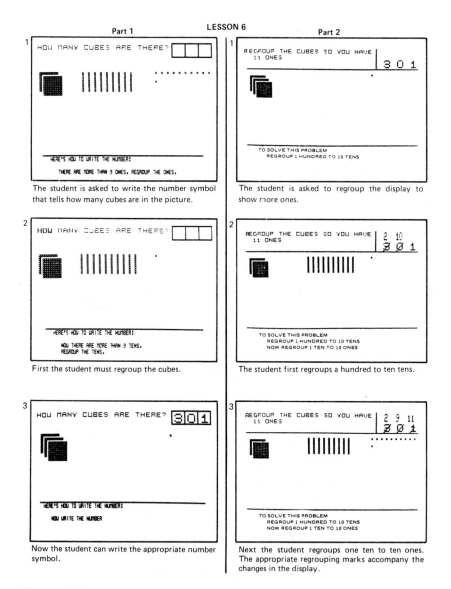

FIGURE 6–9 Linking of manipulatives and the number symbol. (Courtesy of National Council of Teachers of Mathematics)

ously on the symbols. Such mappings tend to prevent students from making renaming errors, such as

$$\begin{array}{r} \overset{6}{\cancel{7}}\ 0\ \overset{14}{\cancel{4}} \\ -3\ 8\ 6 \\ \hline \end{array}$$

because they can "picture" that the value has not been conserved.

Another series of experiences with place value that emphasizes such mappings is contained in the IBM Elementary Mathematics Series. First, students see that 10 tens make 1 hundred, and that 10 hundreds make a thousand (a Dienes block's representation is used; there is also a different sound effect for each place). Second, they repeatedly press a key to "count off" a block's representation of a given number. That is, each block, starting with the thousands, is highlighted as the numeral (which initially is 0000) is updated appropriately. Students then enter the numeral by themselves. If they are incorrect, they are led place by place to type in the correct numeral (as the corresponding blocks are again highlighted). This can be especially helpful for students who have forgotten a zero as a placeholder. After they are successful, students count again, this time without the constantly updated numerals (if they err, the numerals reappear).

In the next activity, students must press keys corresponding to blocks to construct a block representation of a given number. For example, they may have to show 8347 by pressing a key that displays one thousands cube for each keypress eight times, a key that displays a hundreds rod three times, and so on (Fig. 6–10). If they make a mistake, the program offers them a second chance and, if they require more assistance, asks them to tell how many of each place is represented in the numeral. As they respond, the computer displays the correct number of blocks.

Next, students type a numeral given a "number word" such as EIGHT THOUSAND THREE HUNDRED NINETY-EIGHT. If they are incorrect, the block representation is shown. If they need more help, each place is highlighted in turn, as in previous activities (e.g., the words "SEVEN THOUSAND," the seven "thousands blocks," and the numeral "7000" are highlighted simultaneously). The final activity is "Showing Number Words," in which students use the keys to show a block representation of a number word. Later activities offer further help with translating between words and numerals.

These activities have several commendable features:

They are easy to use.
The conceptual model is clear.
A careful sequence of activities is provided.
Help is always available.

What about the objection that these and similar activities are not "concrete?" Recall from the first chapter that students do not abstract mathematics from concrete things but from their *actions* on these things. No Dienes

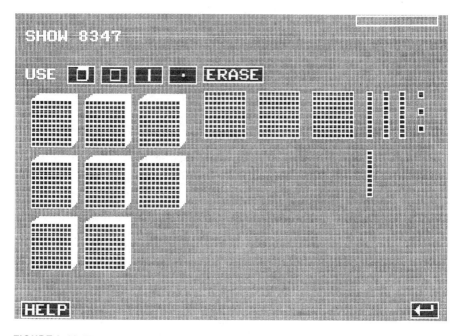

FIGURE 6-10 Place value. (From the IBM/WICAT Elementary Mathematics Series. Used with permission of IBM Corporation/WICAT Systems Inc.)

block "contains" place-value ideas. These ideas are generated from working with these blocks. Ironically, the actual concrete blocks can be so clumsy and the manipulations so isolated one from the other the students see only the trees (manipulations of many pieces) and miss the forest (place-value ideas). Worse, most students never *act* on the blocks much at all; they passively watch demonstrations! Computer lessons such as those described ameliorate this problem: *The concrete activity is mental activity.*

The *Arithmekit* (J. S. Brown, 1983) allows students freedom to explore a mathematical microworld. It represents an attempt to develop a domain-dependent programming language—one that expresses the important conceptual constructs of a task domain without requiring detailed knowledge of programming. In this program, students actually design algorithms by graphically "wiring up" primitives (adders, carriers, etc.) to place-value boxes. Flow of control in the algorithm is also graphically depicted as lines and arrows. Connected to each numerical place-value representation is a Dienes blocks model. Thus, when students have "wired up" an algorithm, they can study its execution in terms of numerical symbols, the blocks, or the correspondence between these two. This allows them to detect errors in the procedure. They can store and replay the workings of their algorithms, permitting them to examine aspects of their own thinking processes. They are free to reproduce standard arithmetic algorithms or to create their own and check them for validity.

Programs such as these give students the opportunity to manipulate place-value models actively while continuously showing them the correspondence between the pictorial model and the arabic numerals. The resulting mappings connect the frame students develop for concrete/pictorial materials with their numerical symbol frame. These frames and their connections help students see the sense, or semantics, as well as the syntax (rote procedures) of place-value algorithms and thus help them to understand, recall, debug, and apply the algorithms.

NUMBER THEORY

Factoring, Primes, and Composites

Factoring Whole Numbers introduces its topic by having students build rectangles with (real) tiles as concepts are simultaneously presented on the computer screen. Students are to find factor pairs by determining the lengths and widths of rectangles of a given area. Tutorials are followed by gamelike activities that rely on application of the skills taught. For example, a later activity demonstrates how to find all perfect squares from 1 to 10,000 through the observations of patterns and relationships. Then students play a game that requires them to make increasingly accurate estimates of the square roots of any number in that range.

In "Taxman" (on *Elementary Vol. I* from MECC) students choose a range of numbers, from 1 to 10, say. Then they select one number in that range, which is added to their score. However, the Taxman (computer) takes all the divisors of that number. If the number has no divisor, the Taxman takes the number. Try the game yourself, or simulate it with a friend; it's more challenging than it first appears.

Students could be introduced to prime and composite numbers through a challenge: Write a Logo program that will find all the divisors of all numbers from 2 to 100. Alternatively, of course, students could use such Logo procedures (provided by the teacher) as a tool. For example, the program in Fig. 6.11, DIVISORS, takes two inputs and prints the divisors of each number between these two numbers, inclusive.

```
DIVISORS 2 50
DIVISORS OF 2 ARE: 1 2
DIVISORS OF 3 ARE: 1 3
DIVISORS OF 4 ARE: 1 2 4
DIVISORS OF 5 ARE: 1 5
DIVISORS OF 6 ARE: 1 2 3 6
DIVISORS OF 7 ARE: 1 7
DIVISORS OF 8 ARE: 1 2 4 8
DIVISORS OF 9 ARE: 1 3 9
DIVISORS OF 10 ARE: 1 2 5 10
DIVISORS OF 11 ARE: 1 11
DIVISORS OF 12 ARE: 1 2 3 4 6 12
DIVISORS OF 13 ARE: 1 13. . . .
```

Why are there more numbers with an even number of divisors than an odd number? Which number has the most divisors? The least?

Students might be led to classify numbers greater than one in two

```
TO DIVISORS :NUMBER.1 :NUMBER.2
 IF :NUMBER.1 > :NUMBER.2 [STOP]
 IF :NUMBER.1 < 0 [PRINT [USE NUMBERS GREATER THAN
    0] STOP]
 TYPE ( SENTENCE [DIVISORS OF] :NUMBER.1 [ARE:] )
    TYPE CHAR 32
 PRINT GET.DIVISORS 1 :NUMBER.1 []
 DIVISORS :NUMBER.1 + 1 :NUMBER.2
END

TO GET.DIVISORS :DIV :NUMBER.1 :DIV.LIST
 IF :DIV > :NUMBER.1 [OP :DIV.LIST]
 IF (REMAINDER :NUMBER.1 :DIV) = 0 [MAKE "DIV.LIST
    LPUT :DIV :DIV.LIST]
 OP GET.DIVISORS (:DIV + 1) :NUMBER.1 :DIV.LIST
END
```

FIGURE 6-11 DIVISORS Logo Program (Terrapin version in Appendix)*

ways, those that have only 1 and themselves as divisors, and those that have additional divisors. These are prime and composite numbers, respectively. Of course, this exploration should be deepened conceptually with other activities, such as using squared paper to form every possible array for each number (e.g., 7 can be made only as a 1 by 7 array; 4 as both a 1 by 4 and a 2 by 2 array).

Challenges: Make the DIVISORS program more efficient in locating primes (e.g., Do even numbers have to be checked? Would the program have to check divisors beyond the square root of the number? Why?). Have the program collect the primes in a list (this list might be used in the next activity).

Examine the factors of 6: 1, 2, 3, and 6. All the factors except the number itself (called the proper factors) sum to 6. Therefore, 6 is called a *perfect* number. If the sum of the proper factors is less than the number, it is *deficient;* if more, it is *abundant.* Write a Logo procedure that uses DIVISORS or its subprocedures to find all the perfect, deficient, and abundant numbers up to 10,000. What number is the most deficient; the most abundant? What characterizes numbers that are relatively more deficient or abundant?

Although the many explorations that can be conducted with primes and composites will intrigue more able learners, all students need to be able to find the prime factors of a number. The PRIME.FACTORIZATION program (see the Appendix) demonstrates a method often use by students. Determine if the number is divisible by the smallest prime number. If so,

---

*It is essential to type Logo programs exactly as given. Usually, this means only careful checking of the letters, numbers, and especially *spaces*. Sometimes, however, long Logo instructions do not fit in one line of this book. For the sake of readability, they have been printed with a special format: Every line after the first line of a long Logo instruction is indented, and no words are split at the end of the line. When *you* type these instructions, some of your words might be split into parts at the end of the line. This is all right; just keep typing. Most important, do *not* press the RETURN key until the end of the final indented line.

add the prime to the list of factors and try the same prime as a divisor again until the dividend is no longer its multiple. Then try the next-largest prime. Continue this process until the dividend is itself a prime.

Challenges: Write a Logo program that creates a Sieve of Eratosthenes. Guess how many primes there are to 1000 and use the PRIME.FACTORIZATION procedures to check. Investigate Goldbach's Conjecture—that every even number greater than 2 can be found by adding only two primes (e.g., $8 = 3 + 5$). This conjecture has not yet been proven; can students find an exception? Can a Logo program be written to check all even numbers within a certain range?

Two other useful concepts stem from this study. The greatest common divisor (GCD; also called greatest common factor) of two numbers is the largest number that is a divisor of both numbers. One method of determining the GCD is to find all the divisors of each number (e.g., for 16, {1, 2, 4, 8, 16}; for 24, {1, 2, 3, 4, 6, 8, 12, 24}), determine the shared divisors (i.e., the intersection of these sets: {1, 2, 4, 8}), and choose the greatest common divisor (8). A Logo program that uses this method is GCD.SETS. A much faster tool is GCD.EUCLID, a separate program that uses the Euclidian algorithm (see the Appendix for each). Challenge: Write a Logo program that finds the GCD of two numbers utilizing the PRIME.FACTORIZATION procedure. (*Hint:* use an INTERSECT procedure.) This would find and then multiply the prime factors contained in both numbers (e.g., {2, 2, 2} for 16 and 24).

This will be important in the study of fractions, as the simplest way to reduce a fraction to its lowest terms is to use the GCD as a divisor of the numerator and the denominator. For example, 16/24 in lowest terms is

$$\frac{16}{24} \div \frac{8}{8} = \frac{2}{3}$$

The least common multiple (LCM) of a number is the smallest multiple of two or more numbers (i.e., the least common denominator when applied to fractions). The program LCM checks each multiple of one of two numbers and outputs the first that is also a multiple of the second number (see the Appendix). For example, given 6 and 9, it would first check if 9 was a multiple of 6, then 18; because it is a multiple of 6, it would output 18. Challenge: Write a Logo program that uses another process, such as finding the LCM by determining the prime factors of each number; the LCM is the product of the prime factors with the highest powers (e.g., $6 = 2^1 + 3^1$; 9 $= 3^2$; so LCM $= 2^1 \times 3^2 = 18$).

Palindromes

Palindromes are words, sentences, or numbers that read the same backward as forward (e.g., "mom," "Able was I ere I saw Elba," or 19891). It is interesting that if a number is *not* a palindrome, one can usually produce one by adding the number to its "reverse" and repeating the process until a palindrome appears (e.g., $84 + 48 = 132$; $132 + 231 = 363$, a palindrome). Challenges: Write a Logo program that reverses the digits of any number, checks if the number is a palindrome, and if not, tries to produce a palindrome in the manner described. What number requires the largest number of steps to produce a palindrome? Can you find that that never does? Find a formula for the number of palindromes of n digits. Check the conjecture that every palindrome with an even number of digits is divisible by 11. Why should this be true? Other investigations in number theory might involve even and odd numbers or divisibility.

It is important to note that any such Logo program can be used in different ways by students of varying ability. Students who are more able in mathematics and/or programming might construct such procedures on their own, or at least modify them. Others might discuss how the procedures work. All students could learn to use them as tools for exploring topics in number theory. For example, they might have the programs list (and possibly count) all the primes within given ranges, such as 1–10, 11–20, 21–30, ...; or 1–100, 101–200, ...; and look for patterns. Or they might list them in different ways, actively searching for their own patterns. The same could be done for perfect, deficient, and abundant numbers. Whether constructing, modifying, studying, or "merely" using the programs, students can be involved in "learning to be mathematicians versus learning about mathematics."

Spreadsheets can be used to explore topics in number theory. For example, they might be used to generate the Fibonacci sequence, where each new term is the sum of the previous two (in the screen display below, A7 is defined as A5 + A6, and so on). Students can search for patterns in this sequence. One sixth-grade student duplicated the "Difference" column from the polygon exploration (see Chapter 3) and found the interesting result shown in column B below (what is the relationship between columns A and B?).

```
B16(V)  (A16-A15)


            A              B

 1 |  FIBONACCI   DIFFERENCE
 2 |
 3 |       1
 4 |       1             0
 5 |       2             1
 6 |       3             1
 7 |       5             2
 8 |       8             3
 9 |      13             5
10 |      21             8
11 |      34            13
12 |      55            21
13 |      89            34
14 |     144            55
15 |     233            89
16 |     377           144
```

Other patterns might be found: What is the pattern of even and odd numbers? Those divisible by 3? By 4, 5, 6, or 7?

Interestingly, the ratio of successive terms approaches the "golden mean" (or "divine proportion"), as column C demonstrates. The golden mean is the ratio between the sides of a "golden rectangle," believed by the ancient Greeks to be the most beautiful four-sided figure. If the short side of this rectangle is 1 unit long, the long side is 1.61803 . . . units.

C16 (V) (A16/A15)

	A	B	C	D
1	FIBONACCI	DIFFERENCE	RATIO	RATIO RECIP.
2				
3	2			
4	7	5	3.5	.2857143
5	9	2	1.285714	.7777778
6	16	7	1.777778	.5625
7	25	9	1.5625	.64
8	41	16	1.64	.6097561
9	66	25	1.609756	.6212121
10	107	41	1.621212	.6168224
11	173	66	1.616822	.6184971
12	280	107	1.618497	.6178571
13	453	173	1.617857	.6181015
14	˙733	280	1.618102	.6180082
15	1186	453	1.618008	.6180438
16	1919	733	1.618044	.6180302

The Greeks found this ratio repeatedly in nature. Ask students to compare the golden mean to the ratio of the length of their forearms to that of their hands (tip of middle finger to wrist) or their height to the "height" of their navels! Students might research the occurrences of the Fibonacci sequence and the golden mean in biology and music (a useful reference is Thornburg, 1983).

As column D showed, the inverse of the ratio approaches the ratio minus 1. Why this should be so is discussed in Chapter 9. Here we will conclude by noticing that changing the first two numbers—those that start the sequence—alters the sequence, but curiously, the ratio approaches the golden mean in a similar manner.

It is important to reiterate that students do not have to construct every (or any) spreadsheet definitions themselves. Templates could be provided to students, who would change the data parameters and observe the results, looking for patterns (see Chapter 3).

Whether constructing hypotheses about classifying rules, searching for patterns and relationships, creating new procedures to operate on place-value representations, or delving into topics in number theory, students engaged with activities such as those illustrated here are playing a *generative* role in learning. They are constructing mathematical questions and answers

D16 (V) (A15/A16)

	A	B	C	D
1	FIBONACCI	DIFFERENCE	RATIO	RATIO RECIP.
2				
3	1			
4	1	0	1	1.0
5	2	1	2	.5
6	3	1	1.5	.6666667
7	5	2	1.666667	.6
8	8	3	1.6	.625
9	13	5	1.625	.6153846
10	21	8	1.615385	.6190476
11	34	13	1.619048	.6176471
12	55	21	1.617647	.6181818
13	89	34	1.618182	.6179775
14	144	55	1.617978	.6180556
15	233	89	1.618056	.6180258
16	377	144	1.618026	.6180371

to share with their peers and teachers. They are constructing mathematical understandings for themselves.

SUGGESTED READINGS

Hansen and Sweng's (1984) NCTM yearbook includes several chapters that discuss the use of computers in teaching place-value and number ideas.

Thompson and Van de Walle (1985) provide a useful series of correlated noncomputer and Logo lessons on patterns.

NOTE: The rule for the sequences on p. 161 is: The third number is the average of the first two.

TABLE 6-1 Software: Logical Foundations and Number

Title	Producer	Notes
Number: Multiple Areas		
Basic Math Skills Instructional Series	Control Data	Counting, number concepts. 3–8.
Computer Drill and Practice: Mathematics	SRA	Number readiness, counting, place value, ordering. 1–6.
Fundamentals of Mathematics	Sterling Swift	Reading and writing numbers, sequences, patterns, skip counting. 1–6.
IBM Elementary Mathematics Series	IBM/WICAT	Comprehensive program. Includes the Math Concepts and Math Practice Series. K–8.

Title	Producer	Notes
Kinder Concepts	Midwest	Counting, relationships sequences. P–6.
Knowing Numbers	Learning Well	Counting, relationships. P–1.
Math Concepts I and II	Hartley	Before/after, odd/even, counting by 5's, 10's, etc., less than/greater than, regrouping. 1–5.
Math Rabbit	TLC	Drill (plus) in counting, adding, subtracting, recognition of number relationships, and patterns. Some useful CMI. Recommended. P–2.
Mathematics Activity Courseware (MAC)	Houghton Mifflin	Whole numbers, number theory. 2–8.
Mathematics Assessment/ Prescriptive Edu-Disks	Reader's Digest	Classifying, counting, reading and writing numerals, ordering and relationships, place value. 1–7.
Mathematics Series	Centurion	Counting, number concepts, place value, comparing numbers and arithmetic operations. K–6.
Mathematics Today Practice Diskettes	Harcourt Brace	Counting, number recognition, place value, number theory. A series of 16 practice diskettes presenting drill correlated with the publisher's text series. Embedded in gamelike activites; provide "clues" when students make errors. K–8.
Mathematics Unlimited: Problem Solving	Holt	Problem-solving series with several challenges and minisimulations. For example, first graders help stick patterns into a sticker album; second graders help a space traveler by solving problems in numerical reasoning (e.g., by choosing a door—from those labeled 60, 12, 72, and 15—whose number is odd AND less than 50); more complicated number patterns are presented to older students. 1–8.
Micro-Ed CMA Series	Micro-Ed	Counting, relationships, sequences, place value, K–6.
Number Munchers	MECC	Drill in a game format for five areas: multiples, factors, primes, equality, and inequality. 4 + .
Numbers	JMH	Counting, number sequences, place value.
Numbers: Drills and Games	Sunburst	Place value, sequences, counting. K–3.

(continued)

TABLE 6–1   (Continued)

Title	Producer	Notes
Preschool Disk	Nordic	Counting with voice feedback, connect the dots in decimal, binary, octal, or hexadecimal bases. P–K.
ReadiMath	Davell	Matching, counting, names of numbers, place value, greater/less than. P–2.

Classification, Seriation, Relationships, and Patterning

Simple Discrimination and Classification

Children's Carousel	Dynacomp	P–1.
Colors and Shapes	Hartley	P–4.
Early Games	Springboard	P–1.
Early Childhood Learning Program	Ed. Act.	P–2.
Ernie's Magic Shapes	CTW	P–1.
Flying Carpet	Learn. Tech.	K–2.
Happy Birthday, Pockets!	World Book	Likenesses and differences, matching shapes and numerals. P–K.
Identity 500	Orange Cherry	Identities and number relationships in a race-car game format. 2–6.
KidsTime	Great Wave	One of five activites, "Match-It," allows a choice of difficulty levels, from matching simple pictures, to categorizing, to matrix puzzles. P–2.
KinderComp	Spinnaker	P–K.
Learning With Leeper	Sierra	P–K.
Odd and Even	Bergwall	Students determine whether a numeral is even or odd. 2–4.
Ordinal Numbers	Bergwall	Students name ordinal position of an object, tell what ordinal number comes next. 2–4.
Pockets and Her New Sneakers	World Book	Sorting and classifying. P–K.
Pockets Goes on a Picnic	World Book	Sort objects into categories. P–K.
Preschool IQ Builder	PDI	P–1.
Press	Koeff	P–3.
Shape and Color Rodeo	DLM	P–2.
Shapes and Patterns	Learning Well	Visual discrimination, embedded shapes, and complete-the-pattern; game-change options. P–1.
Shape Starship	Gamco	Matching and sequencing shapes. Some CMI. P–2.
ShapeWorks	Nordic	Matching and discriminating among shapes, patterns, and sizes. Choice

Title	Producer	Notes
		of lesson, shapes, patterns, length of lesson, and objective (learn about: shapes, patterns, size, or a combination of these). P–1.
Size and Logic	Hartley	P–K.
Stickybear Shapes	Xerox	P–1.

More Advanced Classification

Title	Producer	Notes
Category and Classification	Hartley	P–1.
Chaos	Milliken	Capture alien satellites that match the shape and color of a model. K–6.
Code Quest	Sunburst	Find the mystery object given clues embedded in a series of codes. 4–adult.
Discrimination, Attributes, and Rules	Sunburst	A range of programs in discrimination, identifying attributes, inducing rules. See the text. K–6.
Gertrude's Secrets	TLC	Classification, hypothesis formation, and testing. See the text. P–5.
Gertrude's Puzzles	TLC	More challenging version of above. 3–8.
Moptown	Apple	Classifying and hypothesis testing. See the text. K–8.

Seriation and Relationships

Title	Producer	Notes
Bumble Games	TLC	Guess a number in a range. P–5.
Comparing Whole Numbers	Creative Equip.	Equal, greater, and less with numbers to 99, 999, and 9999. K–12.
Early Childhood Learning Program	Ed. Act.	Seriation. P–1.
Elementary Vol. 1—Math.	MECC	Guess a number in a range. 3–5.
Equations and Inequalities	Micrograms	Insert $<$, $>$, or $=$. 4–5.
Fish-Metric	Commodore	Equal, greater, less. 2–6.
Guess the Number	EduSoft	Guess a number in a range. P–2.
Introduction to Counting	EduWare	Ordering by length. P–2.
Less Than, Greater Than	Micrograms	Introduction and practice with $<$ and $>$ symbols. 2–3.
Math Action Game Series	Mindscape	Ordering numbers. K–3.
Math Logic I	Orbyte	Comparing number values. 3–5.
123 Math	Trojan	Relationships between numbers. 1–3.
Number Guess	NTS	Simple number-guessing game (1–100). K–2.

(*continued*)

TABLE 6-1 (Continued)

Title	Producer	Notes
Storybook Friends: Number Relationships	Edupro	Greater, less, equal. K–3.
Patterning		
Arrow Graphics	Milliken	Students are presented with a figure created by a three-move command repeated four times. A move is a direction and a specific number of spaces; R3 is right three spaces. They must type in the three moves the computer used to draw the figure. Three perfect patterns in a row gives children the opportunity to specify the commands themselves and see the computer create their pattern. 2–4.
Guess My Rule	HRM	Finding patterns and expressing them as a rule. 6–10.
KidsTime	Great Wave	Five activites. One, "Dot-to-Dot," involved ordering numerals. Teachers can alter existing puzzles or create their own. P–2.
The King's Rule	Sunburst	Numerical patterns and relationships. 4–adult.
Mickey in the Great Outdoors	Disney	Fill in missing number in sequence. 2–6.
Patterns and Sequences	Hartley	P–K.
Peter's Growing Patterns	Strawberry	Pattern recognition and generation. K–3.
Playing to Learn: Math/Logic Games	HRM	In one of four games, students figure out the operation underlying a series of numbers. 4–12.
Pockets Leads the Parade	World Book	Pattern recognition, copying patterns. P–K.
The Pond	Sunburst	Spatial/numerical patterns. 2–adult.
The Royal Rules	Sunburst	Numerical patterns and relationships; a sequel to *The King's Rule*. Students can create their own rules. 6–adult.
Size and Logic	Hartley	Discrimination of size, linear patterning of pictures. P–1.
Surrounding Patterns	Strawberry	Copying and creating designs. P–6.
What's Next	Strawberry	Patterning with shapes. K–7.
Whole Numbers and Counting		
Aliencounter	Milliken	K–1.
All About Zero	ICEC	Value of zero in counting and concept of "nothing."

Title	Producer	Notes
Arithmagic: Counting	Banbury	P–K.
ArithMatic: Counting	Compu-Teach	Two activities: choose any number and see that many objects, or be shown objects and count them. P–1.
Beginning Math Concepts	Orange Cherry	Counting, number values, comparing numbers. P–3.
Beginning Mathematics Concepts	Brittanica	Counting, greater and less than, and the number line. Some CMI. K–3.
Children's Carousel	Dynacomp	P–1.
Conservation and Counting	Hartley	P–K.
Count and Add	EduSoft	Counting and adding. If students miscount, the program helps. Recommended by EPIE. K–3.
Counting	MECC	K–2.
Counting Fun	Edutek	Drill on counting and numeral recognition. K–1. Other programs by the same publisher are available.
Counting Parade	Spinnaker	Pick up the correct number of animals to match the given number of plants (one-to-one correspondence), can choose single animals or groups. P–1.
Counting Plus	Professor	P–3.
Critter Count	EMC	Simple practice and quizzes. P–3.
Early Learning	Learning Tech.	Three programs, "The Flying Carpet," "Let's Go Fishing," and "Clowning Around," that integrate counting with other skills. P–3.
Early Numbers	Orbyte	Counting. 1–3.
Educational Package III	Micro Learn.	Counting, reading numbers, number comparisons. 3–6.
Elementary Math Mixer	PLATO/WICAT	Counting and comparing. 4–9.
Ernie's Quiz	CTW	P–2.
Essential Mathematics	BertaMax	1–6.
The Grabit Factory	DCH	K–3.
Hobo's Luck	Strawberry	Counting. P+.
Introduction to Counting	EduWare	P–2.
Learning About Numbers	C & C	Several activites. Practice in counting, telling time, and arithmetic facts. Some CMI. Special features for prereaders. P–5.
Learning to Count	ICEC	Number recognition, one-to-one correspondence, and counting. P–1.
Learning with Leeper	Sierra	P–1.

(continued)

TABLE 6-1   (Continued)

Title	Producer	Notes
Math Disk #1	Data Command	Counting. K–3.
Math Action Game Series	Mindscape	K–8.
Math Rabbit	TLC	Several games with multiple levels of difficulty; counting, number/numeral correspondence, greater/less than, equivalence. Well designed. K–2.
Math Whiz Quiz	Dynacomp	
Mathematics A, B, and C	SRA	1–6.
Mathematics—Grade 1	Intellectual	Meaning of numbers; counting money, days of the week, etc. 1.
Mathfinder	Hold	Counting and numeration are part of a comprehensive package. K–6.
Number-Beci	Beci	P–K.
Number Farm	DLM	P–2.
Number Match and Number Match-It	Berta-Max	Match domino pattern with numeral. K–3.
Number/Numeral	Merry Bee	P–1.
Number Sea Hunt	Gamco	Counting, ordering numbers, using illustrations. Some CMI. K–1.
Number Sequencing	Sunburst	K–3.
Number Train	Micrograms	Counting by 1s, 2s, 3s, 5s, and 10s with numbers from 0 to 20 or 0 to 99. 1–2.
Numbers	Dorsett	Tutorials on whole-number concepts, other number systems' arithmetic. 1–6.
Numbers	Lawrence Hall	Counting. P–1.
Numbers 0–9 (also: Numbers 10–100)	Control Data	Tutorials and practice on whole numbers.
Numeration	Scott Foresman	Identification and ordering; place value; comparing; etc., with multidigit numerals. K–3.
Pockets Goes to the Carnival	World Book	Counting, one-to-one correspondence. P–K.
Prereading/Counting	MECC	P–K.
Skip Counting	B5	By 1–10, 15, 20, 25, 50, 100, 1000. 1–5.
Skip Counting	Bergwall	Students determine rule and next number in pattern of numerals. 2–4.
Stickybear Numbers	Optimum	Practice with numbers and counting with large animated cartoon pictures. Recommended by EPIE. P–1.
The Sweet Shoppe	DCH	K–3.
Telemath	Psychotechnics	Counting, naming numbers. K–6.

Title	Producer	Notes
Tinka's Maze	Mindscape	K–3.
Webster's Numbers	EduWare	Counting and pattern recognition. P–3.
Place Value		
Bannercatch	Scholastic	Binary number system embedded in a game. 4–8.
Block It	Elec. Course	Place value with graphic representations of counting blocks.
Building Tens Strategy	Hartley	See text. K–3.
Conceptual 1: Math and the Game of Arragon	Learning Res.	Graphics demonstration of place value, and game involving place-value skills. 1–3 (introduction); 4–6 review.
Elementary Math Package I	Micro Learning-ware	Place, value, number strings, drill.
Expanded Notation	Hartley	Can be adapted to teachers' and students' needs. 2–5.
Face Flash	Milliken	Grouping by tens, subitizing. K–4.
Galaxy II Math Facts	Random House	2–6.
Hodge Podge	Dynacomp	P–2.
IBM Elementary Mathematics Series	IBM/WICAT	In the "math concepts" strand. See the text.
Learning Place Value	CCM	CMI based—Diagnostic tests develop an individualized program of conceptual and drill remediation.
Math Ideas with Base Ten Blocks	Cuisenaire	Counting and place-value notions are developed with pictorial representations of base 10 blocks. 2–7.
Math 1	Psych. Corp.	Testing program. 3–8.
Math Shop	Scholastic	Students help in various stores in a mall by solving problems, each using a specific curriculum concept. For example, in the dairy, students choose the most efficient way to pack a given number of eggs, thereby learning about other number bases. 6–9.
Mighty Math	World Book	Arranging numbers according to place value. 1–5.
Number Factory	Compu-Teach	Place value, renaming in several bases.
Number Factory	HRM	Filling factory "bins" of different bases. 2–6.
Number Systems	MECC	6–9.
Number Words	Hartley	K–5.
Numeration	Scott Foresman	K–7.

(*continued*)

TABLE 6-1   **(Continued)**

Title	Producer	Notes
Place Value 1s 10s 100s	EME	Two basic activities, one an introduction to place value with pictorial Dienes blocks, the other a game in which children trade with a bank.
Place Value and Expanded Notation	Bergwall	Students identify places in 4-digit number and a number represented on an abacus. 2–4.
Place Value Place	Interlearn	Groupings of apples illustrate place-value concepts; a game is also included (make the largest value). 1–6.
Places, Everyone!	NTS	Identifying place value and translating words to digits. 2–5.
Potato Factory	Micro. Wrkshp.	Base numbers. 1–8.

Number Theory

Title	Producer	Notes
Elementary Math Booster	Trillium	Number theory for gifted children. 4–8.
Elementary Vol. 1—Mathematics	MECC	Includes "Taxman," a game involving factoring and recognizing prime numbers.
The Euclid Game	QED	Tutorial and game based on Euclid's method for determining the GCD. Recommended. 4–8.
Even Steven	Micrograms	Help Steven land on even numbers. 1–2.
Fabulous LCM Machine	Micro-Ed	Finding the LCM of three numbers. 5–8.
Factor Blast	Hayden	Factoring whole numbers and primes. 4–8.
Factoring Game—Taxman	Intellectual	Game of identifying factors. 4–8.
Factoring Whole Numbers	QED	Introduction, practice, and game with each of 12 activities covering factoring (primes and composites, LCM, square roots, Euclid's algorithm). E.g., introduces factoring by having students build rectangles with (real) tiles as concepts are simultaneously presented on the screen. Students are to find factor pairs by determining the lengths and widths of rectangles of a given area. Generally useful pattern-searching games. Recommended. 5–8.
Factors and Multiples	Micrograms	Game involving factors and multiples. 5+.
Factors and Multiples	Orbyte	Finding factors and multiples. 4–10.

Title	Producer	Notes
Factoring Whole Numbers	QED	Factoring. 12 diverse programs, including tutorials, drills, exploration, and enrichment. 5+.
IBM Elementary Mathematics Series	IBM/WICAT	Integers. Students begin by pressing left or right arrow keys to "build a bar" to a number on a number line, such as 7 or −4.
Great Times Hotel	Micro-Ed	Factors, common multiples. 2–4. Other programs on related topics include "Guzinta Hotel," "Prime Number," and "Prime Fishing."
The King's Rule	Sunburst	Determine rules. 4–adult.
Magic Math Plus	Recreat.	Number games, tricks, recreations, etc., many with explanations. 6–adult.
Math Skills: Pirate	Diversified	Factors, perfect square, odd/even. Search game requiring student to use deductive logic and math skills to find hidden treasure. 4–8.
Mathdisk One	Univ. Evan.	Prime factorization, number bases, randomness.
Number Munchers	MECC	Provides drill in several related skill areas (identifying multiples, factors, primes, equalities, and inequalities). Students direct creatures called Number Munchers to "eat" all those targets (numbers or arithmetic expressions) that match a criterion such as "multiples of 9," "prime numbers," or "greater than 1." 3+.
Number Systems	MECC	The binary, hexadecimal, and octal systems, and how computers process numbers. 6–9.
Number Theory	JMH	Primes, factors, divisibility, LCM, GCD, square roots. 6–9.
Oil Well	Micro-Ed	Primes. 4–8.
Playing to Learn: Math/Logic Games	HRM	In one game, "Dr. Factor," students earn points by selecting numbers from a number board. All the factors of that number go to their opponent. In "Even Wins," students try to end up with an even number of chips. They remove 1–4 from a pile. 4–12.
Primes and Composite Numbers	Orbyte	Primes and composites in tug-of-war format. 4–10.
Prime Numbers	Athena	Determining whether a number is prime. 3–7.

7

COMPUTATION

THE ROLE OF COMPUTERS IN COMPUTATION

"Computers should be providing individualized, motivational practice in arithmetic algorithms that includes immediate feedback so that students learn these essential skills more efficiently."

"No—that's taking a step backward. Students will no longer need to do tedious computations—they should use the computer to do long division."

What position do you take? Should computers be used to teach the four arithmetic operations—addition, subtraction, multiplication, and division? Or should they be used as calculators to perform these operations for students? As is so often the case, the best answer lies partially between and partially beyond these two positions. *Between,* in that computers can help students become proficient with basic arithmetic processes; however, the presence of computing devices obviates the need to attain a high level of speed with more complex forms (e.g., 95093.658 ÷ 495.6). *Beyond,* in that the computer should be used—even in the realm of computation, much less in mathematics as a whole—for broader and deeper purposes than "computing sums." Let us examine these issues more closely.

We have seen that achieving automaticity in certain basic skills frees processing capacity for higher-level thought. Computers can be used to provide effective and efficient drill with the "facts." Following the principles established in Chapter 1, though, students should receive as much of this experience as possible within the context of meaningful high-level activities.

However, students will *not* need to achieve a level of quick, rote performance in completing complex procedures such as long division. (When was the last time you chose to do a four- or five-digit long-division exercise with the typical school paper-and-pencil algorithm? When was the last time most students saw their parents doing so? But *they* have to in school. Is it any wonder they ask why?) It could even be argued that complex algorithms should *not* be extensively practiced. For example, Moise contends that "algorithmic drill stands alone in the elementary curriculum: it is the only subject whose study ordinarily damages the mentality of the child" (Moise, p. 38, in Hansen & Zweng, 1984). This rather radical proposal will be discussed more fully in a later section on the use of calculators. However, here we may at least agree that (a) long, complex algorithms need not be given as much emphasis in the elementary mathematics curriculum, and (b) mastery of these algorithms does *not* necessarily imply mastery of concepts or applications. This brings us to the final point.

Going *beyond* the mere teaching of basic facts or algorithms, computers should be used to help students develop conceptualizations of computations, utilize appropriate strategies and search for patterns, and apply computational skills. We will examine each of these applications of computers, as well as the application of developing automatic procedural skill when this is relevant.

DEVELOPING COMPUTATIONAL CONCEPTS

Several computer programs for early elementary students attempt to develop concepts of addition and subtraction through a presentation such as the following:

$$\begin{matrix} \bullet \\ \bullet \ - \ \bullet \ = \\ \bullet \end{matrix}$$

Because this graphic is supposed to model "3 − 1 = ___," the student is to type "2." However, children may answer "4," "3" (4 in all, take 1 away), "1," and even "7" ("four balls and three sticks," one youngster explained)! The pictorial model is not appropriate. Neither is the simultaneous introduction of the subtraction situation and the abstract symbols (minus and equal signs).

Better models do not begin with symbols. Instead, they provide valid pictorial representations within a context that motivates students, requires that they think about their responses, and provides realistic and meaningful feedback. For example, one early addition program in ESC Mathematics sequence asks students to help "Gus Plus" save another animated character who is precariously hanging by one hand. Gus and the student build a scaffold together out of boards of length 1 through 10 (these vertical support boards are demarcated in units and are labeled with numerals). Gus might place a board of length 3 on top of a board of length 4 on his side of the scaffold. The student must place a 7-board on her side. If correct, a horizontal platform is placed on top, building up the scaffold. If the student were to select a 6-board instead, Gus would shake his head, move his boards over next to the student's to show that a level platform could not be placed, and ask the student to try again. Later in the program, Gus may choose an 8-

board and the student must choose any two boards that will be of an equivalent length (e.g., 3 and 5).

Note that the representation is concrete and the premature introduction of abstract signs is avoided. Students are motivated to help Gus. Also, they see a *real reason* to add and the feedback they get is intrinsic to the task ... it makes sense. The reward they get—successfully building the tower and ultimately saving Gus's friend—is also intrinsic and satisfying. Finally, the activity involves *problem solving* and significant mathematical ideas; for example, when finding two boards that match Gus's 8-board, students are also dealing with subtraction and the relationship between addition and subtraction. As another example, the IBM/WICAT series *Elementary Mathematics Series* includes addition and subtraction activities that demonstrate how to build up number sentences from pictorially represented stories and then use such sentences to solve problems (see Fig. 7-1).

After a basic notion has been established, symbolic presentations should be mapped onto (related to) the pictorial. For example, in *Stickybear Math,* students might see "9 − 5 = " and, above the "9," nine balls. If they press "5," five balls disappear one at a time (with sound effects to enhance the process) and the remaining four balls move over the numeral "4" in the completed sentence, "9 − 5 = 4."

Unfortunately, on this program, if the student types an incorrect answer, the correct numeral is shown but the balls do not demonstrate the subtraction ... and here is the student that *needs* that assistance! Another

A

B

C

FIGURE 7-1
In this tutorial example, students are first presented with the problem, then shown a subtraction sentence (a). Five balloons are popped, and the students then count the remaining balloons. Each time they press a key, an additional balloon changes color, and the numeral at the right is incremented (b). Finally, the answer, 2, slides over to complete the subtraction sentence (c). Students then perform these steps by themselves, guided by the program (*Elementary Mathematics Series,* IBM/WICAT Systems, Inc.)

program provides pictorial assistance to this student. In "The Bakery" (in *Piece of Cake*) students read about bakers who sell some cakes: "Of their 7 cakes, they sold 4. How many were left?" A picture of 7 cakes is shown. The student has the opportunity to answer using his own methods. If he makes a mistake, however, the program shows the number sentence, "7 − 4 = ?" If the student still needs help, the computer counts out 4 of the 7 cakes. If he still answers incorrectly, 4 cakes move away from the pile. If the student's answer is not correct, the 4 cakes move off the screen, and the computer re-counts the remaining 3 cakes. In this way, progressively more help is pro-vided to the student, as needed, and a concrete model of subtraction is provided.

The *Piece of Cake* program also provides models for multiplication and division. Bakers need to get just the right number of pieces from each of their cakes in "Dividacake." The program provides these hints, as needed: (a) the related multiplication number sentence, say "2 × 5," is displayed; (b) a cake is cut up to show a 2 × 5 array; (c) the same cake is cut up into more separated pieces, with the rows and columns labeled with numerals; and (d) the pieces are counted one by one as a multiplication fact is progres-sively generated (e.g., 2 × 1, 2 × 2, 2 × 3, ...). Finally, the multiplier (5) is moved from its place in the multiplication fact into its place in the corresponding division fact.

Other programs emphasize each step in the algorithm itself, usually with closely supervised digit-by-digit evaluation and feedback (see Fig. 7–2). Some comprehensive programs of this type, which include demonstra-tions, tutorials, practice, and CMI components, include *Elementary Mathemat-ics Classroom Learning System: Whole Numbers; Mathematics Strands, Grades 1–6; Understanding Math Series* (see Tables 2–2 and 7–1). Not all programs of this type, however, encourage relational understanding (i.e., meaningful learn-ing; Chapter 1). If only the steps for manipulating numbers are presented, the program might be encouraging merely instrumental, or rote, learning of a procedure. What might prevent students who have learned subtraction instrumentally from renaming as follows?

$$\overset{5\quad 1}{\cancel{6}00 4}$$
$$-\ 427$$

Nothing; without a meaningful interpretation of place value and subtrac-tion, this process appears reasonable. Students believe they have "followed the rules." But students who *relate* renaming to trading place-value represen-tations such as Dienes blocks or bundles or sticks (see Chapter 6) will under-stand that trading 1 thousand for 10 ones doesn't make sense. For them, renaming/trading has meaning. In Davis's terms, the former students' sub-traction frame is based only on rules for manipulating symbols. The latter students' subtraction frame contains procedures as well; however, they are also *attached* to a meaningful representation involving *actions on things*. (These students also are *monitoring* their subtraction.)

As an illustration, the *Understanding Math Series* has several worthwhile

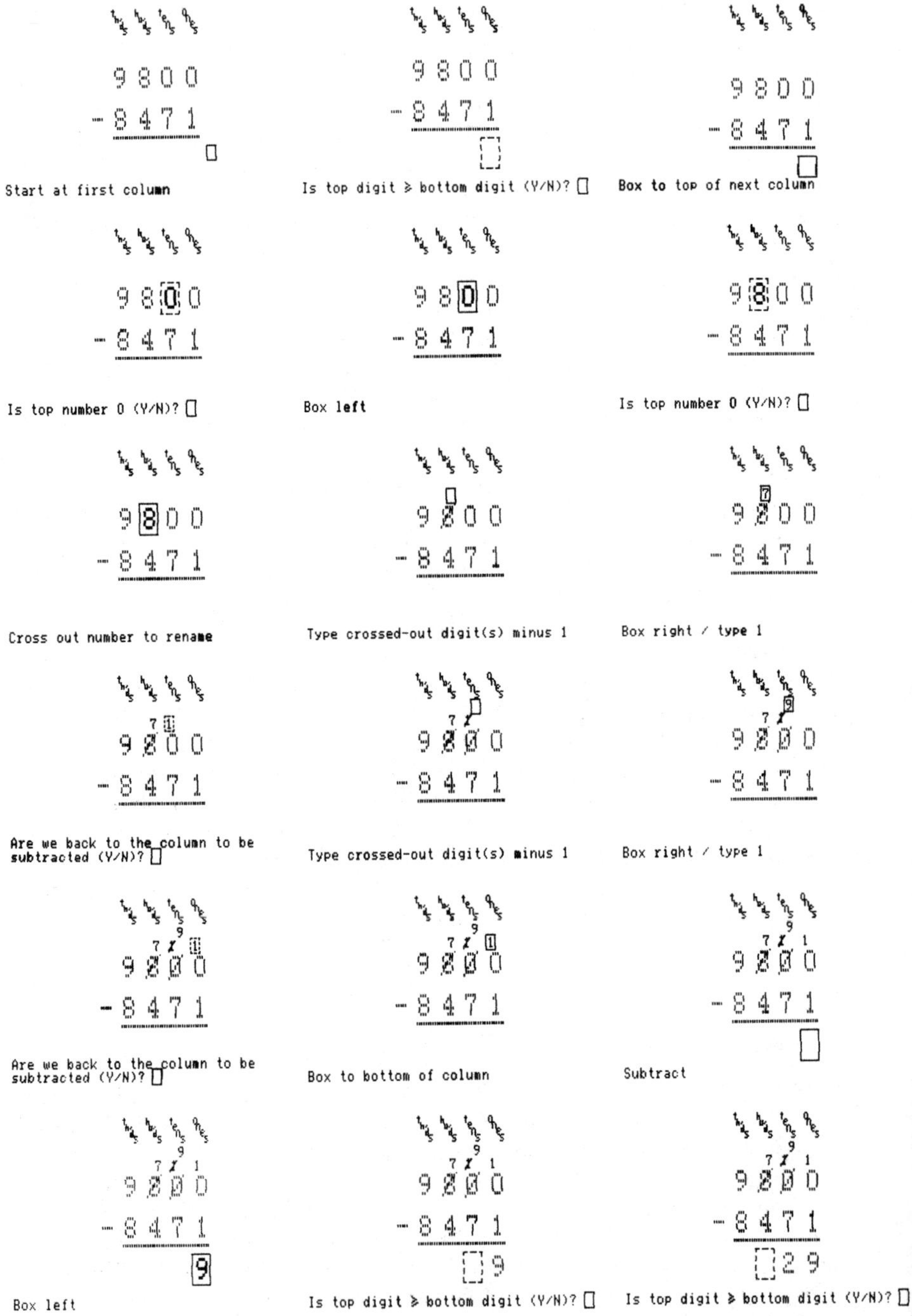

FIGURE 7-2 A sequence from *Microtutor II: Arithmetic Skills.* (Scandura Training Systems)

For details and theoretical rationale, see Scandura, J. M. et al. (1986), ''Intelligent Rule Tutor CBI System for Diagnostic Testing and Instruction, *Journal of Structural Learning, 9,* 15–61.

characteristics. A conceptual model—simplified two-dimensional multibase blocks—underlies the program. Students learn an algorithm first with the blocks, then with blocks and numerals, and finally with numerals only. Assistance is offered. For example, if a student combines 5 tens and 7 tens and types the incorrect sum twice, the program highlights each block in turn to help the student count the 12 tens. If errors are made in trading, the program might count each of the 12 tens again, but highlight 10 of the tens in a different color, thus making the 10 tens → 1 hundred trade perceptually salient. When the trade is made, these 10 tens move to become 1 hundred in the appropriate column.

DEVELOPING STRATEGIES AND SEARCHING FOR PATTERNS

Many students find the "building tens strategy" to be helpful in learning simple addition and subtraction. One activity in a program by that name asks students to type the number of dots that—when taken from the bottom pattern—will make a ten in the top pattern (e.g., they would type "2" for the display in Fig. 7–3a). The dots move; then students are prompted to type the sum (12; see Fig. 7–3b). Subtraction Bridges (in *MAC*) teaches students to "bridge with ten" to solve 13 − 9 by subtracting 13 − 10, then 10 − 9. The ESC sequence in addition teaches such strategies as counting on, building tens, and doubles/doubles plus one.

   An addition activity in *Math Rabbit* asks students to create number patterns in a train. If the starting number of the train (e.g., 20) is a multiple of the number by which the sequence increases or decreases (e.g., 5), students are building readiness for multiplication facts (e.g., students select 25, 30, 35, . . .). If the starting number is *not* a multiple (e.g., 8), a pattern in the units place still emerges (e.g., in the numbers 8, 13, 18, 23, . . .).

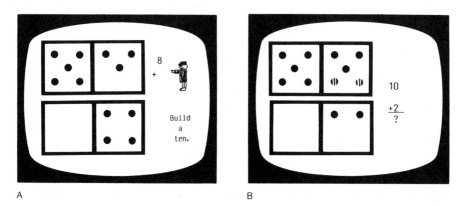

A   B

FIGURE 7–3 From *Building Tens Strategy.* (Reprinted with permission of Hartley Courseware, Inc.)

Patterns in Computation:
A Computer Programming Example

Simple programming projects can lead to a host of explorations. Recall Bobby's FOR/NEXT program described in Chapter 4. The teacher wanted everyone to have a chance to participate in dramatizing the program, so she had the class experiment with changing lines in it. First they changed line 20 to read FOR N = 1 TO 7. Then they changed line 30 to print N + N + N; N + N + N + N; 2 * N. Each of these new programs were checked afterward on the computer. This way, students also learned to use the computer to check on their intuitive and creative ideas. They also explored the patterns that resulted. The teacher printed and posted them for discussion (columns have been labeled for the reader's convenience).

A	B	C	D	E
1 + 1 = 2	1 + 1 + 1 = 3	1 + 1 + 1 + 1 = 4	1 * 2 = 2	
2 + 2 = 4	2 + 2 + 2 = 6	2 + 2 + 2 + 2 = 8	2 * 2 = 4	
3 + 3 = 6	3 + 3 + 3 = 9	3 + 3 + 3 + 3 = 12	3 * 2 = 6	
4 + 4 = 8	4 + 4 + 4 = 12	4 + 4 + 4 + 4 = 16	4 * 2 = 8	
5 + 5 = 10	5 + 5 + 5 = 15	5 + 5 + 5 + 5 = 20	5 * 2 = 10	
6 + 6 = 12	6 + 6 + 6 = 18	6 + 6 + 6 + 6 = 24	6 * 2 = 12	
7 + 7 = 14	7 + 7 + 7 = 21	7 + 7 + 7 + 7 = 28	7 * 2 = 14	

She asked her students to look for patterns. Identify some yourself before reading on. The following is an abbreviated version of some students' observations.

The sums in the first group (column B) are like counting by two's; column C is counting by three's; D is counting by four's. Guided by the teacher's questions, the students figured out that each addend is being increased by one each time; therefore, with two addends, the sums increased by two's, with three addends, the sums increased by three's, and so on. The teacher asked them what the sums for N + N + N + N + N would be. The students guessed 5, 10, 15, . . . and programmed the computer to check their prediction.

They noticed that the sequences of sums of the number sentences (i.e., columns B, C, and D in one row) were replicated within certain columns. That is, the sequence of sums in the first row—2, 3, 4—is also seen in the first column (A), starting with 2. The sequence of sums in the second row—4, 6, 8—is also seen in column B, starting with 4—4, 6, 8. The sequence of sums in the third row—6, 9, 12—is also seen in column C. And the sequence 8, 12, 16 is replicated in column D. The pattern held for the new "5's" column also. Another student noted the equivalence of columns B and E ("Of course. Two one's is the same as one plus one").

Another day, they rewrote the program to print out 10 sums in each series going up to N + N + N . . . N with 10 N's. This time they recorded only the sums.

N	Sums								
	A	B	C	D	E	F	G	H	I
(1)	2	3	4	5	6	7	8	9	10
(2)	4	6	8	10	12	14	16	18	20
(3)	6	9	12	15	18	21	24	27	30
(4)	8	12	16	20	24	28	32	36	40
(5)	10	15	20	25	30	35	40	45	50
(6)	12	18	24	30	36	42	48	54	60
(7)	14	21	28	35	42	49	56	63	70
(8)	16	24	32	40	48	56	64	72	80
(9)	18	27	36	45	54	63	72	81	90
(10)	20	30	40	50	60	70	80	90	100

Students discovered several additional patterns. The 5, 0, 5, 0, . . . pattern in column D was noticed. The digits in column A made a repeating pattern—2, 4, 6, 8, 0, 2, 4, 6, 8, 0, ... So did the digits in column C—4, 8, 2, 6, 0, 4, 8, 2, 6, 0, ... Interestingly, similar patterns were found in E (6, 2, 8, 4, 0, . . .) and G (8, 6, 4, 2, 0). One student remarked: "The C pattern is just every other number in the A pattern." Another found that "the E pattern is just the C pattern going the other way, and the G patterns is just the A pattern going the other way." The teacher challenged them to check if this was always true. They ran the computer programs again up to an N of 100 and found that the patterns held.

One student was disappointed that columns B and F have no patterns. A friend found that they did; you just had to run the series higher to see it.

One major observation was: "Hey, that's just a multiplication table!" The students discussed how that could happen, when they just added. One student explained it this way: "Multiplying is just like adding a number again and again a certain number of times." This led to additional discoveries.

The pattern in column H (the units digits) was identified as "counting backward." The ten's digits were counting forward. One bright student said, "That's because adding nine is almost adding ten, but it slips back one each time." The teacher led the students to see the connection between a number and the product of that number and nine. One girl described the rule: "The ten's digit is one less than the number. The one's digit is the number that you would add to the ten's digit to get nine." The students also found symmetry in the table; for example, the number at F-3 was equal to the number at B-7, and the number at E-5 was equal to the number at D-6.

Another day the students explored N * N (multiplication or squaring a number), and x / x (division). The fact that results for the latter were all the same perturbed some students until they figured out that every number "goes into" itself just one time.

It should be pointed out that these lessons were conducted with only one computer for the entire class (although individuals kept modifying the programs for weeks to come), and without the computer many of the explorations, especially those involving higher numbers, would probably not have been made. The computer also allowed the students to generate the series themselves and therefore understand how the series were generated. Several students were motivated to learn more about mathematics and more abut computer programming through writing similar programs on their own. Recall that an electronic spreadsheet could also be used to generate these patterns.

Spreadsheet patterns. A primary-grade teacher developed an addition table template (similar explorations could be conducted in later grades using a multiplication table template). The first number in the first row and the first column was zero. Then each following number in the top row and in the leftmost column was defined simply as one more than the previous number. On the rest of the table, the intersection of each number was their sum. This allowed students to see how an addition table was generated. They also searched for patterns in the table; for example, each number appears only once in the one's place in any row or column; reading down or to the right is like counting; any number on the upper left half can be matched with one on the lower right (symmetry and the commutative property—3 + 4 = 4 + 3); numbers on diagonal lines heading toward the upper right are the same; and numbers on diagonal lines heading toward the lower right jump by 2's. Even more interesting were the explorations that came as a result of changing the zeros that were the first numbers. One student suggested changing them to 10s; another to − 10s; a third wished to see

	0	1	2	3	4	5	6	7	8	9	10	11	12	13	14
0	0	1	2	3	4	5	6	7	8	9	10	11	12	13	14
1	1	2	3	4	5	6	7	8	9	10	11	12	13	14	15
2	2	3	4	5	6	7	8	9	10	11	12	13	14	15	16
3	3	4	5	6	7	8	9	10	11	12	13	14	15	16	17
4	4	5	6	7	8	9	10	11	12	13	14	15	16	17	18
5	5	6	7	8	9	10	11	12	13	14	15	16	17	18	19
6	6	7	8	9	10	11	12	13	14	15	16	17	18	19	20
7	7	8	9	10	11	12	13	14	15	16	17	18	19	20	21
8	8	9	10	11	12	13	14	15	16	17	18	19	20	21	22
9	9	10	11	12	13	14	15	16	17	18	19	20	21	22	23
10	10	11	12	13	14	15	16	17	18	19	20	21	22	23	24
11	11	12	13	14	15	16	17	18	19	20	21	22	23	24	25

	-10	-9	-8	-7	-6	-5	-4	-3	-2	-1	0	1	2	3	4
-10	-20	-19	-18	-17	-16	-15	-14	-13	-12	-11	-10	-9	-8	-7	-6
-9	-19	-18	-17	-16	-15	-14	-13	-12	-11	-10	-9	-8	-7	-6	-5
-8	-18	-17	-16	-15	-14	-13	-12	-11	-10	-9	-8	-7	-6	-5	-4
-7	-17	-16	-15	-14	-13	-12	-11	-10	-9	-8	-7	-6	-5	-4	-3
-6	-16	-15	-14	-13	-12	-11	-10	-9	-8	-7	-6	-5	-4	-3	-2
-5	-15	-14	-13	-12	-11	-10	-9	-8	-7	-6	-5	-4	-3	-2	-1
-4	-14	-13	-12	-11	-10	-9	-8	-7	-6	-5	-4	-3	-2	-1	0
-3	-13	-12	-11	-10	-9	-8	-7	-6	-5	-4	-3	-2	-1	0	1
-2	-12	-11	-10	-9	-8	-7	-6	-5	-4	-3	-2	-1	0	1	2
-1	-11	-10	-9	-8	-7	-6	-5	-4	-3	-2	-1	0	1	2	3
0	-10	-9	-8	-7	-6	-5	-4	-3	-2	-1	0	1	2	3	4
1	-9	-8	-7	-6	-5	-4	-3	-2	-1	0	1	2	3	4	5
2	-8	-7	-6	-5	-4	-3	-2	-1	0	1	2	3	4	5	6
3	-7	-6	-5	-4	-3	-2	-1	0	1	2	3	4	5	6	7
4	-6	-5	-4	-3	-2	-1	0	1	2	3	4	5	6	7	8

	10	11	12	13	14	15	16	17	18	19	20	21	22	23	24
10	20	21	22	23	24	25	26	27	28	29	30	31	32	33	34
11	21	22	23	24	25	26	27	28	29	30	31	32	33	34	35
12	22	23	24	25	26	27	28	29	30	31	32	33	34	35	36
13	23	24	25	26	27	28	29	30	31	32	33	34	35	36	37
14	24	25	26	27	28	29	30	31	32	33	34	35	36	37	38
15	25	26	27	28	29	30	31	32	33	34	35	36	37	38	39
16	26	27	28	29	30	31	32	33	34	35	36	37	38	39	40
17	27	28	29	30	31	32	33	34	35	36	37	38	39	40	41
18	28	29	30	31	32	33	34	35	36	37	38	39	40	41	42
19	29	30	31	32	33	34	35	36	37	38	39	40	41	42	43
20	30	31	32	33	34	35	36	37	38	39	40	41	42	43	44
21	31	32	33	34	35	36	37	38	39	40	41	42	43	44	45
22	32	33	34	35	36	37	38	39	40	41	42	43	44	45	46
23	33	34	35	36	37	38	39	40	41	42	43	44	45	46	47
24	34	35	36	37	38	39	40	41	42	43	44	45	46	47	48

	-10	-9	-8	-7	-6	-5	-4	-3	-2	-1	0	1	2	3	4
10	0	1	2	3	4	5	6	7	8	9	10	11	12	13	14
11	1	2	3	4	5	6	7	8	9	10	11	12	13	14	15
12	2	3	4	5	6	7	8	9	10	11	12	13	14	15	16
13	3	4	5	6	7	8	9	10	11	12	13	14	15	16	17
14	4	5	6	7	8	9	10	11	12	13	14	15	16	17	18
15	5	6	7	8	9	10	11	12	13	14	15	16	17	18	19
16	6	7	8	9	10	11	12	13	14	15	16	17	18	19	20
17	7	8	9	10	11	12	13	14	15	16	17	18	19	20	21
18	8	9	10	11	12	13	14	15	16	17	18	19	20	21	22
19	9	10	11	12	13	14	15	16	17	18	19	20	21	22	23
20	10	11	12	13	14	15	16	17	18	19	20	21	22	23	24
21	11	12	13	14	15	16	17	18	19	20	21	22	23	24	25
22	12	13	14	15	16	17	18	19	20	21	22	23	24	25	26
23	13	14	15	16	17	18	19	20	21	22	23	24	25	26	27
24	14	15	16	17	18	19	20	21	22	23	24	25	26	27	28

FIGURE 7-4 Altering the addition spreadsheet by changing the initial numbers.

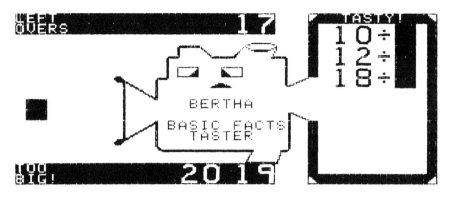

FIGURE 7-5 *Bertha Eats Basic Facts.* What is the divisor? (Copyright © 1984 by Houghton Mifflin Company. All rights reserved.)

what would happen if one was 10 and the other was 0. The results of these explorations, reproduced in Fig. 7–4, allowed students to find and discuss other patterns and discover additional mathematical rules and insights. What patterns can you find? Most of the spreadsheet activities discussed in Chapter 3 also encourage the intelligent application of arithmetic computations.

In "Bertha Eats Basic Facts" (in *MAC*), Bertha gets a taste for numbers that can be evenly divided by 2, 3, 4, or 5. Students feed her numbers. If the number is not evenly divisible by Bertha's divisor, she pops it out as "left over" (i.e., it leaves a remainder). If the number is greater than 9 times her divisor, she pops it out as "too big." If the number is divisible by her divisor, it finds its way into Bertha's stomach, and the student has the opportunity to guess the divisor. For example, one student guessed 17, 10, 20, 12, 19, and 18, yielding the display in Fig. 7–5. What would you guess Bertha's divisor is?

Functions. One teacher used a "carton computer" (see Clements, 1985a) to illustrate the important mathematical concept of function. In fact, this simple model—input, process, output—is virtually the definition of a function. If the carton computer is programmed to add, then students merely input two numbers. The person inside the computer outputs their sum. Students might then program a real computer to be a "function machine."

Logo

```
TO FUNCTION
  PRINT [TYPE IN A NUMBER.]
  PRINT (FIRST READLIST) + 3
  FUNCTION
END
```

For some versions of Terrapin (excluding the Macintosh version):

```
TO FUNCTION
 PRINT [TYPE IN A NUMBER.]
 PRINT (FIRST REQUEST)
 FUNCTION
END
```

BASIC

```
10 PRINT "TYPE IN A NUMBER."
20 INPUT N
30 PRINT N + 3
40 GOTO 10
```

The programs would run like this:

```
TYPE IN A NUMBER.
4
7
TYPE IN A NUMBER.
10
13
TYPE IN A NUMBER.
6
9. . . .
```

Students might run the program and let a friend play it without seeing the program itself. The friend tries to guess the "rule" or function.

APPLYING COMPUTATIONAL SKILLS

Computation should be both (mathematically) meaningful and (practically) significant. This necessitates using computations to accomplish other tasks.

Computation and Logo

Computing within Logo programming. Students programming in Logo use computation for a purpose (recall Fig. 4–7). Of course, using Logo does not ensure accuracy; for example, Linda needed to complete a frame for a house. She had typed FD 50. Noting that the line was too long, she said, "I forgot it was 40," corrected her mistake by typing BACK 9, and explained, "I needed 9 less" (Kull, 1986). However, accuracy will improve (especially as students discover that inaccurate computations often have significant negative ramifications for their procedures!), and students learn important ideas about the concepts, meaning, and usefulness of arithmetic computations.

Logo lessons emphasizing computation. It is, of course, useful to plan specific experiences with Logo that will enhance students' understanding of arithmetic operations. Some critics might say that this is an inefficient approach (compared to traditional CAI or mathematics textbook approaches). Therefore, let us discuss one example in detail, to examine the rationale for this approach to teaching and learning computational concepts.

A nongeometric topic that often presents considerable difficulty for students is the addition and subtraction of integers. In a typical textbook approach, students are provided specific rules for these operations immediately upon introduction of the topic, with a brief reference to a number-line model. For example, "To add two integers with different signs, consider the distance each integer is from zero. Subtract the shorter distance from the longer distance. Then use the sign of the number farther from zero in your answer"; and "To subtract an integer, add its opposite" (Scott Foresman's *Invitation to Mathematics: 8,* pp. 300–303; see also levels 6 and 7). As Davis (1984) points out, good students do not actually code mathematical ideas in such natural language statements. Instead, they actively construct frames that serve as the basis for future processing of similar situations. These frames must be constructed out of experiences, and they "play a major role in shaping our thinking" (Davis, 1984, p. 178). Thus, to grasp a mathematical idea, "we map it into a more concrete representation" (p. 178).

A teacher could extend the textbook's rule-based presentation by engaging students in problem solving in several Logo tasks. This would provide not only a more active exploration of the processes, but also the opportunity to take responsibility in building mental frames, or models, of the operations. For example, after students have had experience moving the turtle, and have discussed the notions that moving forward is analogous to addition, moving back is analogous to subtraction, and subtraction is the inverse of addition, teachers could have students use the simple program LOGO.LADDER (This is actually a simple variation of the FEED.TURTLE program listed in the Appendix.) A number-line "ladder" marked in steps of ten is drawn on the screen, with the turtle positioned at "0." The program asks, "START AT WHAT NUMBER?" If the student types "30," that number is displayed at the bottom of the screen and the turtle is repositioned at that point on the line. Next, the student is reminded that FORWARD is analogous to addition and BACK to subtraction and is prompted to enter a command (such as "BACK 23"). The turtle slowly moves backward 23 units, while its numerical position as displayed at the bottom of the screen is simultaneously decremented. At the end, the screen displays

STARTED AT	COMMAND	NEW POSITION
30	BACK 23	7
30	− 23 =	7

Students are encouraged by the teacher to estimate the answers to exercises such as the following, and then to move the turtle to check (students might use numerical and/or visual approximation in estimating): 30 + 40; 70 − 20; 20 + 20 − 10; 10 + 10 + 10; 34 − 12; 100 − 45; 10 + 48 − 56. Next, students would be queried as to the effects of the commands such as "FD −20" and "BK −50." After constructing hypotheses, they would verify their ideas using the turtle. They might first issue the commands to the turtle without the "LADDER" program in exploring and describing the turtle's actions. Then, using the program, they would solve exercises from their textbook such as $-46 - (-18)$. After they entered -46 as the starting position, and BACK -18 as the command, the turtle would stop moving at -28 and the bottom of the screen would show

STARTED AT	COMMAND	NEW POSITION
-46	BACK -18	-28
-46	- (-18) =	-28

The teacher would then have students solve word problems from their regular mathematics program using the program. For example, one problem from the same textbook series reads "The high temperature in Chicago during April was 21 degrees Celsius. The low temperature was -3 degrees Celsius. How much warmer was the high temperature than the low?" Students might solve the problem by starting at 21, and entering "BK -3," seeing and reading the result: 24.

Students would then solve more exercises and word problems from the textbook without the computer; importantly, the teacher would remind them to think of the turtle's movements when they used the number line provided in the textbook. Class discussions would also emphasize this connection; for example, discussing a text problem of "$-7 + (-8)$", a student might explain: "It's like the turtle starts at negative seven, then moves forward negative eight, which is the same as moving back eight, to negative fifteen." At even higher stages, students would be guided to define procedures, such as SUBTRACT :NUM.1 :NUM.2, which takes two numbers as inputs and moves the turtle forward the distance given by :NUM.1, and back the distance given by :NUM.2. Students could then be challenged to define this procedure several different ways; for example, as forward :NUM.1 and forward ($-$:NUM.2) or the like. They would be asked questions such as whether the net effect of SUBTRACT depends on the order that the inputs are given the procedure (is this true for a procedure ADD as well?).

A more complete microworld has been developed and successfully used to help sixth graders construct meanings for integers and integer addition (P. W. Thompson & Dreyfus, 1988). Here, a turtle walks right and left. Entering an integer or integer expression causes the turtle to walk according to specific rules. For example, entering 50 asks the turtle to walk 50 steps in its current direction; -50 causes the turtle to turn around, walk 50 steps, then turn back around. START.AT -70 asks the turtle at the position -70. Vertical lines mark the turtle's beginning and ending positions. The heavy arrow shows the displacement. Figure 7-6a and b illustrate first entering 50, then -90. If commands are entered on the same line, they are executed one at a time, with a light arrow showing the net effect (Fig. 7-6c). Can you act out the turtle's movement for the fairly complicated problem in Fig. 7-6d?

Such integration of Logo activities into the curriculum will turn students away from the mechanical application of calculations toward the active construction of conceptual understandings and semantic connections

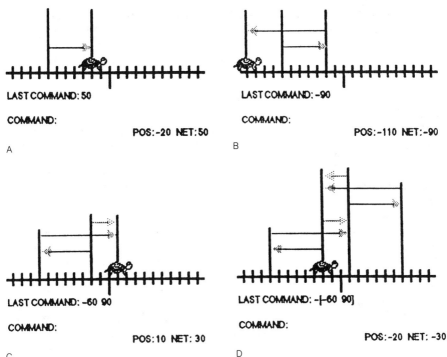

FIGURE 7-6 An integer microworld.

(via frames) which underlie the ability to solve problems within a subject-matter domain.

Arithmetic as a way to more efficient procedures. Place a simple transparency showing a maze over the computer screen. Have students attempt to move from HOME to the star without crossing any lines. They should record each of their moves. Ask them to examine this record and attempt to devise a sequence of fewer moves that would make the turtle travel the same path. Guide them to see how arithmetic can be applied to this problem; for example:

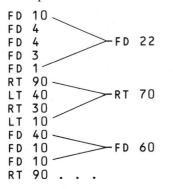

```
FD  10
FD   4
FD   4  ─── FD 22
FD   3
FD   1
RT  90
LT  40  ─── RT 70
RT  30
LT  10
FD  40
FD  10  ─── FD 60
FD  10
RT  90 . . .
```

Encourage them to use this method to make their *own* procedures more efficient and easier to read. Explicitly discuss with the students the mathematical principles and operations that permit such changes (e.g., equivalence, reflexive property, inverse relationships) and other problems in mathematics in which these same techniques and principles are useful.

Multiplication and repeat. Write a simple procedure 3TREES that draws three trees side by side. Ask the students how many trees will appear if they type: REPEAT 2 [3TREES]. Have them try it. Repeat with REPEAT 3, REPEAT 4, and so on, and finally with other procedures such as 2SQUARES or the like that you or your students create. Generalize that multiplication can be seen as REPEATed addition. Have students use similar REPEATs with their own projects, planning or predicting the results. In addition, have them use this way of thinking to solve multiplication problems from their regular mathematics program.

Use the program MULTI.REPEAT (see the Appendix). STARTing the program causes a line segment to be drawn on the screen, with the turtle positioned at one end of the segment. The length of the segment is displayed at the bottom of the screen, along with the length of the turtle's line (0 at the start). Students type in any REPEAT statement that they believe will move the turtle the same length as the given line segment (in the form, REPEAT n [FD d], where n represents the number of times the FORWARD command is repeated and d represents the number of turtle steps the turtle will go forward each time). Each time the turtle moves forward, the display at the bottom of the screen is updated to show the new length of the turtle's line. At the end, the lines and numbers show whether or not the REPEAT statement was correct. If it was, students are challenged to find yet another REPEAT statement that would draw an equivalent line (e.g., for a line of length 120, the following would work: REPEAT 10 [FD 12], REPEAT 12 [FD 10], REPEAT 60 [FD 2], REPEAT 2 [FD 60], REPEAT 6 [FD 20], REPEAT 240 [FD .5], and many others). If the students' attempt was not successful, their previous REPEAT statement is displayed and they are encouraged to try again. In either case, they have the option to try another goal instead. Highlight the multiplicative nature of the REPEAT statement. Challenge students to find "all the combinations of numbers" that create a line of a given length (if decimals are included, there are myriad solutions). The author used this program in a research study with fourth graders. Some of the students' experiences were revealing. Given a goal of 130, Georgia and Tammy stated that they thought that they could use "2," but that they "didn't know how to divide three-digit numbers" (i.e., 130/2). They were "stuck" and could not generate any other solution strategy once the one algorithm they knew failed them. Apparently, flexible mathematical thinking was not called on in the girls' classroom. A good Logo environment does facilitate this type of thinking—minutes later, a second pair created and solved the identical problem. As they explained it, they "went up by tens . . . 50 times 2 is 100, 60 times 2 is 120, and 70 times 2 is 140. So it was between 60 and 70. We tried 65, and 2 times 65 was it!" Georgia and Tammy heard this and later took a more active approach. They had found that REPEAT 10 [FD 13] worked. Georgia said "Let's try 5" and typed REPEAT 5 [FD . . . and stopped.

"Now how far forward?" Tammy said, "Half as many REPEATs, so go twice as far as 13 ... 26." The turtle and its movements gave them a concrete referent for arithmetical compensation (divide one factor by a number, multiply the other by the same number, and the product remains the same). One bittersweet experience ended the day. Jim was very excited about finding "all the ways" to make 24 (the goal he set for himself after 130). He ran up to his teacher who had just entered the room and said: "Look what we're doing! Look what I found! This could really help us, we're doing factors!" (the researchers had not mentioned that term). His teacher (his math teacher, no less) barely turned toward him and said, "Uh-huh. Math class is starting, get in the room." Jim's enthusiasm and spontaneous recognition of the relationship between his Logo and classroom work offered the potential to reinforce both his academic motivation and his appreciation of mathematical ideas ... but the potential went unrealized.

Arithmetic properties (commutativity, associativity, distributivity). Ask students to have Logo evaluate simple statements for equivalence. For example, in response to

```
PRINT 3 * (2 + 4) = (3 * 2) + 4
```

Logo will print FALSE. Include expressions that illustrate the properties of commutativity, associativity, and distributivity, and discuss these properties. Ensure that the connections among these discussions, the computer work, and their succeeding arithmetic work are salient for the students.

Order of operations. Have students examine the following procedure, which combines three numbers using the four basic arithmetical operations. What will be PRINTed?

```
TO COMPUTE
  PRINT 7 + 4 - 2
  PRINT 7 - 4 + 2
  PRINT 5 * 3 - 1
  PRINT 9 - 3 * 4
  PRINT 6 + 4 / 2
END
```

Replace the numbers and operation signs with others to guide the student to discover the order in which Logo performs operations (i.e., the computer first multiplies and divides—left to right; then adds and subtracts—again, left to right). As they are performing similar calculations in their regular mathematics work, ask them: "In what order would Logo perform the operations?"

The most powerful and motivating use of arithmetical operations is applying them to the solution of a real problem. Application of these operations to Logo programming projects represents an intelligent application of arithmetic. Encourage students to continue this practice in their own projects.

Beyond arithmetic: Prealgebra explorations with Logo. Although the study of algebra has been traditionally left for later grades, appropriate computer applications allow elementary students to investigate some of algebra's powerful ideas. For instance, the notion of a variable can be introduced to elementary students (in about third grade and up) quite successfully in constructing "generalized procedures" in Logo (see Chapter 4). Wallace Feurzeig, one of the creators of Logo, is constructing a Logo-based prealgebra course for upper elementary and middle school students (see Feurzeig, 1987, for a full account). In the first component, students are introduced to algebra through Logo projects such as generating gossip, making and breaking secret codes, and writing quizzes. These activities are rich in algebraic ideas, yet their content is meaningful to students. They begin with English, because students have relatively more knowledge of English than mathematical structures and because the English-based activities hold great interest for students. For example, the initial gossip program randomly selects a name from a list of names, an action from a list of actions, and puts the two together into a sentence.*

```
to gossip
 output (sentence who doeswhat)
end

to who
 output pick [sam jane sally bill chris]
end

to doeswhat
 output pick [ cheats [loves to sing] giggles
               [talks your ear off]
               [likes smelly feet]]
end
```

If students were to type "*repeat 4 [print gossip]*," they might see

```
jane talks your ear off
sally giggles
bill loves to sing
chris likes smelly feet
```

Students begin by running, then modifying and extending these simple procedures to create their own gossip. They first alter the name and action lists. Then they might extend gossip to be of the structure "who doeswhat to whom." Such activities illustrate mathematical notions of functions with inputs and outputs and pave the way for a deeper understanding of variables. This leads to simple algebraic programs that present problems such as

```
5 * BOX + 4 = 39
What is the value of BOX?
```

First they learn to have the program choose three numbers (e.g., 5, 7, and 4), compute $5 * 7 + 4$ to get 39, conceal the 7, and output the problem as

---

*Type any instruction such as the long one in the "doeswhat" procedure on *one* line, pressing the RETURN key only when you're done (with "feet]]"). It is printed in this book for readability; yours will appear differently on the screen. Note these procedures are not complete; the PICK procedure must be added.

above, with 7 known to be the answer. Later, they are led to see that there *is* a procedure they can use to solve linear equations, initially working with simple problems such as BOX + 3 = 10. Students often work out standard procedures on their own; one incorporated his knowledge of it within his quiz program:

```
-78 * BOX + +97 = -3023
WHAT IS BOX?
? 35
IT TOOK YOU 33 SECONDS TO ANSWER ME YOU KNUCKLE-
BRAIN # THAT IS SLOW!
WRONG
THE REAL ANSWER IS +40
AN EASY WAY TO GET THE ANSWER IS TO SUBTRACT +97
FROM -3023 AND THEN TRY TO DIVIDE -78 INTO -3120
```

Note that the Logo skills required are taught along the way, as an integral component of the project work, and students are only expected to write fairly simple programs.

The second component introduces standard algebraic notation and the manipulation of algebraic expressions through pictorial representations of algebraic objects and manipulations. The first such environment is an icon Logo in which procedures and functions are represented as machines that may have inputs and an output. This model is introduced from the start to illustrate the functional relationships among procedures. For example, the icon Logo for one student's gossip program is shown in Fig. 7-7. These "machines" can be constructed and "run."

The second environment is a marbles and bags microworld in which bags contain an unknown number of marbles. This is introduced through a well-known guessing game that might be introduced by the teacher as follows.

Think of a number. Don't tell me what it is, just remember it.

Now double it. Add 3 to that. Subtract 2 from that. Double the result.

Now tell me what you have. 50? Then I say your original number was 12. Right?

Students are shown how to do this type of number puzzle by using a notation called marbles and bags. A bag (variable) represents the student's original number. Figure 7-8 illustrates the Logo program. The top half

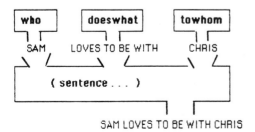

FIGURE 7-7
An icon Logo gossip machine.

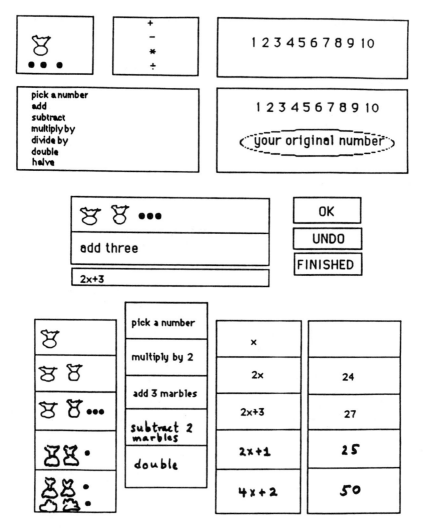

FIGURE 7-8 The marble bag model.

shows the operations (symbolic, as in the top middle window, or in English—"pick a number," "double," etc.) and operands (numbers from 1 to 10 or "your original number") that can be selected. The illustration is of the problem presented above. The bottom windows show the history of the problem in three formats; from left to right: marble and bag, English, algebra. To solve the problem, one works backward (see the final window on the bottom); that is, if 4 bags and 2 marbles equal 50 marbles, then two bags and one marble equal 25 marbles, and so on.

Other exercises include learning to solve inversion problems through a task with turtle geometry. Students are given a list of commands that direct the turtle along a path (only the first part of the path can be seen).

The challenge: Invent a procedure that will bring the turtle back home (i.e., "undo" the series of commands). This, of course, involves constructing a "reverse path" in which each command is the inverse of a corresponding command in the given list. They are then led to see that the process of solving an equation is, similarly, the inverse of the process used in generating it. For example, to generate or "do" the equation $2 * X + 4 = 14$, one:

Starts with X,
Multiplies that by 2,
Adds 4 to that, and
Ends with 14.

Therefore, to solve (or "undo") the equation, one should:

Start ("unend") with 14,
Subtract ("unadd") 4 from that, to get 10,
Divide ("unmultiply") that by 2 to get 5, and
End ("unstart") with X, so $X = 5$.

Thus, the procedure for solving simple linear equations follows directly from that already constructed to reverse the turtle's path.

CAI

CAI materials can also offer experiences in meaningful application of computational concepts and skills. In "Diffy" (in *Arith-Magic*) students select four numbers, which are printed on the screen as corners of a square. Then the students find the difference between each successive pair of numbers. The four differences are placed halfway between each original pair and thus become the corners of the next square. This continues until the number in each corner is zero. Students can be challenged to go beyond just the subtraction. Will the differences always "diff out" or reduce to zero? Does it matter in what order the numbers are placed on the square? Can you find numbers for the corner that maximize the number of moves? In a game from the same package, "Tripuz," the computer chooses three numbers which form the vertices of a triangle. However, these numbers are not shown to the student; instead, question marks show where the numbers are hidden. The computer does show the sums of each pair of vertices between the hidden numbers. The student might see

```
? 11 ?
 9  4
   ?
```

The student has to figure out the hidden numbers. Can you? For older students, the game may be played with multiplication (the numbers shown are the product of the hidden numbers at the vertices). Advanced students might be challenged to figure out a general (algebraic) solution.

Another puzzle format is found in *Teasers by Tobbs*. Students must fill in the missing numbers of addition or multiplication grids. At the lower levels, there is only one correct answer:

+	4	7
3	7	10
5	9	___

+	39	26
54	___	___
48	___	___

At the higher levels, there is no unique solution. The computer tells the students "That will work" instead of "That is correct."

+	32	___
___	87	___
___	___	68

In "Rubi-Quations" (in *MAC*) students must rearrange five arithmetic equations to make them true. They rotate the columns of digits up or down, making as few moves as possible. For example, try the following yourself (a hint to make it easy—only the D and E columns need to be rotated in this example).

A	B	C		D	E
5	×	1	=	1	9
5	+	7	=		2
1	+	8	=		1
4	×	3	=	1	5
3	−	2	=		2

Can you see that moving the D column up two spaces and the E column down two spaces would yield the following?

A	B	C		D	E
5	×	1	=		5
5	+	7	=	1	2
1	+	8	=		9
4	×	3	=	1	2
3	−	2	=		1

CHECKING ANSWERS AND DOING COMPUTATIONS ON MACHINES

Should computers be used to check answers to computations done by students? Should they be used to do the computations, freeing students to engage in solving meaningful math problems which require complex calculations? Yes, especially the latter. However, the smallest and least expensive "computers" we have—calculators—should be used for this purpose, rather than microcomputers. Using a computer for this purpose is like using a crane to move a paper bag.

Is there truth to the concern that students will not learn their basic facts if they use calculators and computers? Research indicates that there is no ground for such worry and that calculator use can increase students' computational power (Shult, 1981; Shumway et al., 1981). Two studies found calculator use motivating and beneficial even for students as young as 5 through 7 (Behr & Wheeler, 1981; Scandura et al., 1978).

If calculators are beneficial, should students still learn their "facts"? Of course. These will always be important. They should also learn better estimation skills and learn to use technology appropriately. They should probably *not* have to learn to perform abbreviated, complex computational algorithms quickly, if at all. In addition, recall Moise's statement about the deleterious effects of such algorithmetic drill. He proposes that "a child should not be forced to do by hand anything that can be done better and more easily with a pocket calculator" (in Hansen & Zweng, 1984, p. 37). Because this amounts to assigning "to the student interminable chores that neither demand nor repay thought," it may damage their inclination to use their intelligence. Moise goes on to say that some critics suggest that the use of a calculator does not teach students about the concept of number, the meanings of the operations, or the reasons why the machine gives the correct answer, but he answers that "this objection is a nullity, because the [paper and pencil] *algorithms are also worthless in all three of these respects*" (p. 37, emphasis added).

DEVELOPING AUTOMATICITY

Many of the programs discussed so far provide practice on basic facts as they teach students to apply their knowledge. However, in accordance with the principles developed in Chapter 1, achieving automatic procedural skill sometimes requires specifically designed drill. There are many programs available for this purpose (see Table 7-1). One well-designed arcade-type program, *Math Blaster,* was discussed in Chapter 2. In another, *Alien Addition,* students encounter invading spaceships, each of which has an addition problem on it. They must load their laser cannon with the correct answer and "equalize" the spaceships before they can land. Consonant with good drill practices, students must be both fast and accurate. Unfortunately, the computer's capability to generate problems tailored to each student's needs is not utilized. Programs that do present "just the facts students need"—that is, have good management systems—are available, although they vary in the quality of their presentations (see Tables 2-2 and 7-1).

DIAGNOSIS OF COMPUTATIONAL ERRORS

Recall from Chapter 2 that computer programs have been written that can accurately diagnose students' mistakes in computation. J. S. Brown, Burton, and VanLehn's program, "Debuggy," can explain the reason for the underlying error in students' subtraction processes rather than simply identifying the procedural mistake. Their theory holds that students' errors are of different types. Slips are careless, unintentional errors that we all experience.

Bugs are systematic errors. Consider the following hypothetical student's work (adapted from VanLehn, 1981):

306	80	183	702	3005	34	251
−138	− 4	− 95	− 11	− 28	−14	− 47
78	76	88	591	1087	24	244

This student appears to have difficulty with renaming (or "borrowing"). Specifically, his errors can be precisely predicted if answers are computed using a procedure with a small modification of the correct procedure. This modification is called a "bug," as it is seen to be similar in some ways to a bug, or error, in a computer program which causes it to operate incorrectly. This student has the "borrow-across-zero" bug. It modifies the correct subtraction procedure by skipping over the zero and borrowing from the next column. One can now attempt to predict exactly what the student would answer to new problems. A student may have more than one bug at a time. The student above answered the last two problems incorrectly, but another bug must be hypothesized to account for the error—in this case, the "N − N = N" bug. When the digits in a column are equal, the student writes the number, instead of zero, for the answer. Research has indicated that about one-third of all students who have "buggy" subtraction procedures have more than one bug (VanLehn, 1981).

How do bugs arise? Their *repair theory* postulates that when students get stuck while executing an incomplete subtraction procedure, they are not likely to quit as a buggy computer program might. Rather, they will do a small amount of "patching" to get over the impasse. These local problem-solving strategies, called "repairs," may be as simple as skipping the operation or backing up and trying another path. For example, solving 504 − 286, the student might think, "I can't subtract 6 from 4, so I'll borrow. But I can't take anything away from zero. So I'll go back and subtract 4 from 6 instead." Based on repair theory, the computer program DEBUGGY is as effective as expert human diagnosticians (VanLehn, 1981). Research with DEBUGGY has uncovered additional interesting information. It appears that bugs are not stable; that is, they may appear throughout one test, but disappear on the next. (This has implications for teachers—more practice at just this time may not be warranted, as students may commit to memory a newly invented bug.)

Although DEBUGGY itself is not yet available on microcomputers, a companion program, BUGGY, is. Designed for teacher education, this program simulates a student whose subtraction procedure has bugs. Given problems this "student" has solved, teachers must construct their own theories to find the bugs. They find they must be very careful, as many bugs or combinations of bugs produce the same erroneous solution. For example, a sample dialogue between the computer and a team of student teachers might go like this:

I have chosen a bug. Here is an example of the bug.

17
+ 5
13

Now you can give me problems to determine the bug.

$$
\begin{array}{r} 18 \\ +\ 6 \\ \hline 15 \end{array}
\qquad
\begin{array}{r} 43 \\ +79 \\ \hline 23 \end{array}
$$

Got the Bug!
Please describe the bug.
Student adds the number to be carried into the last column worked in.
Here are some problems to test your theory about the bug.

$$
\begin{array}{r} 21 \\ +39 \\ \hline \mathbf{51} \end{array}
$$

That's not the bug I have. Using my bug:

$$
\begin{array}{r} 21 \\ +39 \\ \hline 15 \end{array}
$$

Try giving me some more examples.

$$
\begin{array}{r} 51 \\ +1707 \\ \hline 21 \end{array}
\qquad
\begin{array}{r} 99 \\ +99 \\ \hline 36 \end{array}
\qquad
\begin{array}{r} 68 \\ +\ 9 \\ \hline 23 \end{array}
$$

Got the Bug!
Please describe the bug that you think I have.
The student is adding all the digits together.
Here are some problems to test your theory about the bug:

$$
\begin{array}{r} 33 \\ +99 \\ \hline \mathbf{24} \end{array}
\qquad
\begin{array}{r} 1091 \\ +\ 60 \\ \hline \mathbf{17} \end{array}
\qquad
\begin{array}{r} 8 \\ +34 \\ \hline \mathbf{15} \end{array}
\qquad
\begin{array}{r} 28 \\ +70 \\ \hline \mathbf{17} \end{array}
\qquad
\begin{array}{r} 15 \\ +17 \\ \hline \mathbf{14} \end{array}
$$

Very good. My description of the bug is:
The student always sums up all the digits with no regard to columns.

Student teachers using this game discovered that errors that may appear to be random may actually be the result of a systematic misconceptualization. Obviously, teachers who understand such bugs are better prepared to help students recognize and remediate them.

An interesting change occurred when some intermediate students used BUGGY. At first, they were disdainful of the computer's simulated errors ("How could anyone be so stupid!"). However, as they used the program, their perceptions changed; they came to see that many mistakes are "logical," at least from one point of view. This helped them see errors (their own as well as those of others) more as bugs to be analyzed and corrected than the result of "stupidity."

We must be careful, however, not to overestimate the explanatory power of programs such as BUGGY. The bugs tend to represent what students do when they have little or no understanding of a certain part of an algorithm. If students were taught in more meaningful ways, such as using Dienes blocks representations (off and on computer), they might not make the same kind of errors.

Another system similarly diagnoses subtraction errors, but is designed for free interaction with students (Attisha & Yazdani, 1983). It describes their bugs and informs them of the required remediation. Janke (1984) has developed a program (*Math Assistant*) which diagnoses students' errors in whole-number algorithms. It is not based on a complex theory as is DE-BUGGY but upon a compilation of student's error types identified in the literature. It provides a list of all such errors consistent with each student's answer. Students of teachers provided with this diagnostic information the program provides showed significantly higher achievement. Several of the drill and practice programs listed in Table 7–1, such as *The Math Machine*, include on-computer placement tests.

SUGGESTED READINGS

Hansen and Zweng's (1984) NCTM yearbook includes several chapters that discuss the use of computers in computation.

Usiskin (1983) presents his point of view about computation and calculators. Many teachers still disagree. Do you?

VanLehn (1981) discusses "repair theory," a challenging but rewarding topic to investigate.

TABLE 7-1   Software: Computation

Title	Producer	Notes
Add-Card	Academic Ther.	Addition fact drill. Student moves graphics to match numerals, then objects regroup and student enters sum. 1–3.
Adding and Subtracting	Gamco	Addition and subtraction. 2–5.
Adding Two Digit Numbers	Resource	Addition, two disks (without and with carrying). 3–5.
Addition and Subtraction	Queue	Addition and subtraction. Available as "0–5" and "6–10". K–1.
Addition and Subtraction	Orange Cherry	Addition and subtraction of whole numbers. K–3.
Addition and Subtraction	Silver, Burdett & Ginn	Basic facts for four-digit numbers with regrouping.
Addition and Subtraction	MCP	Addition and subtraction, conceptual and practice, some CMI. 5–9.

Title	Producer	Notes
Addition B.C.	Opp. Learning	Addition (sums 11–18). 1–3.
Addition in Columns	Amer. Peri.	Column addition. 1–4.
Addition Logician	MECC	Addition with regrouping. Drill with logical problem-solving games as rewards for good performance. 3–4.
Addition Made Easy	Spinifex Software	Addition. Some CMI.
Addition Magic	Deegan	Addition drill and practice. 2–6.
Addition Magician	TLC	Single-digit addition, draw lines around groups of numbers that sum to a target number. Involves much practice in strategy game. 1–4.
Addition 1 and 2	Control Data	Addition properties, meaning of addition, addition facts.
Addition/Subtraction Facts 1	JMH	Addition and subtraction. Beginning levels. K–2.
Addition Table	SVE	Addition. 1–3.
Addition Tables	NTS	Addition. K–2.
Addition with Carry	Micro. Wrkshp.	Addition. Some CMI.
Addition with Carrying	PDI	Addition. 2–6.
Add/Sub	Boston Ed.	Addition and subtraction with various levels of difficulty. Optional regrouping. K–2.
Adventures with Negative Numbers	IBM	All operations with negative numbers in adventure-game format.
Andy and the Math-a-sizer	Aladdin	All operations. If incorrect, solution is shown on a "blackboard." K–8.
Academic Skills Builders	DLM	All operations. Six programs can be adjusted in difficulty, pacing, etc. (although there is no CMI). 1–7.
Arith-A-Tackle	Micro Learn.	All operations; drill in game format. Speed and complexity adjusted to past performance. 1–6.
Arith-magic	QED	Substraction in a motivating, problem-solving-oriented framework (e.g., DIFFY, TRIPUZ, and magic squares). 2–9.
ArithMatic: Addition and Subtraction	Compu-Teach	Addition and subtraction facts. Teacher can choose to do facts that progress by 1 or those in a "facts family." K–3.
Arithmekicks	Houghton Miff.	Multiplication and division. Some estimation practice. Gamelike format. 3–6.
Arithmetic: Addition (and Subtraction)	Acorn	Graphically portrays addition as counting. P–2.

(continued)

TABLE 7-1 (Continued)

Title	Producer	Notes
Arithmetic Classroom	Sterling Swift	All operations. Tutorials and practice, using sound pictorial models. Similar to Elementary Mathematics Classroom Learning System, but without the CMI component. 4–8 (Also available from DCH.)
Arithmetic Doctor	Ed. Act.	Diagnosis and remediation in all operations, with CMI.
Arithmetic Drill	EMC	All operations. Automatically adjusts difficulty level. 1–6.
Arithmetic Fundamentals	BLS	All operations. 2–5.
Arithmetic Games	SRA	All operations in game formats emphasizing thinking strategies. 4–adult.
Arithmetic Racing	Math Software	All operations. Game to develop speed and accuracy; assumes facts known. 4–11.
Arithmetic Skills	Scandura	See MicroTutor II: Arithmetic Skills.
ArithmeTic Tac Toe 3D	RG Comp. Wrk.	All operations in 3D tic tac toe format. 1–8.
Arithmetic Teacher	H & E	All operations; timed. 1–5.
Arithmetic Tutor	Bluebirds	Addition and subtraction. Some CMI. 1–2.
Arithmetickle	Houghton Miff.	Addition and subtraction in a game-like format. 3–6.
As Easy as 2 × 2	AIMS Media	Multiplication. Practice in using multiplication table and two games.
Astro-Grover	CTW	Addition and subtraction. K–2.
Balloon Bandit	Orange Cherry	All operations. 3–8.
Basic Arithmetic	MECC	All operations. Solving simple whole-number problems. 2–6.
Basic Arithmetic	Tandy	All operations. 2–6.
Basic Fact Games	JMH	All operations.
Basic Math Competency	Ed. Act.	All operations, tutorial and drill. 4–12.
Basic Math Facts	Houghton Miff.	All operations. Provides individualized practice on facts via CMI component. See the text. 1–6.
Basic Number Facts	Control Data	All operations. Part of PLATO series; car-race format with automatically adjusted difficulty level. 3–8.
Basic Number Help	Acorn	Addition and subtraction. K–3.
Basic Skills in Math	Opp. Learning	All operations; set of 12 disks.
Basic Skills Math Series	Control Data	All operations. PLATO instructional series; includes CMI. 3–8.

Title	Producer	Notes
Battling Bugs	Milliken	Positive and negative numbers. Students add either positive or negative bugs to keep the "factions" even. 4–8.
Beat the Computer	Ed. Software	All operations. Timed or untimed practice. 6–12.
Beginning Math Series	SVE	All operations. Drill and tutorials with remediation. K–3.
Beginning Mathematics Concepts	Britannica	Addition and subtraction, first with pictures, then numerals and larger numbers. Some CMI. 1–3.
The Big Math Attack	Scholastic	All operations in arcade format. 1–6.
Black-Out	Ed. Software	All operations. Computer rolls three dice for each player, who must combine them with arithmetic operations to match one of 64 numbers. 2–10.
Borrow	B5	Subtraction. 2–4.
Box Series	SVE	All operations. K–3.
Bright and Early: Math Skills	Acorn	All operations. A series of five programs. 1–6.
Building Tens Strategy	Hartley	Addition; some CMI. 1–3.
Bunny Hop	Micrograms	Addition and subtraction drills with hopping bunny. 2.
Calculated Risk	Woodbury	All operations. Adventure game; students must first bargain for supplies (checking that they have not been cheated), then answer arithmetic exercises to advance in the adventure plot. 2–8.
Carry	B5	Addition. 2–4.
Carrying	Renaissance	"Carrying" with visual demonstrations and branching tutorial; also speed drills. 2–8.
Carrying: Regrouping for Addition	Renaissance	Addition of two-digit numbers with regrouping.
CDI:M	SRA	All operations. Abbreviation is for Computer Drill and Instruction: Mathematics. Available with or without CMI; includes animated tutorials, seatwork generator, electronic blackboard. K–12.
Challenge Math	Sunburst	All operations. Three games that motivate students, one emphasizing estimation, another in an "adventure game" format. 1–8.

(continued)

TABLE 7-1 (Continued)

Title	Producer	Notes
Circus Math	MECC	Addition up to four digits and three addends. Includes records of student progress. 2–3.
Classroom Math Games	Gamco	All operations. 4–8.
Color Math	Radio Shack	All operations; adjusts to ability level. 1–8.
Columns	NTS	Column addition game. 2–4.
Commodore Plus Curriculum for Math	Data Command	All operations. 40 programs on five disks. K–6.
Compu-Math Arithmetic	Edu-Ware	All operations, includes CMI. 2–6.
Computational Skills Program	Hough. Miff.	All operations. Diagnosis and prescriptions. Related skills grouped and ordered by difficulty. 1 + .
Computer Math Activities and Computer Math Games	Addison-Wesley	All operations. Activities and games to supplement any text series. 1–9.
Computer Puzzle Works	Continental	All operations (one program for each; sold separately). Students work toward animating a puzzle. 1–4.
Computer Zoo	Micrograms	Addition and subtraction. 1–2.
Counters	Sunburst	Addition and subtraction. P–1.
Counting	MECC	Basic addition. K–2.
Counting Plus	Professor	From simple counting to addition with renaming.
Derby	Micrograms	All operations; horse-race game. 4–6.
Development of Basic Math	SVE	All operations, three levels available separately. 2–8.
Dice 'n' Dominoes	NTS	Addition and subtraction. Choose dice or dominoes to add or subtract. K–2.
The Dig Math Computer	WFF'N PROOF	Based on "Equations: The Game of Creative Mathematics." Diagnosis and games from basic arithmetic to algebra, emphasizing applications. 4–12.
Discovery Adding Machine	Queue	Addition by putting two groups of animals together. Some CMI. P–2.
Discovery Take Away Zoo	Queue	Subtraction by separating two groups of animals. Some CMI. P–2.
Divide and Conquer	AIMS Media	Division of whole numbers; practice in two games.
Division Drill	Teacher's PET	Basic division operations; drill. 4–8.
Division Magic	Deegan	Division drill and practice. 2–12.
Division of Numbers	Orange Cherry	Division. 3–6.

Title	Producer	Notes
Division Practice	NTS	Division. 2–5.
Division Skills	Media Materials	Division lessons in three modes: step-by-step instruction, practice (with help if requested), and mastery quiz. 6–8.
Division Skills	Media Materials	Division, basic facts to two-digit divisors, includes some CMI. 5–8.
Dolphin Math	Houghton Miff.	All operations, includes CMI with diagnosis. 1–8.
Early Addition	MECC	Addition. Little conceptual assistance, keeps student records. 1–2.
Piece of Cake Math	Springboard	All operations; five activities that portray concepts graphically. 1–4.
Early Math	Orbyte	Addition and subtraction. 1–3.
ECLP (Cars)	Ed. Act.	Addition. P–1.
Edupack and Frenzy	Milliken	Subtraction. 1.
Edupack Mathpack I	Comm*Data	All operations; several games. K–3.
The Electric Chalkboard	Heartsoft	Computation drill and practice.
Elementary Math	Scholastic	All operations; tutorials with graphics provided if incorrect answers given. 1–6.
Elementary Math Drill	Alphatel	All operations; drill. Some CMI. 3–5.
Elementary Math Games	PLATO/WICAT	All operations. 1–6.
Elementary Math Edu-Disk	Muse	All operations. Uses graphics and voice. 1–6.
Elementary Math Package I	Micro Learn.	All operations.
Elementary Math Steps	CBS	Addition, subtraction, multiplication. K–3.
Elementary Mathematics Classroom Learning System: Whole Numbers	Sterling Swift	All operations. Demonstration/tutorial of operation, with step-by-step correction of students' errors. Features CMI, including a diagnostic-placement test. Well designed, also available in Spanish. 4–8.
Elementary Mathematics Series	IBM/WICAT	All operations. Contains concept development and practice strands. Generally, valid models and pedagogical techniques in the former. The latter feature step-by-step guided practice (if needed). See text in this and other chapters. 1–8.
Elementary Vol. 1: Mathematics	MECC	"Tens" is a drill on multiplying numbers by multiples of 10. 5–6. "Speed drill" deals with all operations. 2–6.
Equations Challenge Matches	WFF'N PROOF	Matching equations. 4–12.

(continued)

TABLE 7-1 (Continued)

Title	Producer	Notes
Essential Math, Version 2.0	BertaMax	All operations, available with CMI. 1–8.
ESC Mathematics	ESC	All operations. Features meaningful situations, on-line calculator when appropriate, and a variety of operations. Comprehensive program for grades 1–6.
Expression Writer	HRM	All operations. Create numerical expressions to achieve an arithmetic goal. Option to include negative numbers. 4–12.
Fact Track	SRA	All operations. 1–6.
Factors	Bergwall	Students determine which of three numbers is not a factor of a given product. 2–4.
Facts Arcade Games	Gamco	All operations; a different program for each operation. Arcade format. Some CMI. 2–6.
Facts Match Series	BertaMax	All operations. 1–4.
Fast Facts	EduSoft	All operations. 3–10.
Fastmath I and II	NTS	All operations. Two-player drills. K–5.
Fay: That Math Woman	Didatech	All operations; uses a number-line model. 1–4.
Fetchin' Folks	Data Command	Drill matching equations. 2–5.
First Facts—Addition and Subtraction	Academic Ther.	Addition and subtraction (separate programs). 1–3.
1st Math: Main Menu; 2nd Math: Car Race	Stone	Drill on basic operations.
First Men in the Moon Math	Hammett	All operations. Word problems in a moon adventure format. 4–7.
Fishing for Answers	NTS	Addition and subtraction drill. K–4.
Flash Cards	SVE	All operations. K–4.
Flower Power Numbers	HRM	Addition and subtraction. K–3.
Footstep Math	HRM	Addition and subtraction and positive and negative numbers using a number-line model. 2–6.
Frenzy	Commodore	Subtraction and multiplication practice. 2–6.
Fun with Numbers	Micro. Power	Addition and subtraction; beginning levels. 1–3.
Fundamental Math Drill	Random House	All operations; CMI optional. 1–8. (Similar programs also available.)
Fundamentals of Math	Sterling Swift	All operations; drill and tutorial. 3–12.

Title	Producer	Notes
Galaxy Math Facts Game	Random House	All operations. Drill in a fantasy format (see also their *Grand Prix*). Motivating program, with good documentation. Recommended. 1–9.
Getting Ready to Add	MECC	Addition. 1.
Getting Started in Addition	AIMS Media	All operations available.
Gotcha Math Games	Comm*Data	All operations. 1–8.
The Grabit Factory	DCH	Addition and subtraction; arcade drill. K–3.
Grand Prix	Random House	All operations. 2–6.
Grating Method of Multiplication	Ed. Software	Multiplication. Alternate algorithm. 3–12.
Greased Lightning	Micrograms	Multiplication practice. 4–5.
The Great Number Chase	Milliken	All operations. Maze in which student must move to a combination of operations and numbers to reach a target number; involves strategic choices. Students can design their own mazes to play. 3–8.
Green Jay Arithmetic Series	QED	Addition and subtraction. A bean frame is used to introduce the concepts. Some CMI is available. K–3.
Guinness World Records	SVE	All operations (one program for each). 4–6.
Gulp!!	Milliken	Addition and multiplication. Basic drill; answer 20 basic fact problems before the little fish is eaten by the bigger fish. 2–6. (Milliken's *Frenzy* is similarly designed for subtraction and division.)
Heath Mathematics Software	DCH	All operations. Pictorial demonstration, then drill with CMI; supplements Heath mathematics textbooks. 1–4.
Hey, Taxi	Media Materials	All operations. Word problems in situations involving running a taxi. 1+.
Highrise Math	Word Assoc.	All operations. Provides drill in single-digit arithmetic operations in an arcade-style format. Students are to construct several number sentences equivalent to a target number. Some strategic thinking required (which, for some students, might overwhelm the arithmetic skills involved). K+.

(continued)

TABLE 7-1   (Continued)

Title	Producer	Notes
IBM Elementary Mathematics Series	IBM/WICAT	Comprehensive program. Includes the Math Concepts and Math Practice Series. Includes conceptual models for "facts" and step-by-step guides through algorithms. K–8.
Inequalities	Bergwall	Students solve unequal number sentences. 2–4.
Integer Arcade	HRM	Addition and subtraction of positive and negative numbers to control the depth of a submarine. 4–8.
Integers	SVE	All operations with integers. 5–9.
Integers/Integer Fast Facts	EduSoft	All operations with positive and negative numbers. Wide range of options with corrective feedback. 4–12.
Introduction to Addition and Subtraction (and available with multiplication and division)	Concept Ed.	All operations with positive and negative numbers at three ability levels. K–4.
Jeni Math	JR Software	All operations. Program is designed for the home, as it's personalized for one student. 1–3.
Jumping Math Flash	Mindscape	Addition, subtraction, multiplication, and division. Some CMI. 1–4.
K-8 Math Program	Radio Shack	All operations. Complete sequence of activities, including drill and testing and sequencing components; CMI is optional. Carefully correlated with six popular basal text series. K–8.
K–8 Math Worksheet Generator	Radio Shack	All operations. Comprehensive worksheet generator cross-referenced with six popular basal text series. K–8.
The King's Rule	Sunburst	Determine rules. 4–adult.
Learning about Numbers	C&C	All operations. Drill in a fantasy setting: be a hero or heroine; help a person or the troll! P–4.
Learning Mathematics	Queue	Addition and subtraction with decimals. 5–6.
Learning to Add and Subtract	Learning Tech.	Single-digit addition and subtraction with picture clues. P–3.
Let's Have Fun Subtracting	Resource	Subtraction. 1–3.
Little Professor's Math	Professor Corp.	Addition and subtraction. P–3.
Long Division	Micro. Wrkshp.	Division with one- to three-digit divisors. Apple version has some CMI. 1–6.

Title	Producer	Notes
Long Division	Scholastic	Division with one- to three-digit divisors. 3–6.
Long Division Made Easy	Spinifex Software	Division. Some CMI. 3–9.
Long Multiplication Made Easy	Spinifex Software	Multiplication. Some CMI. 3–9.
Make a Number	NTS	All operations; find as many ways as possible to make a target number. 2–4.
Marblemath	DCH	Multiplication and division. 3–6.
Mastering Math Series	MECC	All operations. A series of programs. Records kept of individual student performance; diagnostic systems are also available. 1–4.
Math Action Game Series	Mindscape	All operations. K–8.
Math Adventures with Mickey	Walt Disney	All operations; word problems. 4–8.
Math Amazing	Light 8	Addition and subtraction; drill on single-digit exercises. 1–3.
The Math Arcade	Math Arcade	Addition and subtraction; some CMI. 1–6.
Math Arcade Games	Orange Cherry	All operations; three games. 1–8.
Math Archery	Davell	Writing arithmetical expressions to come close to a "bull's-eye."
Math Assistant	Scholastic	All operations. Error analysis. Version I identifies 20 addition and 20 subtraction errors (version II is similar for multiplication and division). Can be used for drill (with feedback consisting of hints pinpointing errors) or as a diagnostic test. CMI component. 3–6.
Math Baseball	Ed. Act.	All operations. 2–6.
Math Basic Facts—Drill and Testing	Sysdata	All operations. Some record keeping. 3–6.
Math Blaster	Davidson	Motivating arcade format. Can choose level or put in your own problems to be practiced. Favored by many. 1–7.
Math Bowl	Micrograms	Addition in bowling game format. 4–5.
Math Busters	Spinnaker	Equations with positive and negative numbers; monster game format. 5–12.
Math Challenge I	Orbyte	Addition and subtraction. 3–5.
Math Challenge II	Orbyte	Calculating expressions. 5–7.

(continued)

TABLE 7-1 (Continued)

Title	Producer	Notes
Math Circus	Ventura	All operations. K–6.
Math Computation Series	IBM	All operations. 6–12.
Math Concepts Series	IBM	All operations. K–8.
The Math Connection	Sunburst	All operations, drill in game format, demanding some analysis and deduction. 3–8.
Math Conqueror	Ed. Act.	All operations. 4–6.
Math Courseware Series	Scott Foresman	All operations. A series of programs offering tutorials and drill with animation illustrating the processes. 1–8.
Math Double Drill	Cardinal	All operations. K–6.
Math Facts	Commodore	All operations. 1–4.
Math Facts 4	Aladdin	All operations. Drill from basic facts to three-digit numbers. K–8.
Math Facts Games	Opp. Learning	All operations; arcade format.
Math Facts and Thinking Games	Berta-Max	All operations; basic facts. 3–8.
Math Facts Level II	T.H.E.S.I.S.	Addition and subtraction. 1–3.
Math Facts Match	Berta-Max	All operations. Choose the equation that would produce a given answer. 3–8.
Math Football	Gamco	All operations in a football game format. Some CMI.
Math for All Ages	Aquarius	All operations. Some CMI. K–9.
Math Fun	Newberry Software	Addition, subtraction, multiplication, division, games with grids, decimal place.
Math Gallery	Beh. Eng.	All operations. "Shoot" correct equations (not the incorrect ones). 2–6.
Math Game	MECC	All operations. 2–6.
Math Grades K-3; 4–6.	Data Command	All operations. Series of three disks for primary, three for intermediate. K–3, 4–6.
Math Helper	Idaho	All operations. 1–5.
Math I	Pers. Com. Art	All operations. 1–8.
Math Ideas with Base Ten Blocks	Cuisenaire	All operations are developed through pictorial representations of base ten blocks. Good reinforcement if the model was first developed concretely in class. 2–7.
Math in a Nutshell	Learning Tech.	All operations; choose the correct signs $(+, -, \times, /)$ to complete number sentences. 3–6.

Title	Producer	Notes
Math in the Real World	Intellectual	All operations; application to real-life problems.
Math Invaders	Winners Circle	All operations. Fact practice emphasizing speed and accuracy; for slower students, special mode eliminates time pressure. Some CMI. K–6.
The Math Machine	SouthWest	All operations. Includes CMI with diagnostic testing, arcade game reinforcement (optional). P–6.
Math Magic	Mindplay	Addition and subtraction with several levels of difficulty. P–2.
Math Man	Scholastic	All operations, including concepts such as commutativity, in arcade format best suited to the individual user. 1–6.
Math Marauders!	Micrograms	Addition in arcade format. 2–7.
Math Mastery	Random House	Addition and subtraction. 1–2.
Math Mastery Series	Gamco	All operations. Automatic placements; CMI. 3–8.
Math Maze	DCH	All operations; students maneuver a fly chased by a spider through a maze in a search for answers to number sentences. Various levels of difficulty; your own mazes can be stored. 2–6.
Math Milage	CBS	Multiplication. 2–4.
The Math Path	Milliken	All operations; also analysis of basic facts, factoring. Students construct input–output "machines" with numbers and operations. 3–8.
Math 1	Per. Com. Art	All operations. Easy to use; wide range of difficulty. 1–8.
Math Power	Orange Cherry	Mental arithmetic. 5–8.
Math Power Program	I/CT	All operations. Tutorials and practice. 1–6.
Math Practice Series	IBM	All operations; drill with help. 1–8.
Math Rabbit	TLC	Addition and subtraction; readiness for multiplication. Also patterning, different names for a number. Several games with multiple levels of difficulty. Some useful CMI. Well designed. P–2.
Math Regrouping Games	McGraw-Hill	Addition and subtraction regrouping. Low evaluation from EPIE. 4–6.
Math Run	Avant-Garde	All operations, drill. 1–6.

(continued)

TABLE 7-1   (Continued)

Title	Producer	Notes
Math Sequences	Milliken	All operations. Includes record keeping with pre- and posttests (allowing computer placement in the sequence) and a worksheet generator. 1–8. (Now called "Revised Math Sequences"; also comes in a multiple loading form without CMI)
Math Shop	Scholastic	Students help in various stores in a mall by solving problems, each using a specific curriculum concept, including all operations. 6–9.
Math Skill Builders	Comm. Skill	All operations; CMI. 3–8.
Math Skill Games	McGraw-Hill	All operations. 4–6.
Math Skills	Britannica	All operations. 1–6.
Math Sports Package	Opp. Learning	All operations.
Math Strands/Math Skills	CCC	All operations. Drill designed to reflect content in current textbooks. Extensive CMI component. Substantial research evaluation. 1–8.
Math Strategy	Beh. Eng.	All operations. Teaches a strategy for memorizing facts through visualization. Some authoring. 1–7.
Math Study Center	TYC	Subtraction and multiplication. Limited authoring. 1–8.
Math Tutor	Comm*Data	All operations; graphic aids. 3–6.
Math Tutor	Micro Learn.	All operations; 25 difficulty levels. 1–6.
Math Tutor	Telephone	All operations. 3–9.
Math Voyager	CLS	All operations; pictorial models that are generally sound (although one tens model may need to be explained). K–8.
Math Wars	SouthWest	All operations in arcade format. 2–10.
Math Whiz Quiz	Dynacomp	All operations. P–6.
Math With Microman	Microgram	Addition and subtraction; two-digit with regrouping. 3–4.
Math Wizard	Unicorn	All operations. Includes speech. 1–5.
Math World Commander	Orange Cherry	All operations. 3+.
Mathemagician	Micro SPARC, Inc.	Five games, five levels, multiplication, division, addition, subtraction.
Mathematics Action Games	Scott, Foresman	All operations. Two for each of three levels: K–3, 4–6, and 7–8.
Mathematics Activity Courseware (MAC)	Houghton Miff.	All operations. Generally well planned, correlated with Houghton Mifflin's mathematics series. 2–8.

Title	Producer	Notes
Mathematics Assessment/ Prescriptive Edu-Disks	Reader's Digest	All operations, includes CMI. 1–7.
Mathematics Courseware Series	Mindscape	All operations; graphically illustrates concepts. K–6.
Mathematics Courseware	Silver Burdett	Lesson/practice/game cycle for each topic. K–8.
Mathematics for Primary Series	Aims Media	All operations. Review and test. Some CMI. 3–6.
Mathematics for the C-64	Opp. Learning	Primary and elementary programs.
Mathematics: Grade 1	Intellectual	Addition and subtraction; CMI. 1.
Mathematics Series	Centurion	All operations. K–6.
Mathematics Skills Software	Addison-Wesley	All operations. 1–8.
Mathematics Software	Amer. Sys. Dev.	All operations. K–12.
Mathematics Software	Media Materials	Division. 6–8.
Mathematics Strands	CCC	All operations. Extensive CMI component permits a highly individualized program of drill and practice, with digit-by-digit evaluation and feedback. Long history of development and research on effectiveness. A major investment, this system utilizes a minicomputer (CCC MICROHOST) to drive up to 128 terminals, which can include several types of microcomputers already in the school. Also available on Sony microcomputers. Some courses may be taken from the students' homes using Touch-Tone phones. 1–6.
Mathematics Today Practice Diskettes	Harcourt Brace	All operations. A series that presents drill correlated with the publisher's text series. Embedded in gamelike activities; provide "clues" when students make errors. K–8.
Mathematics Unlimited: Problem Solving	Holt	Problem-solving series with several minisimulations and challenges dealing with computation. For example, first graders help Honeybear along a number line (avoiding the bees, landing on the honey) by completing number sentences. In "Safari Story," fifth graders have to load four bundles of gifts on each of two elephants so that they carry as much weight as possible, without exceeding their limit. Several activities have students attempt to

(continued)

TABLE 7-1   (Continued)

Title	Producer	Notes
		find the shortest route to travel to all points on a map. 1–8.
Mathfacts	B5	All operations. 1–5.
Mathfacts 4	Alladin	All operations. K–8.
Mathfinder	Holt	All operations. K–6.
MathFlash	Palantir	All operations. Electronic flash-cards. Scorekeeping. 1–3.
MathQuest	Jadee	Addition and multiplication facts. K–5.
Mathsheet	Houghton Miff.	All operations. Easy-to-use worksheet generator, correlated with Houghton Mifflin's basals, but usable with other texts. 1–8.
Mathware System "S"	Mathware	All operations; CMI. 2–8.
Mathworld Commander	Orange Cherry	All operations. 2–8.
Matt the Cat Math 1	Dynacomp	Addition and subtraction with one- and two-digit numbers. 2–3.
Meg-A-Math Series	Media Materials	Addition, subtraction, and multiplication.
Mel's Math Machine	CASA	All operations. Computer supplies a number, and the student races against the clock to create as many expressions as possible which equal that number. 1–10.
Meteor Math II	Brauer	Facts tables in space adventure-game format. 1–6.
Mickey in the Great Outdoors	Walt Disney	All operations. 2–6.
Micro Addition (other operations available)	Hayden	Counting and addition of whole numbers with animated pictures. K–5.
Micro-Math	ETA	All operations. Demonstrations and practice; automatic level adjustment. K–8.
Micro Math for Kids	Hayden	Two programs, microAddition/microSubtraction and micro-Multiplication/microDivision. Utilizes graphics and animation to teach operations with single-digit numbers and drill with two-place numbers. P–2.
Micro Math Magic	Deegan	All operations; CMI. 2–6.
Micrograms Math Games	Micrograms	All operations. Drill games. 3–6.
Micropower Elementary	Modern Curr.	All operations. 1–3; 4–6.
MicroTutor II: Arithmetic Skills	Scandura	All operations. Comprehensive tutorial and drill with well-designed CMI, including diagnosis, individualiza-

Title	Producer	Notes
		tion, and step-by-step instruction through carefully sequenced skill levels (see Chapter 2). "Meaning" level, however, starts with numerals in expanded notation, not graphics. 2–8.
Middle School Mathematics	MCP	All operations; concepts and skills. Inexpensive software developed by teachers. 6–9.
Mighty Math	World Book	Addition, subtraction, multiplication. Mighty Math World Book. All operations in a game format. Choice of levels. 1–5.
Milt's Math Drills	Hartley	All operations. Some CMI. K–4.
Mind Warp	Micro Power	All operations. 2–6.
Minit/Maxit/Targit	Milliken	Addition and subtraction. Students try to find the minimum or maximum number, or a target number by selecting numbers from a grid and adding (subtracting) the selected number to (from) their score. Involves strategic choices. 2–6.
Missing Math Facts	Gamco	All operations; fill in missing component. 3–6.
Mr. Math Arithmetic Tutor	Term	All operations. Students work problems on screen; solution demonstrated if necessary. Some CMI. 1–5.
Mixed Math Exercises	Centurion	All operations; mental computations. K–6.
Mixed Numbers	Media Materials	All operations. 1–6.
Monkey Math	Scholastic	All operations in arcade format. 1–3.
Monster Math	IBM	Addition. 1–6.
Monstrous Addition	Opp. Learning	Addition to three digits. 3–4.
Multi-BECi	Boston	Multiplication. 2–4.
Multi-fun	Ed. Soft. Cons.	Multiplication. 2–4.
Multi-Play-Cation	Class Tech.	Multiplication.
Multipix	NTS	Multiplication facts and graphic representation of grouping. 2–4.
Multiplication	MCP	Multiplication. Several activities, including drill and conceptual work, some CMI. 5–9.
Multiplication	Orange Cherry	Multiplication of whole numbers. 3–6.

(continued)

TABLE 7-1 (Continued)

Title	Producer	Notes
Multiplication and Division	Silver Burdett & Ginn	Basic facts for two- and three-digit division. Tutorials. 3–6.
Multiplication: Basic Concepts	Control Data	Multiplication. Tutorial and practice on algorithms and properties. 1–12.
Multiplication Magic	Deegan	Multiplication drill and practice.
Multiplication Puzzles	MECC	Multiplication. Drill and practice aimed at whole-number multiplication from basic facts through one-digit times three-digit multiplication with regrouping. Based on the mastery learning concept, students are guided to choose programs of increasing difficulty as they successfully complete 80% of each set of problems. 3–4.
Multiplication Table	SVE	Multiplication facts. 1–6.
Multiplication Tables	IBM	Multiplication tables. 3–6.
Multiplication Tutor	Computer Island	Multiplication tutorial. 3–6.
Multiply/Divide	Moses	Multiplication and division; numbers to 120. 3–4.
Multiplying Single Digits	Resource	Multiplication. 1–3.
Nimble Number Facts	DCH	All operations. 1–5.
Number and Shape Recognition	Learning Well	Includes addition and subtraction. P–2.
Number Builder	Commodore	All operations. An arcade format, but one that develops thinking skills. 5–8.
Number Chase	SRA	All operations. 2–8.
Number Cruncher and Function Machine	Berta-Max	Equations and functions. 3–9.
Number Facts	Gamco	All operations with multiple levels of difficulty. Arcade game reward. Some CMI. 2–6.
Number Jumper	Micro-Ed	Adding a series of numbers quickly. 1–4.
Number Magic	Triton	All operations. Drill with color displays. 1–6.
Number Sea Hunt	Gamco	Addition, subtraction using illustrations. Some CMI. K–1.
Number Stumper	TLC	Addition and subtraction; recognizes multiple solutions and encourages mental computation. 1–5.
Number Tumbler	M & M	All operations. 2–6.
Numbers of Fortune	Fortune	All operations. Gamelike. 1–6.
Numbers on Parade	Micro Power	Multiplication tables. 2–5.
1-2-3 Digit Multiplication	Micro. Wrkshp.	Multiplication; some CMI. 3–9.

Title	Producer	Notes
Order of Operations	Micro. Wrkshp.	All operations. 4–10.
Overflow I	Micro. Wrkshp.	All operations. Overflow a bucket game. 1–4.
Path Tactics	MECC	Practice in the basic operations on whole numbers in a problem-solving race game setting. Can promote strategic thinking as well. Seven levels. K–6.
Peanuts Math Matcher	Random House	All operations. 2–7.
The Pet Professor	Cow Bay	All operations; some CMI. 3–8.
Piece of Cake Math	Springboard	All operations; uses pictorial models. 2–7.
Pinball Math	Taylormade	All operations. 1–6.
Plato Match Series	Plato/WICAT	All operations. 1–7.
Playful Professor	Screenplay	All operations. 1–6.
Plot-a-Point	World Book	Provides practice in adding, sub-tracting, and multiplying, and in simple plotting of points. The arith-metic operations utilize a number line. For example, in multiplying, students are allowed to press a key to move a cursor in "jumps"; that is, for 6 × 28, they would move it forward 28 units with each of six keypresses. 1–5.
Prescriptive Math Drill	Hartley	All operations; drill with CMI. 1–4.
Primary Math Tutor	Comm*Data	Addition and subtraction. 1–4.
Prism Math 1	Psych. Corp.	All operations; a testing program for monitoring progress. 3–8.
Progressive Math Series	CompEd	Addition and subtraction. Some CMI. K–3.
Put Together, Take Away	Media Materials	Addition and subtraction. 1–4.
Puzzle Works: Circus Subtraction and Animal Addition	Continental	Addition and subtraction. Fill in a grid to see a picture. 1–3.
Pythagoras and the Dragon	Krell	All operations. Fantasy game in which player gets clues based on speed and accuracy of completing math problems. 3–12.
Quations	Scholastic	All operations. Create number sen-tences in a crossword-type format. 4–8.
Quotient Quest	MECC	Division, some with remainders. 4.
Quotient Quiz	Teacher's PET	Division. Which number divided by 4, 5, and 7 results in a given re-mainder?

(continued)

Title	Producer	Notes
Race Car 'Rithmetic	Unicorn	All operations in race-car format. K+
Salina Math Games	Ed. Act.	Multiplication with some management. 3–9.
Schoolhouse Arithmetic Series	Schoolhouse	All operations. Includes testing. 1–10.
Ships Ahoy	Unicorn	All operations. K–8.
Shipshape Math	Data Command	All operations in a game format. 4–8.
Simple Addition	Resource	Addition. 1–3.
Simple Division	Resource	Division. 1–3.
Six Second Club	Micrograms	All operations. Fact drill.
Slam Dunk	Micro-Ed	Subtraction. 2–5.
Snoopy to the Rescue	Random House	Addition in fantasy format. 3–12.
Soccer Math	Scholastic	Addition, subtraction, and multiplication. 3–8.
Soft Text: Math	Continental	All operations. Computer programs and paper activites. Some CMI optional. 1–6.
Software for Basic Math	Love	All operations. Tutorials, tests, games, and some CMI. 1–6.
Solving Addition and Multiplication Problems	MCE	Addition and multiplication word problems.
Space Equations	Opp. Learning	Arcade drill. 4–8.
Space Math	Learning Well	All operations; some CMI. 1–6.
Space Probe: Math	Walt Disney	Multiplication and division in space adventure. 2–8.
Space Subtraction	MECC	Subtraction. Five involving whole-number subtraction from "facts" to three-digit minus three-digit numbers without regrouping. 1–3.
Spaceship	MECC	Addition of two groups, sums 1–10. P–2.
Spark-80 Mathematics	Precision	All operations. 103 disks with tutorials, drills, games, assessments, and some CMI. K–8.
Speed/Bingo Math	Commodore	All operations in game format. 1–6.
Speedway Math	MECC	All operations. Three games providing practice in basic facts. CMI component for 250 students. 1–6.
Stickybear Math	Weekly Reader/ Optimum	Addition and subtraction drill. Responding correctly allows the student to help Stickybear get out of various "sticky" situations. Animated objects at introductory lev-

Title	Producer	Notes
		els; automatic adjustment of difficulty with limited CMI. 1–4.
Stickybear Math II	Weekly Reader/ Optimum	Multiplication and division drill. Automatic adjustment of difficulty with limited CMI. 7 +.
Storybook Friends	Edupro	Addition and subtraction. K–3.
Subcat	Moses	Subtraction. 1–3.
Subtraction	Micro. Wrkshp.	Subtraction; some CMI. 1–8.
Subtraction: Basic Concepts	Control Data	Subtraction. Tutorials and practice on meaning of subtraction and facts. 1–9.
Subtraction Made Easy	Spinifex Software	Subtraction. Some CMI. 2–6.
Subtraction Magic	Deegan	Subtraction drill and practice. 2–6.
Subtraction Minus	The Professor	Introduces subtraction with and without regrouping. P–2.
Subtraction I and II	Resource	Subtraction. 3–5.
Subtraction Puzzles	MECC	Subtraction with regrouping. 3–4.
Subtraction Skills	Control Data	Subtraction. Review drill and applications. 1–9.
Subtraction Safari	Opp. Learning	Subtraction (minuends to 10). 1–3.
Subtraction Superheroes	Opp. Learning	Subtraction to three digits. 3–4.
Subtraction with Renaming	Bergwall	Subtraction of three-digit numbers. 2–4.
Success with Math	CBS	All operations on different disks. Algorithms illustrated step by step, analyses of errors. 1–8.
Sum Ducks	Spinnaker	All operations. 4–7.
Supermath II	Ed. Sys. Soft.	All operations; some CMI. 1–7.
The Sweet Shoppe	DCH	Addition and subtraction. K–3.
Talking Software	AIMS	All operations with speech. 3–6.
Tandy 500	M & M	All operations. Facts drilled in race-car format. Some CMI. 1–3.
Targets	Sunburst	All operations in a problem-solving format—student must combine a pair of numbers with operations to generate a target number. 4–adult.
Teacher's Aide	Dyncomp	All operations. Drill. 1–6.
Teasers by Tobbs	Sunburst	All operations. Good arithmetic practice in a problem-solving format. See text. 4–10.
Telemath	Psychotechnics	All operations; multiple games and activities for drill and practice. K–8.
Think Tank 1 & 2	Opp. Learning	Application of operations to word problems. 4–8.

(continued)

Title	Producer	Notes
Times	Teacher's PET	Multiplication. Timed drill. 3–6.
Times Tables	NTS	Multiplication. 2–5.
Tinka's Mazes	Mindscape	Addition. K–3.
Tink's Subtraction Fair	Mindscape	Subtraction. 1–4.
Treasure Cove Math	Opp. Learning	All operations.
A Treasure Hunt of Facts	Jostens	Addition and subtraction with speech. 1–6.
Tricks to Fast Mental	Zypcom	All operations. Mental arithmetic. 5+.
Trillium Basal Math-Ware	Trillium	Evaluation and management system for Macmillan Mathematics Textbook Series M. Administers tests and provides practice. See Chapter 2. 1–6.
Two-Minute Warning	Micro-Ed	Subtraction. 2–5.
Understanding Math	CCM	All operations are taught in four separate programs in this series. CMI, including survey and diagnostic tests that develop an individualized program for each student and the incorporation of both conceptual development activities and drill. See the text. 2–6.
U.S.S. Subtraction	Opp. Learning	Subtraction (minuends 11–18). 1–3.
WhizCalc I	World Book	All operations; drill. 5–12.
Whole Number Arithmetic	Ed. Micro. Sys.	All operations; modifiable. 2–8.
Whole Numbers: Practice	Control Data	All operations. Well-designed drill in a pinball-game format. 5–8.
Wonderful Wizard	CLC	All operations. P–6.
Word Problem Puzzles	Deegan	Student sets up addition, subtraction, multiplication, and division problems after reading problem.

FRACTIONS, DECIMALS, PERCENT, RATIO, AND PROPORTION

As with too many topics, students frequently have difficulty learning fraction and ratio concepts because they have been rushed too quickly to symbolizations and operations without developing solid conceptual understandings. Computer materials should make this situation better, not worse.

For example, children should have significant amounts of experience with conceptual models of fractions (i.g., manipulatives and pictures) and oral representations (a spoken "one-third") before dealing with symbols ("⅓"). Computer programs that rely too soon and too heavily on such written symbols and that fail to take advantage of graphic models are inappropriate for the introduction of fraction concepts and skills. Computer programs that provide *mappings* between *different* meaningful conceptual representations of fractions as well as between these representations and symbolic representations and symbol manipulation rules (e.g., multiplication), however, may serve appropriately as a bridge between the pictorial and the symbolic. They may help students solve problems relationally, rather than instrumentally sifting through all the rules they know—most of which are meaningless to them—in an attempt to find one that might work.

CAI: TUTORIALS AND DRILLS

In that light, let's examine Equality and Inequality (from the *Fraction Bars Computer Program*). All concepts are illustrated with pictorial fraction bars. For example, the first activity on the equality disk, "match two fraction bars," starts with two examples. One is shown in Fig. 8–1. The use of pictorial representations of fractions (the bars) is helpful, although it should be remembered that any single representation has weaknesses. For example, with bars it is easy to loose sight of what is "one," that is, the unit.

It is imperative that the graphic representation of fractions be concep-

EXAMPLE 1

THESE TWO FRACTION BARS HAVE THE SAME
SHADED AMOUNT. BOTH BARS ARE HALF
SHADED.

WHEN TWO BARS HAVE THE SAME SHADED
AMOUNT, THEIR FRACTIONS ARE EQUAL.

$$\frac{2}{4} = \frac{3}{6}$$

PRESS ⎡ RETURN ⎤.

FIGURE 8-1
An example from the *Fraction Bars
Computer Program.* (Scott Resources Inc.)

tually clear to students. How would you evaluate a sequence from the addition activity in *The Fraction Factory* (Fig. 8–2)?

One package that generally presents sound models—and has students act on those models— is the *IBM Elementary Mathematics Series.* In "Fraction Strips," students are shown a nonpartitioned whole and asked to mark 1/3 on a similar strip below it. (Answers that are "close" are accepted.) In the

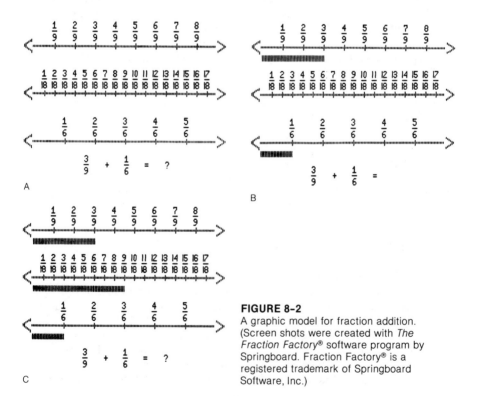

FIGURE 8-2
A graphic model for fraction addition. (Screen shots were created with *The Fraction Factory®* software program by Springboard. Fraction Factory® is a registered trademark of Springboard Software, Inc.)

next activity, they similarly shade the correct fraction of a set (3/4 of a set of 4, 8, or 12, etc.).

Students using "Comparing Fractions" see two fractions to the left of two unmarked fraction strips. They attempt to indicate which is greater. As feedback, they are shown the partitioned, shaded representations (Fig. 8–3). They then perform the inverse of the first activity, as they build a whole given a fraction. Other activities extend these skills and introduce comparisons on a pan balance, building equivalent fractions (Fig. 8–4) and simplifying fractions. Importantly, students work with the conceptual models first as a basis for later numerical manipulation.

To develop abilities involving addition and subtraction with fractions, a fraction strip model is presented. Students have to decide what "equal parts" to mark off on a number line (e.g., the common denominator). If they are incorrect, they receive graphic and written feedback showing them that, for example, "You cannot find the answer in fifths."

Similarly, the sequences with arithmetic operations with decimals allow children to use a decimal model to subtract (Dienes blocks graphically represent decimal numbers). Students press single keys to create ones, tenths, and hundredths. They can "break" (regroup) any of these at any time that is necessary (Fig. 8–5). Finally, they "recolor" to show subtraction.

Such lessons help students form close links between meaningful graphic representations and fractional symbols. Students are forming a frame for fractions that includes many relationships between different frac-

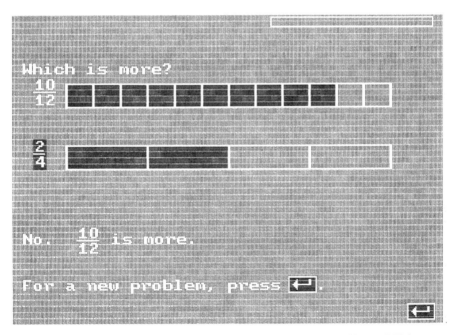

FIGURE 8-3 Feedback provided by the Comparing Fraction activity. (IBM/WICAT Systems Inc.)

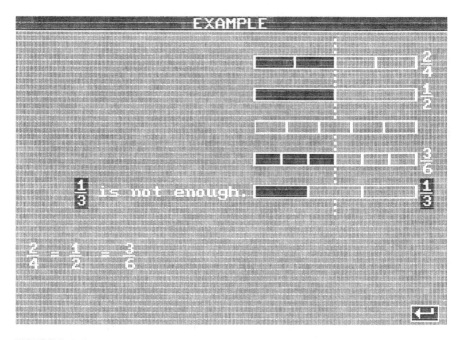

FIGURE 8-4 Building equivalent fractions. (IBM/WICAT Systems Inc.)

tional ideas. Students virtually take apart fraction ideas and put them back together, and in so doing begin to build up an organized *structure* for understanding and solving fraction problems. Let us not forget: The graphic model must be sound, but students do not abstract the mathematical idea from such models, but from their *actions* on these models. "Concrete activities" *are* beneficial, but this phrase should refer to students' mental activities, not to manipulatives.

Interactive video programs have the potential to offer especially effective representations. Bejar and Swinton (1984) have created interactive

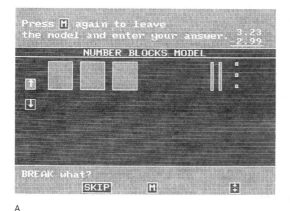

A

FIGURE 8-5

A Dienes blocks model is used for subtracting decimals. Sample screens show one student breaking or regrouping the 3.23. In (a), (b), and (c) a ones block is being broken into 10 tenths blocks. In (d) one of these tenths blocks has been broken into 10 hundredths blocks, which are moving one-by-one up to the top of the screen. (IBM/WICAT Systems Inc.)

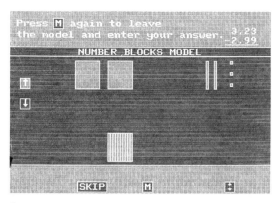

B

FIGURE 8-5 (*Continued*)

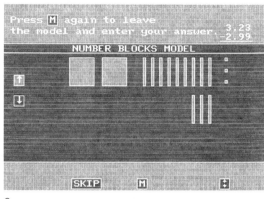

C

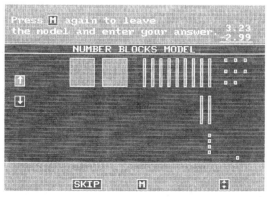

D

videodisk programs for teaching fractional concepts to third and fourth graders. Motivation is engendered by embedding the lessons in a series of dramatic sketches about a space crew on a rescue mission. The video production is similar to that of educational TV programs, but interactive video allows the students to be directly involved in the action by having to solve fractions problems related to the ongoing action. Another promising videodisk series is *Mastering Fractions/Mastering Decimals and Percents.* These minicourses cover a wide range of basic concepts, especially those with which students frequently have difficulty. The program follows a whole-class demonstration model. Teachers control the videodisk with a remote keypad. First, the class watches a dynamic video tutorial. The narrator then asks questions, and the teacher stops the presentation to allow students to work the problem. Depending on the students' success, the teacher can branch to any segment of the lesson to illustrate a point or provide remediation. A particular strength of the videodisk format is the potential for presenting conceptually clear pictorial models.

Fraction Concepts: Other Examples.

"Darts," and the many imitators it has spawned, is an example of a game in which the mathematics is intrinsic to the content and structure of the activity. In it, students explore the placement of rational numbers on the number line. They shoot darts at balloons attached to the number line by estimating their positions on the line (Fig. 8–6). These estimates can be in the form of fractions, decimals, mixed numbers, and expressions. When a dart hits the line, students receive significant mathematical feedback that goes beyond "right or wrong." They see how their guesses relate to other positions on the line. They can use this information to correct misconceptions (such as "$-1\frac{1}{2}$ will be between -1 and 0") and as a valuable referent for their next guess (e.g., "That 3/8 was just a little too high. I bet 5/16 will get it"). It opens the way for serendipitous learning, as when a student first guessed 3/4 and then 6/8 and discovered the darts hit the same point. Another student was startled to find that there was a number between 6/7 and 7/8! Finally, it encourages the construction of strategies, such as using the width of a pencil for a unit (which might be 1/15 on the number line), or purposely shooting 1/5, 2/5, 3/5, and 4/5, regardless of the balloons' placements, just to get reference points.

Number Quest challenges students to find a number that the computer has choosen at random. For example, in "Fractions" and "Decimals" children see a number line from 0 to 1 and must find a fraction or decimal in as few guesses as possible. In "Decimals," the computer chooses a three-place decimal number. Students then guess a number (e.g., .5). The program then provides numerical and graphic feedback by showing the more constrained interval at the bottom of the screen and darkening that interval in the original 0 to 1. This continues—after each place is determined (starting with the tenths), a new number line is created illustrating the darkened segment of the segment above it (e.g., the second line in Fig. 8–7 shows the darkened interval from 0.9 to 1, which is expanded on the third line to show the further narrowed interval of 0.94 to 0.95, which is likewise expanded

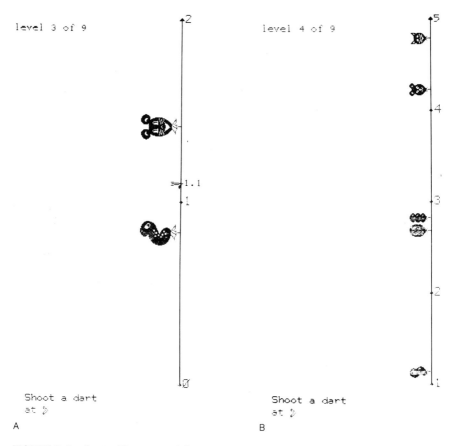

FIGURE 8-6 *Darts.* (Courtesy of Control Data Corporation)

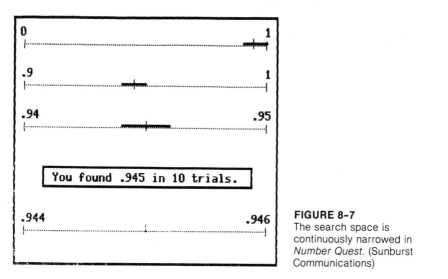

FIGURE 8-7
The search space is continuously narrowed in *Number Quest.* (Sunburst Communications)

on the third line, and so on). This illustrates the continuously narrowing search space. Students who use these games often are surprised to discover that there are numbers between 0.35 and 0.36 (or between 3/4 and 7/8) or that 0.128 is not larger than 0.3.

Get to the Point includes three activities addressing that same problem—children's misconceptions regarding order of magnitude of decimals. In "Point of Order," students are presented with two numbers. The challenge is to type a number between these two "endpoints" as many times as possible. When a correct number is typed, that number becomes one endpoint; the number from the old interval to which it was closest becomes the other (e.g., given the interval between 0.355 and 0.905 as in Fig. 8–8, if the student typed 0.478, the new interval would be 0.355 to 0.478). Therefore, to play the game as long as possible, the student must understand the ordering of decimal numbers and must be able to choose numbers that fall as near as possible to the center of the interval (e.g., choosing 0.630 would have left a larger interval and thus would have prolonged the game).

Another activity, "Point in Question," provides practice in arithmetic operations with decimals, emphasizing the placement of the decimal point. It presents problems such as "1.6 ÷ ? = 0.4". If students respond with "0.4," they are shown:

$$1.6 \div ? = 0.4$$
$$1.6 \div 0.4 = 4$$

and are asked to try again.

In "Fraction Clues" (*Mathematics Activities Courseware*), players take turns comparing two fractions, such as 7/8 and 7/10. If they answer correctly immediately, they get 3 points. If they hesitate, a unit fraction and an equivalent fraction clue are given (Fig. 8–9a). A correct answer now is worth 2 points. After another hesitation, more elaborate hints are supplied (Fig. 8–9b). A correct answer now earns 1 point. If the player is incorrect or runs out of time, no points are earned.

Arithmetic Operations: Other Examples.

Several programs provide step-by-step instruction followed by practice. For example, in *Success with Math,* a tutorial then proceeds through each step of a sample problem, asking the student to decide on the proper step

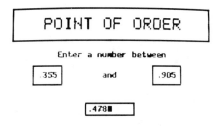

FIGURE 8-8
Get to the Point. (Sunburst Communications)

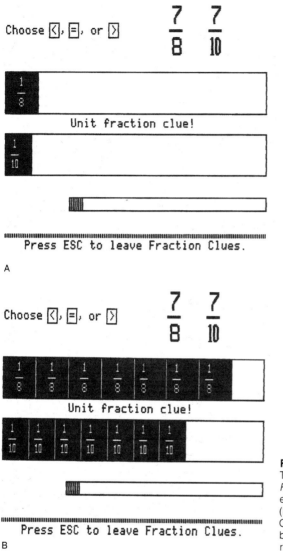

A

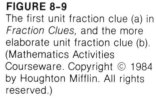

B

FIGURE 8-9
The first unit fraction clue (a) in *Fraction Clues,* and the more elaborate unit fraction clue (b). (Mathematics Activities Courseware. Copyright © 1984 by Houghton Mifflin. All rights reserved.)

(e.g., change to least common denominator, add, reduce, etc.). After one incorrect choice, a hint is given; after two, the correct answer is provided. After each problem, a summary of errors is listed. A similar summary is provided after a problem set. In a similar vein, recall the example from the tutorial/drill program *Adding Fractions* in Chapter 2.

Mathematics Activities Courseware (MAC) includes several gamelike activities at varying levels. Players in "Fraction Hunt" have to capture six intervals on a number line between 0 and 10. To their present fractional number they add or subtract one fraction from a given set of eight fractions. Sometimes, of course, it is necessary to plan a combination of operations that will land the marker in the interval. This activity also reinforces estimation of fractional sums and differences. Teachers are advised to discuss some strategies; for example, given $3\frac{2}{7} - 1\frac{1}{2}$, students might reason that 1/2 is greater than 2/7, so the difference will be less than $3 - 1 = 2$. But the difference will be greater than $1\frac{1}{2}$ because $3 - 1\frac{1}{2} = 1\frac{1}{2}$. Therefore, the difference is between $1\frac{1}{2}$ and 2.

At the upper skill level, "Closing In" (on *Mathematics Activities Courseware*) challenges students to improve the accuracy of a decimal factor estimate within a set time limit. For example, with a goal **30.21 × N = 96.672,** a pair of students might substitute in turn:

30.21 × 3	= 90.63		
30.21 × 3.1	= 93.651	Closer	This player gets 1 point.
30.21 × 3.4	= 102.714	Further	This player's opponent gets 1 point.

Students should be guided to use increasingly sophisticated strategies (see Chapter 10). For example, an (intuitive or explicit) understanding of the distributive law might have helped the student who saw his opponent guess 3.1. Seeing that the product had to be about 3 higher (i.e., 96.672 − 93.651), and noticing that 3 is about one-tenth of 30.21, a logical estimate would have been one-tenth (0.1) higher than the previous guess: 3.1 + 0.1 or 3.2. In fact, that estimate would have yielded the exact answer and two bonus points.

Ratio and proportion. "Equal Ratios" from the *IBM Elementary Mathematics Series,* presents a recipe for baking two cakes. Included in this recipe are 3 cups of flour. The activity then shows a picture of 2 cakes with 3 cups of flour and describes the ratio as 2:3. It says, "For 4 cakes, you would need 6 cups of flour." The ratio of cakes to flour is 4:6. 2:3 and 4:6 are equal ratios. This is extended to 6:9. Students are then asked to type a ratio equal to a given ratio.

The problem-solving program *Gears* can be formalized as a proportion problem (a proportion is a statement that two ratios are equal). Students select the number of gears they wish to line up and the number of teeth for each gear. Then, given the number of rotations of the first gear, they are to predict the direction and number of times the last gear will rotate (Fig. 8–10). Before reading on, try to figure out the relationships (even without the aid of the computer simulation!).

FIGURE 8–10
Gears. (Sunburst Communications)

The direction of rotation, of course, depends only on whether there is an odd or even number of gears (as each gear reverses the direction of rotation of the one driving it). The number of times the last gear will rotate depends on a composition of proportions. Generally, the proportion governing the relationship of two gears is

$$\frac{t}{T} = \frac{R}{r}$$

where t and T are the number of teeth and r and R are the number of revolutions in a given time period for the smaller and larger gears, respectively. Therefore, in Fig. 8–10, if the first gear on the left (with 9 teeth) is turned 10 revolutions, the second (with 5 teeth) will turn 18 revolutions ($5/9 = 10/r$, $5r = 90$, $r = 18$). How many times will the gear on the right (with 13 teeth) turn?

What's missing?   Many of the activities discussed to this point demand the use of problem-solving skills. Too often missing, however, is the provision by the computer of a link between symbols and a conceptual (usually graphic) representation for rational numbers. This link is especially necessary in feedback for errors, and it is here that it is least likely to be seen. Also frequently missing is an "intelligent" analysis of the errors students are making, with appropriate remediation. It can be hoped that software with these characteristics will begin to appear. Regardless, teachers need to ensure that students connect the symbols for rational numbers to a conceptual model and to use the knowledge they have about mathematics to evaluate the reasonableness of their results.

LOGO EXPLORATIONS

As we have discussed, there is no reason to attempt to explore every topic with Logo just for its own sake. Logo should be used when it makes a unique contribution. It would seem, therefore, that common fractions would be the last topic we would approach with Logo. After all, most versions of Logo normally express fractions in decimal form, and, if ⅓ is typed, Logo immediately applies division, returning a decimal approximation of ⅓, such as 0.333333333. (*Object Logo* for the Macintosh is a notable exception; given ⅓ + ½, it returns ⅚.) Although these difficulties exist, interesting and worthwile Logo explorations can be designed. If not the most palpable application of Logo, these explorations do illustrate the inherent flexibility of the language and the way Logo challenges can lead to creative solutions.

One teacher demonstrated procedures she had written to draw a bar (rectangle) of specific dimensions and to return to the "starting" position on the bar (Fig. 8–11a). She challenged her students to recreate these procedures and then challenged them to construct as many ways as they could to partition the bar into equal parts. They began with just two parts. After sharing their solutions, the class discussed the advantages of each, as well

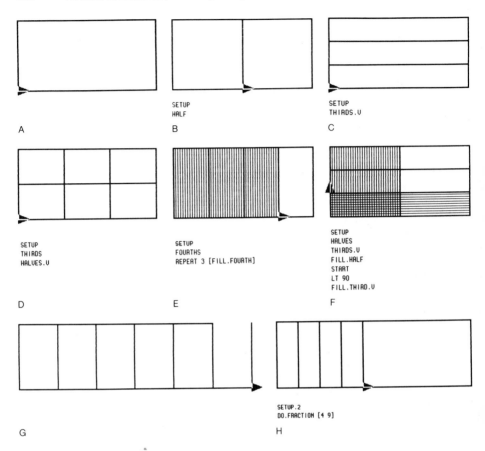

FIGURE 8-11 Logo fractions.

as the merits of different names for the procedure. HALF emerged as one good way (Fig. 8-11b).

Then they wrote procedures to partition the bar into other numbers of equal parts and procedures to partition the entire bar (e.g., THIRDS and FOURTHS). They discussed generalizations such as:

As the number that named the procedure (e.g., FOURTH, SIXTH, EIGHTH) increased, the distance the turtle initially goes forward—and thus the size of the piece—decreased.

To write a procedure to partition the whole bar, such as EIGHTHS, you always REPEATed EIGHTH 8 times (i.e., 8 EIGHTHS make 1 whole).

Students then compared fractions, especially to find those that are equivalent (each fraction was actually drawn in a different color; unfortunately, this feature—along with the more essential feature of animation—

cannot be reproduced in this book). For example, typing THIRD, then START, then SIXTH SIXTH (or, REPEAT 2 [SIXTH]).

At this point, students printed their fractional figures, cut them out, labeled them, and used them as manipulatives in their regular classroom work as well as for planning future Logo explorations. Many students made their own uniquely sized fraction bars; useful discussions followed the question: "Will we all get the same answers?" (Of course, work with other manipulatives preceded this Logo work.)

A student suggested that procedures could be constructed that partitioned the bar vertically (e.g., THIRD.V, Fig. 8–11c). After the class accepted the challenge and wrote and explored these procedures, they combined the horizontal and vertical partitionings to look at equivalent fractions from a new perspective; for example, typing THIRDS and HALVES.V might illustrate that 1/3 is equivalent to 2/6 (Fig. 8–11d). With further work and teacher guidance, students generalized that both the numerator and denominator may be multiplied or divided by the same number to generate equivalent fractions (e.g., try THIRDS and HALVES, then THIRDS and THIRDS.V, and so on).

The teacher posed some fractional problems such as "Tammy, Chuck, and Jill each ate a fourth of a candy bar. How much was eaten in all?" Students showed their solutions by typing instructions similar to SETUP FOURTH FOURTH FOURTH. Some saw that REPEAT 3 [FOURTH] was another solution, and noticed that it was another way of representing three-fourths. Others wrote procedures to fill, or shade in, a given unit fraction (Fig. 8–11e).

One student typed HALF, then START (to return to the "beginning") and THIRD. She was interested in the difference between the two, which was smaller than the THIRD. She typed FOURTH, but was disappointed. She started over and tried SIXTH. It worked. The turtle landed exactly on the "half" mark.

The horizontal and vertical partitionings also served well to illustrate multiplication of fractions. For example, Fig. 8–11f shows how a pair of boys represented 1/2 × 1/3 = 1/6.

A small group of bright children thought of generalizing the fraction procedures to work with any fraction. But what fractional notation can we use? If students type 2/3, a division occurs. We need a different representation. Logo's lists work well. A fraction might be represented as a list: 2/3 as [2   3]. Then we need some basic tools. NUMERATOR and DENOMINATOR are simple but useful for writing understandable procedures.

```
TO NUMERATOR :FRACTION              [Outputs the numerator of
                                     any fraction it is given
                                                (as a list)]
 OUTPUT FIRST :FRACTION
END

TO DENOMINATOR :FRACTION
 OUTPUT LAST :FRACTION
END
```

```
PRINT NUMERATOR [3   5]
3
PRINT DENOMINATOR [3  5]
5
```

Now the students needed to construct the fraction. Their procedure DO.FRACTION repeats UNIT.FRACTION a number of times equal to the numerator of the fraction. DO.UNIT.FRACTION is the generalization of THIRD, FOURTH, and the like. Working on these initial procedures, students saw that they were always dividing the width of the bar by the denominator of the fraction, then turning, drawing a line, and turning back. This is precisely what the procedure does.*

```
TO DO.FRACTION :FRACTION
  REPEAT (NUMERATOR :FRACTION) [DO.UNIT.FRACTION
  :FRACTION]

END

TO DO.UNIT.FRACTION :FRACTION
  FD (:WIDTH / DENOMINATOR :FRACTION)
  LT 90
  FD :HEIGHT BK :HEIGHT
  RT 90
END
```

Of course, these procedures also need SETUP.2 and START.2 procedures to show the unit, give values to such variables as :WIDTH and :HEIGHT, place the turtle, etc.
They are:

```
TO SETUP.2
  MAKE "HEIGHT 120
  MAKE "WIDTH 360
  HOME
  START.2
  UNIT.BAR
END

TO START.2
  HT
  PENUP
  HOME
  BK 59
  RT 90
  BK 215
  ST
  PENDOWN
END

TO UNIT.BAR
  REPEAT 2 [(FD :WIDTH ) LT 90 (FD :HEIGHT ) LT 90]
END
```

Most proper fractions could now be expressed easily (e.g., Fig. 8–11g). Previous procedures such as "thirds" now becomes simply DO.FRACTION [3   3] (with a START.2 to return the turtle to the starting position). One boy made a serendipitous discovery when, in an effort to type DO.FRAC-TION [5   6], he mistakenly entered DO.FRACTION [6 5] (see Fig. 8–11h). After some puzzlement, he figured out what had happened, and even duplicated his result with REPEAT 6 [FIFTH].

The teacher asked all her students to use these procedures to compare fractions with the same numerators but different denominators (e.g., 2/3 and 2/4), with the same denominators but different numerators (e.g., 2/5 and 3/5), and with different numerators and denominators (e.g., 3/5 and 2/3). Where possible, generalizations were made (e.g., if the numerators are the same but the denominators are different, the fraction with the smaller denominator is greater).

These procedures generate simple graphics, but they can encourage and support complex learning. Why is this type of work valuable?

The construction of the procedures is valuable in relating work with fractions to that with Logo, especially in the creation of one's own fractional representations with mathematical and computational symbols.

It combines two important representations, the rectangular region and the number line. In the latter, fractions as the length of segments are emphasized rather than as names for points. This helps avoid confusion for students. Importantly, it is also a dynamic representation.

Relational understanding is necessary in solving the problems and in translating between representations (e.g., THIRD THIRD; REPEAT 2 [THIRD]; DO.FRACTION [2   3]; etc.). Instrumental manipulation of numerical representations such as 2/3 would not suffice.

Fast, accurate manipulations can be made once the procedures are developed, encouraging explorations and extensions. In addition, procedures themselves can be altered easily and almost instantly redrawn. Students can try out several ideas in minutes with precision.

How would one perform arithmetic operations on numerical fractions directly in Logo? This would be helpful—those who work with computers have usually been frustrated at one time or another by decimal approximations of fractions. With the list representation we discussed, it is possible. As a complement to NUMERATOR and DENOMINATOR, a procedure called FRACTION, which takes two numbers as inputs and outputs our fractional representation, will be helpful (see Fig. 8–12 for all procedures).

```
SHOW FRACTION 3 5
[3 5]
```

It might also be helpful to print this fraction in the form 3/5. This can also be accomplished.

```
PR.FRACTION FRACTION 3 5
3 / 5
```

```
TO FRACTION :NUMERATOR :DENOMINATOR
OUTPUT LIST :NUMERATOR :DENOMINATOR
END
```

Makes a fraction (a list) out of any numerator and denominator it is given.

```
TO PR.FRACTION :FRACTION
TYPE NUMERATOR :FRACTION
SPACES 1
TYPE "\/
SPACES 1
TYPE DENOMINATOR :FRACTION
PRINT "
END
```

Prints a fraction (given as a list) in the form "3/5."

In some versions of Logo, the backslash "\" allows you to print special characters, such as spaces and division signs.

```
TO SPACES :NUMBER
REPEAT :NUMBER [TYPE "\ ]
END
```

Types a given number of spaces (type a space after the \).

```
TO REDUCE :FRACTION
LOCAL "DIVISOR
MAKE "DIVISOR GCD NUMERATOR :FRACTION DENOMINATOR
  :FRACTION
OUTPUT FRACTION ( NUMERATOR :FRACTION ) / :DIVISOR
  (DENOMINATOR :FRACTION ) / :DIVISOR
END
```

REDUCEs a fraction to its lowest terms.

Finds the GCD of the numerator and denominator (type all on one line).

Outputs the fraction produced by dividing the numerator and denominator by the GCD.

```
TO GCD :NUMBER1 :NUMBER2
IF NOT :NUMBER2 > 0 [OUTPUT :NUMBER1]
OUTPUT GCD :NUMBER2 REMAINDER :NUMBER1 :NUMBER2
END
```

Euclid's algorithm for finding the greatest common divisor.

```
TO MULTIPLY.FRACTIONS :FR.1 :FR.2
LOCAL "NUM LOCAL "DEN
MAKE "NUM ( NUMERATOR :FR.1 ) * ( NUMERATOR :FR.2 )
MAKE "DEN ( DENOMINATOR :FR.1 ) * ( DENOMINATOR :FR.2 )
  OUTPUT REDUCE FRACTION :NUM :DEN
END
```

Multiplies two fractions and outputs the product in lowest terms.
Store the product of the numerators.
And the denominators.
Output the REDUCEd form of the FRACTION created by these.

```
TO ADD.FRACTIONS :FR.1 :FR.2
LOCAL "NUM LOCAL "DEN
MAKE "NUM
      (NUMERATOR :FR.1) * (DENOMINATOR :FR.2 )
    + (DENOMINATOR :FR.1) * (NUMERATOR :FR.2 )

MAKE "DEN
      (DENOMINATOR :FR.1) * (DENOMINATOR :FR.2 )
  OUTPUT REDUCE FRACTION :NUM :DEN
END
```

Multiplies two fractions and outputs the product in lowest terms.
Store the sum's numerator. This is the sum of the numerators of the addends; here we assume that they are *renamed* to be fractions with a like denominator, which is.....
Store the sum's denominator—the product of the denominator of the two addends.
Output the REDUCEd form of the FRACTION created by these.

FIGURE 8-12 Fraction manipulation procedures.

We could immediately write a multiplication procedure, which could simply multiply the numerators and denominators of two fractions, producing a result such as the following:

```
SHOW FIRST.MULTIPLY.FRACTIONS [1 2] [2 5]
[2 10]
```

or

```
PR.FRACTION FIRST.MULTIPLY.FRACTIONS [1 2] [2 5]
2 / 10
```

But let's wait. We may want to have our answer in lowest terms. We'll put a REDUCE operation in our multiplication procedure (Fig. 8–12) and then think about how we might create it. For this purpose, GCD comes in handy (this is GCD.EUCLID from Chapter 6). Once we have found the greatest common of the numerator and denominator, we simply need to divide both the numerator and denominator by that number and create a FRACTION from the results (Fig. 8–12).

```
SHOW REDUCE [6 8]
[3 4]
```

or

```
PR.FRACTION REDUCE [2 8]
1 / 4
```

Now we can multiply more elegantly (using procedures from Fig. 8–12).

```
PR.FRACTION MULTIPLY.FRACTIONS [1 2] [2 5]
1 / 5
```

It is imperative that students check these (and all other) procedures with manipulatives or even with the previous "bar" Logo procedures. Adding fractions is a bit more involved. One way is to find the sum of two equivalent fractions, as in

$$\frac{1}{3} + \frac{2}{5} = \frac{5}{15} + \frac{6}{15} = \frac{11}{15}.$$

Note that the new denominator is the product of the denominators of the factors, and each numerator is renamed by multiplying it times the denominator of the other factor. Figure 8–12 shows the corresponding Logo procedure, which utilizes REDUCE to output the sum in its lowest terms.

```
PR.FRACTION ADD.FRACTIONS [1 2] [1 6]
2 / 3
```

Some students might wish to return to their original, "written word" representation of fractions. They might write procedures such as

```
TO ONE.HALF
  OP [1 2]
END
```

```
TO ONE.THIRD
  OP [1 3]
END
```

This allows such instructions as

```
PR.FRACTION (ADD.FRACTIONS ONE.HALF ONE.THIRD)
5 / 6

PR.FRACTION (MULTIPLY.FRACTIONS ONE.THIRD ONE.HALF)
1 / 6
```

Can you write a procedure that more closely mirrors the traditional approach of using the least common denominator, instead (recall the LCM procedure in Chapter 6)? Can you invent procedures for division (write two, one using GCD and one "invert and multiply" using MULTIPLY.FRACTIONS)?

Why should students write Logo procedures which perform algorithms they can already work on paper?

> When students are learning new reasoning skills, it is helpful to apply them first to topics about which they already have some knowledge and intuition.
>
> Students may become more conscious of the rules behind manipulations. Programming helps make such rules explicit and promotes a "debugging" approach to the application of these rules.
>
> A powerful idea from computer science is being introduced incidentally and informally: *data abstraction.*

We have created a new type of object in Logo, a fraction, just by defining procedures that "glue together" a numerator and a denominator to form a fraction (FRACTION), called *constructors,* and that select the numerator and denominator from a fraction (NUMERATOR and DENOMINATOR), called *selectors.* Notice that all other procedures we write do not have to know how fractions are made. They use only these three basic procedures. In the method of data abstraction, we separate those parts of the program that deal with how a representation of fractions is constructed from those parts that actually use the fractions.

However, there is an important warning: Such Logo explorations are not easy, especially the latter ones that use lists. They are appropriate if students have substantial Logo experience and easy access to a knowledgeable teacher. Even the initial tasks of drawing fractional representations may not be appropriate for Logo novices. In this case, *teachers should develop the procedures,* then assign tasks for students to complete using these procedures (of course, more advanced students could always be asked to modify or extend them). Students do not have to develop all the procedures. In fact, for many, too much attention can be diverted to procedure writing and too little given to the mathematics involved. This is especially true if students have not worked with Logo as a tool for doing mathematics in all preceding grades. Students must work at the *correct level of representation.* For example, developing a "pie" procedure for representing fractions would waste many students' time in the complexity of developing the procedure. They might benefit, however, from using procedures already developed by the teacher. *Give students any and all tools they need to work on the mathematics they need.*

Ratio and proportion can be studied in the context of typical work with turtle geometry. For example, during a project we conducted (Clements & Merriman, in press), one pair of bright third graders were creating a city. They had constructed one building but wanted to revise the procedure so that it would draw buildings varying in size. Initially, they used two variables, for the height and width. However, there were problems. For example, the "shape didn't always look right" (Fig. 8–13a). Worse, with other buildings the windows were either "weird" (Fig. 8–13b) or "ridiculous" (Fig. 8–13c) according to the students' evaluations. They were introduced to the

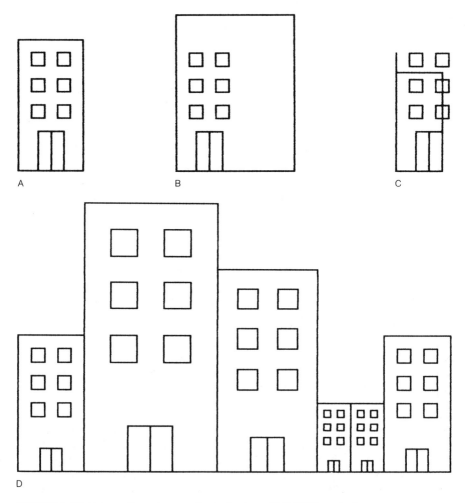

FIGURE 8-13 Using ratio and proportion in the Logo BUILDING procedure.

notion that all the lengths in the procedure had to be expressed in terms of their relationship to one another (in proportion).

They reconceptualized the procedure as one based on one input only—the width of the building. They figured that the height would be two times the width. Windows posed the biggest challenge. Cathy finally figured that "there's two distances across for the windows, then three more for spaces—between the left side and the first window, between the windows, and between the right side and the second window. That's five. The windows will be the width divided by 5 and so will the spaces." Similar reasoning led to the final procedures (Fig. 8–14). The final city scene—filled with proportional buildings—is shown in Fig. 8–13d.

```
TO BUILDING
 RECT 100 50
 RT 90
 FD 16
 LT 90
 RECT 30 8
 RT 90
 FD 8
 LT 90
 RECT 30 8
 RT 90
 BK 24
 LT 90
 FD 90
 RT 90
 REPEAT 3 [WINDOWS]
 LT 90
 BK 30
END

TO WINDOWS
 REPEAT 2 [PU FD 10 PD
    SQUARE 10 FD 10]
 PU BK 40
 RT 90
 FD 20
 LT 90
END

TO SQUARE :SIDE
 REPEAT 4 [FD :SIDE RT 90]
END

TO RECT :HEIGHT :WIDTH
 REPEAT 2 [FD :HEIGHT RT 90
    RTFD :WIDTH RT 90]
END
```

```
TO BUILDING.2 :WIDTH
 RECT :WIDTH * 2 :WIDTH
 RT 90
 FD :WIDTH / 3
 LT 90
 RECT :WIDTH / 3 :WIDTH / 6
 RT 90
 FD :WIDTH / 6
 LT 90
 RECT :WIDTH / 3 :WIDTH / 6
 RT 90 BK :WIDTH / 2
 LT 90
 FD :WIDTH * 9 / 5
 RT 90
 REPEAT 3 [WINDOWS.2
    :WIDTH / 5]
 LT 90
 BK :WIDTH * 3 / 5
 RT 90
 FD :WIDTH

 LT 90
 PD
END

TO WINDOWS.2 :SIDE
 REPEAT 2 [PU FD :SIDE PD
    SQUARE :SIDE FD :SIDE]
 PU BK :SIDE * 4
 RT 90
 FD :SIDE * 2
 LT 90
END
```

FIGURE 8-14 The BUILDING procedure. The initial procedures are on the left; the final procedures are BUILDING.2 and WINDOWS.2.

CAI and Logo approaches to the study of fractions often differ considerably, even in their goals. However, both should help students establish valid conceptualizations of fractions and fractional procedures. Both should promote relational understanding.

SUGGESTED READINGS

Behr, Wachsmuth, Post, and Lesh (1984), in this and several other articles, describe students' development of ideas about rational numbers. What implications do their findings—especially those concerning misconceptions—have for the use of computer programs?

TABLE 8-1   Software: Fractions, Decimals, Percent, Ratio, and Proportion*

Title	Producer	Notes
Add/Subtract Fractions	JMH	Addition and subtraction of fractions with like and unlike denominators.
Adding Fractions	Scholastic	Practice in the steps of adding fractions. 5–8.
Addition and Subtraction of Fractions	Courses by Com.	Concepts and skills in addition and subtraction of fractions and mixed numbers. Some CMI, including mastery tests and diagnostic placement tests.
Adventures with Fractions	MECC	Ordering unlike fractions, tutorial and gamelike practice. 5–8.
Adventures with Decimals, Fractions, and Negative Numbers	IBM	Decimals, fractions, and negative numbers in game format.
Arithmetic Classroom	Sterling Swift	Lessons on basic concepts, comparing and rounding, and the four operations. Tutorials and practice, using sound pictorial models. Similar to Elementary Mathematics Classroom Learning System, but without the CMI component. Recommended. 4–8. (Also available from DCH as the "New Arithmetic Classroom.")
Basic Math Competency: Fractions	Ed. Act.	Tutorial and practice on addition, subtraction, multiplication, and division of fractions. Some CMI. 4–6.

*Note: Many CAI programs that provide tutorials and practice on computations with fractions and decimals were listed on Table 7–1.

Title	Producer	Notes
Batting Average	Amer. Peri.	Uses batting averages as setting for practice with converting fractions to decimal equivalents. 5–8.
Blast Off, Lightning	Schoolhouse	Addition and subtraction of decimals. 4–9.
Cannon Attack	Schoolhouse	Multiplication and division of decimals. 4–10.
Compare Fractions I and II	Teacher's Pet	Drill on comparing two fractions through cross-multiplication and computation of common denominators, but no graphics and limited help. 5–9.
Comparing Decimals	Micrograms	Inserting $<$, $>$, or $=$ between two decimal numbers. 5+.
Compubar	Milliken	Adding and subtracting bar lengths. 4–8.
Concentration	Milliken	Equivalent fractions in a concentration-game format. 4+.
Decimal	Cow Bay	Search for patterns in a decimal equivalent after inputting the numerator and denominator of a fraction. 5–8.
Decimal—%	Teacher's Pet	Drill on conversion of decimals and percentages. 5–8.
Decimal Discovery	DLM	Drill on decimal concepts in arcade setting.
Decimal Series	JMH	Separate programs. Includes: Representing decimals; finding the smallest or largest of given decimal numbers; estimation and rounding; all operations on decimals with emphasis on placement of the decimal point. 3–8.
Decimal Concepts and Skills	Courses by Computers	Meaning and use of decimals, including operations. Tutorial and practice segments. Some CMI, including mastery tests and diagnostic placement tests.
Decimal Concepts/ Operations	Mathware	Concepts and operations. 4–8.
Decimal Conversion 2	JMH	Converting decimals to common fractions. 3–8.
Decimal Dungeon	Unicorn	All operations. Arcade game format. 5–9.
Decimal + and −	Teacher's Pet	Addition and subtraction drill to hundredths. 6–8.

(continued)

TABLE 8-1   (Continued)

Title	Producer	Notes
Decimal X	Teacher's Pet	Multiplication. 4–12.
Decimal Skills	Media Materials	All operations with decimals. Students enter all subcalculations. Can get step-by-step instruction via a "help" key. Some CMI. 6–8.
Decimal to Fraction	JMH	Tutorial in converting decimals to fractions. 4–8.
Decimals	Control Data	Designed to develop ability to perceive and define distances using fractional numbers. Variation of the "darts and balloons" activity. Well designed; includes CMI. 3+.
Decimals	Gamco	Two packages, one on addition and subtraction, the other on multiplication and division. Students work exercises on paper and enter their answers. Some CMI. Adventure-game rewards. 2–8.
Decimals	JMH	Converting, estimating, rounding, and comparing decimals.
Decimals	Micro. Wrkshp.	A series of programs, including all operations with decimals. Drill with some tutorial. 5–8.
Decimals	Orbyte	Identify largest number and match fractions with decimal names. 5–6.
Decimals	Peachtree	All operations, percentage, rounding off, and conversion.
Decimals	QED	Tutorial and game/exploration activities. Reading decimals; multiplying and dividing by multipliers of 10; addition, subtraction, multiplication, and division; fractional equivalents primes and common multiples; pi; etc. (advanced) 5–12.
Decimals	Silver Burdett & Ginn	Computation of fraction and conceptual tutorial. 4–8.
Decimals: Addition and Subtraction	Gamco	Addition and subtraction of decimals. Guided drill. Some CMI. 3–8.
Decimals: Addition, Subtraction, Multiplication, and Division	NTS	All operations; tutorial and drill. 5–9.
Decimals Drill Program	MSS	All operations and converting fractions and decimals. 5–7.
Decimals Equivalent	Orybte	Writing fraction, decimal, and per-cent names to find a lost treasure. 5–6.

Title	Producer	Notes
Decimals I and II	Microphys	All operations (two on each program). Drill; reports student performance. 4–8.
Decimals, Per Cent, and Fractions	NTS	All conversions. Tutorials and drills. 5–9.
Decimals, Percents, Ratios and Proportions	Media Materials	All operations with decimals; finding the percent of a number, finding a base number, and percent word problems; writing ratios and proportions in context, solving word problems. Some CMI. 6–8.
Decimals: Practice	Control Data	A version of the "darts" game for locating the decimal number for a point on a number line. 4–6.
Decimals Primer	Merit Audio	Decimal and money skills. 4–8. Other packages in the series include "Decimals–Percent Practice."
Decimals: Terminology and Concepts	Control Data	Meaning, all operations, and applications for decimals. 3–8.
Dolphin	Houghton Miff.	Wide range of skills covered in this comprehensive program. 1–8.
Edu-Ware Decimals	EduWare	All operations and rounding with decimals. Some CMI. 4–8.
Edu-Ware Fractions	EduWare	All operations on fractions. Some CMI, including diagnostics. 4–8.
Elementary Mathematics Classroom System: Fractions and Decimals	Sterling Swift	See "Arithmetic Classroom."
Elements of Mathematics	Elec. Course.	Adding, reducing simple and complex fractions. Drill with some CMI, including useful instructor management options. 5–12.
Essential Mathematics	BertaMax	Drill on wide range of topics. Some CMI available. Fraction and decimal topics are grades 3–9.
Fast-Track Fractions	DLM	Drill on fraction concepts in arcade setting.
Figuring with Fractions	Micrograms	Introduction, operations, equivalent fractions. 5–7.
Fraction Action	PLATO/WICAT	Fraction exercises. 4–9.
Fraction Action	Unicorn	All operations in arcade-game format. 4–5.
Fraction and Mixed Number Recognition	EduSoft	Recognition of fractions and mixed numbers. Name the shaped portion of a display. 1–10.

(continued)

TABLE 8–1   **(Continued)**

Title	Producer	Notes
Fraction and Mixed Number Concepts	Courses by Computers	Meaning and use of fractions and mixed numbers. Tutorial and practice segments. Some CMI, including mastery tests and diagnostic placement tests.
Fraction Bars Computer Program	Scott Resources	Seven disks covering the fraction concepts of basic concepts, equality, inequality, addition, subtraction, multiplication, and division. See the text. 3–12 (probably intended as remediation in higher grades).
Fraction Drill	Math Arcade	Drill with some CMI.
Fraction Factory	Springboard	Fraction concepts and arithmetic operations. Increasing levels of hints, graphic aids. 3–9.
Fraction Fever	Spinnaker	Fraction concepts, including graphic representations and equivalent fractions, in arcade format. The documentation is somewhat brief in explaining the game. 2+.
Fraction Flip	SouthWest	Drill in concentration-type game format; identifying a pictorial representation of a fraction (and equivalent fractions) and, on level 2, decimal equivalents. Limited informative feedback. 5–8.
Fraction Frenzy	Orbyte	Addition, subtraction, multiplication. 4–10.
Fraction Fuel-up	DLM	Word problems in space game format. Reducing, renaming, and finding equivalent fractions; addition and subtraction of fractions and mixed numbers with like and unlike denominators. Some CMI. 3–8.
Fraction Fun I & II	Deegan	Develops skills in understanding, writing, and working with fractions.
Fraction Fun with Fraction Man	Edu-Link	Fraction concepts in drills and a game. 4–6.
Fraction Machine	SouthWest	Wide range of fraction skills. Drill with some diagnosis and CMI. 4–9.
Fraction Math Quiz	Creative Tech.	Multiple-choice drill on fraction concepts. 3–12.
Fraction Skills I and II	Orbyte	Writing fractions. 4–10.
Fraction Tutor	Telephone	Identifying illustrated fractions. 4–9.
Fraction Tutor	J. Weston Walch	Drill, despite the title, on identification of, and arithmetic operations on, fractions. Recommended only for the former. 4–8.

Title	Producer	Notes
Fraction Tutorial	Opp. Learning	All operations and reducing. Step-by-step tutorial with circle and square representations of fractions. Some CMI. 5–8.
Fraction + and −	Teacher's Pet	Addition and subtraction. 5–8.
Fraction ◊	Teacher's Pet	Multiplication. 5–8.
Fractions	Bergwall	Students determine and write fractions of geometric shapes. 2–4.
Fractions	Control Data	Practice identifying fractional intervals in a dart-game format ("Darts"). Well designed; includes CMI. 5+.
Fractions	Dorsett	Arithmetic operations with fractions, changing fractions to decimals, percents concepts, word problems. 4–8.
Fractions	Ed. Act.	All operations. Step-by-step tutorials and practice. Some CMI. 4–6.
Fractions	PDI	Arithmetic operations, equivalent fractions, decimal fractions, proper and improper fractions, etc., with voice narration. 4+.
Fractions	Peachtree	Definitions, denominators, and all operations. 4–12.
Fractions	QED	Tutorial and game/exploration activities, with some placement testing. 5–8.
Fractions	Micro. Wrkshp.	A series of programs including all operations with fractions. Drill with some helpful tutorial sequences but no graphics to aid conceptualization. 5–8.
Fractions	Silver Burdett & Ginn	Computation of fractions and concepts. 4–8.
Fractions: A Review Course	Random House	Fraction concepts and operations. 6+.
Fractions and Mixed Numbers	Scholastic	Step-by-step guidance on arithmetic problems with fractions and mixed numbers. 4–9.
Fractions: Addition and Subtraction	CBS	Part of the Success with Math Series. Drill of fractions with unequal denominators. At each step in the process, student must select the next procedure (e.g., change to least common denominator, add, or reduce). Provides reports to student on errors made. 5–8.

(continued)

TABLE 8-1   (Continued)

Title	Producer	Notes
Fractions: Addition and Subtraction (also Multiplication and Division)	Control Data	All operations; tutorials and practice.
Fractions, Decimals, and Percent	SVE	All operations, changing fractions to percents, word problems, and other topics (six-disk set). 6–8.
Fractions/Decimals	Control Data	Identifying fractional or decimal intervals between numbers on a line (variation on "Darts"). 4–6.
Fractions Diagnostic	Computer Island	Tutorial on operations. 4+.
Fractions Drill Program	MSS	All operations and reduction. 4–7.
Fractions Package	Micro-Ed	Equal fractions, mixed numbers and improper fractions, adding and subtracting. 4–8.
Fractions Series	NTS	Lowest common denominator and all operations. 5–7.
Fractions Tutor	Computer Island	Addition, subtraction, and multiplication. 4–6.
Fun Fractions	Taylormade	All operations and reducing fractions. Drill. 4–9.
Galaxy Math Facts Game	Random House	Drill in a fantasy format (see also their *Grand Prix*). Motivating program, with good documentation. 5–8.
Gears	Sunburst	Select the number of gears to line up and number of teeth for each gear. Given the number of rotations of the first gear, predict the direction and number of rotations for the last gear. 4+.
Get to the Point	Sunburst	Order of magnitude of decimals. Provides practice in ordering, challenges students to estimate and compute with decimals at varying levels of difficulty, then presents game in which students search for a mystery decimal chosen by an opponent. 5–9.
Growgains' Fractions	MECC	Ordering fractions with like denominators or like numerators, tutorial and gamelike practice. 5–8.
IBM Elementary Mathematics Series	IBM/WICAT	Comprehensive program. See the text.
Intermediate Math Skills	Orange Cherry	All operations on fractions, decimals, and percentages. 3–8.
Introduction to Decimals on the Computer	Ed. Act.	All operations with decimals. Especially for slow learners.

Title	Producer	Notes
Introduction to Fractions	Concept Ed.	Fraction concepts, operations, and conversions. 2–6.
Introduction to Fractions	Moses	Addition. 4.
The Language of Math (module 7)	Krell	Rates and ratios related to everyday situations.
Learning and Practicing with Decimals	RSI	Calculations and word problems with decimals. 5–7. Others in the series cover discounts and percents.
Learning Mathematics	Queue	Place value in decimal numbers; one part of a larger package. 5–6.
Mastering Fractions	Systems Impact	Videodisk 35-lesson minicourse. Individual, small group, or whole class.
Mastering Decimals and Percents	Systems Impact	Videodisk 15-lesson minicourse. Individual, small group, or whole class.
Mastering Mathematics: Decimals	Continental	All operations and word problems. Tutorials and drill. Some CMI. 5–8.
Math Action Game Series	Mindscape	Fraction and decimal practice in a bowling-game format. K–8.
Math Adventures with Mickey	Disney	Decimals and problem solving. 4–8.
Math Blaster	Davidson	Motivating arcade format. Can choose level or put in your own problems to be practiced. 1–7.
Math for Everyday Living	Ed. Act.	Fractions and percents in real-life situations. 4–6.
Math Marvels	Houghton Miff.	Decimal concepts. 3 + .
Math Masters	Houghton Miff.	Fractions and ratios; three games. 3 + .
Math Power Program	I/CT	Fractions, decimals, and percents are a part of this program. 1–6.
Math I	Pers. Com. Art	Fraction concepts and operations.
Math Shop	Scholastic	Students help in various stores in a mall by solving problems, each using a specific curriculum concept. In the jewelry shop, students are to choose the two decimal weights that, when summed, yield the desired quantity of gold. 6–9.
Math Skills: Elementary and Junior High	Britannica	Fractions, decimals, percents, ratios, and graphing. 4–9.
Math Wars	SouthWest	Fraction and decimal concepts in arcade-game format. 2–10.
Mathematics Activity Courseware	Houghton Miff.	Several activities in this series involve fractions, decimals, percent, ratio, and proportion. For example, level 3 includes a decimal skip-

(*continued*)

Title	Producer	Notes
		counting activity; level 4, activities on comparing fractions and estimating decimal addition and subtraction; level 5, activities involving equivalent fractions, addition and subtraction of mixed numbers, multiplication of fractions (area model), comparison of decimals, and multiplication of decimals; level 6 activities involve decimal concepts, multiplication of decimals, relationship of fractional and decimal representations, all arithmetic operations on fractions, and percents (see the text). Complete documentation, including corresponding worksheets. Coordinated with Houghton Mifflin's text series. 2–8.
Mathematics Courseware Series	Scott Foresman	Fractions, decimals, percents. Demonstration followed by drill. The fractions programs include activities on identifying what fraction of a whole and of a set is shaded, writing the numeric form of a fraction from pictures or words, writing equivalent fractions, solving word problems involving fractions, arithmetic operations on fractions, equivalent fractions, mixed numbers, etc. Similar programs for decimals and percents. 1–8.
Mathematics Software	Media Materials	Decimals, mixed numbers, and percent. 6–8.
Mathematics Strands	CCC	Strands on fractions and decimals. 4–8.
Mathematics Today Practice Diskettes	Harcourt Brace	Most concepts and skills. The series presents drill correlated with the publisher's text series. Embedded in gamelike activities; provide "clues" when students make errors. 2–8.
Mathfinder	Holt	Fractions, decimals, percents, proportions. K–6.
Mathware System "S"	Essertier	Some CMI.
McCoco's Menu	Computer Island	Select items from restaurant menu and add the prices in decimal form. 4–6.

Title	Producer	Notes
McGuffey's Fractions/ Decimals	Creat. Comm.	All operations on decimals, conversions, etc. 4–6.
Meaning of FracTions	CAE	Series of programs focusing on skills of writing a fraction from a description and demonstrating a fraction by creating a picture, manipulating objects, or selecting an appropriate representation. 1–6.
Metric I: Fundamentals of Decimals	CCM	Closely guided practice on "lining up the decimal point" in arithmetic operations. 3+.
Middle School Mathematics	MCP	Fraction, decimal, percent, and ratio concepts and skills. Inexpensive software developed by teachers. 6–9.
Micrograms Decimal Series	Micrograms	Introduction, all operations, and conversions. 5–7.
Middle School MCP	MCP	Variety of disks/activities on fractions and decimals.
Mister Math Fraction Arithmetic Tutor	Term	All operations. 4–7.
Mister Math Fraction Concepts Tutor	Term	Problems with fractions. Drill with step-by-step solutions to problems. 3–6.
Mixed Numbers	Media Materials	Converting mixed numbers to improper fractions, comparing mixed numbers and all operations. Step-by-step tutorial and drill. Some CMI. 5+.
Mixed/Improper Fractions	JMH	Representing and converting mixed and improper fractions.
Multiplication and Division of Fractions	Courses by Com.	Concepts and skills in multiplication and division of fractions and mixed numbers. Some CMI, including mastery tests and diagnostic placement tests.
Multiplying Fractions	Scholastic	Practice in the steps of multiplying fractions. 5–8.
The New Arithmetic Classroom	DCH	Comprehensive coverage, including concepts, arithmetic operations, and problem solving with fractions, decimals, and percents. Tutorials and drill. CMI. K–8.
Partial Fractions	Sunburst	Multiplication and division of fractions. Five levels. Teachers' options available. 4–8.

(continued)

Title	Producer	Notes
Percent Concepts and Skills	Courses by Com.	Meaning and use of percent, including finding the percent of a number. Tutorial and practice segments. Some CMI, including mastery tests and diagnostic placement tests.
Percentages	Ed. Act.	Tutorials and practice on percentage concepts and skills, including relationships to fractions and decimals. 4–9.
Percentages 1 and 2	Queue	Percentages, fractions, and decimals. Practice and games.
Percents	JMH	Representing, writing, and estimating percents, and solving rate-base-percentage problems. Other programs include "Percent-Base," "Percent-Rate," "Percentage." 3–8.
Percents	Media Materials	Rewrite percents in lowest terms, solve simple equations by division, solve simple proportions. Step-by-step tutorials and drill. Good documentation. Some CMI. 6–8.
Percents and Decimals	Dorsett	Conversions, rounding. 4–6.
The Pet Professor	Cow Bay	Fractions and decimals, all arithmetic operations. Demonstration and test modes. CMI is optional.
Pick the Numbers	DCH	Two games providing practice in ordering decimals and fractions along a number line (0–1). Student must pick the numbers in correct order while avoiding barriers. In the first game, they must select the number with the smallest value; in the second, the number represented by a question mark on the number line. Beginning and advanced levels; choice of fractions, decimals, or both. 4–7.
Pizza Fractions	HRM	Slicing pizza into fractional parts. 4–7.
PLATO Math Series	PLATO/WICAT	Decimals and fractions. 1–7.
Pre-Fractions Math Package	Micro-Ed	Introductory concepts, such as multiples, divisors, primes and prime factors, GCF, LCM; 2–6.
Problem Solving: Fractions and Decimals	Courses by Com.	Solving word problems with fractions and decimals. Tutorial and practice segments. Some CMI, in-

Title	Producer	Notes
		cluding mastery tests and diagnostic placement tests.
Proportions and Percents	QED	Tutorials and games on proportions and percents. 6–10.
Ratio, Proportion and Percent	Control Data	Tutorials and practice on multiple topics, including definition and application of ratio, proportion, and percent with a review drill. 3–7.
Ratio, Proportion and Percent	Silver Burdett & Ginn	Application of concepts. 5–8.
Ratios and Proportions	Ed. Act.	Several programs. Uses situations such as padlocks and keys to introduce ratio; simplifying ratios, solving proportions. Some diagnostics built in. 5–12.
Ratios and Proportions	JMH	Short tutorials and drill. 6–12.
Ratios and Proportions	Media Materials	Readiness skills, and using data to write ratios and proportions and to solve problems. Some CMI. Good documentation. 6–8.
Recognizing Fractions	Teacher's Pet	Identifying fractions from pictures. 3–6.
Salina Math Games	Ed. Act.	Several activities on topics such as finding equivalent fractions, operations with fractions, comparing fractions, reducing fractions, finding the fractional part of a number, mixed fractions, etc. Some CMI. 3–9.
Same	Teacher's Pet	Addition and subtraction of fractions with same denominators. Practice with some remedial tutoring. 4–8.
Shipshape Math	Data Command	Includes equivalent fractions, matching exercises in a game format. 4–8.
Simple Fractions	JMH	Representing, comparing, and reducing fractions.
Starship Alert	Opp. Learning	All arithmetic operations and reducing. Students must solve fraction problems to save a space city. 5–8.
Success with Math	CBS	All operations with fractions and decimals on different disks. Algorithms illustrated step by step, analyses of errors. 1–8.
Telemath	Psychotechnics	A variety of activities and games. 4–6.
Turtle Trot	Micrograms	Equivalent fractions. 5–6.
Tutorcourse	BLS	Wide range of skills. 5–8.

9

GEOMETRY
AND MEASUREMENT

GEOMETRY

Do you use geometry or arithmetic more often? (Are you saying, "I don't use geometry at all"?) You probably use arithmetic frequently. But consider: How many times have you arranged furniture, relying on your ability to visualize spatial relationships and your intuition about shapes and how they fit together? Have you estimated whether a particular container would hold some amount of leftovers? Have you given or asked for directions, employing such notions as distance, right and left turns, traffic circles, and parallel streets? Packed a car trunk or kitchen shelf? Arranged pictures? Appreciated architecture?

Even young students bring to the classroom myriad experiences with geometry. They have navigated, built, and played in a world filled with geometric shapes. Geometry's visual nature provides definite pedagogical advantages. It also contributes to a strong foundation for learning arithmetic and algebra. With all these advantages, you might think that geometry would hold a special place in the curriculum. In fact, there are serious problems with the geometry instruction in too many schools.

What's Wrong with the
Current Geometry Curriculum?

Geometry is a core subject in mathematics. According to extensive evaluations of mathematics learning, such as the National Assessment of Educational Progress (NAEP), there has been a "failure of students to learn basic geometric concepts" (Carpenter et al., 1980, p. 25), especially geometric problem solving. This poor performance is due, in part, to the current elementary school geometry curriculum. Indeed, geometry should be the study of objects, motions, and relationships in a spatial environment. Geometry instruction should develop geometric ideas, spatial visualization, and geometric problem-solving ability (Clements & Battista, 1986). First experiences with geometry should emphasize informal study of physical shapes and their properties and have as their primary goal the development of students' knowledge and intuition about their spatial environment. Subsequent experiences should involve analyzing and abstracting geometric concepts and relationships in a more formal setting. However, even a cursory glance at most elementary mathematics texts indicates that their major focus is on recognizing and naming geometric shapes and learning to write the proper symbolism for simple geometric concepts. There is little opportunity for geometric problem solving. There is little chance to develop students' spatial thinking, a commodity that has primary importance in the geometry curriculum (NCTM, 1980). There is little opportunity for students to analyze and reconceptualize geometric ideas. It is no wonder that after experiencing such an impoverished geometry curriculum in elementary school, many high school students do not have the necessary geometric intuition and background for a formal deductive geometry course. They are also not adequately prepared for the later study of important ideas such as vectors, coordinates, transformations, and trigonometry. Indeed, the current elementary geometry curriculum illustrates the "instrumental-oriented" curriculum discussed in Chapter 1.

Another deficiency in the current curriculum is that it does not always emphasize the topics or conceptualizations of topics that are most useful in the later learning of mathematics. For instance, the concept of angle normally encountered in elementary school is that of a union of two rays with a common endpoint—the same formal definition used in high school geometry. However, in trigonometry and calculus, an angle is thought of as a rotation. Existing elementary school geometry curricula do not address this second aspect of the angle concept, even though the latter aspect seems more closely related to navigation, "one of the most widespread representations of the idea of angle in the lives of contemporary Americans" (Papert, 1980, p. 68). In fact, interviews with third- and fourth-grade students suggest that students' first notions about angle are connected with navigation (Clements & Battista, 1988).

What should we be doing in geometry? Geometry instruction aided by the computer should be, paradoxically, both more and less formal than geometry as usually presented in schools. *More,* because it should allow students to go beyond the simple naming of shapes that comprises far too much of elementary geometry. Students should explore the properties of these shapes and begin to analyze these properties and their relationships. *Less,* because it should not stress anything like the deductive reasoning of two-column proofs that usually accompany this type of analysis in the later study of geometry. You know, the exercises in which students consider theorems that they already believe are true (because the teacher told them they were) and attempt to "prove" this truth (only because the teacher told them to, not because they felt any need for or interest in the task) by memorizing sequences of arguments that they often do not fully understand. Rather, students should generate and test hypotheses that are meaningful to them. Computers can play an important role in such a revised curriculum. They can motivate students to tackle significant geometric problems and provide the tools needed for their solution. They can serve as essential bridges between real-world manipulative experiences and more formal geometry.

CAI

Mrs. Harrison thought she had a geometric genius in her class. She had asked Erin what the shape in Fig. 9–1a was. The youngster had responded, "It's a triangle. That's a shape with three angles and three sides that meet at the vertices." Taken aback, Mrs. Harrison drew Fig. 9–1b and asked again, receiving a similar answer. Confidently, wishing everyone in the class to hear the definition a third time, she drew Fig. 9–1c and asked Erin, "And this is a triangle, is it not?" Erin said, flatly, "No." Disappointed, Mrs. Harrison asked, "Is it a shape?"

"Yes."

"Does it have three angles?"

"Of course."

"Does it have three sides?"

"Uh-huh."

"Do they meet at the vertices?"

"Yeah."

"Well, then, why isn't it a triangle"

"It's standing on its head!"

Even children well versed in definitions hold such misconceptions. Of course, orientation in space is irrelevant to the definition of a triangle. But narrow, static textbook presentations often reinforce such misconceptions. Examples are numerous. It might not be a triangle for a student if one angle is too large or too small, or if it "hangs over" (i.e., an obtuse triangle with a short side as its base). Or, it must be a triangle if any three points are connected by line segments, or if any three line segments are connected at their endpoints (can you find exceptions?).

Exploring Triangles provides several programs designed to help students construct clear conceptions, or schemata, about triangles. "Random Triangles" helps students recognize any three-sided polygon as a triangle and realize that size and orientation do not determine whether a polygon is a triangle. It generates three points that do not lie on a straight line and connects them to form a triangle. This initial experience is extended in "Three Points," wherein students choose three points on the screen. When the third point is plotted, a triangle is formed unless the three points lie on a line, in which case students read: "NOT A TRIANGLE! DO YOU SEE WHY?"

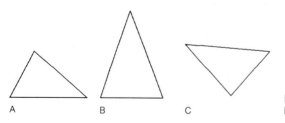

A   B   C

FIGURE 9-1
Erin's triangles.

The goal of the next activity, "Constructing Triangles," is to convince students that the sum of the length of any two sides of a triangle must be longer than the third side. Students choose three line segment lengths and manipulate them on the screen. Two of the segments can be rotated around the vertex at which they connect to the third (Fig. 9–2a). If a triangle cannot be made, copies of the lengths are animated to illustrate that the two shorter lengths are not longer than the third side (the right segment moved up next to the left segment at the bottom of Fig. 9–2b).

Students playing *Trap-A-Zoid* must construct a variety of polygons so as to trap (enclose) a small creature (a "zoid") before it moves from the left side of a grid to the right. They connect lines on the grid to block its path. These lines, however, must finally form a specific polygon. Once the zoid is trapped inside a polygon, a point is earned for the student. When seven such points are earned, the student advances to the next level.

Even young children can use appropriate geometry programs. In fact, one study showed that kindergartners benefited equally from computerized and a teacher-directed programs for learning about shapes (von Stein, 1982). Perhaps more promising, however, is a different approach to developing such abilities. Working with preschoolers, Forman (1986) found that certain graphics programs offer a new, dynamic way of drawing and exploring geometric concepts. For example, a "Boxes" function allows children to draw rectangles by stretching an electronic "rubber band." Using this stretching process gives children a different perspective on geometric figures. The area fill function, which fills closed regions with color, prompts children to reflect on such topological features as closure as the consequences of *actions,* rather than merely as characteristic static shapes. The power of such drawing tools lies in the possibility that children will internalize the functions, thus constructing new mental tools.

Thus, numerous other programs are available for teaching geometric concepts (see Table 9–1). They range from drill to tutorial to more exploratory approaches. Whatever type best suits your teaching need, any geometry

TO FORM A TRIANGLE

TWO SIDES TOGETHER MUST BE LONGER

THAN THE THIRD SIDE.

BASE :	⋯⋯⋯⋯⋯⋯⋯⋯	75	BASE :	⋯⋯⋯⋯⋯⋯⋯	75
LEFT :	⋯⋯⋯⋯	45	LEFT :	⋯⋯⋯⋯⋯	45
RIGHT :	—	25	RIGHT :		25
A			B		

FIGURE 9-2 Try getting these sides to form a triangle! (*Exploring Triangles,* Encyclopedia Britannica Educational Corp. Distributed by Looking Glass Learning Products, Inc.)

program should help students build complete and accurate frames and avoid misconceptions.

Coordinate graphing. The *Elementary Mathematics Series* introduces co-ordinate graphing in an active way by having students move a cursor (an "X") around a grid, marking the point, and naming the point in another way as "over 2, up 3," or—a shorter way—as (2, 3). They then construct and label several points, finally connecting them to create figures. Such games (e.g., Hurkle) are designed to develop the ability to describe location with a coordinate and to establish horizontal and vertical references. Several programs have variations of the game battleship, such as *Naval Battle*. In Fig. 9-3, a student is placing her ships to begin play. They will be hidden after each has been placed. Then each player specifies coordinates in an attempt to sink the other's ships. Of course, students should also engage in similar noncomputer activities. For example, a class might use the array of desks as a coordinate system ["Student at desk (3,5) please call out the next coordi-nate," or "All students whose coordinates sum to 6 please stand up"]. They might also extend their work to street maps and coordinates on the globe.

Those recently introduced to Logo sometimes are not aware that a complete set of instructions for using coordinate geometry are available in addition to those of standard turtle geometry. Students might draw pictures based on coordinates. Other activities include using the turtle's coordinate system as a computerized geoboard and writing procedures that replicate string art. As an example of the latter, Fig. 9-4 presents a procedure that takes four inputs, the initial X and Y coordinates for the starting point and ending point for each line segment. The graphic suggestion of a circle, and

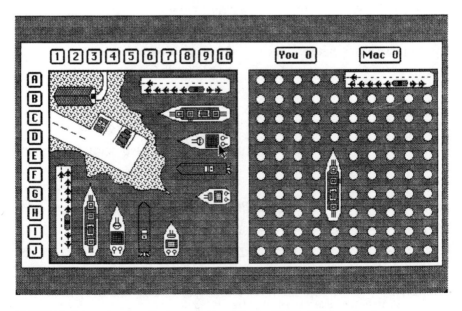

FIGURE 9-3 Learning coordinates with *Naval Battle*. (Nordic Software, Inc.)

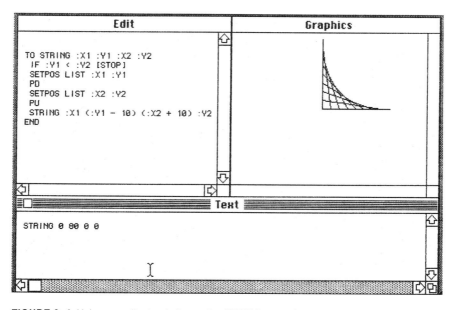

FIGURE 9-4 Using coordinates in Logo: the STRING procedure.

the many interesting designs that can be created, are motivating for many students. Figure 9–5 illustrates a design that is produced by combining four simple variants of STRING. Can you write the three missing ones? (*Hint:* Those producing the left side merely use a negative X coordinate; those on the bottom "move":Y1 in a different direction.)

Spatial visualization. The ability to manipulate images mentally is shared by many who are talented geometers. Several programs provide experiences with this ability. For example, students might design "products" in the *Factory*. Given a picture of the way the product should appear, they

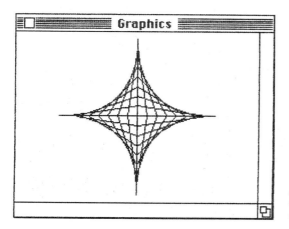

FIGURE 9-5
A design that was produced by combining four simple variants of STRING.

reconstruct the sequence of machines and processes used for its creation (Fig. 9–6). Recall that one class worked with an in-class, concrete assembly line to dramatize the sequencing of machine operations that created a product. This helped many of the students form mental models of these processes, especially that of rotation.

The *Super Factory* extends these explorations to three dimesions. A cube is built by students. They rotate it and place different pictures or designs on each side. This introduces them to the three-dimensional aspects of the two-dimensional representation of the cube. The next step is to design a similar cube with a "planning sheet." Then students are shown a cube that is rotated to show all sides. The challenge is to re-create the cube on a planning sheet and, when finished, display it alongside the model.

Number Quest includes two binary search activities in two- and three-dimensional space. In the latter, for example, students have to enter X, Y, and Z coordinates in an attempt to find a point within a three-dimensional figure. The program responds to their guesses by redrawing the search space, shading in the volume in which the hidden point lies, and labeling the corners that represent the lowest possible remaining values for each coordinate and the highest possible values (Fig. 9–7).

Tangrams Puzzler allows students to manipulate simple geometric shapes with simple commands (slides and turns) so to form a picture. The shapes appear on the left, their number codes on the top right, and the goal picture on the bottom right (Fig. 9–8). Students can ask for a clue; the position of one shape is shown (Fig.9–8 shows such a clue—the position of one triangle is revealed). They can also see the answer (i.e., the picture would show the placement of each shape) or the solution (i.e., each shape on the left move into the correct position). Students can use a permanent set or they can construct and use their own set.

Motions (or transformations) are basic geometric processes. In addition, work in this area can have a positive impact on students' spatial visualization abilities. Mathematically, a transformation is a one-to-one correspondence, or mapping, between a set of points on a plane and themselves; between a shape and an image of that shape. In the elementary grades, they are better thought of as *motions*. We will discuss three important motions.

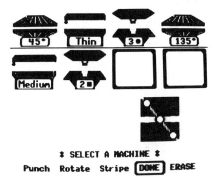

FIGURE 9-6

In *The Factory,* students rotated the product 45 degrees, made a thin stripe, punched three round holes, rotated another 135 degrees, made a medium stripe, and punched two square holes. (Sunburst Communications.)

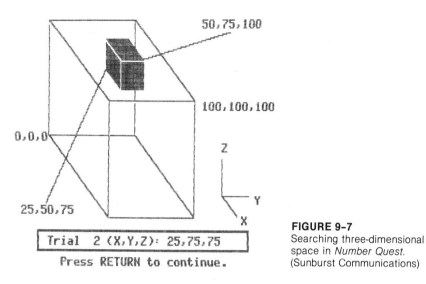

FIGURE 9-7
Searching three-dimensional
space in *Number Quest.*
(Sunburst Communications)

In a *slide* (formally, a translation) each point in a shape is "slid" along a line (i.e., each point moves the same distance and direction). In a *turn* (rotation) each point is turned a certain number of degrees about some point (i.e., each point is moved along an arc whose center is the turn center). In a *flip* (reflection) each point is "flipped" over a line (i.e., each point is reflected across some line in the plane).

One property of these motions is that they always move a figure to a figure with the same size and shape (i.e., a congruent figure). For this reason, they are called *rigid motions.* They are the only motions that have this prop-

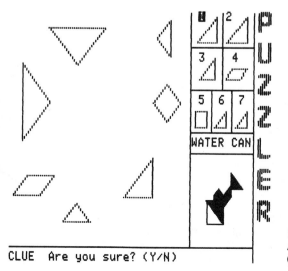

FIGURE 9-8
A clue in *Tangrams Puzzler.*
(Milliken)

erty; therefore, any motion that produces congruent figures must be a slide, flip, turn, or some combination of them.

In *Funky Chicken*, students practice two-dimensional motions while trying to position a chicken so that it will catch a fly. They might be told, for instance, that the flies will make five moves:

1. Flip over vertical line.
2. Flip over horizontal line.
3. Turn counterclockwise 180°.
4. Flip over horizontal line.
5. Flip over horizontal line.

The students would visualize the effects of the motions on the flies, then choose a sequence of motions for the chicken that would put it in a position to eat the flies (see Fig. 9–9). Can you determine the surprisingly simple sequence for the chicken on this problem?

The object of *Tip 'N Flip* is to find the moves (flips and turns) that will transform a pattern so that it matches the pattern given by the computer. Students must mentally flip and turn the pattern until they believe they know the correct sequence of moves. They can use a scratch pad that allows them to turn and flip the pattern, although each scratch pad move costs one point.

Similar experiences can also be made available in Logo, especially with the provision of microworlds such as MOTIONS. The Logo program carries out rigid motion transformations of the plane. Students issue commands to perform turns and flips and compositions of these motions. They can also define a new motion in terms of existing ones. In most of the activi-

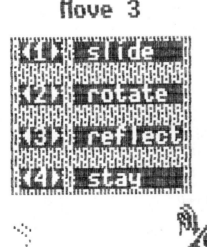

FIGURE 9–9
Motions in *Funky Chicken*. (Encyclopedia Britannica Educational Corp. Distributed by Looking Glass Learning Products, Inc.)

ties, students specify a motion for a flag, predict where it will move the flag, instruct the computer to perform the motion, and compare their prediction with the result. They then receive visual and numeric feedback. Students might be provided additional challenges:

1. Use the motions to create as many different symmetrical figures as you can.
2. Here is a transparency that duplicates the computer screen and the flag. Tape it to your screen and determine the motions required to move the computer's flag from its initial position on top of that on the transparency.

The first few such challenges might involve a single motion. More difficult are combinations of motions. The most difficult is to find the three or fewer motions that are always sufficient! The full Logo language presents a wide range of opportunities for geometric explorations. We consider them next.

Logo and Geometric Construction Programs

Geometry, as studied in Logo, is substantive rather than factual; it promotes relational rather than instrumental understanding, and is thus fundamentally different from the geometry presented in current elementary school texts. To see this, consider the concept of rectangle. In the usual elementary geometry curriculum, students are required only to be able to identify a visually presented rectangle (a first-level, or visualization, activity in the van Hiele hierarchy). In Logo, however, students can be asked to construct a sequence of commands (a procedure) to draw a rectangle. This forces them to make their concept of rectangle explicit. They must analyze the visual aspects of the rectangle as a whole and make conclusions about its component parts (a second-level van Hiele activity). In the words of Papert: "The computer allows, or obliges, the child to externalize intuitive expectations. When the intuition is translated into a program it becomes more obtrusive and more accessible to reflection" (1980, p. 145). With proper teacher guidance, this program can then be used as material "for the work of remodeling intuitive knowledge" (p. 145). That is, by designing a rectangle procedure or program, students are beginning to form an abstract definition of a rectangle (a third-level van Hiele activity); they are externalizing their intuitive ideas about rectangles.

Writing procedures to construct geometric shapes helps students analyze the properties of those shapes. Running the program on the computer allows them to test the validity of their definition, to reflect on their conceptualization. Through such experiences, not only are students progressing into higher levels of geometric thinking in the van Hiele hierarchy, they are building conceptual structures or schema about rectangles that can be useful in other situations, such as drawing quadrilaterals, triangles, or regular polygons, and are thus learning geometry relationally.

So, the point of using activities such as Logo and geometric construction programs is to emphasize "doing geometry" and solving geometric problems rather than learning geometry facts. Students seek questions as much or more than answers. They investigate rather than memorize.

Because some of the best Logo explorations are not teacher centered, and because possible applications of Logo to geometry instruction are virtually limitless, only a few examples of Logo activities can be offered here. Additional ideas are provided in the suggested readings at the end of the chapter.

The SINGLEKEY program introduced in Chapter 4 is not merely a way to introduce young children to Logo. It can also be used for many interesting geometric explorations. (In fact, in the one-to-one correspondence of commands and graphic steps, students are experiencing the concept of function at an intuitive level.) Remember that each F is equivalent to FD 10, each R to RT 30, and so on. The following activity uses these simple commands to explore regular polygons, patterning, similarity, and congruence.

Ask students to predict what the following pattern of SINGLEKEY commands will draw: FFFLLFFFLL . . . (try this yourself before reading on!). Have them try this on the computer. The result is a six-sided polygon with all sides the same length and all angles the same measure (a regular hexagon; see Fig. 9–10a). Predict and verify the following patterns: FFFRRFFFRR . . . (Fig. 9–10b); FFFFLLFFFFLL . . . (Fig. 9–10c); and FFLLFFLL . . . (Fig. 9–10d). In what ways is the figure created by the second pattern the same as the original (same size and shape)? Different (orientation)? How does the third compare to the original (same shape; larger)? The fourth (same shape; smaller)? What shape would you predict for FFFFFLLFFFFFLL . . . (Fig. 9–10e)?

Review the original hexagon. Have students predict and verify the figure created by FFFLFFFL . . . (this produces a different shape—a 12-sided figure called a regular dodecagon; Fig. 9–10f). Point out that one L yielded a twelve-sided figure; two Ls a six-sided one. What would three Ls yield (i.e., FFFLLLFFFLLL . . .)? Students may predict a triangle; however, this pattern actually creates a square (Fig. 9–10g). What produces a triangle (FFFLLLLLFFLLLLL . . . ; an equilateral triangle, Fig. 9–10h)? How would you create a larger triangle? Smaller?

Have students create their own patterns of commands, predict what figure will be constructed, and verify their predictions. They might also define the figures as procedures and use them to construct additional designs. Reinforce the concept that regular polygons with similar turns are similar in shape. The number of Fs determines the size of the figure.

Following are some examples of additional explorations:

1. How many identical small squares does it take to construct a square with sides twice as long as the original square? Triangles? Pentagons (five sides)? Hexagons?

2. What shape do you predict will be created by each of the following patterns? Can you create an interesting modification of these patterns? (To save time,

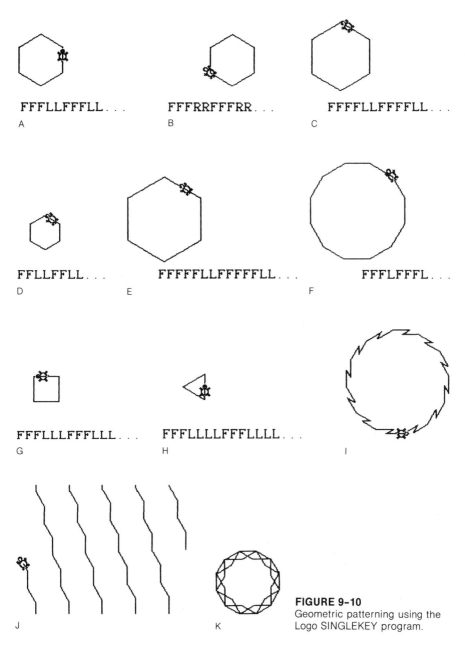

FFFLLFFFLL...
A

FFFRRFFFRR...
B

FFFFLLFFFFLL...
C

FFLLFFLL...
D

FFFFFLLFFFFFLL...
E

FFFLFFFL...
F

FFFLLLFFFLLL...
G

FFFLLLLFFFLLLL...
H

I

J

K

FIGURE 9-10
Geometric patterning using the
Logo SINGLEKEY program.

guide students to define one or two segments of the pattern as a procedure;
then call that procedure repeatedly.)*

```
FFLFFRRR . . .
FFLFFR . . .
FFLLLFFRRR . . .
FFLBBRRR . . .
FFLBBRR . . .
FFLBRR . . .
FFLBBLFFR . . .
FFLFFLBR . . .
```

Why do some patterns close (returning to the starting point), whereas
others do not close (moving increasingly farther from the starting point)?
Can you find patterns within the patterns? Later, students might be challenged to draw these shapes using regular Logo instructions. (Indeed, the
entire exploration could easily be conducted with the regular Logo commands, REPEAT, FD 10, BK 10, RT 30, and LT 30.)

A popular and worthwhile Logo exploration concerns procedures to
draw any regular polygons. A few days before beginning such an exploration, one teacher purposely had challenged her students with a version of
the "Multiplication and REPEAT" activity from Chapter 7. For this challenge, the students had to write as many instructions in the form REPEAT
4 [RT 90] that would rotate the turtle "completely around" as they could.
This provided a valuable supportive experience when the students tackled
the challenge of writing a procedure that would draw regular polygons. The
reason for this should become clear. To begin the exploration, the teacher
guided the students in listing the basic information from each of the procedures they had already generated.

Shape	Instruction	
triangle	REPEAT 3	[FD 40 RT 120]
square	REPEAT 4	[FD 40 RT 90]
pentagon	REPEAT 5	[FD 40 RT 72]
hexagon	REPEAT 6	[FD 40 RT 60]

From this, they constructed a table. The last column, which represents
the product of the previous two columns, was added last, as a result of students' search for patterns.

Shape	# Sides	# of Turns	° Turn	Total ° in Turns
triangle	3	3	120	360
square	4	4	90	360
pentagon	5	5	72	360
hexagon	6	6	60	360

Thus, it could be seen that each figure contained a total of 360° rotation
("Of course!" proclaimed one girl, "It's got to go all the way around!"). Some

*Figures 9–10i–k were produced by three of these patterns. No "answers for the teacher" this
time! Try to match them to the commands. Draw what the others will produce.

members of the class remained unconvinced. The teacher had them use the slow RT procedure (see Chapter 4) in several of the REPEAT instructions, gradually reducing the size of the input to FD:

```
REPEAT 6 [FD 30 RT 60]
REPEAT 6 [FD 20 RT 60]
REPEAT 6 [FD 10 RT 60]
REPEAT 6 [FD 5 RT 60]
REPEAT 6 [FD 0 RT 60]
```

The students saw that the turns remained the same; as the length of the sides was reduced to zero, the "complete turn" was quite evident.

The teacher then asked: "Will this be true for any closed shape, or only for regular polygons?" Debate was lively, with neither side convincing the other. The teacher had students construct as many closed figures as they could, keeping track of the rotations. Some students proclaimed that they had found shapes that contained less than 360°; however, others pointed out that they had forgotten to turn the turtle back to its original heading. One boy found a shape (an "arrowhead") that he said had 540°:

```
TO ARROWHEAD
  FD 120
  RT 150
  FD 120
  RT 150
  FD 44
  LT 90
  FD 44
  RT 150
END
```

After examining the procedure, however, a classmate pointed out that one of the turns was a LEFT. "That's going around the other way. It should be subtracted." Indeed, this yielded 360°.

The teacher directed attention back to the table. She asked, "How would we fill in the next row, for a hexagon?" Students quickly filled in the first, second, and—not quite as quickly—the last column. The teacher said: "How could we find the correct turn?"

hexagon 6 6 ? 360

Soon, the students decided it must be 360 ÷ 6, or 60°. A few seconds at the computer verified their idea. After several other shapes had been generated, one student finally said, "There's got to be a faster way!" "How?" "Can't the computer do the division?" "Try it!" Groups of students worked together toward a solution. After each group discussed their ideas, the following was voted "most elegant":

```
TO POLY :NUM.SIDES :LEN.SIDE
  REPEAT :NUM.SIDES [ FD :LEN.SIDE RT 360
                    /:NUM.SIDES]
END
```

An aside: In the traditional textbook approach, the concept of regular polygon is defined, examples and nonexamples are provided, and students are required only to discriminate examples accurately from nonexamples. These activities force students to analyze their conception of a regular polygon, searching for a way to reconceptualize it in terms that they can "explain" to the turtle via the Logo language. The procedural definitions enhance students' understanding of regular polygons. More important, they are engaged in geometric problem solving, in "doing mathematics."

After polygons are explored, polyspirals should not be missed. Polyspirals are "polygons" that increase in size as they are drawn. For example:

```
TO POLYSPIRAL :SIDE.LENGTH :TURN
  IF :SIDE.LENGTH > 50 [STOP]
  FD :SIDE.LENGTH
  RT :TURN
  POLYSPIRAL (:SIDE.LENGTH + 2) :TURN
END
```

For some versions of Terrapin (excluding the Macintosh version):

```
TO POLYSPIRAL :SIDE.LENGTH :ANGLE
  IF :SIDE.LENGTH > 50 STOP
  FD :SIDE.LENGTH
  RT :ANGLE
  POLYSPIRAL (:SIDE.LENGTH + 2) :ANGLE
END
```

Do you see a connection between this type of procedure and the arithmetic sequence procedures from Chapter 6? What drawings look most interesting to you? One young child observed: "The neatest ones are not quite a regular turn, like 90. It's almost like they keep trying to be a square, but they can't quite do it" (e.g., POLYSPIRAL 5 86). This child is learning the magic and the logic in the factors of 360 such as 10, 30, 45, 90, 120, and so on, and in the nonfactors such as 17 and 119.

In these types of explorations, it is important to discuss the difference between exterior angles (the angle through which the turtle turns, 120° for those in an equilateral triangle) and interior angles (the traditional measure of an angle, 60° for the angles of an equilateral triangle). Their relationship is equally important. They are supplementary; they sum to 180°. Thus, if an interior angle of 45° was desired for a right isosceles triangle, the turtle would turn 135°.

Some educators view such differences between turtle geometry and traditional elementary school geometry as confusing, and therefore as a disadvantage of Logo. Although the issues must be addressed, this is not necessarily true. First, if one had to choose one of the two perspectives, turtle geometry often is the more potent of the two. We have just seen an example. Using traditional internal angles, the sum of the angles of a triangle is 120°; of a square, 360°; of a pentagon, 540°; and so on. There is a pattern—the sum of the interior angles = (the number of sides − 2) × 180—but it does little to empower us. In comparison, the total turtle turn theorem is consistent, powerful, and widely applicable. However, there is no need to choose. If teachers discuss the two perspectives and their relationships, both are enriched. There is evidence that, given such a learning environment, concepts from both perspectives can develop in such properly structured Logo environments (Clements, 1987).

Consider another exploration. Students commonly believe that a square is not a type of rectangle (whose sides are all the same length), or that a rectangle is not a parallelogram (whose angles measure 90°). These three quadrilaterals all "look different," and appearance is the only way students initially have to think about shapes (this is the first, or visualization, level of van Hiele). Unfortunately, what they are taught in textbooks often does little to correct this misconception.

To begin a Logo exploration of these ideas, ask your students to draw several different parallelograms. For example, one such procedure might be

```
TO PARALLELOGRAM
  FD 30
  RT 135
  FD 50
  RT 55
  FD 30
  RT 135
  FD 50
  RT 55
END
```

Have them keep track of the amount of turn they used as the inputs to the RT or LT commands. Encourage them to keep a table, such as

First and third turns	Second and fourth turns
135	55
145	35
120	60

and so on.

Have them find a pattern. If they don't immediately do so, prompt them: "If I wrote a parallelogram procedure with one turn of 60°, what would the other turn have to be?" Ask them how they figured out the answer. After discussion, have them express their idea in a formal way in a procedure. Eventually, they could also specify inputs for the length of each pairs of sides; for example:

```
TO PARALLELOGRAM :TURN :LENGTH1 :LENGTH2
  FD :LENGTH1
  RT :TURN
  FD :LENGTH2
  RT 180 - :TURN
  FD :LENGTH1
  RT :TURN
  FD :LENGTH2
  RT 180 - :TURN
END
```

Discuss this work, emphasizing the following basic ideas. First, the turns that create opposite angles of a parallelogram are, of course, equal. Because the Turtle Total Turn Theorem shows us that the turtle turns a total of 360°, this means that adjacent angles of a parallelogram must sum to 1/2 of 360°, or 180°. Second, when the turtle turns $n°$, then $180° - n°$ (i.e., when it turns 180° in all), it is heading in the "opposite" direction. The line segments it creates will therefore be parallel.

Challenge the students to figure out what types of figures they can make with this procedure (e.g., a rectangle? rhombus? kite? triangle? trapezoid? square? etc.). Summarize that if one can draw one type of quadrilateral (e.g., rectangle) as a special case of another (e.g., a parallelogram with right angles), then the rectangle is a special kind of parallelogram. Because a rectangle is always created when the input (TURN) is 90°, students should be led to conclude that a rectangle is a special type of parallelogram. If, in addition, the other two inputs for the lengths of the sides are equal, a square is always drawn. Thus, a square is a special type of rectangle, and, of course, is also a special type of parallelogram. However, no trapezoid can be drawn with the PARALLELOGRAM procedure, so trapezoids are not parallelograms. And so on.

These activities encourage students to start focusing on the relationships between figures and to start logically ordering figures, thus thinking at the third level. One could even write one in terms of the other:

```
TO RECTANGLE :LENGTH1 :LENGTH2
 PARALLELOGRAM 90 :LENGTH1 :LENGTH2
END

TO RHOMBUS :TURN :LENGTH
 PARALLELOGRAM :TURN :LENGTH :LENGTH
END

TO SQUARE :LENGTH
 RECTANGLE :LENGTH :LENGTH
END
```

and so on.

Other examples of properties of figures that might be explored in a similar manner include: opposite sides of squares and rectangles are parallel; opposite sides of a parallelogram are equal in length; opposite angles of parallelograms are equal; and adjacent angles in a parallelogram are supplementary (sum to 180°). In fact, older students might discover that:

> For: FD :dist1 RT :turn1 FD :dist2 RT :turn2 FD :dist3
> If: :turn1 + :turn2 = 180
> Then: the first and third line segments will be parallel.

Can you see why this might be true? One student explained that "the turtle is heading in the exact opposite direction." There is another pattern for parallel lines, using one right turn and one left turn. What is the "rule" for this pattern? Students checked parallellism by having Logo SHOW HEAD-

ING; the headings of parallel lines are either the same or have a difference of 180°.

Certain geometric explorations might occur in the context of Logo microworlds. The transformations microworld, MOTIONS, has already been discussed. Procedures that allow students to perform similar transformations on any Logo procedure are provided in Clements and Battista (1988).

Logo can aid in geometric explorations of all kinds. After engaging his students in several noncomputer explorations of pi (the ratio of the circumference of a circle to its diameter), one teacher asked how they might approximate pi on the computer. Among several solutions offered was the following. Write a procedure that draws a "circle" (actually a polygon), then a half circle (i.e., it goes "half way around again"). The X coordinate there will provide a measure of the diameter. [This assumes that you started at HOME, the origin. If you believe this use of the X coordinate will not be clear to your students, have them draw the circle, turn RT 90, hide the turtle, and through successive approximation, move the turtle to a point on the circle opposite the starting point. Summing all their "moves" will yield an approximation of the diameter.] Divide the circumference (perimeter of the polygon) by this diameter. The procedure and one "run" are shown in Fig. 9–11.

By decreasing the input to RT and increasing the number of repetitions, a close estimate can be computed. For example, using REPEAT 36 [FD 5 RT 10] as the approximation of the circle yields

```
THE ESTIMATES ARE
CIRCUMFERENCE 180
DIAMETER 57.15026
PI 3.14959
```

If you have patience, using REPEAT 36000 [FD .01 RT .01] gives 3.14159, an excellent approximation.

However, even this exploration could have been improved. Students may still not understand why this rather odd ratio appears in circles. The teacher might have asked them to explore the relationship between the

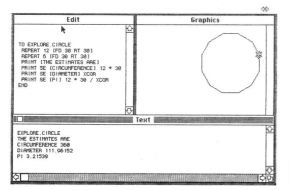

FIGURE 9–11
Estimating the value of pi.

length of the diagonal in a variety of figures. For example, a similar procedure for squares might be

```
TO EXPLORE.SQUARE
 RT 45
 REPEAT 4 [FD 30 RT 90]
 REPEAT 2 [FD 30 RT 90]
 PRINT [THE ESTIMATES ARE]
 PRINT SE [PERIMETER] 4 * 30
 PRINT SE [DIAGONAL] XCOR
 PRINT SE [RATIO IS] 4 * 30 / XCOR
END
```

```
EXPLORE.SQUARE
THE ESTIMATES ARE
PERIMETER 120
DIAGONAL 42.42641
RATIO IS 2.82843
```

Interestingly, with different-size squares, the ratio remained the same
(why did the "circle" procedure yield increasingly accurate estimates?). The
ratio for hexagons was 3. Guess what the ratio for a figure with more than
six sides might be; then try it yourself. Do you see what's happening? We're
starting to approximate a circle, and the ratio is approaching . . . !

Why was the ratio constant for each type of figure? Each set of shapes
we investigated were similar. Ratios of corresponding parts of similar
shapes remain constant. Because circles are all similar, the ratio of their
circumferences to their diameters will always be the same. And we can see
that it will be a number that's a bit more than 3. Pi.

One enrichment mathematics topic that lends itself to Logo explorations combines the topic of this chapter, geometry, with that of Chapter 8,
ratios. The ancient Greeks believed the golden rectangle to be the most
beautiful four-sided figure and used it extensively in their architecture (e.g.,
the Parthenon) and sculpture. It has many additional interesting geometric
properties. Recall that the short side of the rectangle is considered to be 1
unit in length, the long side is 1.61803 . . . units. Interestingly, if a square is

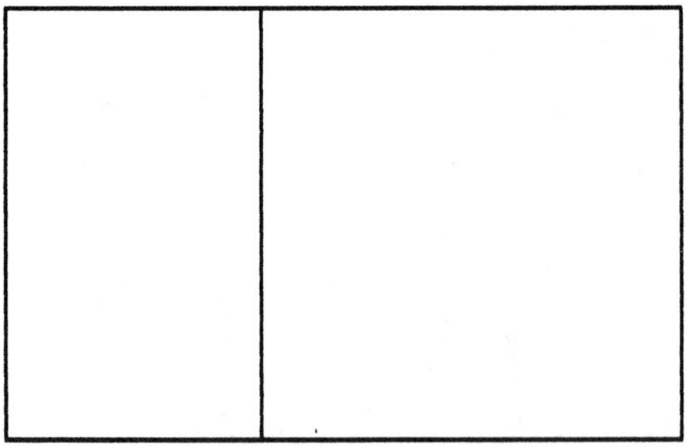

FIGURE 9-12
A golden rectangle.

removed from a golden rectangle, the remaining rectangle is also a golden rectangle (Fig. 9–12).

Because the square was assumed to have a length of 1 unit, the short side(s) of the new rectangle has a length of about: $s = 1.61803 - 1$ or 0.61803 unit. But it also is a golden rectangle, so $1.61803 = 1/s$; transformed, $s = 1/1.61803$. Because $s = 0.61803$ and $s = 1/1.61803$, we find that the golden mean minus 1 equals the reciprocal of the golden mean, just as we discovered in the initial spreadsheet exploration.

Of course, a square could be removed from this new rectangle, creating another golden rectangle, and so on, ad infinitum (Fig. 9–13). This reapplication of the same rule to successively smaller cases certainly suggests recursion. In fact, the Logo program that generated this figure uses recursion and the golden mean (the turtle was turned RT 90 before the procedure was executed).

```
TO GOLD.RECT :SHORT.SIDE
  FD :SHORT.SIDE * 1.61803
  RT 90
  FD :SHORT.SIDE
  RT 90
  FD :SHORT.SIDE * 1.61803
  RT 90
  GOLD.RECT :SHORT.SIDE / 1.61803
END
```

Finally, if connecting quarter circles are draw within each square, the result is an approximation of a logarithmic (or proportional) spiral (Fig. 9–14). This is one of the common spirals in nature (e.g., shells). The Logo program that produces this spiral is (CURVE.LT draws a quarter circle):

```
TO SPIRAL :RADIUS
  CURVE.LT :RADIUS
  SPIRAL :RADIUS / 1.61803
END
```

Each segment of the spiral, of course, is smaller than the one before, in proportion to the golden mean.

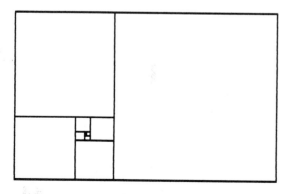

FIGURE 9-13
An infinite number of golden rectangles could theoretically be constructed with this recursive process.

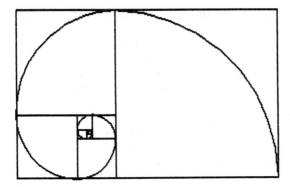

FIGURE 9-14
A spiral based on the same proportions as Figures 9–12 and 9–13.

Geometric Construction Programs

Several programs allow students to carry out and explore geometric constructions. These provide a complementary approach to Logo experiences for older students. For example, with the *Geometric preSupposer*, the computer is used for constructions possible with a straightedge and compass: points, segments, angles and angle bisectors, triangles, quadrilaterals and other polygons, circles, perpendiculars, parallels, and so on. In addition, students can measure lengths, circumferences, areas, and angles, and can perform arithmetic combinations on these measures, such as the sum of two angles, the square of the length of a segment, or the ratio of two areas. Importantly, all of these operations can be conducted simply and accurately.

If only one computer is available, the *preSupposer* can be used in posing and answering questions with the class as a whole. With more access to computers, students can work individually or in small groups as the teacher helps them analyze their observations. Often, the ideal situation is a combination of these approaches. What might students do with the *preSupposer?*

One class was challenged to find a way to locate the center of any regular polygon. Two of their solutions are shown in Fig. 9–15. The creators of the program asked students to make a parallelogram from a triangle, believing themselves that there was but one approach. The students surprised them by inventing several solutions: reflecting the two equal sides of an isosceles triangle onto the third side; adding parallel lines to each of any two sides of a triangle; bisecting the three sides of a triangle and connecting the points; and others.

Other challenges that might be presented include:

Draw several quadrilaterals. Connect the midpoints of each of the sides. What kinds of figures are created? (See Fig. 9–16.)

Draw a polygon with three sides and compute the sum of its interior angles. Repeat this process for polygons with four, five, six, seven, and so on, sides. Find a generalization about the number of sides of a polygon and the sum of its internal angles.

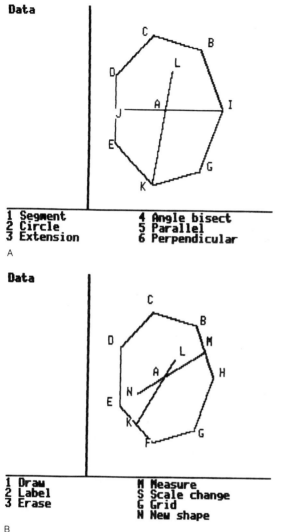

Data

1 Segment
2 Circle
3 Extension
4 Angle bisect
5 Parallel
6 Perpendicular

A

Data

1 Draw
2 Label
3 Erase
M Measure
S Scale change
G Grid
N New shape

B

FIGURE 9-15
The *preSupposer* can be used to locate the center of any regular polygon by: (a) finding the intersection of two angle bisectors, and (b) finding the intersection of the perpendicular bisectors of two sides. Can you think of other ways? (Sunburst Communications)

Invent your own categories for classifying geometric shapes (e.g., one student uniquely and correctly defined an obtuse triangle as one in which the largest angle was greater than the sum of the other two angles!).

(After discussing the concepts of similarity and congruence): Measure the angles and sides of several triangles generated by the program to answer these questions: Are all acute triangles congruent? Are they similar? How about obtuse triangles? Right? Isosceles? Equilateral?

Construct as many different congruent shapes as you can in an equilateral triangle, a square, a rhombus (e.g., construct one or two diagonals in the latter two). Do the same methods work for other polygons?

Data

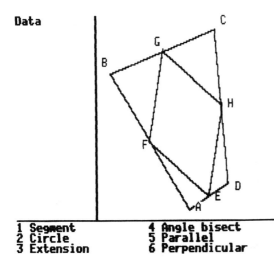

1 Segment	4 Angle bisect
2 Circle	5 Parallel
3 Extension	6 Perpendicular

FIGURE 9-16
Connecting the midpoints of
each of the sides of a random
quadrilateral seems to produce
a special figure. Will it always do
so? (Sunburst Communications)

Of course, students should still work with pattern blocks and geo-boards, and could perform constructions with straightedges and compasses. The use of construction programs should build on these concrete psycho-motor experiences. Students use the construction programs to extend and begin to formalize their initial concrete experiences. The computer allows constructions to be performed more easily, more rapidly, and more accurately. As construction procedures can be saved and almost instantly reapplied to new figures, generalizations are created and tested much more efficiently. In fact, most students would not maintain an interest in reperforming long series of constructions on paper to generate and test generalizations. As with Logo, the computer program serves as a bridge between the concrete and intuitive on one hand, and the abstract and formalistic on the other.

Other construction programs can be used with younger, as well as older, students. For example, the *IBM Elementary Mathematics Series* is for a complete CAI sequence for grades 1 through 8 based on a construction tool kit. The tools are in three basic categories. The first, CONSTRUCT, includes traditional Euclidean construction tools. Students can draw and label segments, lines, rays, polygons, angles, circles, midpoints, parallels, and perpendiculars. In the second, TRANSFORM, they can alter figures. Commands include translate, rotate, reflect, "pull" (e.g., lengthen or shorten a figure along one dimension proportionately), scale (e.g., "make the figure larger," but similar, to the original), and others (e.g., allowing the original figures to be kept or not). The third, "V-Draw," is a simple Logo-like component of the system. These commands can be used effectively to teach concepts. For example, the series introduces isosceles triangles by having students pull an equilateral triangle, and rectangles by having them pull a square.

In lessons for the earliest grades, students are introduced to the tools. They draw lines and line segments. From their first sessions with the program, they use transformations such as scale and pull to compare shapes and dimensions (see Fig. 9–17). They use simple Logo-based commands to draw polygons and pictures. This is not a full Logo environment; but as a hybrid CAI/construction program, it does provide students guidance at each point in their work. A particular strength of this series is that students are not only carefully guided and checked; most lessons end with an "Explore" segment, in which students are encouraged to use the tools available and the new concepts to draw something, experiment with ideas, or meet an open-ended challenge. For example, one lesson teaches students about points, lines, and line segments by developing these concepts while letting students construct them. Then several exploratory (nonguided) activities are provided. Students first connect four points with lines or segments in any way they please. Next, they are provided with points A through L arranged in a circle. Again, they connect these points to create a design interesting to them; then they fill the regions so constructed with color (see Fig. 9–18 for parts of this sequence). Other exploratory activities in this unit

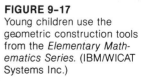

FIGURE 9-17
Young children use the geometric construction tools from the *Elementary Mathematics Series*. (IBM/WICAT Systems Inc.)

FIGURE 9-17 (*Continued*)

GUIDED PRACTICE
To make the shape longer, press U for pUll.

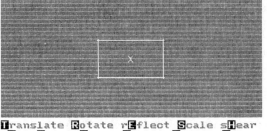

Translate Rotate rEflect Scale sHear pUll Point N-gon Circle Define Keep

C

The shape is longer.

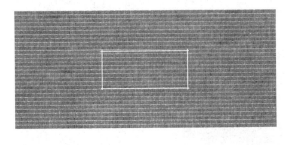

D

EXPLORE: When finished, press SKIP.
Use these points (or add points of your own) to draw segments.

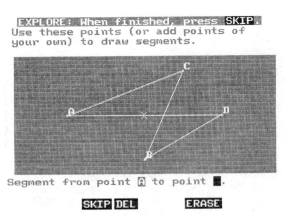

Segment from point A to point B.

SKIP DEL   ERASE

A

FIGURE 9-18
Creativity in geometry. (IBM/
WICAT Systems Inc.)

Any number of lines can be drawn
through one point.

FIGURE 9-18 (*Continued*)

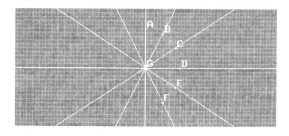

B

This design
has many
intersecting
lines.

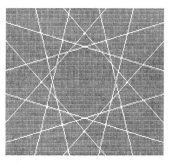

C

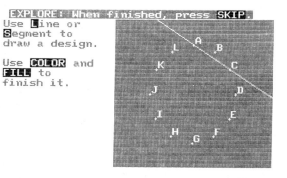

Stand by . . . updating your bookmark

D

include using certain figures, such as triangles and circles, to create designs; the reflect and translate commands to draw a congruent figure, and the *N*-gon (regular polygon), scaling, rotate, translate, and reflect commands to draw pictures. The computer emphasizes the dynamic aspect of such transformations (Fig. 9–19). This cycle of conceptual development with guided practice and exploratory activities holds promise for ameliorating the problems in the learning of geometry as described previously, and for developing relational understanding and positive attitudes.

A few other examples illustrate these points. Students learn about par-

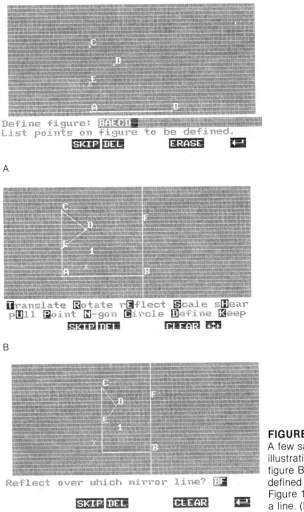

FIGURE 9-19
A few sample screens illustrating a reflection (flip). The figure BAEDC must first be defined (and thus named as Figure 1) and then reflected over a line. (IBM/WICAT Systems Inc.)

allelograms while constructing them via pairs of intersecting parallel lines. Appropriate constructions are conducted for other quadrilaterals. Similarly, for triangles, students use construction commands to create the various types (e.g., constructing an isosceles triangle by rotating one segment while keeping the original line, or preimage, and connecting the endpoints that do not intersect). Samples of work on rectangles are shown in Fig. 9–20.

It would not at first seem that computers could be of much assistance teaching about solids. However, this series includes a sequence that allows students to construct, for example, a two-dimensional representation of rectangular prisms by drawing a regular polygon, copying and translating it, and connecting the corresponding vertices (see Fig. 9–21).

FIGURE 9–19 (Continued)

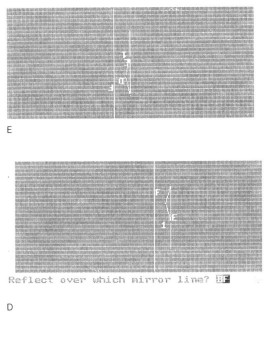

E

D

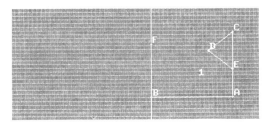

F

These are rectangles.

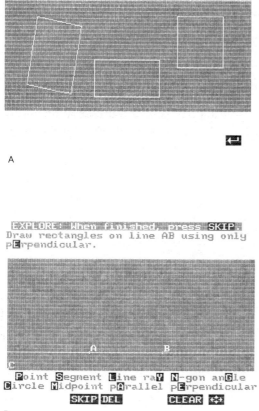

A

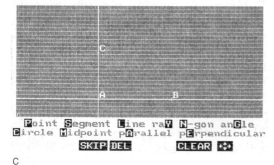

B

C

FIGURE 9-20
Work with rectangles (sample screens). First students are shown several rectangles (a). They then use the LINE command to draw line AB. They are asked to use the PERPENDICULAR command to construct two perpendiculars to that line (b and c). They are challenged to think about the resulting parallelism (d and e). They then measure the angles (f) and read (g). Finally, they are challenged to draw a parallelogram with only one right angle (h). Can they do it? (IBM/ WICAT Systems Inc.)

Side AF is parallel to side CD. Think about how this can be shown to be true.

FIGURE 9-20 (*Continued*)

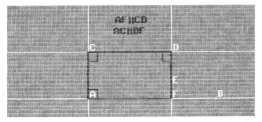

D

Similarly, side AC is parallel to side DF because they are both perpendicular to side CD.

E

Use **MEASURE** to find the measure of ∠AFD.

∠AFD = ▓▓▓°

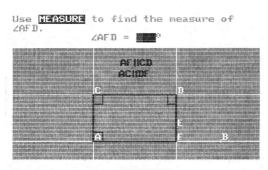

To measure, press **MEASURE**.

F

All four of the angles of parallelogram
ACDF are right angles.

FIGURE 9-20 (*Continued*)

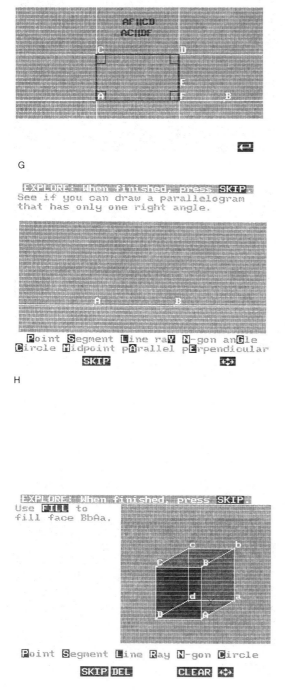

G

H

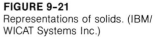

FIGURE 9-21
Representations of solids. (IBM/
WICAT Systems Inc.)

A final programming example will show that with an extensible language like Logo, you can "have it all." A set of mathematics "utility" procedures, called GEOTOOLS, has been created (Clements & Battista, 1988). These procedures permit students in a Logo environment to label points with letters and to measure line segments and angles, thus enabling them to utilize these ideas to solve geometric problems in the dynamic environment of Logo. Specifically, procedures include:

POINT is a command that takes one letter as input. It moves the turtle to a random position on the screen and labels that point with the letter.

LINE.SEGMENT is a command that takes two letters as input. It draws a line segment between two points previously labeled with those letters.

LENGTH is an operation that takes two letters as input. It outputs the distance between the two points previously labeled with those letters.

MEASURE.ANGLE is an operation that takes three letters as input. It outputs the measure of the angle labeled by those letters.

The following activities use these procedures to investigate concepts from the standard geometry curriculum in an exploratory fashion.

Write a procedure that randomly labels three points on the screen, A, B, and C, and then draws angle ABC. Draw a random angle with this procedure. Estimate the measure of this angle, then use MEASURE.ANGLE to check yourself. Repeat several times.

Clear the screen and label this position A. Move the turtle forward 50 and label this point B. Turn right any number of degrees and move the turtle FD 50. Label this point C. Use the MEASURE.ANGLE procedure to find the measure of angle ABC. How does this number compare to the angle "turned" by the turtle at point B? Repeat.

Write a procedure that picks three points at random and draws a triangle with these points as vertices. (Such a procedure might be

```
TO RANDOM.TRI
  POINT "A
  POINT "B
  POINT "C
  LINE.SEGMENT "A "B
  LINE.SEGMENT "B "C
  LINE.SEGMENT "C "A
END
```

Ask students if this will always produce a triangle.)

Use your RANDOM.TRI and MEASURE.ANGLE to measure all three of the triangle's angles. Repeat this several times, keeping records. What do you notice about the sum of a triangle's angles? (Repeat for other polygons. Compare this with the sum of the exterior angles.)

Write a procedure that draws a scalene triangle. (This can be difficult in Logo without always starting and ending at HOME. With these procedures, students can label A, go forward any amount, label B, turn any amount, go forward any amount, and label C. Giving the command LINE.SEGMENT "C "A will complete the triangle. Finally, the LENGTH and MEASURE.ANGLE procedures can be used to find the measures needed to write traditional Logo procedures to draw this triangle. This method can be used for other types of triangles and other types of polygons.)

Nevertheless, at the risk of repeating ad nauseam, concrete manipulative materials such as solids and geoboards should not be forsaken. Discussion of such real exemplars should emphasize real-world applications: Why is a sphere such an important shape? What makes it so suitable for games? (Because it rolls due to its perfect symmetry about a point.) Why is it used for water tanks? (Because it holds more water for the material it takes to build it than any other shape.) Why aren't milk cartons spheres? (Because other considerations, such as packing, stability on a surface, etc., enter the picture.) Why are bowls shaped the way they are? (Why might corners be inappropriate for mixing bowls?) What about the shape of cereal boxes?

In two or three dimensions, students should be involved with four representations of every geometric idea. They should use classroom manipulatives, examine the physical world, examine and draw diagrams, and learn names and definitions. Computers can serve in crossing the bridge from the concrete to the abstract. They can also promote the development of spatial visualization and geometric problem-solving ability (Clements & Battista, 1986).

MEASUREMENT

Measurement is the process of assigning a number to a physical property of an object for purpose of comparison. Measurement instruction should follow a sequence of phases. First, students should become aware of an attribute. They manipulate objects and engage in activities that give meaning to an attribute that will later be measured. For example, a teacher observing young children building a block building might comment as to its height and width, the amount of rug it covers (area), and the amount of room inside it (volume). Increased awareness almost invariably leads to increased motivation for comparison, the second phase. Students physically compare objects, developing concepts such as "longer than" or "same length." The third phase involves measuring with nonstandard units. Measuring involves two steps: (a) choosing a unit of measure and (b) determining how many units "fit in" the object. To help students focus on both steps, initial experiences should use multiple copies of nonstandard units (e.g., pieces of unused chalk laid end to end). This can be followed by iterations of a unit (one piece of chalk laid down several times, with the endpoints marked). Fourth, standard units should be used (e.g., multiple unmarked metersticks laid end to end). Fifth, standard measuring devices should be introduced.

Where do computers fit into this sequence? Generally, it seems they are appropriate only during the later phases, and even there their usefulness might be questioned. Let's examine some programs to answer the question further.

CAI for Geometric Measurement

In *Elementary Mathematics, Vol. 1,* students are shown a line segment and are asked to estimate its length in centimeters or millimeters. But how can this be accurate when screens vary in size? Any program in which students measure pictures on the screen should have calibration procedures. For instance, students might measure an object and type in its length, allowing the computer to adjust the length of all future objects to ensure accuracy. For example, "Metric Paths" (from *Mathematics Activity Courseware*) asks students to measure a segment with a flexible millimeter ruler before playing an estimation game. Once the screen has been calibrated, paths of two to five segments are displayed. Students must estimate their length in centimeters within 10 seconds.

Geometry and Measurement asks children to use a metric ruler to determine length and perimeter of figures drawn on a simulated geoboard. Area is taught as counting the geoboard squares contained in a figure (figures with diagonal lines are segmented first). In *Area and Perimeter* the movement of blocks into a rectangle demonstrates the idea that area is defined in terms of unit squares. Students are then asked to give the area of a rectangle given the lengths of two adjoining sides. If they are incorrect or ask for help, they are given assistance first in the form of a grid and then in the form of an appropriate multiplication sentence. Finally, the answer is provided.

The "Rectangle Factory" uses animation to demonstrate that the parallelogram can be made into a rectangle by cutting it and rearranging the pieces. Students then create parallelograms by entering the lengths of the base, the height, and the leg and are guided in determining their area. Last, they are shown an animated reminder that parallelograms with the same height have the same area.

In a similar manner, area is introduced by the *Elementary Mathematics Series* by having students fill all the squares inside a rectangle with color and count how many squares there were. They are told: "The area of the rectangle is 15 square units." The counting-based introduction is far more pedagogically sound than the typical early introduction of area formulas (e.g., $A = L \times W$), as it helps to avoid common conceptual errors such as counting unit segments (e.g., for a 2×3 grid, counting the 10 segments of the perimeter to determine the area) or "points" (e.g., counting each point on the perimeter, including the corners, which also yields an "area" of 10). After concepts have been developed, the program related the area formula to the counting model. As is typical of this series, students learning about angular measure are actively involved in drawing angles of various sizes.

Other programs do not ask students to measure directly that which appears on the screen. *Explorer Metros: A Metric Adventure* provides practice in estimating metric reference measures without attempting to show actual units on the screen. As such, it is appropriate for practice only after students have had concrete measurement experiences. In this adventure game students explore a space colony and encounter situations requiring them to make choices based on estimations of metric measures. For example, they might see Fig. 9–22. Unless they have an extremely large net and quite a bit of assistance, running away appears to be an excellent option! A useful option the program includes is for teachers or students to write their own "encounters," using the pictures provided. Thus, material that matches the needs and interests of students may be added.

Experiences such as these can contribute to students' ability to measure small linear distances, to conceptualize area, to estimate quantities, and the like. Nevertheless, there are clear limitations. They remain inappropriate for the earliest phases of measurement instruction. Even in the later levels, however, there are problems. For example, measuring line segments on a screen is a limited experience. Measurement of such attributes as volume, weight, or temperature seems impossible.

One way to ameliorate such problems is to use the geometric construction programs, most of which have the ability to report measurements of any segments or angles constructed by the student. For example, the *Elementary Mathematics Series* introduces perimeter by having students draw a figure, determine the length of its sides with the MEASURE command, and find its perimeter. Following the introduction of area as counting square units (as described in the preceding section), the series has students MEASURE the length and width of rectangles and apply the formula to determine the areas. Areas of complex figures are determined by segmenting them into rectangles. Angle measure can also be reported.

Logo programmers, of course, deal with angle and distance measurements constantly. Only the former, however, is expressed in standard units. Experiences with area measure might also be designed by the teacher. Another way is to use the computer as a measurement device with real-world objects.

Computer laboratories: A promising approach.   Packages exist that allow the computer to serve as a laboratory instrument. *AtariLab,* for example, might be used to measure the temperature of hot water. A probe—a small device connected to the computer—is placed in the water. The program displays a graphic thermometer registering this temperature. Then, as the water cools, a new picture moves out of and away from the first one, reveal-

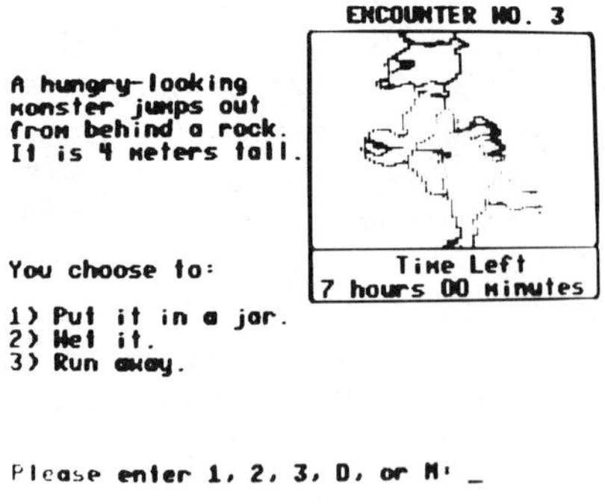

FIGURE 9-22
Metric estimation in *Explorer Metros.*
(Sunburst Communications)

ing a lower temperature. Time segments are also displayed. This continues, as a row of graphic thermometers visually display the phenomenon of cooling. Then, at command, the tops of the "mercury" in the thermometers are connected by lines, portraying a line graph of the process. Even young children can control the temperature readings (with their hands, hot and cold water, etc.) and read the corresponding graphs. They see the relationship between their own sensory impressions and the graph. (Note, however, that most laboratories now sold are basically designed for students in middle school and above.) Unlike simulations of measurement, this computer application allows students to experience the process of measurement and extends their knowledge of it via computer.

Computer laboratories (or Microcomputer-Based Lab, MBL) like *Atari-Lab* gather data directly from the environment with low-cost probes, or transducers. A *transducer* is a device (like a telephone) that gathers energy in one form (sound waves) and translates it into another (electrical impulses). Computer laboratory transducers measure physical attributes, translate these measures into electrical impulses the computer can read (usually the "game port" into which joysticks are plugged), and display them on the screen.

Computer programs with such transducers provide students with the ability to measure and explore their environment to a much greater degree than traditional instruments (although the latter should be experienced first, as always). Students can measure the attributes of temperature, velocity, light level, sound, force, and so on. For example, the temperature inside and outside the classroom could be taken every hour, around the clock, for a week. This information could be automatically saved, graphed, and printed. Older students might use photocells and timers to plot the velocity of a toy car as it moves down a ramp and across a tabletop. Speed calculations under different conditions can then be made. The measurements can be displayed instantly in a variety of forms, saved to disk as desired, graphed, and statistically analyzed or transformed. This approach also eliminates some of the tedium of collecting copious measurements over an extended period. Students instead can concentrate on hypothesizing and analyzing.

Money and Time

Several programs listed in Table 9–1 provide practice with money. For those that involve coin recognition, it is important that the coins be represented accurately. Some of the programs on computers with better resolution have reasonably clear depictions of coins. For example, *CoinWorks* for the Macintosh contains seven lessons. In the first, students enter the total amount shown in coins. If desired, help can be requested. As each coin is pointed to by the student (with a mouse), the computer counts the total. In other lessons, students select coins to match a given amount, count coins to determine if they have enough money to buy a given item (see Fig. 9–23), compare the value of sets of coins, select the fewest possible coins to make a purchase, and make change.

In *The Magic Cash Register* students play store using an on-screen cash

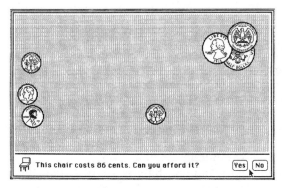

FIGURE 9-23
Counting money with *CoinWorks.*
(Nordic Software)

register. The program begins by asking students to "cash in." They are to get toy money, sort it into a box, and enter the amount of each denomination into the computer. The cash register's drawer is updated to mirror these amounts. Students then sell items—whatever they wish, actually. They type the name of the item, the number the customer desires, and then the total price. They must then determine that total by multiplying. If they make an error, the program informs them of the probable nature of the mistake (e.g., "multiplication fact" or "decimal point"). It then offers to assist them in one of four ways: setting up the problem (vertically), printing the problem on paper, highlighting all the digits that were wrong, or providing a step-by-step demonstration of the algorithm. (Note that students can bypass all computation through an option that has the cash register perform all calculations.) When all purchases have been made, they total the sale. Then they tell the program how much money the customer is giving them and make change, in both cases, specifying the number of each coin and bill. If they make change correctly, the program still might tell them they were correct, "but there is a better way," and offer to show them. A receipt is printed at the end of the transaction. When the students are finished, they cash out, compute total income, and view a skill report. Other simulations emphasize economic concepts and principles to a greater degree. See the discussions of *Lemonade* in Chapter 10, *Run for the Money* in Chapter 11, and *Survival Math* in Chapter 2 (several simulations from this package, such as "Hot Dog Stand" and "Smart Shopper Marathon," emphasize money and economics more than did the one described in that chapter).

Similarly, several programs offer practice "telling time," employing both conventional dial (analog) and digital clocks. *ClockWorks* provides practice in setting digit clocks to match traditional clock (hands), or vice versa, or setting either given time expressed in words (see Fig. 9–24). Other lessons include counting by fives, concepts/terms such as "quarter til," and solving word problems. Users have a variety of choices, such as time interval used (hour, half-hour, quarter-hour, 10 min, 5 min, minutes). A similar program in *Learning About Numbers* presents both a conventional clock and a digital watch. Students manipulate the hands of the clock to match a digital display. Difficulty is automatically adjusted, starting from time on the hour and advancing to stating time in word form.

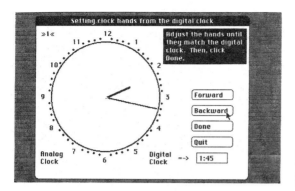

FIGURE 9-24
Telling time with *ClockWorks*.
(Nordic Software)

Of course, more dynamic experiences with time might be presented via the computer laboratories, which allow students to measure, record, analyze, and graphically display measurements against time (as in the temperature example described previously). As with geometry and geometric measurement, the most effective use of the computer is in enabling students to have more powerful encounters with mathematics and with their world.

SUGGESTED READINGS

Billstein, Libeskind, and Lott (1986), Clements and Battista (1988), Martin and Bearden (1985), and **Thornburg (1983)** provide additional suggestions for teaching geometry with Logo.

Moore (1984) provides sequenced lessons on learning geometry with Logo, on blackline masters that can be duplicated for students.

C. S. Thompson and Van de Walle (1985) provide ideas for geometry lessons with Logo, emphasizing patterning.

TABLE 9-1 Software: Geometry and Measurement

Title	Producer	Notes
	Geometry	
Aestheometry	MECC	Shows how curves can be drawn from a series of straight lines. 3–12+.
Arith-Magic II	QED	Area and perimeter. Three games: Squ/area, The Rectangle Game, and Per/area game. 4–10.
Arrow Graphics	Milliken	Spatial visualization and patterning. Students observe a pattern of arrow and reprogram the path. Reward is the opportunity to specify one's own pattern. 2–4.

(continued)

TABLE 9-1 **(Continued)**

Title	Producer	Notes
Basic Math Competency: Measuring with a Ruler, Perimeter, Circumference, Area	Ed. Act.	Tutorial and practice on the topics listed. Some CMI. 4–6.
Basic Skills Math	Control Data	Tutorials and drills on geometry: plane figures, figure comparison, three-dimensional figures, and applications problems. 3–8.
Building Perspective	Sunburst	Spatial perception game. Students view depictions of buildings of different height, viewed from the side. They must visualize what the top should look like. To do this, they must develop a step-by-step process, including the removal of buildings to see what lies behind. Recommended, especially if used in conjunction with concrete materials. 4+.
Bumble Games	TLC	Sequence of six games that develop number lines, graph plotting. Recommended. P–4.
Bumble Plot	TLC	Sequence of five graphing and problem-solving programs, from number-line problems to using positive and negative numbers to name points in a four-quadrant grid. Recommended. 3–8.
Creativity Unlimited	Sunburst	Students use shapes, motions, and symmetry to create aesthetic and mathematically interesting designs. 3+.
Cube Builder	HRM	Visualization of three-dimensional shapes and the connection between length, area, and volume as the scale of an object is changed. Students manipulate unit cubes to build their own shapes. They can enlarge or rotate their constructions. Two challenge sections are provided; e.g., one asks students to deduce a three-dimensional object from two-dimensional views. 6–12.
Elementary-Geometry	MECC	Several activities in each of several volumes, usually including tutorials and quizzes. E.g., Vol. 3 includes drill on geometric shapes, practice calculating area and perimeters. 6+ (note that the volumes do not

Title	Producer	Notes
		represent a sequence). Vol. 8 covers points, lines, and angles. 3–5. Vol. 9 includes defining parallel, perpendicular, and intersecting lines and different types of triangles. 4–6. Vol. 10 provides tutorials on the area and perimeter of quadrilaterals. 4–6.
ESC Mathematics	ESC	Spatial relationships, classifying, pattern development, figures, solids, and coordinate mapping. A comprehensive program for grades 1–6.
Euclid	Compu-Teach	Introduces concepts necessary for later study of proof, such as congruence, corresponding parts.
EUCLID	Univ. Evans.	Enables students to perform elementary constructions such as points, lines, circles, angle bisectors, perpendiculars, parallels, etc.
The Factory	Sunburst	Students create geometric "products" on an assembly line by sequencing a series of machines (e.g., a 90° right rotation, a hole-punching machine, etc.). A supplementary book of activities is available. 4+.
First Shapes	First Byte	Introduction to shapes. A series of learning modules, including shape identification, constructing toys from shapes (e.g., "What shape should the robot's head be?"), finding a described shape, and matching shapes. Unique is the program's extensive use of speech (requiring no additional hardware or software). P–3.
Flip Flop	Milliken	Transformation geometry; can one figure be moved to look exactly like another? Recommended with reservations by EPIE. 2–6.
Flying Carpet	Learn. Tech.	Recognize and count geometric shapes created by a genie. K–2.
Funky Chicken	Britannica	Transformational geometry activity. See the text. 4–8.
GEO-Pool and GEO-Billiards	CAE	Simulations that develop skill in estimating angles. Includes an on-screen "sight" which players may

(continued)

TABLE 9-1   (Continued)

Title	Producer	Notes
		use to project the direction of a shot before the ball is actually "hit." 5+.
GEOART	Ventura	Concepts in geometry and art: names and characteristics of common geometrical figures, perimeter and area, drawing game (transformations), designing graphics. 4–12.
Geography	Micro. Wrkshp.	Practice the four cardinal map directions by navigating a neighborhood. 3–8.
Geometric Concepts	Courses	Concepts of lines, segments, rays, angles, triangles, rectangles, squares, circles, and polygons. Tutorial and practice. Some CMI. 6–9.
Geometric preSupposer	Sunburst	A tool for geometric construction and exploration. Introduces simple constructions that are usually made with a straightedge and compass. Students experiment with combinations of constructions and measurements. Other programs in the series focus on triangles and quadrilaterals. For older and/or talented students. 6+.
Geometry	Dorsett	Tutorials on areas of triangles and rectangles and the Pythagorean theorem. 6–12.
Geometry	JMH	Five programs on angles, triangles, lines, quadrilaterals, and congruent figures.
Geometry Alive!	Ed. Act.	Fundamentals, area of polygons, circles. Tutorials with help (and some humor). Some CMI. 4+.
Geometry and Measurement	Control Data	Practice problem sets on classifying polygons and terms related to circles.
Geometry and Measurement Facts	Bergwall	Basic geometric concepts and metric and English measurement. 2–4.
Geometry! Part I	K–12 Micro.	Montessorian approach to polygons and spatial reasoning. Four activities illustrate and give graphic meaning to the geometric concepts of point, line, angle, plane, triangles, quadrilaterals, and other polygons; provide practice in spelling these terms; present quizzes; and in the most creative of the activi-

Title	Producer	Notes
		ties, provide a drawing tool that allows students to draw representations of these geometric constructs in any combinations to create designs and pictures. K–5.
Geometry With Logo	Metier	Concepts of point, line, ray, line segment, angle, and congruence are taught in a turtle geometry environment. 5–10.
Gertrude's Secrets	TLC	Classification of shapes. P–5.
Gertrude's Puzzles	TLC	More advanced classification of shapes. 3–8.
Golf Classic	Milliken	Angle and length estimation in game; players determine how golf ball should be hit. 4–8.
Graphing and Geometry	Commodore	Ordered pairs and plotting on a four-quadrant plane and shapes and rotations. Tutorial and drill. 4–9.
Grid Locations	Bergwall	Plotting points on a grid. Concepts and applications. 2–4.
Grid Search Games	Creative	Coordinate systems in pursuit-and-capture game format. 4–9.
Gridlock	2-Bit	Cartesian coordinates. 3–9.
IBM Elementary Mathematics Series	IBM/WICAT	Comprehensive program. Includes the Math Concepts and Math Practice Series. K–8.
Leo's Links	Chalk Board	Design and play imaginary golf courses using lines and shapes. 4–12.
Logic Builders	Scholastic	Visualization and patterning. Students create or copy a geometric "web" by maneuvering five spiders, each of which draws one shape. 2–6.
Mathematics Activity Courseware (MAC)	Houghton Miff.	Several activities for different grade levels. Level 2 includes "Snake in the Grass" (estimating centimeters). In level 3, "Sliding Twins," asks students to be the first to match pairs of congruent figures. In "Figure Fast," at level 4, players choose a figure that is congruent to a target figure (which may be turned or flipped). In level 5's "Same Shape—Same Size," students use slides, flips, and turns to move one figure to coincide with its

(continued)

TABLE 9-1 (Continued)

Title	Producer	Notes
		congruent partner. A similar, albeit slightly more difficult activity, is level 6's "Slide–Flip–Turn."
Mathematics Today Practice Diskettes	Harcourt Brace	Several concepts and skills. Presents drill correlated with the publisher's text series. Embedded in gamelike activities; provide "clues" when students make errors. K–8.
Middle School Mathematics	MCP	Plane and solid geometry concepts and skills. Inexpensive software developed by teachers. 6–9.
Planes	Ventura	Several programs on shapes, perimeter, area, transformations, etc. 4–8.
The Right Turn	Sunburst	Predict and experiment with transformations. Recommended. 4+.
Shape Grabber	Commodore	Geometric shapes. 1–4.
Symmetry	Bergwall	Students locate symmetric figure. 2–4.
Symmetry	Queue	Creating symmetrical patterns; transformations.
Super Factory	Sunburst	An extension of *The Factory* to three dimensions. Problem-solving strategies and spatial visualization are developed in a three-dimensional version of *Factory*. Students rotate a cube in three dimensions, placing pictures on its faces. They can create their own designs, or be challenged to construct a given design at four levels of difficulty. Good documentation, including classroom lesson plans; 5–adult.
Tangrams Puzzler	Milliken	Rearrange seven shapes cut from a square to duplicate a given figure. 4+.
Telemath	Psychotechnics	A variety of activities. K–6.
Tip 'N Flip	Sunburst	Specify the flips and turns needed to move a pattern so that it matches a given design. See the text. 4+.
Trap-A-Zoid	DCH	Constructing polygons and other geometric skills taught in a game format. Recommended with reservations by EPIE. 4–8.
Voyage of the Mimi	Holt	A comprehensive program by Bank Street College with an ecological

Title	Producer	Notes
		theme (whales). Pertinent here are the modules "Introduction to Computing" and "Maps and Navigation." In the first, the student might be a captain of a ship trying to free whales with a minimum of Logo commands (FD, BK, LT, RT). Other similar activities extend the experience to other commands, drawing, and so on. "Maps and Navigation" teaches mathematic equations, plottings of latitude and longitude, triangulations, and the use of a compass.

Measurement

Geometric Measurement and Weight

Title	Producer	Notes
Area and Perimeter	Britannica	Several activities. See the text. Intermediate and above.
Area and Perimeter	Computer Island	Solving area or perimeter problems. 6+.
Area and Perimeter	Micrograms	Practice in calculating area and perimeter of squares and rectangles. 5–6.
Area of a Rectangle	CBS	Begins with concept of area; guides students to find the formula for area of a rectangle. 3–8.
Arith-magic II	QED	Activities with area and perimeter that build initial concepts and sound measurement ideas while simultaneously developing a foundation for understanding of other mathematical topics.
Basic Math Competency Skill Building	Ed. Act.	Multiple programs; one is "Measuring with a Ruler: Perimeter, Circumference, and Area." Includes how to read a ruler, formulas to find perimeter and area of polygons, and pi. 4+.
Basic Skills Math Instructional Series	Control Data	Tutorials and drills on measurement: linear, area, volume, and capacity. Includes applications problems. 3–8.
Clock Works	MECC	Drill in reading and setting analog and digital clocks. 1–3.
Comparison Kitchen	DLM	Identifying the region with less area. P+.

(continued)

TABLE 9-1 (Continued)

Title	Producer	Notes
Concepts of Measurement	Courses by Com.	Measurement of perimeter and area of simple polygons and of time. Tutorial and practice. Some CMI.
Distance Problems	Computer Island	Using distance formula to solve word problems. 6+.
Elementary Vol. 1: Mathematics	MECC	Several activities dealing with metric estimation and converting from one metric unit to another. 2-6.
ESC Mathematics	ESC	Begins with an emphasis on making comparisons, shifts to nonstandard units, then standard metric and English units. (Also includes money, time, and temperature.) A comprehensive program for grades 1-6.
Explorer Metros: A Metric Adventure	Sunburst	Estimation of metric measurements in adventure format (not actually a simulation, as is stated in the documentation). See the text. 4+.
Fish Scales	DLM	Teaches how height, length, and distance are measured, and how measurement is used to compare.
Geoboard Geometry and Measurement	Cuisenaire	Reading a ruler, measuring line segments, constructing parallel and perpendicular lines, and finding the area and perimeter of polygons. Actual measurement of line segments and figures drawn on a simulated geoboard on the screen. 3-10.
Geometric Concepts	Borg-Warner	Tutorials and practice with measurement concepts and formulas for triangles, squares, rectangles, parallelograms, and other polygons. Some CMI. 6-9.
Geometric Concepts: Area and Perimeter	Jostens	Practice with geometric concepts and formulas. 6-9.
Geometry and Measurement	Control Data	Practice problem sets on metric length, perimeter and area, angle of measurement, and volume and surface area of solids. PLATO materials. 6-9.
Geometry and Measurement Facts	Deegan	Drill with some CMI. 2-6.
Golf Classic	Milliken	Determine the angle and distance for golf shots. 4+.
IBM Elementary Mathematics Series	IBM/WICAT	Comprehensive program. Includes the Math Concepts and Math Practice Series. K-8.
Inches and Centimeters	Amer. Peri.	Measuring length. 5-10.

Title	Producer	Notes
Math Strands/Math Skills	CCC	Metric and U.S. measurement. Drill designed to reflect content in current textbooks. Extensive CMI component. Substantial research evaluation. 1–8.
Mathematics Activity Courseware (MAC)	Houghton Miff.	Several activities for different grade levels. Level 4 includes "Area Estimation." "Centipede Races," an estimation activity involving area and perimeter, is at level 5. Students at level 6 are asked to estimate lengths in centimeters in "Metric Paths," and to estimate angles in "Learning All the Angles."
Measurement: Length, Mass, and Volume	Focus Media	Measurement of length, mass, and volume. Tutorials and problems. 5–12.
Measurement: Basic Skills	Control Data	Tutorials and practice on a variety of topics. 1–6.
Measurements	Dorsett	Estimating measurements and telling time. 4–6.
Measures Drill-and-Practice Program	MSS	Drill on U.S. and metric systems. 6–9.
Measures 'n' Metrics	Orbyte	Identifying units of measure in game format. 3–5.
Measuring with a Ruler: Perimeter, Circumference, Area	Ed. Act.	How to measure with a ruler, separate lessons on perimeter for polygons, squares, rectangles, and triangles; circumference; and area of rectangles, squares, triangles, and circles. 5–8.
Metric	JMH	Metric prefixes and units of length, mass, capacity, and temperature. Emphasizes changing from one unit to another and providing examples of measuring familiar objects.
Metric and Problem Solving	MECC	Drill in metric units, estimation, and conversion. 2–6.
Metric Conversion	Micro. Learn.	Utility to convert metric and U.S. measures. 3–12.
Metric I-V	CCM	Metric measurement. Simulations and drill on fundamentals, units, applications, and linear units. Comprehensive coverage with valid use of graphics. 5+.
Metric Mathematics	MECC	Estimation, conversion, estimation of metric measures. 4–6.

(continued)

TABLE 9-1   (Continued)

Title	Producer	Notes
Metric Mind	Creative Tech.	Converting to and from metric units. 3–9.
Metric Program	Professor Corp.	Converts U.S. and metric measures. 5+.
Metric Series	CCM	A series of five tutorial/practice programs. Includes Metric I: Decimals (arithmetic operations on decimals); Metric II: Math Applications (volume and weight); Metric III: Units of Measurement (includes conversion between units); Metric IV: Linear Units (reading and using a metric ruler by moving a line to the proper position next to a ruler; also perimeter); and Metric V: Area/Density Measurements.
Metric Skills I and II	Hartley	Length, mass, and capacity. Some CMI; teacher modifiable. 4–8.
Metric System Tutor	Cygnus	Use of metric units with placement test. 6–12.
Metric/English Conversion	Ed. Micro. Sys.	Metric/English (U.S.) conversions. 4–8.
Metrics	Moses	Concepts of metric measurement and conversion. 4–7.
Metrics: Measuring Length	Spectrum	Tutorial and practice. 5–7.
Micrograms Metric Series	Micrograms	Introduction and practice with conversions. 5–7.
Middle School Mathematics	MCP	A collection of activities on measurement, sold together or separately, including perimeter, circumference, area of rectangles, and volume. 6–9.
Perimeter	Bergwall	Students calculate perimeter of a polygon. 2–4.
Perimeter, Area, and Volume	JMH	Perimeter and area of polygons, circles (circumference and area), surface area and volume of three-dimensional figures.
Perimeter, Area, Volume	Gamco	Area, perimeter, and volume. Combines drill, arcade-style reward, and some CMI.
Ruler Measurement	JMH	Measuring by centimeters. 1–6. Others include "Ruler Fraction," "Ruler Inches," "Ruler Objects Inches," etc.
SI/Metric Literacy	EME	Length, area, volume, mass density, acceleration, force, large and small units, temperature. Tutorial.

Title	Producer	Notes
Volume	Micrograms	Volume of cubes, cylinders, cones, pyramids, and prisms. 6+.
Weights and Measures	Persimmon	Weight and measure conversions. 6-12.
Weights and Measures	T.H.E.S.I.S.	Reading scales and converting. 1-4.

Money

Amusement Park	SRA	Simulation of operating an amusement park, including buying equipment and food, advertising, and paying staff.
Banker's Run	Orange Cherry	Coin values, addition. Players race through bank vault in search of coins that sum to given withdrawal amount. 3-8.
Cash Register	Program Design	Making change. 4-6.
Change Maker	Micro Learn.	Practice in making change. 1-6.
CoinWorks	Nordic	Seven lessons on dealing with coins (see the text). The coins to be used, the total amount of money encountered, and the length of the lesson can be set by the user. Voice is available. All lessons can be printed on paper as well. 1-4.
The Coin Changer	Heartsoft	Coin tutorial and drill and practice.
Donald Duck's Playground	Sierra	Helping Donald earn money to pay for, and buy parts for, a playground. 2-5.
Elementary Vol. 1: Mathematics	MECC	Change is an activity on making change with the computer providing a random purchase price and amount paid. 3-5.
Essential Math Skills: Computing Tax	Media Materials	Computation with taxes: sales, federal, property, etc. 4-12.
Learning & Practicing with Money	Resource	Drill and tests in money problems. 5-7.
Learning to Count Money	Mercer	Three programs, how to count coins, shopping trip, and check-out (change). 4-6.
Lifeskill Math in the Marketplace	Media Materials	Comparison shopping. 4-12. Others in the series include "Skills at Work," "Computing Income," etc.
Magic Cash Register	Avant Guard	Simulation of a cash register; includes buying and selling. 3-6.

(continued)

TABLE 9-1   (Continued)

Title	Producer	Notes
Math for Everyday Living	Ed. Act.	Real-life math and business skills with some simulation. 1–6.
Math for the Young Consumer	Orange Cherry	Drill with all operations in consumer problems; e.g., choosing the best buy, gross and net income, etc. K–3.
Math Shop	Scholastic	Arithmetic, problem solving, and estimation skills in a setting as a salesclerk in a mall. 1–9.
Mathematics Activity Courseware (MAC)	Houghton Miff.	Several activities, such as "Making Money," a game for second graders involving choosing coins that equal a given amount. The series extends from 2–8.
Mathematics Unlimited: Problem Solving	Holt	Problem-solving series with several minisimulations dealing with geometry and measurement. For example, students in fifth grade might have to determine how many cans of water it would take to make enough artificial snow to cover ski slopes (without also covering a judging area); or decide when each of three secret agents at different locations have to begin his or her journey so that they all meet with a spy at a specified time. 1–8.
McCoco's Menu	Computer Island	Select items from restaurant menu and add the prices in decimal form. 4–6.
Money	B5	Counting coins drill. 2–4.
Money	Gamco	Computations skills involving money. For special-needs students as well; some CMI.
Money Addition	Amer. Peri.	Drill in addition of money. 4–7.
Money and Time	SVE	Drill on counting coins and comparing their values; moves clock hands to correspond to a time line. K–4.
Money Manager	Computer Age	Simulation of personal finance. 5–12.
Money Master	Medsystems or K-12 MM	Counting money and making change in maze format. 2–4.
Money! Money!	Hartley	More and less, determining amount shown, counting money, making change, and solving problems. Teacher modifiable. "Not recommended but may meet some needs": EPIE. 1–5.

Title	Producer	Notes
Money Squares	Gamco	Money skills in tic-tac-toe format. Some CMI.
Money/Time Adventures of the Lollipop Dragon	SVE	Application games provide practice in money and time-telling skills. Computer programs plus filmstrip package. K–3.
Purchase Power	Computer Age	Tutorial on making consumer decisions. 5–12.
Run for the Money	Scarborough	A fantasy simulation in which students crash-land on the planet Simian and sell a product to make enough money to leave. See Chapter 11. 4+.
Sales and Bargains	Computer Island	Finding discounted prices. 5+.
Sam's Store	AIMS Media	Simulation of a shopping trip, counting change.
Shopping Spree	M & M	Practice horizontal addition of three- to five-digit addends. 1–4.
Stock Market Math	Orange Cherry	Simulation of trading of stocks and bonds. 4–8.
Using Money & Making Change	Orange Cherry	Value of coins and currency, operations with money, making change, running a cookie shop. 2–4.
The Whatsit Corporation	Sunburst	Simulation of running a small franchise for six months. Students conduct a market survey, consult an economist, borrow money, order inventory, hire salespeople, set prices, advertise, pay taxes, etc. Throughout they keep their own records, calculating, estimating, and using formulas in the process. Thus, mathematics is used as a tool for making business decisions. Recommended by a review in the *Arithmetic Teacher*. 6–12.

Time

Calendar Skills	Hartley	Multiple tutorials and exercises on time measurement. Teachers can create their own lessons. 1–4.
Clock	B5	Drill on intervals of 1 hour, quarter-hour, 5 minutes, and 1 minute. 1–4.
Clock	Hartley	Convert between digital and dial clock and setting clock to match

(*continued*)

TABLE 9-1 (Continued)

Title	Producer	Notes
		common expressions such as "nine thirty-five." Tutorial included. 1–4.
Clock Program	Opp. Learning	Enter either digital or dial clock time, given the other.
Clock Works	MECC	Drill on telling time with analog and digital clocks. Some CMI. 1–3.
ClockWorks	Nordic	Five lessons dealing with clocks (see the text). The time interval to be used and the length of the lesson can be set by the user. Voice is available. Worksheets can be printed. All lessons can be printed on paper as well. 1–4.
Learning About Numbers	C&C	One activity, "Let's Tell Time," presents a dial clock and a digital watch together; students manipulate the hands of the clock to match a digital display. K–4.
Mathematics Activity Courseware (MAC)	Houghton Miff.	Several activities for different grade levels. Level 3 includes "Before and After"; given a digital and dial clock, students calculate a time some minutes in the future and express it as minutes before or after an hour. In "It's About Time," level 5, students race to discover the same random, mystery time. They add or subtract one of 16 times to their own "starting" time and are told whether the resulting time is earlier or later than the mystery time.
My Very Own Calendar	Opp. Learning	Prints out personalized calendar for each student. 1–3.
Spelling and Time	MicroSPARC	Included Time Teacher—moving hands on clock face and digital read-out.
Tadpole Tutor	MicroSPARC	Includes three mathematic programs for young children, such as Apple Time Tutor.
Telling Time	Gamco	Drill in telling time with arcade game reward. Digital and dial time included. Hour, half-hour, and 5-minute intervals. Some CMI. 2–4.
Telling Time	Orange Cherry	"Hours of the Day" and "Minutes in an Hour." P–3.
Telling Time	Random House	Drill and practice activities on

Title	Producer	Notes
		hours, half-hours, and quarter-hours. K–2.
Telling Time—Aim	Aim	Drill on learning time on a dial clock. 1–3.
Tick Tock Tale	Hickory Stick	Identifying time. 1–2.
Time and Distance	JMH	Three activities: "Ruler Fractions," "Clock" (time on hour, half-hour, and quarter-hour), and "Calendar."
Time and Money	Deegan	Drill with some CMI. 2–6.
Time and Money	Silver Burdett and Ginn	Tutorial and practice. K–4.
Time Explorers	Gamco	Drill in telling time in adventure-game format. Some CMI.
Time Master	Garlinghouse	Telling time and relating specific times to life's important events. K–3.
Tommy the Time-Telling Turtle	Heartsoft	Telling time in one-hour, 30-minute, 15-minute, five-minute, or one-minute modules.
Using a Calendar	Hartley	Presents a picture of a calendar, along with information and questions. Teacher modifiable. 3–5.

Computer Laboratories

Title	Producer	Notes
AtariLab	Atari	Hardware and software provided for temperature measurement.
Bank Street Laboratory	Holt, Rinehart	All hardware and software provided. Extension cords can be used to move probes farther from the computer.
MBL Kit	Cross	All hardware and software provided.
Science Toolkit	Broderbund	All hardware and software provided. Temperature, light, timer.
Temp (and others)	CDL	An organization dedicated to MBL. Sells their own and others' packages. A good place to start.

10

STATISTICS, GRAPHS, PROBABILITY, AND ESTIMATION

STATISTICS, TABLES, AND GRAPHS

Every day, newspapers, magazines, and television programs present stories whose argument is based on data presented as raw numbers, percentages, or graphs. Too often, this portion of the story is misinterpreted, doubted, or ignored. In a world increasingly inundated with data and its representation, and increasingly dependent on accurate interpretation of these data, students must develop certain skills and concepts. From their first years in school, students should participate in gathering information or data, and representing it in some way. This is statistics—the collection, organization, interpretation, and presentation of large amounts of data or information. "Reading, interpreting, and constructing tables, charts, and graphs" is one of the 10 basic skills identified by the NCSM (1977). Furthermore, it is recognized that for students to achieve full understanding and mastery of these tools, it is necessary for them to collect and interpret their own data. However, limited time and resources frequently constrain this activity.

Computer Aids

For convenience of display and interpretation, data are often organized in tables and graphs. Several programs assist students in understanding, reading, and (most importantly) constructing attractive, accurate, and flexible tables and graphs.* The first section of *Exploring Tables and Graphs*

---

*If you're saying, "I'm surprised he didn't remind us that the first graphs children make should not be computer graphs," then I've done an adequate job. You're on track already. Space prohibits listing all the interesting graphing experiences that students should have with materials such as blocks, unifix cubes, and graph paper. A few are mentioned in an upcoming section, however.

provides brief tutorials and examples. In some examples, students play several rounds of a computer game briefly and see how their scores would be tabled and graphed. In others, interesting information (about the lengths of rivers, or frog jumps, or sports statistics) is presented in tabular and graphic form. In still other examples, students are prompted for the information. For instance, in the introduction to area (pie) graphs, they are asked how many hours they spend in each of several activities: sleeping, eating, playing, school, TV, and an optional "other" category. Based on this information, the program presents "a table of how you spend your day." It then asks students to label the source line (last two lines) with their name and the date, and finally displays an area graph, explaining: "Each little pie slice shows one way in which you spend your day." It asks students questions, such as which activities they spent the most (or least) time on, and so on. It concludes that "an area graph is a good way to compare the parts of a whole." Similar activities are presented for bar, picture, and (on the level 2 version only) line segment graphs.

In the second section, students are led to construct their own graphs from information provided by the program. For instance, using the table on speeds of mammals given by the program (the same table used in a tutorial example on the first side), they might decide to construct a bar graph (Fig. 10-1).

Students can also construct tables and then create graphs based on these tables, from data they provide. One class surveyed the preferences of all the fifth graders in their school and entered the data into a table (Fig. 10-2). Then they had the program construct a picture graph based on that table. The program originally had each picture represent 7%, but the students decided that this made it difficult to determine the actual percent for each flavor. They changed this first to 10 (but then strawberry and cookie appeared the same) and finally to 5 (Fig. 10-3). Their teacher encouraged them to compare different types of graphs. They constructed area (pie) and bar graphs from the same table within minutes, and discussed the relative merits of each type (Fig. 10-4).

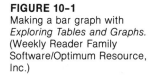

FIGURE 10-1
Making a bar graph with
Exploring Tables and Graphs.
(Weekly Reader Family
Software/Optimum Resource,
Inc.)

```
FAVORITE ICE CREAM FLAVORS

FLAVOR   |PERCENT |        |

VANILLA  |35

STRAW.   |10

CHOC.    |42

COOKIE   |8

BANANA   |5


SOURCE:   MR.  BATTISTA'S CLASS'
SURVEY OF THE FIFTH GRADE.
```

FIGURE 10-2
A table of peer preferences.

```
FAVORITE ICE CREAM FLAVORS

VANILLA  ♟ ♟ ♟ ♟ ♟ ♟ ♟

STRAW.   ♟ ♟

CHOC.    ♟ ♟ ♟ ♟ ♟ ♟ ♟ ♟ ♟

COOKIE   ♟ ♟

BANANA   ♟

   ♟ = 5

SOURCE:   MR.  BATTISTA'S CLASS'
SURVEY OF THE FIFTH GRADE.
```

FIGURE 10-3
Changing the representation.

Representations of Data

This ability to change the type of representation quickly and effortlessly allows students to explore the appropriateness of each type. It is also useful in illustrating that the way data are presented significantly affects the impression given by a graph. For example, the teacher who showed a computerized graph of one student's progress (Fig. 10–5) asked what impression it gave of Ryan's mastery of his facts. Then she changed the range of the vertical axis, and within seconds the students observed the same information presented in the same type of graph, with only this single alteration (Fig. 10–6). But the discussion revealed that the students received a different impression of Ryan's progress and gained a deeper understanding of data representation.

In this way, students understand more fully fundamental concepts of different data representations and their effects on interpretations of data. This improves their ability to interpret data and information of vital importance to society, which is increasingly reported in the form of graphs and charts by news media and others. It also develops their ability to use this tool in solving a wide variety of problems.

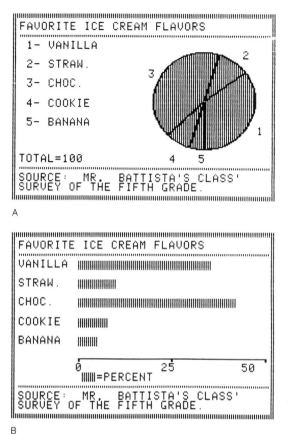

A

B

FIGURE 10-4
Which type of graph best serves
to communicate?

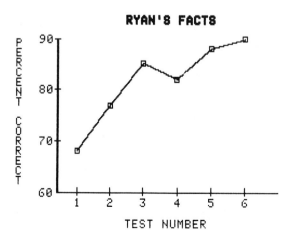

FIGURE 10-5
A graph of one student's progress.

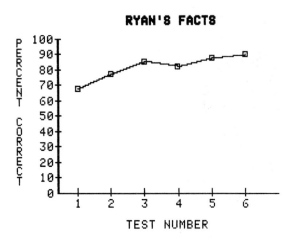

FIGURE 10-6
What impression does this modified graph give? (Weekly Reader Family Software/ Optimum Resource, Inc.)

Foundational Experiences

Young children should solve their first graphing problems concretely. For example, they might choose a type of cracker for snack (e.g., given three different brands/shapes), then lay them on a napkin, creating columns for each type. In this way a real three-column graph is constructed. As another example, newborn guinea pigs might be weighed once a week by placing each animal in one side of a balance scale and enough inch cubes in the other to balance it. Each week the inch cubes could be stacked and the column labeled with the date. When the guinea pig is fully grown, the columns constitute a graphic representation of its growth in terms of weight.

Following these concrete graphs, children might make picture graphs, wherein each student draws a picture of his or her choice on a piece of paper and pastes it in the correct column of a graph. After numerous types of experiences such as these, students can be taught to use the computer to make graph construction easier and more exact. The first experiences with such use should involve constructing both physical (or pictorial) and computer graphs of the same information. For example, what time do you like best at school: reading, language, math, spelling, art, gym, science?; or, what is your estimation of the number of pencils in the pencil container (graph estimates; count the pencils, bundling groups of 10 with rubber bands; compare to estimates); how many crayons in the crayon tub (similar procedure; is the variance less as we become better estimators?)?

Whether graphing is done with real objects or computer programs, development of many essential abilities must be guided by the teacher. For example, identifying the question that is being asked and the process that might be used to answer it, identifying different techniques for collecting data, sorting out relevant and irrelevant data, distinguishing between biased and unbiased samples of data, and detecting common statistical errors.

Integration with Other Subjects

Meaningful graphing can also be conducted as teachers integrate this activity with social studies and science units. Students can collect the data themselves (through actual observation and/or library work), then graph and interpret them. For example, as soon as the students come to school, have them take the temperature of several ice cubes. Every half-hour, they should take the temperature again. This information can be used to construct a line segment graph (Fig. 10–7). What is the temperature after 1 hour? Two hours? What is the trend—what appears to be happening with the rate of temperature change? (Note that temperature change might also be simulated, as with Micro-Dynamo; see Chapter 4.)

Similar statistical analyses might even be applied to other computer programs, such as simulations. For example, "Sell Lemonade" (from *Elementary Vol. 3*, MECC) is a beginning-level economics simulation in which students decide on a daily basis how much lemonade to produce each day (at an initial cost of 2 cents per glass), how many advertising signs to make (at a cost of 15 cents each), and what price to charge per glass so as to maximize their assets.

Beyond such economics concepts of production, advertising, price, assests, and profits, properly structured experiences with "Sell Lemonade" can develop problem-solving skills such as observing; constructing hypotheses; collecting, organizing, and displaying data; and testing those hypotheses. To ensure the development of these skills, teachers need to lead children to go beyond trial-and-error stategies. In fact, one problem with programs such as "Sell Lemonade" is that they allow children to accumulate earnings over an endless series of trials. Therefore, the most money often is earned not through intelligent strategy choice, but through mindless repetition of a moderately successful combination. A teacher might therefore give students the goal of maximizing profit over a limited number of days.

Initially, however, trial-and-error strategies are valuable to "get a feeling for" the simulation and its variables and to form initial hypotheses. For example, students might theorize that the more signs you make, the more glasses of lemonade are sold. The teacher could have them collect data determining the number of glasses sold when 0 to 6 signs are made. After the teacher emphasized that they must hold the other variables constant while the number of signs is changed, the students decided to keep the price at 9 cents and the number of glasses made at 40. They found that all 40 glasses

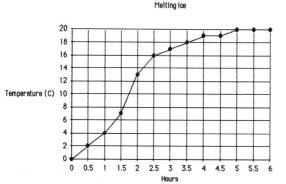

FIGURE 10-7
A graph of temperature change.

```
╔═══════════════════════════════════════════╗
║ GLASSES SOLD FOR EACH # OF SIGNS          ║
║ # SIGNS │40 MADE │50 MADE │60 MADE        ║
║ 0       │32       32       32             ║
║ 1       │40       45       45             ║
║ 2       │40       50       52             ║
║ 3       │40       50       57             ║
║ 4       │40       50       60             ║
║ 5       │40       50       60             ║
║ HOW MANY GLASSES OF LEMONADE SOLD         ║
║ AT 9 CENTS FOR 1-5 SIGNS.                 ║
╚═══════════════════════════════════════════╝
```

FIGURE 10-8
On constructing this graph, students concluded that using only four signs would be optimal. (Weekly Reader Family Software/Optimum Resource, Inc.)

were sold with just one sign; making more was a waste. They repeated the experiment, raising the number of glasses made to 50 and then 60 (given initial assets of $2.00, they could not conduct the experiment making, say, 100 glasses). They organized their results in tabular form with *Exploring Tables and Graphs* and concluded that only four signs were necessary (see Fig. 10-8).

The next step was to figure out the optimal price to charge. First deciding that four signs and 60 glasses might be the best choice, students collected data on the number of glasses sold and the profit gained when from 1 to 15 cents was charged per glass. This information was graphed. It was clear that—under those conditions—the best price to charge was 10 cents (Fig. 10-9). The teacher challenged the students to consider whether the profit could be improved at all. Similar graphs were produced for 60 glasses and three signs (less profit), 55 glasses and three signs (more profit—$3.80—because only 55 glasses were sold anyway), 55 glasses and three signs (less profit, because only 53 glasses were sold, a loss of $0.20, whereas the fourth sign cost only $0.15), and so on. The teacher also challenged them

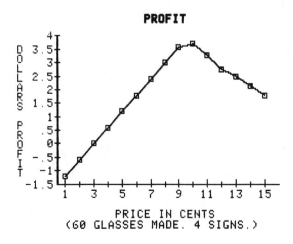

PROFIT

FIGURE 10-9
The best price appears to be 10¢. (Weekly Reader Family Software/Optimum Resource, Inc.)

to answer other questions: Is $0.10 always the best price? What if the cost to produce lemonade increases to 4 cents per glass (as indeed it does in the simulation)? What if one of the random events occur (e.g., hot or cool weather)? What if assets are increased so that 100 glasses could be made? If you must make 80 glasses at the cost of 4 cents per glass, how many signs will sell the most glasses? Yield the greatest profit?

Other Statistical Analyses

Although statistical data are discussed (albeit infrequently) in elementary school, statistical concepts such as the mean (average) or median are often not introduced until the later grades. However, computer programs can help make such concepts meaningful to elementary students. The use of computerized tables and graphs can be used to introduce concepts such as the range (the difference between the greatest and least numbers) and three measures of central tendency: the mean (arithmetic average), median (the "middle number" in the ordered data), and mode (the number that occurs most frequently). Often, graphing programs have statistical components that will provide this information (of course, students should be introduced to these concepts concretely; e.g., using blocks to graph data and finding the average by evening the columns).

Have students collect the heights of all the children in their grade, and the grades one lower and one higher than their grade (they might best organize in groups to accomplish this task). They could then use a graphing program to display a bar graph for all the children, and for each of the three grades separately. Ask them to compare and contrast the graphs. What trends are noticeable? (For example, do the graphs suggest the familiar "bell-shaped curve"? How do they deviate from it?) Which is more variable? What is the mode, median, and mean? Students also might redisplay the data by sex, or collect information on weight for comparative purposes. Much of this type of work can be organized with the help of an information management system, as discussed in Chapter 3.

Students often have difficulty understanding how one extreme number can affect the mean, or average, of a group of numbers. Have students enter figures representing people's wages, heights of girls and boys, prices of houses in a neighborhood, or the like, and investigate the effects of an extreme value. Discuss which measure of central tendency—the mean, median, or mode—is most appropriate for a given situation. For example, for the prices of real estate in a neighborhood with many middle-range houses and two $250,000 houses, the median or mode would be more appropriate. Students could easily see this by examining the figures from the statistics program.

As with the use of other utility programs, one of the main advantages of this activity lies in the freedom and interest it generates for "productive playing" or experimenting with the data they have collected. Simultaneously, students are learning a real-world application and they are developing an intuition for fairly complex mathematical ideas, similar to the intuition a young child develops for an understanding of the relationship between the heights and widths of containers by pouring water or sand from one container to the other. They can do this because the computer conducts the complex calculations while the students immediately see the results of the graphs or calculations they requested. At a later time, they will understand more fully the mathematical basis for the calculations—but now they are building an intuition about them that they might not have developed without the support of the computer and the program.

Logo Programs for Statistics

Many of these utilities that collect, analyze, and display data can be provided by simple computer programs typed in or constructed by teachers and/or older students. Two such Logo programs are provided in the Appendix. The first assists students in conducting a survey of categorical data. For example, two of Mrs. Jones's fifth-grade girls conducted a survey of eye colors. They loaded the program SURVEY.CATEGORICAL (for a survey using categories), typed *COLLECT.DATA*, and engaged in the following interaction:

```
WHAT IS THE DATA'S NAME? (ONE WORD)
>EYE.COLOR.JONES

WHAT ARE THE CATEGORIES?
IF ORDER IS IMPORTANT, TYPE THEM IN
ORDER. USE SINGLE WORDS FOR EACH, WITH
SPACES IN BETWEEN. PRESS <RETURN> WHEN
FINISHED. >GREEN BLUE HAZEL BROWN
VIOLET GRAY

ARE YOU GOING TO ENTER NUMBERS
(D)IRECTLY OR HAVE THE PROGRAM DO A
(S)URVEY? >S

WHAT IS THE QUESTION YOU WISH TO ASK?
WHAT COLOR ARE YOUR EYES?

THE EYE.COLOR.JONES SURVEY...
--------------------------------------------
WHAT COLOR ARE YOUR EYES?

  CHOOSE ONE OF THESE:

  GREEN BLUE HAZEL BROWN VIOLET GRAY
    ...OR TYPE "STOP" TO QUIT

BROWN...
```

Here the program continued to request the information from each student who sat down. At any time, new information can be added (by typing ASK). When each student in the class had participated, the originators typed *REPORT "EYE.COLOR.JONES* and saw:

```
SEND REPORT: (S)CREEN OR (P)RINTER? > P
```

Whereupon the program printed the information on paper.

```
REPORT ON DATA: EYE.COLOR.JONES

THE CATEGORY(IES) WITH THE GREATEST
FREQUENCY WAS (WERE): BROWN
WITH A FREQUENCY OF: 13

THE CATEGORY(IES) WITH THE LEAST
FREQUENCY WAS (WERE): VIOLET GRAY
WITH A FREQUENCY OF: 0

THE RANGE OF THE FREQUENCIES IS: 13

NAME NUMBER %       GRAPH (EACH * = 4%)
----------------------------------------
GREEN      7    28   *******
BLUE       4    16   ****
HAZEL      1    4    *
BROWN     13    52   *************
VIOLET     0    0
GRAY       0    0
```

Note that "number" is the number of students having that color eyes, "%" is the percentage, and the asterisks form a simple histogram. Questions that could now be answered included: What is the most frequent eye color? The least frequent? What percentage of students have blue eyes? and so on.

The two girls decided to compare the results with the other first-grade class. Because those students could not enter their eye color on the computer that week, the girls recorded the data on paper and entered it (D)I-RECTLY by category. Typing *REPORT "EYE.COLOR.SPICER* and specifying the printer, they obtained these results:

```
REPORT ON DATA: EYE.COLOR.SPICER

THE CATEGORY(IES) WITH THE GREATEST
FREQUENCY WAS (WERE): BROWN
WITH A FREQUENCY OF: 14

THE CATEGORY(IES) WITH THE LEAST
FREQUENCY WAS (WERE): VIOLET
WITH A FREQUENCY OF: 0

THE RANGE OF THE FREQUENCIES IS: 14

NAME NUMBER %       GRAPH (EACH * = 4%)
----------------------------------------
GREEN      5    17   ****.
BLUE       8    27   ******.
HAZEL      2    7    *.
BROWN     14    47   ***********.
VIOLET     0    0
GRAY       1    3    .
```

(The period at the end of the graph for some rows signified some fraction of 4%.)

This inspired two boys to do a similar comparison of the two class' grades on a unit test. They used the second Logo program, SURVEY.NUM-ERICAL (see the Appendix), which provides a more extensive analysis of numerical data. After entering the grades, they asked for similar reports. In this case, the program does considerably more work, including sorting the data (which were not entered in order) and providing additional descriptive statistics. The printouts can be seen in Fig. 10–10.

The boys noticed that the "typical" grade (central tendency), as measured by the mean, median, and mode, were not too different, with Mrs. Spicer's class scoring slightly lower. However, there was a difference in how close the two class's scores were to the center. The graphs showed that the scores of Mrs. Spicer's students were spread out more. This is reflected in the greater range (40 versus 20) and standard deviation (about 11.4 versus 6.5). In a "normal" or "bell-shaped" distribution, about two-thirds of the scores are within 1 standard deviation of the mean. That is, about 20 of Mrs. Spicer's students would probably score between 65 and 87 (indeed, 21 did so; how accurate is this approximation for Mrs. Jones's class?). So whereas the mean, median, and mode show us the center, the range and standard deviation tell us how "bunched together" or spread out around the average the scores are.

Such procedures might be used by younger children or students with no programming experience to help them gather, organize, and describe data. Benefit could also be gleaned as more capable students study and modify the procedures to gain a fuller, process-based understanding of mathematical concepts such as frequency, percent, variable, mean, and median, as well as computer science/problem solving concepts such as sorting algorithms, recursion, and conditionals. More advanced students might write their own computer programs to analyze and display data. One obvi-

```
SORTING...
THE SORTED DATA FOR GRADES.JONES ARE:

70 70 70 70 75 75 75 75 75 80 80 80
80 80 80 85 85 85 85 85 85 90 90 90


THE NUMBERS(S) WITH THE GREATEST
FREQUENCY (THE MODE) WAS (WERE): 80 85
WITH A FREQUENCY OF: 6

THE NUMBER(S) WITH THE LEAST
FREQUENCY WAS (WERE): 90
WITH A FREQUENCY OF: 3

THE RANGE OF THE FREQUENCIES IS: 3
```

FIGURE 10-10 A printout from the Logo program SURVEY NUMERICAL.

```
NUM. FREQ.  %    GRAPH (EACH * = 4%)
------------------------------------------
70      4    17   ****.
75      5    21   *****.
80      6    25   ******.
85      6    25   ******.
90      3    13   ***.
```

THE RANGE OF THE DATA IS: 20

THE MEDIAN IS: 80

THE MEAN IS: 79.7916

THE STANDARD DEVIATION IS: 6.50738

SORTING...
THE SORTED DATA FOR GRADES.SPICER ARE:

55 55 60 60 65 65 65 70 70 70 70 75 75 75 75
80 80 80 80 80 80 85 85 85 85 90 90 95 95 95

THE NUMBER(S) WITH THE GREATEST
FREQUENCY (THE MODE) WAS (WERE): 80
WITH A FREQUENCY OF: 6

THE NUMBER(S) WITH THE LEAST
FREQUENCY WAS (WERE): 55 60 90
WITH A FREQUENCY OF: 2

THE RANGE OF THE FREQUENCIES IS: 4

```
NUM. FREQ.  %    GRAPH (EACH * = 4%)
------------------------------------------
55      2    7   *.
60      2    7   *.
65      3    10  **.
70      4    13  ***.
75      4    13  ***.
80      6    20  *****
85      4    13  ***.
90      2    7   *.
95      3    10  **.
```

THE RANGE OF THE DATA IS: 40

THE MEDIAN IS: 77.5

THE MEAN IS: 76.3333

THE STANDARD DEVIATION IS: 11.442

FIGURE 10-10 (Continued)

ous extension to the procedures in the Appendix is a set of procedures that would enable the turtle to draw bar graphs of the data. Or, a procedure could be written that would combine two sets of data.

Another method of collecting such data is by statistical sampling of populations. As with most samples and opinion polls reported in the media, this involves selection of a random sample, often accompanied by the definition of a proper representation of each stratification of a wider population. For example, each of several groups of students could draw a random sample from one grade at their school. Each group of students would collect and record data, graph and analyze their results, and make predictions as to the characteristics of the population sampled. Then all groups' data could be combined and reanalyzed.

Graphing and statistics programs make the display and analysis of data almost effortless; therefore, students can attend more completely to the interpretation of the information.

PROBABILITY

Foundational Experiences

Students' first classroom experiences with probability should not be on the computer. Familiar situations and language should be used to establish basic concepts, such as likely, unlikely, certain, uncertain, and impossible events. Discussions such as that generated by asking: "There are 24 students in the room. If I picked one name out of a hat to determine who would be first in line, what is the chance it would be Rita? If there are 12 girls, what is the chance it would be a girl?" At intermediate grade levels, the formula *probability = number of favorable outcomes / number of possible outcomes* (given that all outcomes are equally likely) could be developed.

CAI Extensions

A teacher might extend such initial explorations of probability by altering spinners used in a classroom game (e.g., one might be 3/4 white and 1/4 black). She might ask: "If your marker was white, which spinner would you rather use? Why?" Students could then spin each and keep a record of the results. The teacher would guide them to hypothesize a relationship between the areas of the colored regions of each spinner and these results. The class data could be aggregated and discussed.

Then students could use "Draw Your Own Spinner" (*TABS-MATH;* Damarin, in Hansen and Zweng, 1984) to construct similar spinners on the screen. These spinners would then generate and automatically tabulate much more data than the paper spinners. In another activity in this set, students are shown "Three Spinners" and the data generated by one of them. They must determine which of the three is being "spun" by the program. If they are successful, they are given increasingly challenging problems. In other activities, students can construct spinners of different shapes and sizes. In one, they can specify the probabilities of the program choosing rock, scissors, or paper, to determine a winning strategy (e.g., if they choose paper and manipulate the spinners to give a high probability of rock and a low probability of scissors). In another, two students must examine a multi-colored game board to construct spinners that will maximize their chance of being first to finish around the board. Another program in the series, *Probability Games*, consists of simulated coins, dice, and marble games. Their purpose is to provide intuitive experience with probability concepts. "In the Bag" is a simple experiment with random sampling with replacement. Students decide how many marbles to put in a bag and how many times to draw marbles from the bag. The program places that many in the bag, without telling the students how many are green and how many purple. It then randomly draws marbles (replacing each marble drawn before drawing another), recording how many of each color were drawn. At this point, the students may guess how many of each color marble are in the bag or they may proceed to draw more marbles. Students learn that the number of draws one has to make is dependent on the number of marbles in the bag and that one can be easily misled by a small number of draws (for larger numbers, one needs many more draws than marbles in the bag). "Math Casino" is a set of games based on dice and coins. The simplest, "Over/Under," asks students to predict whether a roll of two die will be more than 7, equal to 7, or less than 7. Another game addresses the *mis*conception that the probability of an event is dependent on previous events; that is, the erroneous idea that flipping five heads with a fair coin increases the chances that the next flip will yield a tail (or another head). Others allow students to predict the roll of dice or toss of a coin, graph a great number of throws of dice, and so on.

Students playing *The Jar Game* are presented with two jars that contain gold (their) and green (the computer's) candy. They must choose the jar where a fly will probably land more often on the gold candy (i.e., the jar with the greater ratio of gold). If they do, they receive 2 bonus points. Then the fly buzzes randomly from one piece to another, landing when the students press the RETURN key (they cannot influence the outcome by timing the keypress). A gold landing earns them 1 point; a green landing earns the computer 1 point. A round ends after 10 landings; 50 points wins the game. At first, choices are relatively obvious (e.g., gold ratios of 2/5 and 3/5); however, on more difficult problems, students learn that a greater number of gold candies does not guarantee success (e.g., a jar with a gold ratio of 4/8 has more gold candies, but fewer gold landings, than one with a ratio of 2/3).

Logo Extensions

Students familiar with computer programming might write their own simple simulations of probability experiments. The following Logo procedure simulates any number of coin tosses (see the Appendix for the Terrapin version).

```
TO TOSS.COIN :NUMBER.TOSSES
  MAKE "HEADS 0
  MAKE "TAILS 0
  REPEAT :NUMBER.TOSSES [IF (RANDOM 2) = 1
                         [MAKE  "HEADS :HEADS + 1]
                         [MAKE "TAILS :TAILS + 1]]
  PRINT (SENTENCE [AFTER] :NUMBER.TOSSES
    [TOSSES, THE RESULTS ARE:]
  PRINT (SENTENCE :HEADS [HEADS AND]
    :TAILS [TAILS.] )
END
```

If the student types TOSS.COIN 1000, the computer might print

```
AFTER 1000 TOSSES, THE RESULTS ARE:
492 HEADS AND 508 TAILS.
```

Another short challenge: Study the following procedure.

```
TO WANDER
  FORWARD RANDOM 10
  RIGHT RANDOM 360
  WANDER
END
```

What will the turtle's path look like? Where will it probably be after 5 seconds; 1 minute; 10 minutes (especially pertinent question if your Logo has a WINDOW primitive, which allows the turtle to "wander off the screen")? Have everyone run WANDER for 30 seconds, stop the program, and record the coordinates of their turtle. What are the average coordinates? Why does it lurk so close to home so often?

Let's put some limits on our wandering turtle. Pretend that the turtle would "flip a coin" to decide whether to turn RT 30 or LT 30 and then go FD 10. How many possible paths would it take if it took two such steps? We could write procedures to take each step (TAKE.STEP in Fig. 10–11). Then WALK would repeat this procedure a given number of times; two in this first case. We're not sure how many such paths there are, so we have WALK

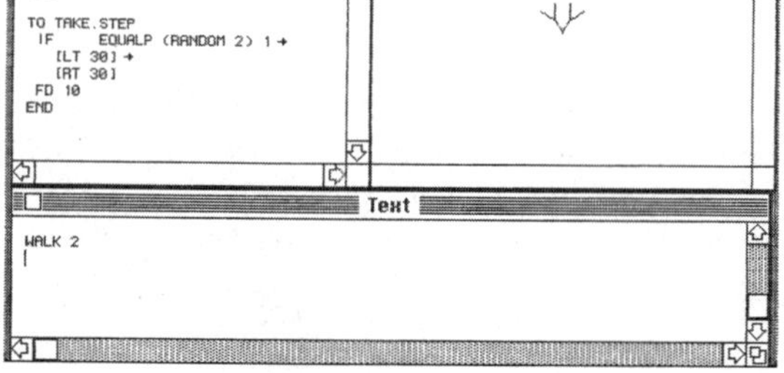

FIGURE 10–11
The WALK Logo program puts limits on the wandering turtle.

call itself recursively until we're satisfied that all the paths have been found. (When we do figure out how many paths for each number of steps, could we then use REPEAT instead of recursion with our present randomized procedure? Why not?) Finding all the paths appears fairly simple in the case of two steps (see the graphics window in Fig. 10–11). But things get rather complex for three, four, five, or nine steps (Fig. 10–12). How can you be sure that all paths have been drawn? Can you see the number patterns resident in these designs?

Graphing and Probability

Graphing activities might be expanded into explorations with probability. For example, students might use the bar graph they constructed displaying the frequency of occurrence of each letter in a class textbook to generate probable occurrence of each letter. This is experimental probability, determined by observing and counting outcomes from a sample. These probabilities could be used to predict how many times the letter would appear in 1000 letters from the same, or another, book. These probabilities might be used to "break secret codes" (students might read a detective story, *The Gold Bug* by Edgar Allen Poe, to see how this technique is applied). As a second example, the students observing traffic flow might also record the

A   B

C   D

FIGURE 10–12 For more than two steps, determining "all the paths" is more difficult.

number of people in each car during the rush hour. They could then express the probability that a car traveling on the road during that time is carrying, say, three people. Whenever more complex information is being collected from a sample, students might use a computerized data base management system (or the Logo programs described above) to record, sort, and tabulate the information (see the next section for examples).

One of the ten basic skill areas deals with probability and "using mathematics to predict" (NCSM, 1977). Statistics and probability programs can help students learn to collect, organize, interpret, and present data; understand randomness and gain intuition about chance events; and generate and test hypotheses and solve problems. It is important to structure these experiences in such a way that students construct basic frames for statistics and probability concepts and problem situations. The frames should be utilized and expanded in real-life and other interdisciplinary applications and thus will be the foundation upon which later, more mathematically rigorous work will build.

ESTIMATION

The use of computers and calculators has increased the importance of the skill of mental estimation—students must be able to determine whether a mechanical computation is reasonable, as it is easy to make a mistake in entering numbers and operations. Additionally, in daily life people use estimation more often than paper-and-pencil computation. The NCTM has recommended that "teachers should incorporate estimation activities into all areas of the program on a regular and sustaining basis" (1980, p. 7). Recall that "estimation and approximation" and "alertness to the reasonableness of results" constitute two of the ten basic skill areas identified by the NCSM (1977). Despite these convincing arguments, estimation remains one of the most neglected areas of the curriculum.

Estimation should be done quickly and mentally. Research indicates that most students are poor estimators and that the few good estimators use a variety of strategies. Reys and others (1982) have identified three basic processes good estimators use:

1. *Reformulation* is the process of altering numerical data to produce a more mentally manageable form by rounding (rounding 474,257 / 8127 to 480,000 / 8000 and estimating the answer as 60); using the leftmost numbers (for 87,496 + 92,503 + 90,454 + 98,102 + 85,492 adding 8 + 9 + 9 + 9 + 8 to obtain an estimate of 430,000); or substituting numbers [for (347 × 6) / 43 substituting (350 × 6) / 42 to obtain 350 / 7, or 50].

2. *Translation* involves changing the structure of the problem (for 87,496 + 92,503 + 90,454 + 98,102 + 85,492, figuring that "all the numbers are close to 90,000, so it would be 90,000 times 5 or about 450,000").

3. *Compensation* is the process of adjusting the estimate upward or downward to correct variation caused by reformulation or translation (increasing the estimate slightly because the numbers were rounded down).

Thus, teachers should search for computer programs that develop these basic processes, as well as those involved in estimation of area, distance, and so on. It has also been found that children can be taught to use valid estimation strategies in a short period of time, that computers can help deliver this instruction, and that replacing computational drill by estimation instruction does not decrease computational skills (Schoen et al., 1981). However, it is important to recognize that these skills must be taught explictly.

The TAB-Math estimation materials focus on whole number multiplication and division (Damarin, in Hansen & Zweng, 1984). Several levels of difficulty are available, defined by the magnitude of the numbers and the discrepancy allowed between the estimate and the result of the computation. Exploration is encouraged; for example, in a "Bull's Eye" program, a problem is presented ("estimate 37 × 54"), and one ring in the bull's-eye target is lit to indicate the closeness or quality of the estimate.

In the real world, judgment of estimation quality is often dependent on context. Therefore, other programs place students in situations such as shopping and car racing, in which underestimates and overestimates have different consequences. For instance, an underestimate of a race's distance produced from the provided rate and time prevents the car from completing the race.

Estimation Invasion includes two games that require good estimates of products. Invaders slowly descend, shooting the students' factor (this gradually uncovers the hidden numbers). If students' estimates are too high or low, they lose one of their three spaceships (on the left of Fig. 10–13). The more accurate the estimates are, the more invaders the players' spaceships destroy and the more points they earn (in Fig. 10–13, the guess of 40,000 shot all the invaders and gained 240 points). A "nondestructive" version of the game "Magic Garden" is also included in the package.

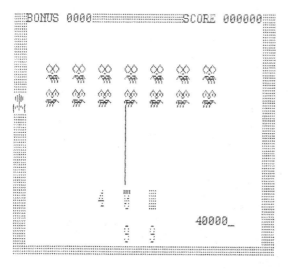

FIGURE 10-13
Estimation Invasion game. (Encyclopedia Britannica Educational Corp. Distributed by Looking Glass Learning Products, Inc.)

In a program in *Challenge Math* children must first choose which of three arithmetic problems will give the largest answer, then compute only that problem. Points are awarded both for the computation and the estimation (Fig. 10–14). *Power Drill* provides practice in estimation and successive approximation. A problem is presented in any of the four arithmetic operations at one of three levels of difficulty, for example: $38 \times ? = 5548$. If the students' answer is far off, say 10, the program would respond, "Way too SMALL" and provide a hint: "Think about $40 \times ? = 6000$." If the students then respond with 150, the screen would display

$$0.10 \text{ is way too SMALL!}$$
$$38 \times ? = 5548$$
$$38 \times 150 = 5700$$

The students would then attempt to improve their estimates. An entry of 145 would produce the following:

$$38 \times 145 = 5510$$
$$38 \times ? \quad = 5548$$
$$38 \times 150 = 5700$$

This process continues until the students "zero in" on the correct factor (146). The total number of tries it took to arrive at this answer is displayed. The documentation exhorts teachers to encourage students to estimate rather than compute, to avoid making a second estimate "from scratch," but rather to estimate how far their first estimate was off, and to develop estimation strategies. For example, they could be guided to see that while increasing the value of a missing addend or factor increases the result, increasing the value of a missing subtrahend or divisor decreases the result. Place value should also be emphasized. Given $319 \times ? = 74,646$, students could see that a three-digit number would have to be multiplied by a multiple of 100 to generate a five-digit number. Because $7 / 3$ is about 2, a likely first estimate would be 200. This yields 63,800. The difference between 74,646 and 63,800 is about 10,000. How many 319s are there in 10,000?—about 30, so the next estimate might be 230, and so on.

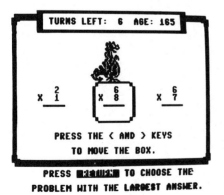

FIGURE 10–14
Estimating computations in *Challenge Math*.
(Sunburst Communications)

As stated, students should estimate many types of quantities. *Estimation* provides several activities involving discrete and continuous quantities for primary-grade children. The first program has a train moving toward, and then through, a tunnel. The student attempts to stop the train when it passes over an arrow placed randomly by the program. The speed of the train can be varied. In "Junk Jar," students select a certain object with which they would like to fill the jar. The program then displays a random-sized jar and the students etimate how many of the chosen objects will fit in it. The computer then drops that number into the jar. Finally, three "Bug Tracks" activities teach estimation of linear quantity. Students might guess how many bugs will fit along a "trail" or which of two trails is longer, or they draw a trail as long as one the program drew. For each, the program places bugs on each trail to provide feedback.

In *Golf Classic* students play golf, determining first the angle a golf ball should be hit and then the number of units for distance. Bright (1984a) has shown that this game can increase skill in angle estimation. However, there was no dependable effect on distance estimation in the study. Bright warned that distortion on the monitor may be detrimental to length estimation (horizontal shots appear to involve a different scale than vertical shots) and that the instruction provided on the computer must be integrated with classroom instruction, lest the two interfere with each other.

Students are engaged in a variety of mental exercises in *Estimating and Common Sense*, such as rounding whole numbers and decimals to estimate answers to arithmetic problems; deciding if a sum is less than or more than 100; and visually estimating lengths, areas, and volumes. In one activity, students are asked to estimate answers by rounding or changing one or both of the numbers in an arithmetic problem. They are advised to decide first which numbers to alter. The program provides examples: For $23 / 4$ it is suggested that 23 be changed to 24 to yield an estimate of 6, whereas 29×37 is rounded to $30 \times 40 = 1200$. Then they are asked to estimate the answers for problems such as 14.7×1.8, 7.8×3, and $9.08 / 2.99$. The computer provides feedback on their estimates.

In other activities, students are guided to estimate areas of composite figures by breaking a figure into manageable parts (the areas of which are provided) and mentally determining the area as the sum of those parts. Given a map with a scale, they must estimate various distances between cities, determine "which city is three times as far from A as B is," and solve problems such as "A car left city H at 9:00 a.m. and averaged 80 km per hour; about what time did it arrive in C?" To judge the reasonableness of results, they are asked if a situation "makes sense," such as "There are 120 girls in the sixth grade. One day, over half of them wore miniskirts to school, 63 of them wore blue jeans, and 22 of them were absent."

Statistics, probability, and estimation are, of course, natural partners. Students in a class might stand at different locations in the building in the morning and record the hair color of 10 people. After constructing a table and graph with a computer program, they could estimate the probability that any student at the school has blond or brunette hair. Of course, they might also collect information in additional categories (e.g., wears glasses, color of clothes, color of eyes, etc.). They could then enter this information into a computerized data base management system (see Chapter 3), have the DBMS sort and tabulate the information, and generate graphs and estimated probabilities for each category.

Of course, estimation should be encouraged whenever it is appropriate. Logo programming often requires estimation of the measure of both distances and angles, especially for students who lack advanced geometric concepts. For example, to determine the length of the final side of a right isosceles triangle (e.g., FD 40 RT 90 FD 40 RT 135 FD ?), younger students not yet able to use the Pythagorean theorem or a trigonometric function might use the estimation strategy of successive approximation. It has been found that even first-grade Logo programmers improve in their use of visual estimates of linear quantities, and gradually rely more on self-constructed "standard units" of measure and mathematical determinations as the year proceeds (Clements, 1985a; Kull, 1986). For example, one girl explained her "units" approach: "In your mind, if you had to go this far and you know about that much was 10 turtle steps (holding her thumb and finger about 1 cm apart) . . . that looks like 1, 2, 3, 4, 5, 6, 7 . . . so what's 7 times 10 and that was 70" (Clements, 1987). Even early, primitive strategies can lead to significant discoveries. One mathematically below-average English boy tried to turn the turtle through a right angle with a "homing in" using the commands: LEFT 40 LEFT 20 LEFT 10 LEFT 20. Having added the inputs, he waited until another right angle was required and then announced the solution LEFT 90, much to the surprise of his peers and teacher (Noss, 1984).

Finally, students could use, modify, or construct Logo procedures that provided practice on estimation (see the Appendix). Interaction with the program might be as follows:

ESTIMATE

```
38 * N = 3230
```

```
WHAT IS YOUR ESTIMATE?  > 80
```
(The student has been encouraged to think "What times 40 equals 3200?")

```
38 * 80 = 3040
38 *  N = 3230
```
(The student thinks, "I'm about 200 too low. That would be about six 33s or five 40s. But 38* N must end in

```
WHAT IS YOUR ESTIMATE?  > 85
```
a zero, so I'll try 85.")

```
38 * 85 = 3230
```

```
THAT'S IT EXACTLY!
```

Notice that it would be very easy for students to alter the program. Some ideas would be to (a) have the program use larger or smaller numbers, or decimals; (b) change the operation to addition, subtraction, or multiplication; (c) change the structure of the problem from a missing factor to a missing product; (d) add a timer to discourage exact computation; (e) create a two-player game with score keeping; and (f) alter the program to inform the users of the proximity of their estimate (e.g., within 10%, 20%, or the like). In this way, students get "three in one"—programming, problem solving, and practice (see Clements, 1983).

Statistics, graphing, probability, and estimation are areas in which computers can help teachers broaden the evolution of their mathematics curriculum. Table 10-1 lists some CAI software in these areas.

SUGGESTED READINGS

Hansen and Zweng's (1984) NCTM yearbook includes several chapters that discuss the use of computers in probability and statistics.

Reys and others (1982) discuss the strategies good estimators use. How could you assist your students' development of such strategies with and without computer programs?

TABLE 10-1   Software: Statistics, Tables, Graphs Probability and Estimation

Title	Producer	Notes
Statistics, Tables, and Graphs		
Averages: Mode, Median, Mean	Control Data	Measures of central tendency. 6–9.
Bar Graph	Micro-Ed	Graphing drill. 4–10.
Bar Graphs	Bergwall	Interpreting negative and positive number values on bar graphs. 2–4.
Basic Math Competency Skill Building	Ed. Act.	Math skills, including graphs, statistics. Some CMI. 4+.
Bumble Games	TLC	Sequence of six games that develop number lines, graph plotting. Recommended. P–4.
Bumble Plot	TLC	Sequence of five graphing and problem-solving programs, from number-line problems to using positive and negative numbers to name points in a four-quadrant grid. Recommended. 3–8.
Descriptive Statistics	Courses	Tutorial with practice; upper grades or enrichment.
ESC Mathematics	ESC	Concept and skill development with charts, tables, graphs, probability, and some beginning statistics. A comprehensive program for grades 1–6.

Please note that many of these programs are appropriate only for students in grades 6 and up, or for enrichment in the higher intermediate grades.

(continued)

TABLE 10-1 (Continued)

Title	Producer	Notes
Exploring Tables and Graphs	Weekly Reader/ Optimum	Tutorials, examples, and games to introduce tables and graphs and tools to allow students to construct their own (see the body of the text). Recommended. 1–6.
Graphic Math	Orbyte	Practice in reading and interpreting bar and coordinate graphs. 3–5.
Graphing	MECC	Shows how ordered pairs create computer graphics as screen is compared to a map. 6–9.
Graphing Is Fun	Aquarius	Graphing. 4–8.
Graphmaster	HRM	Introduction to labeling, altering, and plotting graphs. Uses on-screen tables and calculator. 5–12.
Graphs Tutor	Computer Island	Reading, using, and making graphs and charts. 5–8.
Math Grapher	ECS	Plotting of functions.
Mathematics Unlimited: Problem Solving	Holt	Problem-solving series with several minisimulations. For example, sixth-grade students might manage a music band and have to decide how many tee shirts of each of five sizes to order for a giveaway for the next concert. They need to figure out each quantity based on expected audience size, a graph showing the percent of people that wear each size, and a margin-of-safety error (the difficult level involves the use of ratios). Most of the activities demand considerable estimation; for instance, given a total distance from one cliff to another and the distance of a rock to the other cliff, estimate (via subtraction using first digits only) the correct distances to jump to the rock (grade 3), or choosing two song sequences for an album that meet conditions (e.g., total length of each side and balance of fast/slow). 1–8.
Measurements	Dorsett	Graphs and estimating measurements. 4–6.
Middle School Mathematics	MCP	Statistics and graphing concepts and skills. Inexpensive software developed by teachers. 6–9.
Plot-a-Point	World Book	Plotting coordinates. 1–5.

Title	Producer	Notes
Problem-solving with Scrooge McDuck	Disney	Reading graphs and estimating. 4–8.
Reading Graphs	Micrograms	Introduction of different kinds of graphs. 5–9.
Relating Graphs to Events	Conduit	Graphing as a description of physical phenomena. 5–12.
Statistics	JMH	"Real world" application of statistical data.
Tables	Bergwall	Students make tabulations by reading tally marks on tables. 2–4.
Telemath	Psychotechnics	80 math programs. K–8.

Probability

Chance It: Probability Simulation	Trillium Press	Eleven simulations for exploring probability. 5–9.
Mathematics Activities Courseware	Houghton Miff.	
Pig	NTS	Probability game. 2–5.
Playing to Learn: Math/Logic Games	Queue	Grades 6 and up.
Probability	Bergwall	Students determine probability of an event in fraction and phrase form.
Probability	Control Data	Grades 6–9.
Probability	MECC	Simple coin simulations and surprising game activities that motivate a deeper student of expected events in rolling dice. 6–9.
Probability: Concepts and Skills	Courses	Tutorial with practice. 6–9.
Spinners and Slugs	Scott, Foresman	Buildling probability tables to predict appearance of numbers on spinners or dice. 5–8.
TABS: Pete's Probability Raffle	Britannica	Simulation of a raffle. 5–9.
TABS: Probability Games	Britannica	A set of simulated coins, dice, and marble games designed to provide intuitive experience with probability concepts. 4–9.

Estimation and Rounding

Answer Matches	Media Materials	Reasonableness of answers. 6–9.
Approximation, Estimation, and Standard Form	Queue	Quick and accurate estimation skills.

(*continued*)

TABLE 10-1 (Continued)

Title	Producer	Notes
Arithmetic Games	SRA	
Building Estimation Skills	Cuisenaire	Rounding and estimating arithmetic operations in a hidden-picture format. 4–8.
Bull's-Eye	Britannica	Provides estimation practice in the form of a game of darts. Users can alter the type of problem, the size of numbers, and the difficulty (percentage of error permitted).
Challenge Math	Sunburst	See text.
Elementary Vol. 1: Mathematics	MECC	Activities on estimating metric measures and on rounding numbers to the nearest multiple of 10. 2–6.
Elementary Vol. 4: Math/Science	MECC	Estimating with arithmetic exercises. 4–6.
ESC Mathematics	ESC	Estimation, including number sense, measurement, and computational estimation. Strategies such as front-end estimation, compatible numbers, and rounding. Also mental computation. A comprehensive program for grades 1–6.
Estimath	Micro Power	Estimating answers to arithmetic exercises. 4+.
Estimating and Common Sense	Data Command	See text.
Estimation	Britannica	Estimating products, and rounding.
Estimation	MCEP	Estimating distance, speed, quantity, and length. P–1.
Estimation	MECC	Multiplying and dividing whole numbers and decimals. Also, students use the "Heartbeat" and "Shopping" programs to apply estimation skills to practical situations. 6–9.
Estimation at the Races	Britannica	Provides estimation practice within the context of the relationship between distance, rate, and time. In "The Swimmer," students might be presented with the distance and time for a swim meet, and would have to estimate the rate. Graphic feedback is provided for the estimate.
Estimation Invasion	Britannica	Estimation of solution to problems in arcade-game format. See the text. 6–10.

Title	Producer	Notes
Estimation Skill Builder	EduSoft	Estimate answers to arithmetic operations in arcade-game format. 5–12.
Golf Classic	Milliken	Angle and length estimation. 4+.
Guesstimator	Micro-Ed	Estimating what proportion of a rectangular region has been filled. 3–8.
IBM Elementary Mathematics Series	IBM/WICAT	Estimation and rounding. As an example, in "Order to 10,000," students see a hole on a line between 4334 and 5350 and a hand holding a seed. They read: "Try to plant a seed in the hole. Type a whole number." For each wrong answer a seed is dropped in the corresponding position and a plant grows marked with a numeral. Thus, through successive approximation, the student determines the specific number required. In a similar activity, "Desert Garden: Thousands," students may round 4356 to the nearest hundred to place a rain cloud over the point. If correct, rain helps a plant grow.
Math Skills	Britannica	Grades 6–9.
Math Skills	Diversified	One program teaches rounding skills. 3–7.
Math Strategies: Estimation	SRA	Computational strategies for dealing with large numbers. 4–9.
Math Concepts I & II	Hartley	Rounding. 2–6.
Mathematics Activity Courseware	Houghton Miff.	A package of activities for each grade level designed to provide experiences in estimation, computation, and problem solving. 3–8.
Mathfinder	Holt	Estimation is one part of this comprehensive package. K–6.
Playing to Learn	HRM	Estimation in one of four games. Students estimate the number of "bubbles" in one group after being told how many there are in another. 4–12.
Problem Solving with Scrooge McDuck	Disney	Estimation and graphing. 4–8.
Round Up, Round Down	Britannica	Presents four tutorial and practice programs on rounding up, rounding down, and the mixture of these

(continued)

TABLE 10-1 (Continued)

Title	Producer	Notes
		strategies for estimating products. For example, given 83 × 68, student are taught to round 83 to 80 and 68 to 70, multiply 80 × 70 to obtain an estimate of 5600, and to realize that in this case, the estimate may be greater or less than the actual product.
Rounding	Bergwall	Students round 2-digit numbers. 2–4.
Rounding	Gamco	Rounding whole and decimal numbers. Some CMI. 4–6.
Rounding/Estimating Facts	Deegan	Drill, practice and reinforcement.
The Shark Games	Interlearn	Estimating with coordinates. 3–8.
Tabs Math: Estimation Invasion	Britannica	Estimation by rounding factors in a multiplication equation. 6–8.
Tabs Math: Round Up, Round Down	Britannica	Practice rounding numbers. 5–9.

11

DEVELOPING A COMPREHENSIVE PLAN

I hope you accepted the book's invitation to look seriously at some visions of mathematics and mathematics education. We have discussed theories of learning mathematics, and we have discussed practice—software programs—in the light of those theories. To put all this into practice, however, we need to answer a few more questions: When should computers be used? How can we integrate computer use into classroom routines? How can we integrate computer-enhanced mathematics with other subjects? How can computers contribute to the mathematics education of students with special needs? In this final chapter we suggest some answers to these questions. To make these answers easy to find and use, most have been organized in the form of lists of guidelines and suggestions.

WHEN TO USE COMPUTERS

Steps in Deciding when to Use Computers

To repeat a theme that has been woven throughout this book: Computers are a means, not an end. They should be used when they make a special contribution to children's learning of mathematics. The following steps serve as a guide:

1. Determine what should be taught (see Chapter 1).
2. Establish a relative priority among these topics. You might also ask: Which topics that I taught last year need improvement? Were there areas I missed completely? Why? What type of students need extra challenge or help? How might I better individualize my instruction? Also, establish a priority to develop reflective, meaningful thinking (recall Chapter 1).

3. Determine whether computers can make a contribution to the teaching and learning of each topic.

4. Make a commitment to serious integration of these computer applications into your mathematics program.

5. Evaluate software and different computer applications that may help achieve the objectives and that complement other teaching approaches (especially work with manipulatives). Will the programs allow you to teach better than you could without a computer? Will they develop automatic or reflective mathematical thinking, as appropriate?

In considering when to use computers, it is also valuable to determine what a computer should *not* be.

It is *not a replacement for a teacher.* It is a tool for teachers and students. You must decide how it is to be used. It can help you find better ways of teaching, but it does not replace you.

It is *not a panacea.* Serious questions about present-day mathematics education can and should be raised (recall Chapter 1). Computers can help answer some of these questions. However, they cannot and should not answer them all. More important, the questions should first be addressed—as we did in the first chapter—without considering computers. Initial thought should center on children and mathematics.

It is *not merely an adjunct.* At the same time, if computers are seen as "a better overhead" or "an interactive version of TV or programmed learning," their full potential will not be realized. Their use should not be as one more adjunct, "stuck onto" the existing program. They should become an integral part of the elementary mathematics program. They should become a catalyst for evolutionary change in that program.

INTEGRATING COMPUTER USE INTO CLASSROOM ROUTINES

When you have decided when and how to use the computer and are ready to begin, consider taking the following steps:

1. Become familiar with the computer and the programs yourself first.

2. Involve administrators and parents. Show them what you are doing. Enlist their support for a problem-solving approach.

3. Select housing and management strategies.

4. Introduce the computer gradually. Actually, it is usually best to limit yourself to one (or at most two) programs at a time. Similarly, expect independent, individualized work from students gradually. Prepare them for independence, and increase the degree of such work slowly. Give equal amounts of time to students (about one hour per week minimum, depending on the type of use).

5. Gradually spread out to other applications.

6. Remember that preparation and follow-up are equally necessary for computer activities.

Managing Computer Use

Scheduling.   In one school, two kindergartens shared a computer. One of the teachers loaded a different program into the computer every day for "free play" time, so the computer served as another interest center. She challenged the children to invent a fair way to take turns. They decided to make a list each day. Each child had the responsibility to cross off his or her name and then, when finished, figure out who was next and tell that child. The other teacher set up a creative computer center, partitioned somewhat from the surrounding areas and located next to another carrel where volunteer parents worked with the children. The parent checked whose turn it was and made sure that the child was off to a good start. Sometimes the teacher asked the parent to encourage certain children to use a particular type of program to shore up needed abilities. This system utilized the computer throughout the entire day.

In the same school, another teacher allowed her older students to sign up for two half-hour sessions per week at a computer learning center. Several two-hour blocks of time were set aside for whole-class and makeup sessions. She, too, wisely gave students responsibility for scheduling. A colleague of hers similarly had students sign up for several sessions per week; however, his sign-up sheet included whole-class discussions and reading groups that precluded use of the computer. In addition, he prescribed specific lessons for the students. However, students were also free to sign up for self-directed work before and after school, during lunch or recess hours, and in any "unclaimed" hours. Eventually, he even organized student computer clubs.

Other teachers conduct the scheduling themselves. They map out their week, schedule students who might benefit more from computer experiences during whole-class lessons, schedule the remaining students for small-group work, and leave other time slots open for changes and whole-class computer discussions. Setting up a management system during small-group instruction is especially useful.

An important aspect of good teaching is to engage children in meaningful activities when you work with small groups. For example, you might teach a group while other pupils are working on activities independently, so that your group will not be interrupted. Using a timer (some computer programs include one; a kitchen timer will suffice) and a list of names, students can work independently for a predetermined period and alert the next student on the list when their time is up. The next child resets the timer and the program and does his work. Once set up, this organizational scheme can run for several weeks without requiring additional teacher time or effort. How long should each child spend on the computer? As discussed, a drill and practice program might best be used for 10 to 15 minutes per child. However, larger blocks of time should be planned if the computer is to be used for simulations, problem-solving programs, or programming— about 30 to 45 minutes.

Scheduling work with a simulation: An example.   A teacher might start using a simulation by dividing the class into four for five teams. The room would be arranged so that these groups of five or six students can work together both at the computer and at their desks between turns at the computer.

The teacher might then schedule two class periods per week for the work. Initially, the work would alternate between (a) reading background material, discussing the material as a group, and possibly completing a correlated written assignment; and (b) actually working with the computer, recording information from the program, and planning the next move. Once the simulation was well under way, both sessions could be dedicated to work with the computer. When the groups have made substantial progress, they would share their findings in a whole-class discussion.

Grouping

Many ways to use a program.   Simulations such as the *Search Series* can be set for use with individual students, say if the computer is located in a resource center. Other programs lend themselves to whole-class or small-group work. For example, using a problem-solving program such as *Discover* (see Chapter 5) in a classroom or laboratory with several computers available, two to four students might work together over about five class sessions to meet the challenges posed by the computer. At appropriate times, the teacher would call the students together to discuss their progress or solutions and exchange strategies.

With only one computer in a class, the teacher might set up the program with a large monitor so that all students can see the screens. One effective method of integrating with the program is to have students take turns running the program as the rest of the class watches and advises. Even on a seemingly individual program like *Gertrude's Secrets* (see Chapters 5 and 6), this strategy could be used. For example, when solving a 3 × 3 array puzzle, one student could "send" Gertrude for the puzzle pieces. When the three "clue" pieces are placed in the array on the computer, the rest of the class could place three paper cutout pieces on duplicated sheets at their seats. They could then solve the problem as the pattern is completed on the computer. For a more complex problem-solving program, the class might observe, do the analyses, and follow through testing their hypotheses in groups. Three to four class sessions might be sufficient for this arrangement.

As these examples have shown, group work is an important component of high-quality computer education. The remainder of this section offers suggestions for such work.

Working with Others

First, a reminder: Basic ideas for helping students work in groups on Logo and problem-solving programs were offered in Chapters 4 and 5. Many of these are also appropriate for work with other computer programs. The following suggestions are meant to supplement, not repeat or replace, the ideas offered in those chapters.

Working in groups

1. Clearly specify group tasks.
2. Emphasize that each member has unique abilities.
3. Establish rules with students. For example:
   A. Each member of the group listens to the others, and everyone in the group participates.
   B. Each member must help anyone else in the group who asks for assistance.
   C. Each group must decide on an approach: groups may differ in their approaches.
   D. Any group member should be able to explain the solution strategy the group decided on.
4. Use Leslie Thyberg's "ask three before me" rule for working with Logo and other problem-solving programs.
5. End group work with a discussion. Convey that alternative solutions are valuable and accepted.
6. Form new groups occasionally, so that students have the opportunity to work with other students.

Peer teaching. Peer teaching is a proven method of increasing achievement. Combining within-class or cross-age tutoring with computer tools can garner the benefits of both. Help students to use simple tutoring skills (especially to avoid merely "giving the answer"); a most effective way is by modeling appropriate methods. Tutors should also be familiar with the software and with the skills. Provide assistance for, and supervision of, the tutors.

Encourage spontaneous peer teaching by asking "What are you working on? What did you try already? You could ask Sandy; she had a similar problem." Students often ask others without their teacher's suggestion. Some teachers have certain students (interestingly, not always those with the highest grades) serve as weekly "expert" resource people for other students needing assistance.

Individualization. The use of computers in promoting individualized instruction has been discussed throughout this book. This is just a reminder that the first step in providing for individual differences is to be aware of those differences. Students differ with regards to:

Level of conceptual and procedural knowledge in each topic.

Ability to grasp mathematical relationships. Some children take a long time just to understand the relationship between inverse operations (multiplication and division); gifted children see even complex relationships quickly.

Need for learning experiences at the concrete or symbolic levels.

Need for different types of motivators.

Whole-class discussions. At specified times, the class should gather together around the computer and discuss programs, problems, and solutions. Interaction is guided by the teacher, for example, in a Logo session, the teacher might ask: "What else could be made from that figure?" "Can you figure out what would make Holly's program work?" "Chantz, would that help you with your program? How?" "Could Nancy make her program different? How?" "Nancy, are you going to build more onto your work? What?" "Class, how might he do that?" "That's a tough one. No one seems to have an answer. Let's put tape on the floor to draw the design. You tell Terry how to walk the pattern while I write what you say on the board." "How is this similar to other programs we have made? How is it different?"

This is an excellent time for the teacher to note strengths, areas of need, directions for future work, interests, and the like. She notices that Holly is growing in self-confidence and initiative, that Chantz might profit from working a bit with Holly or the teacher to get him "over the hump," and that several students may be ready for an introduction to random selections. She makes a note to conference briefly with these students tomorrow. Maybe she can suggest a project that will require this; with the right hints, they just might discover the need for it themselves! She observes that several students are still enjoying just "fooling around" with variations of their procedures, whereas others are planning elaborate projects, and two seem hesitant to experiment.

The teacher's role. In all the aforementioned situations, and in your own interactions with your students, recognize that new ways of acting, interacting, thinking, and relating will be demanded of you. Don't expect to "get it right" the first time. It will be difficult at times, but rewarding.

Using Computer Laboratories or Resource Centers

Some schools house the computers permanently in a computer laboratory, often located in the media or resource center. Children come a class or half a class at a time, or individually. Reservation and circulation of materials are handled through the media specialist. Advantages of this arrangement may include (a) efficient use of limited computer resources, and (b) availability of enough computers for group lessons with a hands-on component. Disadvantages may include (a) need for additional staffing, (b) scheduling problems, (c) lack of integration with classroom work, and (d) teachers' feelings that they are not in touch with the computer program.

If you decide on a computer lab, consider the following suggestions:

1. Utilize parent helpers.
2. Provide volunteers with a list of explicit directions, including:
   How to turn on the computers, load programs, care for equipment.
   Location of materials, including manuals.
   Expected behavior on part of students.
   Procedures for selecting programs and keeping track of students' work.
   What to do if helpers are unable to attend (have a substitute list).
   Helping students—when to intervene, how much assistance to give, how to give assistance (e.g., Socratic questioning rather than direct telling), providing encouragement, and so on.
3. Consider networking several computers, connecting them to one large hard disk for efficient loading of programs, management, and so on.
4. Have specific schedules, rules, and responsibilities, and stick closely to them.

5. Provide room for desks so that students can work with noncomputer material, whether that be in conjunction with the computer work or other work, as they await their turn on the computer.

Although this procedure may provide a temporary answer to scarce computer resources, one computer housed in each classroom is an absolute minimum (with two to four a realistic minimum) to totally integrate computers into the curriculum. Ideally, therefore, a laboratory should supplement, not replace, computers in the classroom. In addition, arrangements should be made to allow for lower computer/student ratios when necessary. The ideal situation is to have one computer for every three or four students. Teachers and administrators must work toward these minimal (and eventually toward maximal) goals. The ultimate goal is to provide students with access to whatever computers they need to develop their full potential.

Teaching with Computers: Some Reminders

Introduce computer programs in a "clear and clean" manner.
> Begin with an interesting activity or display.
> Present critical information quickly.
> Write important instructions on a poster near the computer or on a handout that students can read before and during their use of the computer.
> Develop peer experts for each program. Post a list of their names.

Computer activities must be embedded in an effective teaching/learning paradigm.
Use concrete and other noncomputer materials before, during, and after computer use, coordinated with that use.
Use inquiry teaching whenever appropriate.

1. Inquiry-teaching strategies can be used with computer and noncomputer problem-solving activities. They might be adapted as teachers (a) input their own examples into computer programs that allow such "authoring," (b) introduce a new program, (c) intervene when students are "stuck" as they're working on a program, (d) engage children in follow-up discussions, and so on.
   Collins and Stevens (1983) found that effective teachers used such techniques as:
   - Carefully selecting positive and negative exemplars. Introductory examples should be paradigm cases. For instances, in teaching the distributive property, the example $7 \times 5 + 3 \times 5 = ?$ is particularly good, because: (a) 7 and 3 sum to 10, so the 5 appears significantly in the answer (50); (b) the 5 appears in the same position in both parts of the number sentence; and (c) the 5 is different from all other digits.
   - Varying cases systematically. This emphasizes particular details. For instance, a teacher might vary the multiplier, changing $7 \times 5 + 3 \times 5 = ?$ to $7 \times 8 + 3 \times 8 = ?$ (Notice that the multiplier still shows up in the answer, 80). Then the addends could be varied, first as in $70 \times 5 + 30 \times 5 = ?$ or $6 \times 8 + 4 \times 8 = ?$ then as in $14 \times 5 + 6 \times 5 = ?$ (do you see why?), and finally $12 \times 4 + 7 \times 4 = ?$
   - Selecting counterexamples. If students believe the series 2, 4, 8 must continue with 16, a teacher might suggest 14 instead. (Can you see why?)
   - Forming and evaluating hypotheses (recall Chapter 5).

- Tracing consequences to a contradiction. This is illustrated by Socrates' Meno dialogue, in which Socrates leads the slave boy to discover that doubling both sides of squares yields a figure with an area consisting of four of the original squares, rather than two as the boy had predicted.

2. Use effective questioning strategies:
   - Use precise, concise, and clear questions.
   - Balance convergent and divergent questions.
   - Convergent questions are familiar; they ask for the "one right answer." Balance these with divergent questions, such as:
     What do you notice about ... ?
     What if we did the opposite ... ?
     Did you try ... ?
     What did you mean ... ?
   - Also ask questions that ask students to "prove it." For instance, students who completed an addition exercise with renaming might "prove" their answer with popsicle sticks or blocks. A variety of situations call for students to justify their responses, to answer questions that begin with "Why."
   - Include concrete and abstract questions, as appropriate.
   - Wait at least three seconds after asking a question. Rowe (1978) has shown that with a wait time of three or more seconds, the quality and length of students' responses increase dramatically. Students also ask more questions themselves and are less likely to fail to respond—especially the slow learners.
   - Direct the question to an individual *after* the question has been asked.
   - Use questions that encourage students to keep thinking. They encourage students to interact with each other and to become contributors to classroom learning. For example:
     Can you explain how you worked out that answer?
     Why do you think your way (or your answer) is better than (another)?
     Let's hear an argument (defense) of each position (method, answer, etc.).
     Can you find an exception, a situation in which it doesn't work?
     I'm not sure. Prove it to me.
     Does everyone agree with that answer? (Ask this just as frequently following correct answers as following incorrect answers, when there is only one correct answer.)

3. Avoid:
   - Explaining everything yourself.
   - Emphasizing product rather than process.
   - Forcing exploratory computer programs into traditional modes.
   - Listing too many suggestions (just checking to see if you're still with me!).

Essential whole-group sessions: A reminder. We have found that teachers often omit a critical phase of teaching and thus unwittingly impair the effectiveness of their students' work with computers. Students work with simulations, but never gain insight into the phenomenon simulated; they work with Logo, but never learn much about geometry. Why? What is the missing ingredient? Usually, it is the omission of whole-group discussion sessions following computer work.

Take Logo as an example. In well-designed introductory activities, students may gain worthwhile intuitive experience with geometric ideas (see Chapters 4 and 9), but, left to themselves, they often do not *reflect* on this experience, and thus they never become aware of the ideas or their useful-ness. Little geometry is actually learned. If, on the other hand, the teacher follows the computer experience with whole-group discussions of the activi-ties, powerful learning can occur. The teacher's role in such discussions is to bring the objects of study (in this example, geometric ideas, relationships, and patterns) to a conscious level of awareness and have the students dis-cuss them in their own language. Once students have demonstrated their awareness of an idea and have discussed it in their own words, the teacher introduces the relevant mathematical terminology.

The sharing of viewpoints among students should be emphasized. In the context of such discussions, the teacher provides feedback regarding the completeness and accuracy of the students' conceptualizations. In this way, premathematical frames developed during intuitive work on the com-puter (e.g., turning the turtle) are developed further with the aid of lan-guage; they are attended to, elaborated, and embellished. That is, the stu-dents' discussions *focus attention* on the concepts and thus bring them to a more explicit level of awareness.

In our example, students might become aware of the idea that they can think of the measure of an angle as a turtle rotation from one side of the angle to the other. Such a focus helps develop their *angle frame*. (Recall that frames are conceptual structures storing ideas, situations, etc.; see Chapter 1.) Discussions serve to *elaborate* the frames by interrelating them with other frames (e.g., turtle turning is related to angle measure). Finally, frames are *embellished* with language through the provision of labels and descriptions. Ultimately, the frames can be *operated on*—recognized, ana-lyzed, related to other frames, and used as tools for understanding formal geometric concepts and solving geometric problems, such as analyzing and constructing a given shape (Clements & Battista, 1988).

Discussions should also follow more advanced work. After students have had substantial experience solving problems in a certain area, they need to summarize all they have learned about the objects of study, integrat-ing that knowledge into a coherent network of frames that can easily be described and applied. The language and conceptualizations of mathemat-ics are used to describe this network. The teacher's role in these discussions is to encourage students to reflect on and consolidate their geometric knowledge, with an increasing emphasis on the use of mathematical struc-tures as a framework for consolidation. Finally, the teacher summarizes the consolidated ideas by embedding them in the structural organization of mathematics. An example of such a consolidation in the area of turtle geom-etry is the formulation of the "rule of 360" (see Chapter 9).

It is easy to be enthusiastic about students' on-computer work and therefore neglect other essential phases of teaching. Easy, but dangerous. *Remember to use whole-group discussions to promote elaboration and summarization.*

Checking yourself: What type of integration?   One final caveat: Integra-tion should not mean subjugating the software, or more important, subju-gating new approaches to learning and teaching, to traditional curricula and teaching approaches. Effective use of computers must involve the re-conceptualization and extension of the present educational environment.

Integration here means the construction of connections, not assimilation to a traditional paradigm.

INTEGRATING MATHEMATICS WITH OTHER SUBJECTS

Quality use of computers permits, and even encourages, breaking down some of the traditional barriers between subjects. Several excellent computer applications transcend such barriers and thereby lend more depth, validity, relevance, and interest to each discipline.

Mathematics and the Sciences

Several computer applications that integrate the study of mathematics with other sciences have been described throughout this book. For example, the subject matter of data bases usually comes from the physical or social sciences (review Chapter 3). Similarly, creating simulations of real-world phenomena with Micro-Dynamo, students are engaged in theorizing and experimenting across several subject-matter areas, including mathematics, science, sociology, and others (see Chapter 4).

The *Search Series* (McGraw-Hill) provides problem-solving environments that combine social studies, mathematics, and science. It also presents an excellent opportunity for cooperative work. For example, only one computer is needed. It manages the activities of several groups of students—determining each group's changing situation, giving them information, and recording their activities and progress (even overnight, for the duration of the activity). One group at a time is called to the computer, where they are shown information for a limited time only. They must cooperate and work together if they are to glean the needed information.

In *Geography Search,* students use mathematics as a tool in a social studies exploration. Each group is a crew of a ship attempting to find the Lost City of Gold in an uncharted New World. They must stave off hunger and piracy to find gold, which they will sell. Each crew member has a specific job, such as determining the depth of the water, recording wind direction and temperature, finding the position of the ship (navigation), and keeping records of provisions. Often the recording process involves translations of units or scaling. To be useful, all this information must be recorded correctly and synthesized. This involves arithmetic calculations, maps, geometry (e.g., a wind direction might be 125°), and, of course, problem solving and teamwork. The crew must determine an initial course of sail; any course within 90° of the wind heading will not result in much progress. They then obtain a report of their progress (available on the screen for a limited time only!) and make their next move.

Their ship's position is calculated from "home time," shown on the ship's clock when the sun is directly overhead. Students watch a shadow grow shorter toward noon. When it is at its shortest, they must record the time on the clock to determine the home time. This reading must then be converted into minutes past noon. For example, 2:24 represents 144 minutes past noon, which gives the latitude. If they do not record this number, they will not know where they are or which way to go.

The screen also displays sightings of other ships or land on a compass grid. The crew uses this information to determine the relative distance. A map is used to record this information and to build up a map of the New World. This, of course, requires that students utilize such mathematical ideas and processes as coordinates, scaling, angle measure, estimation, making tables and graphs, and breaking a problem down into parts.

Other critical information includes the rate of consumption of supplies, determined by careful completion of the provision report. The crew might average several days' consumption to determine the amount of provisions that should be purchased for the return trip (the length of which must also be estimated).

Run for the Money (Scarborough) is fantasy simulation in which students crash-land on the planet Simian. They must make enough money to repaint the shield on their spaceships so as to be the first to blast off again. To make money, they purchase raw materials and make products to sell to the Simians. In the process, they must utilize such economic concepts as supply and demand, competition, production, advertising, bidding, and pricing. Players view the results of each week's effort (i.e., receive feedback) and then predict what will happen during the coming week. Of course, teachers should make the concepts visible through questioning: What effect does advertising have on sales? How about pricing? Can prices be set so high that advertising's effect is nullified? Recall other programs designed to teach economic concepts, such as *Survival Math* and *Lemonade Stand.*

Chapter 5 discussed several programs that integrated problem solving, mathematics, and science. Two of them, *Discover* and *The Incredible Laboratory,* are designed to teach certain processes used in scientific investigation. Another is *Rocky's Boots* (TLC). Imagine a laboratory of machine parts, batteries, and wires in which children can safely construct and explore mechanisms that will discriminate between objects. In this electronic Tinker Toy set, students learn about how electrical devices can be connected and about the world of logic. The building blocks are wires, machines, sensors, logic gates, flip-flops, and other electronic components—the building blocks of a computer. These can be picked up, moved, and connected. The rules are those of formal digital logic. Children might try to build a machine that kicks diamonds or circles out of a moving line of shapes (Fig. 11–1). These tasks may be supplemented with even more specific science and logic activities (adapted from Burch and Aaronson, 1985). They are intended to help students learn to understand how computers work, read schematic diagrams, build complex circuits, solve problems with logic, and see how logic is used to make decisions in mathematics, digital electronics, and language arts.

1. Have students build circuits with batteries, bulbs, and switches. Like computers, bulbs have only two states: on and off. Students could build a circuit in which both switches must be closed before the bulb will light (the switches would be connected one after the other in a series). This models an AND gate in computers and in *Rocky's Boots.* They could then construct a model of an OR gate,

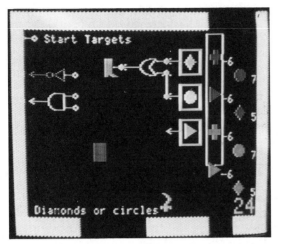

FIGURE 11-1
Building a machine that kicks diamonds or circles out of a moving line of shapes with *Rocky's Boots*. (The Learning Company)

in which the light would go on if either of the switches were closed (the switches would be connected side by side in parallel). They might then draw simple schematic circuits (Fig. 11-2). Similarities and differences between this representation and that in the computer program might be discussed. Finally, charts might be constructed:

Series Circuit/AND Gate			Parallel Circuit/OR Gate		
Switch A	Switch B	Light	Switch A	Switch B	Light
On	On	On	On	On	On
On	Off		On	Off	
Off	On		Off	On	
Off	Off		Off	Off	

Can you complete the charts? For example, the series circuit/AND gate light is on if switch A is on and switch B is on. The light is off if switch A is on and switch B is off.

2. From these two basic circuits, many more complicated circuits can be built. Try to construct and complete a chart for the circuit drawn in Fig. 11-2. Can you think of a real-world and/or computer programming example where this logic would apply? For a challenge, design circuits that demonstrate that (A AND B) OR (A AND C) is equivalent to A AND (B OR C).

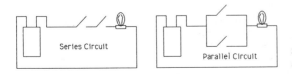

FIGURE 11-2
Simple schematic circuits analogous to computer gates.

3. Discuss logic in "real-world" language situations. For example, pose this problem. Pretend you know that the following two statements are true:
    If it feels warm outside, then I am dreaming.
    If I am dreaming, then either I am tired or I am asleep.
    Now, for the questions below, circle Y if you think the answer to the question is yes, and N if you think the answer to the question is no.
    If I am awake and I am not tired, could it feel warm outside?
    If it feels warm outside and I am awake, must I be tired?
    Alter the statements and questions by adding NOTs, changing ORs to ANDs, and so on (e.g., If I am awake or I am tired, could it feel warm outside?). How do these changes affect the outcomes?
4. After classification activities such as those in the Gertrude programs (see also Chapters 5 and 6), challenge students to depict rules such as "Put all the pieces that are blue and not square together" with the symbols from *Rocky's Boots* (Fig. 11–1).
5. Actually design, build, and test the logic of a logic circuit on a computer chip (see Burch and Aaronson, 1985, for details).

What we are now discussing, of course, is computer science. Approached wisely, it provides obvious tie-ins with mathematics. (What might be less wise? Possibly detailed information about a particular brand of computer or other such information of limited generality.) For example, the history of calculating devices (abacus, Napier's bones) can be integrated with a study of place value and numeration systems. Computer programming and noncomputer mathematical algorithms might also be compared.

Another example of integration across subject-matter areas is *The Voyage of the Mimi* (from Holt). This package for grades 4 through 6 covers several subject-matter areas; it also utilizes several media. Its heart is a television series: 13 short dramatic episodes of a scientific adventure story and 13 documentary-style segments called expeditions. The adventure story follows four children who accompany two scientists and a captain on a research expedition to study humpback whales. The episodes and the documentaries alternate, the first raising questions and motivation, the second providing scientific and mathematical information. For example, one episode ends with the crew shipwrecked, and the captain suffering from hypothermia; the documentary involves scientists studying how the human body reacts under stressful environmental conditions.

Other instructional material includes a teacher's guide, a book for students that supplements the television series, wall charts, and four learning modules that include software programs. In the first, students use Logo commands to explore geometry and programming in games based on navigation and to design patterns. The second includes three computer games and a simulation emphasizing basic map skills (including triangulation to locate a lost vessel). For example, one game has students read a map's mileage scale, steer a ship to a heading given by a compass, and compute the speed and time needed to journey to a given destination. The third involves ecosystems. Students set up an aquarium and engage in related activities, such as calculating the population density of snails in the aquarium. The fourth utilizes computer laboratory tools (recall Chapter 9). Students gather, display, and record data to perform a series of physical science experiments such as measuring the effect of chalk dust on light intensity. They then read about how the ocean absorbs light and how whales' eyes are adapted to operate with low levels of light.

Thinker is an experimental program designed to forge relationships among areas such as science, mathematics, and planning (Bransford et al., 1986). A computer is used to control a videodisk containing a ten-minute passage of a popular film, such as *Raiders of the Lost Ark*. Students first view the passage. From a menu, the teacher then selects one of ten short segments, which is redisplayed. Students attempt to identify evidence of the hero planning ahead (e.g., entering a cave with a pack and its contents), and receive feedback from the computer. In another set of lessons, the hero is unable to eliminate a problem, which he must therefore solve. Students attempt to identify the potential problem (the light-beam trap) and suggest and evaluate various strategies for solution. One goal is to have students notice the degree of effective problem solving and planning that is implicit in movies and everyday life. Mathematical content is also studied. For example, *Thinker* uses computer graphics to allow students to take measurements (the height of the cave entrance and the width of the pit might be measured based on standards such as the hero's height) and thereby solve problems. They might ask whether the hero could realistically have jumped over the pit, or about the size and speed of the large rock that chases him out of the cage. They might question his wisdom in replacing a solid gold statue the size of a ½-gallon milk carton with a small bag of sand. Would they weigh about the same? The computer provides tools, information, and feedback. Students become more interested in density tables when they use one to estimate the statue's weight as 60 pounds. They also think about other implications. Is the idol truly gold? If so, how did people carry it so easily? If not, why the fuss over it?

A Word about Projects

LEGO/Logo projects (mentioned briefly in Chapter 4) represent an excellent blend of mathematics and science. Both Logo and LEGO are construction sets in which basic building blocks are combined to construct complex structures. Often, students build a robot, elevator, or kitchen appliance, test it to check that it works, add a motor, attach the motor to the computer, add touch or light sensors for feedback, and then explore the actions of the construction. In this way, they might conduct time trials of LEGO/Logo vehicles or control LEGO amusement park rides. One student explored controlled vibration as a way of getting a robot to "walk." Others experimented with necessary trade-offs between speed and power.

LEGO/Logo explores relationships between control and feedback, between external stimuli and sensors, allowing children to think about robotics, systems, and even intelligence. Recall also what was said about the project approach. Projects of this type often integrate mathematics and other sciences. Most important, they have the potential to profoundly influence children's engagement with mathematics and learning. But computers do not offer the first opportunity for such projects. Indeed, from John Dewey's school, to England's Nuffield project, to USMES (Unified Science and Mathematics for Elementary Schools), there have been many such project-oriented approaches. What does this mean? First, there are sources of excellent projects, computer and noncomputer, offering numerous ideas for teachers. Second, however, experience with this approach shows that it is not easy.

It would probably be a mistake to alter your time allotment radically right from the beginning. Might you, instead, encourage children to work on projects during a free period? As a club? In class, a couple times a week, completing only one or two projects during a semester? Experiment, and have your children experiment. What do you and your students learn? Does the class feel different during such explorations? How might they be built on, extended?

Mathematics and the Arts

Several programs we have already seen intrinsically integrate mathematics and the arts. For example, students developing Logo projects are combining the geometric and the aesthetic. Similarly, both artistic and mathematical elements are involved in such programs as *Aestheometry, Geometry, Logic Builders,* and *Patternmaker* (see Chapter 9). For instance, students using *Patternmaker* design and explore tesselation patterns. They build patterns of as many as 64 squares. Then they create clones of their original design, operating on them with flips, slides, and turns, to produce beautiful color patterns. They learn about fundamental artistic and mathematical concepts such as symmetry, patterning, balance, and design. Thus, they are simultaneously using mathematics to solve artistic problems, and the graphic arts to solve mathematical problems.

Even music software offers opportunities for meaningful application of mathematics and logical problem solving. *Songwriter* (Scarborough) can be used at many levels of sophistication. Children can easily compose and edit music of their own making. They set the fractional length of a note (e.g., a quarter or eighth note) by using the number keys, possibly in combination with an arithmetic operation. Thus, fractions are used and illustrated—via sound and graphics—in a meaningful way. Similarly, many versions of Logo allow students to write music-producing procedures. These can be used to show the mathematics in music and the connections between the two fields.

MEETING SPECIAL NEEDS

A victim of cerebral palsy speaks his first words by choosing words presented on the computer screen under his control. Programming in Logo elicits the first active exploration and communication for an autistic child. Computers are helping provide support for children with special needs in two basic ways: compensatory and instructional.

Compensatory Aid

Computer technology is quickly becoming the most powerful pros-
thetic device, compensating for a wide range of disabilities (for details, see
Clements, 1985a).

Sensing.   Computers have been connected to devices that present
words as vibrations on the abdomen, and thus sound recognition is learned
similarly to conventional language. Soon a microprocessor placed behind
the ear will translate sound into impulses sent directly to the auditory nerve
for the profoundly deaf.

Controlling.   The advent of computer recognition of speech will increase the applications of computer control of appliances, telephones,
lights, doors, typewriters, and other everyday devices. Bedridden people
will control any electrical device in the home from a central location.

Communicating.   By choosing words from computer screen menus,
children who were without speech can communicate in person or over the
phone.

Instructional Aid

Helping the teacher of the special child.   Computers can be useful in
creating mandated Individualized Education Programs (IEPs), reducing the
time needed for drawing up such a plan from several days to a few hours.
It is, of course, still a tool; people make the final decisions as to what should
be included. But it can help by analyzing the results of multiple measures
and compiling the information in a usable form. It might also have access
to a data bank—a large collection of goals and short-term objectives—and
allow the users to match any relevant goals to the assessment information
(see the Appendix).

Helping the exceptional child.   Special education has been one area that
has welcomed and integrated technological innovations openly. Research
has demonstrated that exceptional children make substantial gains in mathematics achievement, positive perceptions of school, self-concept, and internal locus of control (Cartwright & Derevensky, 1976; Clements, 1985a; Mevarech & Rich, 1985). When choosing software, avoid the common
misconception that only low-level drill and practice programs are appropriate. Exceptional students need to develop conceptual understandings and
problem-solving skills, too. Sterns (1986) reported that learning disabled
students engaged in their own analyses of the problem situations using
problem-solving programs such as *Memory Castle, The King's Rule,* and *The
Pond* (see Chapter 5 for descriptions). Even children with severe handicaps
have been able to explore the picture-drawing, problem-solving, and mathematical activities that Logo offers. Cerebral-palsied nonverbal students
have created geometric designs. Autistic children who balked at performing
upon others' requests enthusiastically explored the commands that instruct
the turtle. Logo demands that children try things out, be exacting, and respond to feedback—learning by doing things themselves. It emphasizes
process more than product, along with the debugging of processes. Chil-

dren obtain experience with geometry, algebra, and other mathematical ideas, along with reading, writing, spelling, and typing.

Table 11–1 lists numerous programs specially designed for special students. The Appendix lists organizations dedicated to effective computer use with these children.

Gifted and Talented

The lack of appropriate educational programming for the gifted and talented (G/T) in mathematics is a national disgrace. Myths that these students exhibit superiority in all areas and that "they'll do fine anyway" have been exploded by research, but they remain implicit assumptions of too many schools. The underachieving G/T student is a reality, an example of social neglect, and a tragic waste of potential. G/T students should use the computer as a tool to extend their talents. Most of these applications have been described in previous chapters; the G/T child should be guided to use these programs in ways that are broader and deeper. Only a few additional examples are offered here.

The most beneficial (and demanding) application is in the development of meaningful and challenging projects. Students might program in Logo to experiment with and then create microworlds for their own and others' exploration. They might create data bases for use by themselves, by other students in the school, or by G/T students in other schools. They might investigate and compare several counting, calculating, computing, and other symbol-manipulating devices. This could lead to an exploration of binary and other number bases.

Access to computers alone is not sufficient. Without supervision, gifted children often play computer games and do not develop significantly. G/T programs should provide guidance in the undertaking of meaningful projects that provide enrichment of the curriculum.

CAI might also be integrated into the program. For example, *Comp-U-Solve* (Educational Activities) is a collection of logical puzzles. Responses are analyzed after every move, so that students are given feedback regarding their progress toward a goal. "Tricky Trip" is a network puzzle similar to the Königsberg Bridge problem. In "Tricky Trip," you must visit all the cities on a map only one time without traveling over the same road twice (Fig. 11–3). The Worthington Schools (752 High Street, Worthington, OH 43085) have created a series of mathematics and science software for gifted students. CAI could also be used to accelerate the curriculum, helping children who are able to move quickly through the normal subject matter so as to free time for special projects. Some G/T underachievers could use appropriate CAI to close the gap between their achievement and their potential.

Experiences for gifted students should contain subject matter that is so current that it is on the cutting edge of the discipline. Computer technology facilitates this as well or better than any other vehicle, for example, through on-line data bases (see Chapter 3). Gifted children are often isolated from others with similar interests. A modem could expand their world. They could participate in computerized conferences with others interested in the same topics. This could involve both peers and experts of any age.

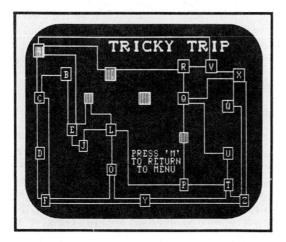

FIGURE 11-3
"Tricky Trip" on the *Comp-U-Solve* disk. (Educational Activities, Inc.)

Computers enable ordinary people to do the extraordinary. They enable extraordinary, exceptional people to do both the ordinary and the extraordinary.

FINAL WORDS

To fully realize the potential that some of the more challenging programs, such as Logo and the tool programs, have to offer you and your students, you must accept the challenge of fundamental change in your own perspective on children, education, and computers. History teaches us that fundamental curriculum change often suffers from two diseases: dilution and corruption. In dilution, educational innovation is "watered down" to "fit" an existing curriculum or the supposedly limited capabilities of the curriculum. Problems are made trivially easy, and the real reasons for the innovation disappear ("Copy this week's Logo procedure" is an example). Corruption distorts the innovation in ways that conflict with the original intent (e.g., teaching problem-solving steps by rote).

To minimize the spread of these diseases, proposed change should, as far as possible, attempt to (a) make life easier for the teacher, (b) make life more fun for the teacher, (c) address a problem the teacher recognizes, and (d) have public support (Burkhardt, Fraser, & Ridgway, 1986). Many computer applications fare well on "b" and "d," but they vary—on "a" and "c" especially. Those that actually try to turn around classroom mathematics—those most strongly advocated here—tend to demand hard work and a new perspective on children and mathematics. Ideally, support for change, including continuing feedback, should be addressed at the school or district level (see Burkhardt et al. for suggestions). However, you can do a lot yourself just by (a) recognizing the deleterious effects of dilution and corruption; (b) keeping your goals clear and specific; (c) forming small (even two-people!) support groups in your school (include your principal and parents as much as possible); (d) changing only one topic or computer application at a time (perhaps only one per year), to ensure its success; and (e) fighting the fear of change.

Too many adults agree that children should discover but fear self-discovery themselves! Too many are also anxious about building evolutionary educational environments for children. They practice "scared eclecticism"—agreeing with the findings of Piaget and cognitive science psychologists, but yet afraid to commit to a new perspective on teaching. Such teachers "stick in" a bit of Piagetian discovery (and a bit of most everything they hear, fearful that they and their students will "miss" something), but cling to the behaviorist notion that children will not really learn material unless teachers "pour it into their heads." Eclecticism is not bad; in fact, no single theory suffices. However, scared eclectics do not attempt to fit a model of learning with an educational goal. As Jerome Bruner has stated: "There is not one kind of learning. . . . But if you see children learning mathematics by rote, you can also say . . . that somebody got confused about models and slipped in an empiricist one in place of a constructivist one" (1985, p. 8). Challenging software offers you opportunities to teach—and your students to learn and construct knowledge—in new and exciting ways.

SUGGESTED READINGS

Clements (1985a), Kelman and others (1983), Pogrow (1986), and **Riordon (1982)** provide suggestions for integrating the computer into the classroom.

TABLE 11-1   Software for Exceptional Students

Title	Producer	Notes
Remedial		
Arithmefacts	EMC	Arithmetic facts drill for moderately handicapped and learning-disabled students. 3–7.
Computer Courseware for the Exceptional Student	Comm. Skill	Includes arithmetic drill with alternative response system for students who have difficulty writing. P+.
Duxbury Braille Translater	Duxbury	Produces Braille from text entered on a computer.
Essential Number Facts	KARD	Math facts for slow learners. Graphic cartoons for motivation, survey tests, and study sheets. 2+.
Income Meets Expenses	MCE	Tutorial and practice in personal-budgeting concepts. Branches for second-, third-, or fifth-grade reading levels. 5–12.
Introduction to Decimals on the Computer	Ed. Act.	Decimal concepts and operations. For slow learners and learning-disabled students. 2–5.

(*continued*)

TABLE 11-1 (Continued)

Title	Producer	Notes
Introduction to Mathematics on the Computer	Ed. Act.	Arithmetic operations. For slow learners and learning-disabled students. 2–5.
Math Assistant	Scholastic	All arithmetic operations. Not written for special populations specifically. Error analysis; can be used for drill (with feedback consisting of hints pinpointing errors) or as a diagnostic test. CMI component. 3–6.
Math Power Program	I/CT	All arithmetic operations. Tutorials and practice develop low-stress algorithms. 1–6.
Money Management Assessment Series	MCE	Basic math skills, money-management concepts. Branches for second- and fifth-grade reading levels. 5–12.
Piat-80	Precision	Interprets results of math subtest of the Peabody Individual Achievement Test, producing IEPs. 1–12.
Remembering Numbers and Letters	MCE	Rapid recognition of numerals. 1–6.
Shape Matching	Conover	Recognition of six shapes. P–K.
Solving Word Problems	Aquarius	Remedial programs on solving word problems. Available at reading levels 1–2, 3–5, and 6–7. 4–10.
Special Skill Builders	Compu-Tations	Number and shape recognition and counting skills. 1+.
Target Math Special Education	Comp. Assisted	Fifty units divided into 14 modules, covering a K–12 special education curriculum. K–12.

Gifted

Title	Producer	Notes
Elementary Math Booster	Trillium	Arithmetic skills, fractions, and number theory for gifted students. 4–8.
EUCLID	Univ. Evans.	Enables students to perform elementary constructions such as points, lines, circles, angle bisectors, perpendiculars, parallels, etc.
Math Worlds	Sterling Swift	Extensive curriculum with many open-ended activities. Emphasizes the role of mathematical thinking, especially patterns, in scientific discovery. Units include Input/Output (functions), Strategies (for playing NIM; students actually write com-

Title	Producer	Notes
		puter programs to play the game at various levels of skill), Business, Sampling, Data Analysis, and Turtle Geometry.
Mathematics Enrichment Software	Univ. Evan.	A wide variety of enrichment topics offered on several disks. Includes number theory, functions, series, geometry, etc. Students can run the programs, but can also change them.
Super Factory	Sunburst	An extension of *The Factory* to three dimensions. Students place pictures on the sides of a cube (see Chapter 9 for more details). 5+.
SuperMath	Sunburst	Games and puzzles for gifted students, including magic squares, math codes, and binary numbers. 5+.

APPENDIX A:
RESOURCES

PUBLISHERS OF SOFTWARE

Note: The abbreviations used in the book are listed first in alphabetical order, followed by the full name of the company in parentheses. If a particular publisher is not found here, refer to listings in computer magazines and books, or ask for assistance at your local computer store or hardware representative. Many, such as Apple and IBM, have extensive catalogs of educational software for their computers. Some publishers, including Dynacomp, Follet, Hammett, Opportunities for Learning, Orange Cherry Media, Queue, Scholastic, and SVE, carry software from many publishers. They might also be contacted.

Academic Ther. (Academic Therapy
   Publications)
20 Commercial Blvd.
Novato, CA 94947

Acorn Software Products
353 W. Lancaster Ave.
Wayne, PA 19087

Addison-Wes (Addison-Wesley)
2725 Sand Hill Rd.
Menlo Park, CA 94025

Advanced Ideas, Inc.
2550 Ninth St., Suite 104
Berkeley, CA 94710

AIMS Media
6901 Woodley Ave.
Van Nuys, CA 91406

Aladdin Software
1001 Colfax St.
Danville, IL 61832

Alphatel Systems Ltd.
11430-168 St.
Edmonton, Alberta
Canada T5M 3T9

American Educational Computer
2450 Embarcadero Way
Palo Alto, CA 94303

American Micro Media
Box 306
Red Hook, NY 12571

Amer. Peri. (American Peripherals)
122 Bangor St.
Lindenhurst, NY 11757

Amer. Sys. Dev. (American Systems
   Development)
P.O. Box 362
13504 Walnutwood Lane
Germantown, MD 20874

Amidon Publications
1966 Benson Ave.
St. Paul, MN 55116

Aquarius (Aquarius People Materials, Inc.)
P.O. Box 128
Indian Rocks Beach, FL 33535

Artworx Software Co., Inc.
150 North Main St.
Fairport, NY 14450

Avant-Garde Publishing
P.O. Box 30160
1907 Garden Ave.
Eugene, OR 97403

Beh. Eng. (Behavioral Engineering)
230 Mt. Hermon Rd.
Suite 207
Scotts Valley, CA 95066

Bergwall Educational Software, Inc.
106 Charles Lindbergh Blvd.
Uniondale, NY 11553

Berta-Max Inc.
3646 Stone Way North
Seattle, WA 98103

B5 Software
P.O. Box 31849
Columbus, OH 43228

BLS, Inc.
Tutorsystems
2503 Fairlee Rd.
Wilmington, DE 19810

Bolt Beranek and Newman
50 Moulton St.
Cambridge, MA 02238

Boston Ed. (Boston Educational Computing,
    Inc.)
78 Dartmouth St.
Boston, MA 02116

Britannica (Encyclopaedia Britannica
    Educational Corp.)
425 North Michigan Avenue
Chicago, IL 60611

Broderbund Software
1934 Fourth St.
San Rafael, CA 94901

Cactusplot Company
4712 E. Osborn
Phoenix, AZ 85018

CADPP (Computer-Assisted Diagnostic
    Prescriptive Program)
Office of Federal Programs
Box 292
Dilwyn, VA 23936

CAE Software Inc.
5225 Wisconsin Ave. N.W., Suite 601
P.O. Box 6227
Washington, DC 20015

C & C Software
5713 Kentford Cir.
Wichita, KS 67220

Cardinal Software
14840 Build America Dr.
Woodbridge, VA 22191

CASA Software
2103 34th St.
Lubbock, TX 79411

CBS Software
383 Madison Ave.
New York, NY 10017
    or
One Fawcett Place
Greenwich, CT 06836

CCC (Computer Curriculum Corporation)
P.O. Box 10080
Palo Alto, CA 94303

CCM (Classroom Consortia Media)
57 Bay St.
Staten Island, NY 10301

CDL (Cambridge Development
    Laboratories)
100 Fifth Ave.
Waltham, MA 02154

Cemcorp
1300 Bay St.
Toronto, Ont.
Canada M5R 3K8

Centurion Industries Incorporated
2000 Broadway
Redwood City, CA 94063

Chalk Board, Inc.
3772 Pleasantdale Rd.
Atlanta, GA 30340

Charles Clark Co., Inc.
170 Keyland Ct.
Bohemia, NY 11716

Classroom Consortia Media
57 Bay St.
Staten Island, NY 10301

CLC (Computer Learning Center)
1775E. Tropicana Ave.
Liberace Plaza, No. 8
Las Vegas, NV 89109

CLS (Computer Learning Services)
1013 Woodbine Circle W.
Galesburg, IL 61401

Commodore
1200 Wilson Dr.
West Chester, PA 19380

Comm. Skill (Communication Skill Builders)
3830 E. Bellevue
P.O. Box 42050
Tucson, AZ 85733

Comp. Assisted (Computer Assisted
    Instruction, Inc.)
6161 28th St., Southeast
Grand Rapids, MI 49506

CompEd
P.O. Box 35461
Phoenix, AZ 85069

Compu-Tations Inc.
P.O. Box 502
Troy, MI 48099

Compu-Teach
78 Olive St.
New Haven, CT 06511

Computer Age Education Inc.
5225 Wisconsin Ave., Northwest
Suite 601
Washington, DC 20015

Computer-Ed
1 Everett Rd.
Carmel, NY 10512

Computer Island
227 Hampton Green
Staten Island, NY 10312

The Computer Learning Center for Children
1775 East Tropicana Ave.
Liberace Plaza, No. 8
Las Vegas, NV 89109

Concept Educational Software
P.O. Box 6184
Allentown, PA 18001

CONDUIT
P.O. Box 388
Iowa City, IA 52244

Conover (The Conover Company, Ltd.)
5684 Shurbert Rd.
P.O. Box 155
Omro, WI 54963

The Continental Press, Inc.
520 East Bainbridge St.
Elizabethtown, PA 17022

Control Data
P.O. Box 261127
San Diego, CA 92126

Coral Software Corp.
P.O. Box 307
Cambridge, MA 02142

Cosine, Inc.
P.O. Box 2017
West Lafayette, IN 47906

Courses by Computers
108 Sowers St.
State College, PA 16801

Cow Bay Computing
P.O. Box 515
Manhasset, NY 11030

Creative Equip. (Creative Equipment)
6864 West Flagler St.
Miami, FL 33144

Creative Pub. (Creative Publications)
788 Palomar Ave.
Sunnyvale, CA 94086

Creative Tech. (Creative Technical
    Consultants)
P.O. Box 652
Cedar Crest, MN 87008

Cross Educational Software
504 E. Kentucky Ave.
P.O. Box 1536
Ruston, LA 71270

CTW (Children's Television Workshop)
One Lincoln Plaza
New York, NY 10023

CUE (Computer Utilization in Education)
Central Square School District
Main St.
Central Square, NY 13036

Cuisenaire Co. of America, Inc.
12 Church St., Box D
New Rochelle, NY 10805

Cygnet Systems Corp.
8002 E. Culver
Mesa, AZ 85207

Data Command
P.O. Box 548
Kankakee, IL 60901

Davell Custom Software
P.O. Box 4162
Cleveland, TN 37311

E. David and Associates
Small Computer Systems
22 Russett Lane
Storrs, CT 06268

Davidson & Associates
6069 Groveoak Place, No. 12
Rancho Palos Verdes, CA 90274

DCH (D.C. Heath and Company)
125 Spring St.
Lexington, MA 02173

Deegan Learning Materials
P.O. Box 245
Mankato, MN 56001

Degem Systems
8122 Data Point Dr.
San Antonio, TX 78229

Digital Research
160 Central Ave.
Pacific Grove, CA 93950

Disk Depot
731 W. Colorado Ave.
Colorado Springs, CO 80905

Disney Educational Software
P.O. Box 2000
Thornwood, NY 10594

Walt Disney
Personal Computer Software
500 South Buena Vista
Burbank, CA 91521

Diversified Educational Enterprises
725 Main St.
Lafayette, IN 47901

DLM (Developmental Learning Activities)
P.O. Box 4000
One DLM Park
Austin, TX 75002

Dorsett Education Systems, Inc.
P.O. Box 1226
Norman, OK 73070

Duxbury Systems, Inc.
77 Great Rd.
Acton, MA 01720

Dynacomp, Inc.
P.O. Box 18129
Rochester, NY 14618

ECS (Electronic Courseware Systems)
309 Windon Rd.
Champaign, IL 61820

Ed. Act. (Education Activities Inc.)
1937 Grand Ave.
Baldwin, NY 11510

Ed. Micro. Sys. (Educational Micro Systems, Inc.)
P.O. Box 471
Chester, NJ 07930

Ed. Software (Educational Software and Design)
P.O. Box 2801
Flagstaff, AZ 86003

Educational Computer Systems Corp.
10818 N.E. Coxley Dr., Suite E
Vancouver, WA 98662

Educational Media Assoc.
Microcomputer Software
342 W. Robert E. Lee
New Orleans, LA 70124

Edupro
A Division of Knowledge Access, Inc.
445 East Charleston Rd.
Palo Alto, CA 94306

EduSoft
P.O. Box 2560
Berkeley, CA 94702

EduWare Services, Inc.
185 Berry Street
San Francisco, CA 94107

EISI (Educational Instructional Systems, Inc.)
2225 Grant Rd., Suite 3
Los Altos, CA 94022

EMC Publishing
300 York Ave.
St. Paul, MN 55101

EME (E.M.E. Corp.)
Old Mill Plain Road
P.O. Box 2805
Danbury, CT 06813

Encyclopaedia Britannica (*see* Britannica)

Eric Software Publishing
1713 Tulare St.
Fresno, CA 93721

Essertier Software Corp.
921 14th St.
Hermosa Beach, CA 90254

ESC (Education Systems Corporation; formerly ESTC, Education Systems Technology Corporation)
Suite 300
6170 Cornerstone Court East
San Diego, CA 92121

ETA (Educational Teaching Aids)
199 Carpenter
Wheeling, IL 60090

ETC (Educational Technology Center)
337 Gutman Library, Appian Way
Cambridge, MA 02138

Follet Library Book Co.
4506 Northwest Highway
Crystal Lake, IL 60014

Fortune Software Co.
70 Sierra Rd.
Boston, MA 02136

Gamco Industries
P.O. Box 310L3
Big Spring, TX 79720

Gentleware Corp.
2509 Saginaw Trail
Maitland, FL 32751

Great Wave Software
P.O. Box 5847
Stanford, CA 94305

Grolier Electronic Pub., Inc.
Dept. 336
Sherman Turnpike
Danbury, CT 06816

J.L. Hammett Co.
Box 545
Braintree, MA 02184

H & E Computronics Inc.
50 North Pascack Rd.
Spring Valley, NY 10988

Harcourt Brace Jovanovich
School Dept.
6277 Sea Harbor Dr.
Orlando, FL 32887

Hartley Courseware
123 Bridge
Dimondale, MI 48821

Harvard Associates, Inc.
10 Holworthy St.
Cambridge, MA 02138

Hayden Software
600 Suffolk St.
Lowell, MA 01854

Heathsoft
P.O. Box 691381
Tulsa, OK 74169-1381

Hickory Stick, Inc.
P.O. Box 6701, Station B
Albuquerque, NM 87197

Holt, Rinehart and Winston
383 Madison Ave.
New York, NY 10017

Home Computer Software
1035 Saratoga-Sunnyvale Rd.
San Jose, CA 95129

Houghton Miff. (Houghton Mifflin)
125 East Lake St., Suite 104
Bloomingdale, IL 60108
   or
One Beacon St.
Boston, MA 02108

HRM Software (Queue, Inc.)
562 Boston Ave.
Bridgeport, CT 06610

IBM Software
P.O. Box 1328
1000 NW 51 St.
Boca Raton, FL 33432

ICEC (Instructional Computer Equipment
   Corporation)
4740 Hinesley Ave.
Indianapolis, IN 46240

I/CT
Taylor Associates
10 Stepar Pl.
Huntington Station, NY 11746

Idaho Software
1863 Bitterroot Dr.
Twin Falls, ID 83301

Ideal Learning
327 South Marshall Rd., Suite 200
Shakopee, MN 55379

Intellectual Software
562 Boston Ave.
Bridgeport, CT 06610

Interlearn
P.O. Box 342
Cardiff by the Sea, CA 92007

IPASS (Individualized Prescriptive
   Arithmetic Skills System)
Pawtucket School Department
Park Pl.
Pawtucket, RI 02860

Island Software
Box 300
Lake Grove, NY 11755

Jadee Enterprises
1799 Meadowlake Dr.
Charleston, IL 61920

JA-MOR Software
60 River Rd.
Clinton, CT 06413

Jostens Learning Systems, Inc. .
800 Business Center Dr.
Mt. Prospect, IL 60056

JR Software
P.O. Box 2848
Denton, TX 76202

JWW (J. Weston Walch)
321 Valley St.
P.O. Box 658
Portland, ME 04104

KARD Software
P.O. Box 7
St. Ignace, MI 49781

Koeff Creations
Box 762
Seward, AK 99664

Krell Software
Flower Feed Bldg. #7
Suite 1D
St. James, NY 11780

K-12 MM (K-12 Micro Media)
Box 17
Valley Cottage, NY 10989

Kurzweil Computer Products
185 Albany St.
Cambridge, MA 02139

Lawrence Hall of Science
Math and Computer Education Project
University of California
Berkeley, CA 94720

LCSI (Logo Computer Systems, Inc.)
555 West 57th St.
Suite 1236
New York, NY 10019

The Learning Company
(see listing under TLC)

Learn. Cons. (Learning Consultants, Inc.)
690 Lafayette Rd.
Medina, OH 44256

Learning Tech. (Learning Technologies,
Inc.)
4255 LBJ Freeway, Suite 131
Dallas, TX 75244

Learning Unlimited Corp.
P.O. Box 12586
Research Triangle Park, NC 27709

Learning Well
200 South Service Rd.
Roslyn Heights, NY 11577

LEGO Systems, Inc.
Educational Sales Dept.
555 Taylor Rd.
Enfield, CT 06082

Love Publishing Co.
1777 South Bellaire St.
Denver, CO 80222

Macmillan Publishing Co.
866 Third Ave.
New York, NY 10022

M & M Micro
306 Clinton St.
Greenville, PA 16125

Marshware
P.O. Box 8082
Shawnee Mission, KS 66208

Math Arcade (The Math Arcade Library)
Adams Basin, NY 14410-0791

Math City
4040 Palos Verdes Dr. North
Rolling Hills Estates, CA 90274

Mathware
919 14th St.
Hermosa Beach, CA 90254

MCE Inc.
157 S. Kalamazoo Mall, Suite 250
Kalamazoo, MI 49007

McGraw-Hill
1221 Avenue of the Americas
New York, NY 10020

MCET (see Lawrence Hall of Science)

MCP (Microcomputer Curriculum Project)
Price Library School
University of Northern Iowa
Cedar Falls, IA 50613

MECC (Minnesota Educational
Computing Consortium)
3490 Lexington Ave. N.
St. Paul, MN 55126

Media Materials
2936 Remington Ave.
Baltimore, MD 21211

Metier
P.O. Box 51204
San Jose, CA 95151-5204

The Micro Center
Dept. MRI, Box 6
Pleasantville, NY 10570

Microcomputer Resources
2845 Temple Ave.
Long Beach, CA 90806

Micro-Ed, Inc.
P.O. Box 24750
Edina, MN 55424

Micrograms Inc.
1404 North Main St.
Rockford, IL 61103

Micro Learn. (Micro Learningware)
P.O. Box 2134
Mankato, MN 56001

Micro Power (Micro Power & Light Co.)
12820 Hillcrest Rd., Suite 224
Dallas, TX 75230

Microphys Programs
1737 W. 2nd St.
Brooklyn, NY 11223

Microsoft Corp.
16011 NE 36th Way
Box 97017
Redmond, WA 98073-9717

MicroSparc Inc.
Nibble Publications
45 Winthrop St.
Concord, MA 01742

Micro. Wrkshp (Microcomputer Workshops)
225 Westchester Ave.
Port Chester, NY 10573

Midwest Publications
P.O. Box 448
Pacific Grove, CA 93950

Midwest Software
Box 214
Farmington, MI 48024

Milliken Publishing Co.
1100 Research Blvd.
St. Louis, MO 63132

Milton Bradley Co.
(Programs now published by Media
  Materials)

Mindscape
SFN Companies, Inc.
1900 East Lake Ave.
Glenview, IL 60025
  or
MINDSCAPE, INC.
3444 Dundee Rd.
Northbrook, IL 60062

Modern Curriculum Press
13900 Prospect Rd.
Cleveland, OH 44136

Moses Engineering
P.O. Box 11038
Huntsville, AL 35805

(MSS) Microcomputer Software Systems
4716 Lakewood Dr.
Metairie, LA 70002

Newberry Software
304A E. Rosedale
Milwaukee, WI 53207

Nordic Software, Inc.
3939 North 48th
Lincoln, NE 68504

NOVA Software
P.O. Box 545
Alexandria, MN 56308

NTS Software
141 West Rialto Ave.
Rialto, CA 92376

Nystrom
3333 North Elston Ave.
Chicago, IL 60618

Opportunities for Learning
20417 Nordhoff St., Room VC
Chatsworth, CA 91311

Optimum Resources, Inc.
10 Station Place
Norfolk, CT 06058

Orange Cherry (Orange Cherry Media)
P.O. Box 427
Dept. 9
Bedford Hills, NY 10507

Orbyte Software
P.O. Box 948
Waterbury, CT 06720

Palantir Software
12777 Jones Rd.
Suite 100
Houston, TX 77070

Peachtree Software
3445 Peachtree Rd. N.E.
Atlanta, GA 30326

Per. Com. Art (Personal Computer Art)
1007 Far Hills Drive
East Peoria, IL 61611

Persimmon Software
502C Savannah St.
Greensboro, NC 27406

PLATO/WICAT Systems Co.
8100 34th Ave. South
P.O. Box O
Bloomington, MN 55440

The Porter Company
Dept. 2BR
35 Rand Pl.
Pittsford, NY 14534

Precision People, Inc.
3452 North Ride Cir., South
Jacksonville, FL 32217

Prentice-Hall
Sylvan Ave.
Englewood Cliffs, NJ 07632

The Professor
959 N.W. 53rd St.
Ft. Lauderdale, FL 33309

Program Design Inc.
11 Idar Ct.
Greenwich, CT 06830

Proud Products
20083 Mack Ave.
Grosse Pointe Woods, MI 48236

QED (Quality Educational Designs)
P.O. Box 12486
Portland, OR 97212

Queue
562 Boston Ave.
Bridgeport, CT 06610

Quinte Learning Centre Ltd.
290 Larkin St.
P.O. Box 1099
Buffalo, NY 14210

Random House School Division
c/o Gerald R. Brubaker
Highway 86 W., Rt 8, Box 100A
Nosho, MD 64850

Reader's Digest
Microcomputer Software Dept.
Pleasantville, NY 10570

Recreational Mathemagical Software
129 Carol Dr.
Clarks Summit, PA 18411

Renaissance Learning Systems
Tecumseh Bldg.
Jamesville, NY 13078

Resource Software International, Inc.
330 New Brunswick Ave.
Fords, NJ 08863

Reston Publishing Co.
Sylvan Ave.
Englewood Cliffs, NJ 07632

RG Comp. Wrk. (RG Computer Workshops,
Inc.)
37 Marcia Lane
New City, NY 10956

Scandura Training Systems, Inc.
3700 Walnut St.
Philadelphia, PA 19104

Scarborough Systems
25 North Broadway
Tarrytown, NY 10591

Scholastic Inc.
P.O. Box 7503
2931 East McCarty St.
Jefferson City, MO 65102

Schoolhouse Software
290 Brighton Rd.
Elk Grove, IL 60007

Science Research Associates (SRA)
155 Wacker Dr.
Chicago, IL 60606

Scott, Foresman and Company
1900 East Lake Ave.
Glenview, IL 60025

Scott Resources, Inc.
P.O. Box 2121
Ft. Collins, CO 80522

Screenplay
1095 Airport Rd.
Minden, NV 89423

Silver Burdett & Ginn
Customer Service Center
P.O. Box 2649
Columbus, OH 43216

Skillcorp, Inc.
1711 McGaw Ave.
Irvine, CA 92714

CUE SoftSwap
P.O. Box 271704
Concord, CA 94527

SouthWest EdPsych Services
P.O. Box 1870
Phoenix, AZ 85001

Spinifex Software
Robert Barboza
1857 Josie Ave.
Long Beach, CA 90815

Spinnaker Software
215 First St.
Cambridge, MA 02139

Springboard Software
7807 Creekridge Cir.
Minneapolis, MN 55435

SRA (Science Research Associates, Inc.)
927 Woodrow Ave.
North Canton, OH 44720

Sterling Swift Publishing Co.
7901 South IH-35
Austin, TX 78744

Strawberry Hill Knowledge Software
202-11961 88th Ave.
Delta, British Columbia
Canada V4C 3C9

Sunburst Communications Inc.
Room YB7
39 Washington Ave.
Pleasantville, NY 10570

SVE (Society for Visual Education)
Dept. 106-FD
1345 Diversey Parkway
Chicago, IL 60614

Sysdata International, Inc.
7671 Old Central Ave., Northeast
Minneapolis, MN 55432

Systems Impact
4400 MacArthur Blvd. NW
Suite 203
Washington, DC 20007

Tandy Corporation/Radio Shack
1800 One Tandy Center
Fort Worth, TX 76102

TCS/Houghton Mifflin Co.
One Beacon St.
Boston, MA 02108

Teacher's Pet Software
1517 Holly St.
Berkeley, CA 94703

Telephone Software
P.O. Box 6548
Torrance, CA 90504

TERM Computer Services
P.O. Box 725
New Providence, NJ 07974

Terrapin Inc.
380 Green St.
Cambridge, MA 02139

Thorobred Software
10 Olympic Plaza
Murray, KY 42071

TLC (The Learning Company)
6493 Kaiser Drive
Fremont, CA 94555

Trillium Press
P.O. Box 921
New York, NY 10159

Triton Products Co.
P.O. Box 8123
San Francisco, CA 94128
(Has assumed marketing of all TI software)

Trojan Software
728 S. Barnhart Rd.
Troy, OH 45373

True BASIC, Inc.
39 South Main St.
Hanover, NH 03755

TWC (Thinking with Computers)
P.O. Box 22801
Tucson, AZ 85706

2-Bit Software
P.O. Box 2036, Dept. EC1
Del Mar, CA 92014

TYC (Teach Yourself by Computer Software)
2128 W. Jefferson Rd.
Pittsford, NY 14534

Unicorn Software Co.
1775 East Tropicana Ave., No. 8
Las Vegas, NV 89109

Univ. Evan. (University of Evansville Press)
P.O. Box 329
Evansville, IN 47702

Ventura Educational Systems
3440 Brokenhill St.
Newbury Park, CA 91320

Wasatch Education Systems
5250 S. 300 W. Suite 350
Salt Lake City, UT 84107

Weekly Reader Family Software
(Now published by Optimum Resources)
Xerox Educational Publications
245 Long Hill Rd.
Middletown, CT 06457

J. Weston Walch
P.O. Box 658
Portland, ME 04104

WFF'N PROOF Learning Games Assn.
1490 South Blvd.
Ann Arbor, MI 48104

WICAT Systems
748 North 1340 West
Orem, UT 84057

Winner's Circle Education
183 East Main St.
Suite 1331
Rochester, NY 14604

Word Associates
3096 Summit Ave.
Highland Park, IL 60035

World Book Discovery
Electronic Products
Merchandise Mart Plaza
5th Floor
Mail Station 13
Chicago, IL 60654

Zypcom
P.O. Box 3421
Boise, ID 83703

MAGAZINES AND JOURNALS

AEDS Journal and AEDS Monitor
1201 16th St., NW
Washington, DC 20036

Arithmetic Teacher
NCTM
1906 Association Dr.
Reston, VA 22091

Byte
70 Main St.
Peterborough, NH 03458

Classroom Computer News
Intentional Educations, Inc.
341 Mt. Auburn St.
Watertown, MA 02172

The Computing Teacher
International Council for Computers
    in Education
University of Oregon
1787 Agate St.
Eugene, OR 97403

Creative Computing
P.O. Box 789-M
Morristown, NJ 07960

Educational Computer Magazine
3199 De La Cruz Blvd.
Santa Clara, CA 95050

Educational Technology Pub.
140 Sylvan Ave.
Englewood Cliffs, NJ 07632

Electronic Education
Suite 220
1311 Executive Center Dr.
Tallahassee, FL 32301

Electronic Learning (and Teaching
    and Computers)
Scholastic Inc.
902 Sylvan Ave.
Box 2001
Englewood Cliffs, NJ 07632

Instructional Innovator
AECT
1126 16th St. NW
Washington, DC 20036

Microquests
Martin-Bearden, Inc.
Box 337
Grapevine, TX 76051

NLX (National Logo Exchange)
Box 5431
Charlottesville, VA 22905

Scholastic Inc. (Electronic Learning,
    Teaching and Computers, etc.)
730 Broadway
New York, NY 10003

T.H.E. Journal
P.O. Box 992
Aston, MA 01720

PRODUCERS OF HARDWARE

Apple Computer
10260 Bandley Dr.
Cupertino, CA 94017

Atari, Inc.
1265 Borregas Ave.
Sunnyvale, CA 94086

Commodore Computer Systems
1200 Wilson Dr.
West Chester, PA 19380

Heathkit Educational Systems
Dept. 558-872
Benton Harbor, MI 49022

IBM Personal Computers
P.O. Box 1328-D
Boca Raton, FL 33432

Mattel
P.O. Box TLC
Madison Heights, MI 48071

Milton Bradley Co.
Springfield, MA 01101

NEC Home Electronics
1401 Estes Ave.
Elk Grove Village, IL 60007

Radio Shack
1800 One Tandy Center
Fort Worth, TX 76102

RB Robot Corporation
18301 W. 10th Ave., Suite 310
Golden, CO 80401

Sinclair Research Ltd.
50 Staniford St.
Boston, MA 02114

Synetix Inc.
10635 NE 38th Place
Kirkland, WA 98033

Timex Computer Corp.
Waterbury, CT 06720

Zenith Data Systems
1000 Milwaukee Ave.
Glenview, IL 60025

California Library Media Consortium for
   Classroom Evaluation of Microcomputer
   Courseware
San Mateo County Office of Education
Redwood City, CA 94064

EPIE Institute
P.O. Box 839B
Water Mill, NY 11976

Far West Laboratory for Educational
   Research and Development
1855 Folsom St.
San Francisco, CA 94103

The Micro Center
Dept. M G
P.O. Box 6
Pleasantville, NY 10570

MicroSIFT
Northwest Regional Educational Laboratory
300 S. W. Sixth Ave.
Portland, OR 97204

School Microware Reviews
Dresden Associates
Box 246
Dresden, ME 04342

Software Reports
10996 Torreyanna Rd.
P.O. Box 85007
San Diego, CA 92138

Technical Education Research Centers
   (TERC)
Computer Resource Center
8 Eliot St.
Cambridge, MA 02138

ORGANIZATIONS DEDICATED TO SOFTWARE EVALUATION

Apple Journal of Courseware Review
Apple Educational Foundation
20525 Mariani Ave.
Cupertino, CA 95014

ORGANIZATIONS DEDICATED TO THE EXCEPTIONAL STUDENT

Apple Computer Clearinghouse
   for the Handicapped
Prentke Romich Co.
1022 Heyl Rd.
Wooster, OH 44691

Closing the Gap
P.O. Box 68
Henderson, MN 56044

Computeronics Gifted Child Project
925A Miccousukee Rd.
Tallahassee, FL 32303

Creative Educational Services
36 River Ave.
Monmouth Beach, NJ 07750

ERIC Clearinghouse on Handicapped
and Gifted Children
CEC
1920 Association Dr.
Reston, VA 22091

Evans-Newton, Inc.
7745 E. Redfield Rd.
Suite 100
Scottsdale, AZ 85260

Gifted Child Project
Leon County School Board
2757 West Pensacola
Tallahassee, FL 32304

HEX
Richard Barth
11523 Charlton Dr.
Silver Spring, MD 20902

Instructional Systems Group
Scott Instruments Corp.
1111 Willow Springs Dr.
Denton, TX 76201

Learning Tools, Inc.
686 Massachusetts Ave.
Cambridge, MA 02139

Maryland Computer Services
2010 Rock Spring Rd.
Forest Hill, MD 21050

National Rehabilitation Information Center
The Catholic University of America
4407 Eighth St., N.E.
Washington, DC 20017

Project CAISH
3450 Gocio Road
Sarasota, FL 33580

Project Micro-Ideas
1335 N. Waukegan Road
Glenview, IL 60025

SECTOR
Exceptional Child Center
UMC 68
Utah State University
Logan, UT 84322

SpecialNet
c/o NASDSE
Suite 404E
1201 16th St., NW
Washington, DC 20036

Trace Research and Development Center
University of Wisconsin–Madison
314 Waisman Center
1500 Highland Ave.
Madison, WI 53706

Western Center for Microcomputers
in Special Education
Suite 275
1259 El Camino Real
Menlo Park, CA 94025

Zygo Industries
P.O. Box 1008
Portland, OR 97207-1008

DATA BASES
AND NETWORKS

CompuServe Information Service
5000 Arlington Centre Blvd.
Columbus, OH 43220
(614) 457-8600
Communications network for general
purpose

Dialog Information Services
3460 Hillview Ave.
Palo Alto, CA 94304
(800) 227-1927
Communications network with educational
data bases

Directory of Online Information Resources
CSG Press
11301 Rockville Pike
Kensington, MD 20895
(301) 881-9400
Not a data base, but a directory
to data bases

ERIC
Educational Resources Center
National Institute of Education
Washington, DC 20208
(202) 254-7934

MicroSIFT
300 S.W. 6th St.
Portland, OR 97204
(503) 248-6800
Clearinghouse for software

Resources in Computer Education/
  Bibliographic Retrieval Services
  (RICE/BRS)
1200 Route 7
Latham, NY 12110
(518) 783–1161
Data base on software for education

The Source
Reader's Digest Educational Division
Pleasantville, NY 10570
(914) 769–7000

Source Telecomputing Corporation
1616 Anderson Rd.
McLean, VA 22102
Communications network with consumer
  services, data bases, and electronic mail

GENERAL ORGANIZATIONS

American Educational Research Association (AERA)
1126 16th Street, NW
Washington, DC 20036
(202) 223–9845
Includes special-interest group for CAI

Association for Computers in Mathematics
  & Science Teaching
P.O. Box 4455
Austin, TX 78765

Association for Computing
  Machinery (ACM)
1133 Avenue of the Americas
New York, NY 10036
(212) 265–6300

Association for Educational
  Communications and Technology
  (AECT)
1126 16th Street, NW
Washington, DC 20036

Association for Educational Data Systems
  (AEDS)
1201 16th Street, NW
Washington, DC 20036

Association for the Development of
  Computer-Based Instructional Systems
  (ADCIS)
Western University Computer Center
Bellingham, WA 98225
(206) 676-2860

Goal: To facilitate communication between
  developers and consumers of computer
  materials

Boston Computer Society (BCS)
Educational Resource Exchange
Three Center Plaza
Boston, MA 02108
(617) 367-8080

Computer-Using Educators (CUE)
c/o Don McKell
Independence High School
1775 Educational Park Dr.
San Jose, CA 95113

Dataspan
c/o Karl Zinn
109 East Madison St.
Ann Arbor, MI 48104

Educational Computing Consortium of Ohio
  (ECCO)
4777 Farnhurst Rd.
Lyndhurst, OH 44124

Educational Technology Center
c/o Alfred Bork
University of California
Irvine, CA 92717
(714) 883-6945
Middle-school computer materials

EPIE Institute
P.O. Box 620
Stony Brook, NY 11790
(516) 246-8664
Educational technology consumer group

ERIC Clearinghouse on Elementary
  and Early Childhood Education
University of Illinois
College of Education
Urbana, IL 61801
(217) 333-1386

ERIC Clearinghouse on Information
  Resources
Syracuse University
School of Education
130 Huntington Hall
Syracuse, NY 13210

Far West Laboratory
1855 Folsom St.
San Francisco, CA 94103
(415) 565-3035
Information service on many aspects of
  computers in education

Human Resources Research Organization
(HumRRO)
300 North Washington St.
Alexandria, VA 22314

International Council for Computers
in Education (ICCE)
Computer Center
East Oregon State College
LaGrande, OR 97850
Educational users' group

Microcomputer Resource Center
Teachers College
Columbia University
New York, NY 10027
(212) 678-3740

Minnesota Educational Computing
Consortium (MECC)
2520 Broadway Dr.
St. Paul, MN 55113
(612) 376-1101

National Audio-Visual Association (NAVA)
3150 Spring St.
Fairfax, VA 22031
(703) 273-7200

National Council for the Social Studies
(NCSS)
3501 Newark St., NW
Washington, DC 20016

National Council of Teachers of
Mathematics (NCTM)
1906 Association Dr.
Reston, VA 22091
(703) 620-9840

National Science Teachers Association
(NSTA)
1742 Connecticut Ave., NW
Washington, DC 20009
(202) 328-5840

Softswap
San Mateo County Office of Education
333 Main St.
Redwood City, CA 94063
(415) 363-5472
Software exchange; "public domain" software

Technical Education Research Center
(TERC)
3 Eliot St.
Cambridge, MA 02138
Technical educators users' group

APPENDIX B:
LOGO PROGRAMS

Notes on using Logo Programs

It is essential to type these programs exactly as given. Usually, this means only careful checking of the letters, numbers, and especially *spaces*. Sometimes, however, long Logo instructions do not fit in one line of this book. For the sake of readability, they have been printed with a special format: Every line after the first line of a long Logo instruction is indented, and no words are split at the end of the line. When *you* type these instructions, some of your words might be split into parts at the end of the line. This is all right; just keep typing. Most important, do *not* press the RETURN key until then end of the final indented line.

FEED.TURTLE	LCSI version

```
TO START
LOCAL [COM POSITION
    OLDPOSITION NUM HIGHEST
    LOWEST FOOD.LIST FOOD]
CS
PD
SETPC 1
AXIS
ST
```

```
PU
MAKE "COM []
MAKE "POSITION 0
MAKE "OLDPOSITION 0
MAKE "NUM 0
MAKE "HIGHEST 130
MAKE "LOWEST ( - 75 )
PRINTPOSITION
FEED.TURTLE
END
```

```
TO AXIS
HT
LT 90 FD 8 BK 14 RT 90
REPEAT 2 [REPEAT 12 [FD 10 LT 90
    FD 3 BK 6 FD 3 RT 90] BK 120 RT
    180]·
LT 90 FD 12 RT 90
MAKE "FOOD.LIST []
REPEAT 5 [MAKE "FOOD.LIST FPUT
    RANDOM 120 :FOOD.LIST]
MAKE "FOOD FIRST :FOOD.LIST
PU
MARK :FOOD.LIST
END
```

```
TO PRINTPOSITION
CLEARTEXT
PRINT :COM
REPEAT 8 [TYPE "\ ]
TYPE ( SE "OLD: :OLDPOSITION " )
```

```
PRINT SE "NEW: :POSITION
PRINT "
END


TO FEED.TURTLE
CLEARTEXT
PRINT [I'M HUNGRY. HELP ME FIND
    MY FOOD.]
COMMAND
END


TO COMMAND
CATCH "ERROR [RUN.IT GETINPUT]
COMMAND
END


TO RUN.IT :LIST
IF EQUALP (FIRST :LIST) "REPEAT
    [REPEAT FIRST BF :LIST [RUN.IT
    FIRST BF BF :LIST] STOP]
IF MEMBERP FIRST :LIST [BK BACK]
    [MAKE "NUM (MINUS LAST :LIST )]
    [ IF MEMBERP FIRST :LIST
    [FORWARD FD] [MAKE "NUM LAST
    :LIST] [PRINT [TRY AGAIN.]
    COMMAND STOP]]
IF (:POSITION + :NUM) < :LOWEST
    [PRINT SE [TOO LOW. POSITION
    IS] :POSITION COMMAND STOP]
IF (:POSITION + :NUM) > :HIGHEST
    [PRINT SE [TOO HIGH. POSITION
    IS] :POSITION COMMAND STOP]
MAKE "OLDPOSITION :POSITION
MAKE "POSITION (:POSITION + :NUM)
SETY :POSITION
IF MEMBERP :POSITION :FOOD.LIST
    [CHECK.FOOD]
PRINTPOSITION
END


TO GETINPUT
MAKE "COM READLIST
IF EMPTYP :COM [OP GETINPUT
    STOP]
IF NOT (AND (MEMBERP UPPERCASE
    (FIRST :COM) [FD BK FORWARD
    BACK REPEAT]) (NUMBERP (LAST
    :COM)) (EQUALP COUNT :COM 2))
    [PRINT [TYPE FD OR BK AND A
    NUMBER.] OP GETINPUT]
OP :COM
END
```

```
TO PRINTPOS
SETCURSOR 20 20
PRINT :POSITION
END


TO CHECK.FOOD
PRINT [THAT'S ONE OF THEM! LET ME
    SEE..]
WAIT 60
IF :POSITION = :FOOD [FISH PRINT
    [YOU FOUND IT!! CHEW, CHEW,
    SWALLOW.] PRINT [YUMMY!
    THANKS!] THROW "TOPLEVEL]
    [PRINT [TOO BAD. NO FOOD. TRY
    AGAIN.]]
WAIT 120
END


TO FISH
PU
SETPOS LIST - 130 ( :POSITION - 29 )
SETH 30
PD
RARC 80
RT 120
RARC 80
SETH 180
FD 50
END


TO MARK :L
IF EMPTYP :L [STOP]
FD FIRST :L
LT 90 PD FD 12 BK 12 RT 90 PU
BK FIRST :L
MARK BF :L
END


TO RARC :R
REPEAT 9 [RCP :R]
END


TO LARC :R
REPEAT 9 [LCP :R]
END


TO LCP :R
LEFT 5
FORWARD :R * ( 3.14159 ) / 18
LEFT 5
END
```

```
TO RCP :R
RIGHT 5
FORWARD :R * ( 3.14159 ) / 18
RIGHT 5
END
```

```
┌─────────────────────────────────────┐
│ FEED.TURTLE          Terrapin version │
└─────────────────────────────────────┘
```

```
TO START
RANDOMIZE
DRAW
PC 1
AXIS
.GCOLL
ST
PU
MAKE "COM []
MAKE "POSITION 0
MAKE "OLDPOSITION 0
MAKE "NUM 0
MAKE "HIGHEST 130
MAKE "LOWEST ( - 75 )
PRINTPOSITION
FEED.TURTLE
END
```

```
TO AXIS
HT
LT 90 FD 8 BK 14 RT 90
REPEAT 2 [REPEAT 12 [FD 10 LT 90 FD
    3 BK 6 FD 3 RT 90] BK 120 RT 180]
LT 90 FD 12 RT 90
MAKE "FOOD.LIST []
REPEAT 5 [MAKE "FOOD.LIST FPUT
    RANDOM 120 :FOOD.LIST]
MAKE "FOOD FIRST :FOOD.LIST
PU
MARK :FOOD.LIST
END
```

```
TO PRINTPOSITION
CLEARTEXT
PRINT :COM
REPEAT 8 [PRINT1 "]
PRINT1 ( SE "OLD: :OLDPOSITION " )
PRINT SE "NEW: :POSITION
PRINT "
END
```

```
TO FEED.TURTLE
CLEARTEXT
```

```
PRINT [I'M HUNGRY. HELP ME FIND
    MY FOOD.]
COMMAND
END
```

```
TO COMMAND
CLEARINPUT
RUN.IT GETINPUT
COMMAND
END
```

```
TO RUN.IT :LIST
IF FIRST :LIST = "REPEAT REPEAT
    FIRST BF :LIST [RUN.IT FIRST BF
    BF :LIST] STOP
IF FIRST FIRST :LIST = "B MAKE "NUM
    ( - LAST :LIST ) ELSE IF FIRST
    FIRST :LIST = "F MAKE "NUM LAST
    :LIST ELSE PRINT [TRY AGAIN.]
    COMMAND
IF :POSITION + :NUM < :LOWEST
    PRINT SE [TOO LOW. POSITION
    IS] :POSITION COMMAND STOP
IF :POSITION + :NUM > :HIGHEST
    PRINT SE [TOO HIGH. POSITION
    IS] :POSITION COMMAND STOP
MAKE "OLDPOSITION :POSITION
MAKE "POSITION :POSITION + :NUM
SETY :POSITION
IF MEMBER? :POSITION :FOOD.LIST
    CHECK.FOOD
PRINTPOSITION
END
```

```
TO GETINPUT
MAKE "COM REQUEST
IF EMPTY? :COM OP GETINPUT STOP
IF NOT (ALLOF (MEMBER? FIRST
    :COM [FD BK FORWARD BACK
    REPEAT]) (NUMBER? LAST :COM)
    (COUNT :COM = 2)) PRINT [TYPE
    FD OR BK AND A NUMBER.] OP
    GETINPUT
OP :COM
END
```

```
TO PRINTPOS
CURSOR 20 20
PRINT :POSITION
END
```

```
TO CHECK.FOOD
PRINT [THAT'S ONE OF THEM! LET ME
    SEE..]
REPEAT 2000 []
IF :POSITION = :FOOD FISH PRINT
    [YOU FOUND IT!! CHEW, CHEW,
    SWALLOW.] PRINT [YUMMY!
    THANKS!] TOPLEVEL ELSE PRINT
    [TOO BAD. NO FOOD. TRY
    AGAIN.]
REPEAT 3000 []
END


TO FISH
PU
SETXY - 130 ( :POSITION - 29 )
SETH 30
PD
RARC 80
RT 120
RARC 80
SETH 180
FD 50
END
TO MARK :L
IF EMPTY? :L STOP
FD FIRST :L
LT 90 PD FD 12 BK 12 RT 90 PU
BK FIRST :L
MARK BF :L
END


TO RARC :R
 REPEAT 9 [RCP :R]
END


TO LARC :R
 REPEAT 9 [LCP :R]
END


TO LCP :R
 LEFT 5
 FORWARD :R * ( 3.14159 ) / 18
 LEFT 5
END


TO RCP :R
 RIGHT 5
 FORWARD :R * ( 3.14159 ) / 18
 RIGHT 5
END
```

```
┌─────────────────────────────────────┐
│ GUESS.NUMBER.TURTLE                  │
│                         LCSI version │
└─────────────────────────────────────┘

TO START
GUESS.NUMBER
END


TO GUESS.NUMBER
 SETUP
 CLEARTEXT
 MAKE "NUMBER 1 + RANDOM 99
 PRINT "
 PRINT [GUESS THE MYSTERY
        NUMBER.]
 PRINT [IT IS BETWEEN 0 AND 100]
 GUESS.NUMBER.2
END


TO SETUP
 CS
 HIDETURTLE
 SETBG 0
 SETPC 1
 AXIS
 PD
END


TO AXIS
 LT 90
 FD 20
 BK 40
 FD 20
 RT 90
 REPEAT 10 [FD 10 LT 90 FD 3 BK 6 FD 3
        RT 90]
 ARROW
 BK 100
 RT 180
 ARROW
 RT 180
END


TO ARROW
 PU
 FD 20
 RT 90
 FD 20
 RT 90
 PD
 FD 15
 LT 45
```

```
BK 7
FD 7
RT 90
BK 7
FD 7
LT 45
BK 15
PU
LT 90
BK 20
LT 90
BK 20
END


TO GUESS.NUMBER.2
PRINT [WHAT IS YOUR GUESS?]
MAKE "GUESS GET.NUMBER
PRINT "
CHECK.GUESS
END


TO GET.NUMBER
LOCAL [NUM MESSAGE]
MAKE "MESSAGE [PLEASE TYPE A
    NUMBER.]
MAKE "NUM READLIST
IF :NUM = [] [PRINT :MESSAGE
    OUTPUT GET.NUMBER]
IF NOT NUMBERP (FIRST :NUM)
    [PRINT :MESSAGE OUTPUT
    GET.NUMBER]
OUTPUT FIRST :NUM
END


TO CHECK.GUESS
IF OR GREATERP :GUESS 99 LESSP
    :GUESS 1 [PRINT [IT MUST BE
    BETWEEN 0 AND 100]
    GUESS.NUMBER.2 STOP]
TEST EQUALP :GUESS :NUMBER
IFT [GOT.IT]
IFT [STOP]
MAKE "GREATER? GREATERP
    :GUESS :NUMBER
IF :GREATER? [PRINT SENTENCE
    :GUESS [IS GREATER THAN THE
    NUMBER.]] [PRINT SENTENCE
    :GUESS [IS LESS THAN THE
    NUMBER.]]
MARK.GUESS :GUESS :GREATER?
GUESS.NUMBER.2
END
```

```
TO GOT.IT
SETY :NUMBER
RT 90
FD 30
BK 60
PRINT " PRINT SENTENCE :NUMBER
    [IS IT EXACTLY!]
END


TO MARK.GUESS :GUESS :GREATER?
SETY :GUESS
IF :GREATER? [RT 90] [LT 90]
FD 15
BK 15
IF :GREATER? [LT 90] [RT 90]
END
```

```
┌─────────────────────────────────┐
│ GUESS.NUMBER.TURTLE             │
│                 Terrapin version │
└─────────────────────────────────┘
```

```
TO START
GUESS.NUMBER
END


TO GUESS.NUMBER
SETUP
RANDOMIZE
CLEARTEXT
MAKE "NUMBER 1 + RANDOM 99
PRINT "
PRINT [GUESS THE MYSTERY
    NUMBER.]
PRINT [IT IS BETWEEN 0 AND 100]
GUESS.NUMBER.2
END


TO SETUP
DRAW
HIDETURTLE
BACKGROUND 0
PC 1
AXIS
PENDOWN
END


TO AXIS
LT 90
FD 20
BK 40
FD 20
RT 90
```

```
REPEAT 10 [FD 10 LT 90 FD 3 BK 6 FD 3
    RT 90]
ARROW
BK 100
RT 180
ARROW
RT 180
END


TO ARROW
PENUP
FD 20
RT 90
FD 20
RT 90
PENDOWN
FD 15
LT 45
BK 7
FD 7
RT 90
BK 7
FD 7
LT 45
BK 15
PENUP
LT 90
BK 20
LT 90
BK 20
END


TO GUESS.NUMBER.2
PRINT [WHAT IS YOUR GUESS?]
MAKE "GUESS GET.NUMBER
PRINT "
CHECK.GUESS
END


TO GET.NUMBER
LOCAL [NUM MESSAGE]
MAKE "MESSAGE [PLEASE TYPE A
    NUMBER.]
MAKE "NUM READLIST
IF :NUM = [] [PRINT :MESSAGE
    OUTPUT GET.NUMBER]
IF NOT NUMBERP (FIRST :NUM)
    [PRINT :MESSAGE OUTPUT
    GET.NUMBER]
OUTPUT FIRST :NUM
END
```

```
TO CHECK.GUESS
IF ANYOF :GUESS > 99 :GUESS < 1
    PRINT [IT MUST BE BETWEEN 0
    AND 100] GUESS.NUMBER.2
    STOP
TEST :GUESS = :NUMBER
IFTRUE GOT.IT
IFTRUE STOP
MAKE "GREATER? :GUESS >
    :NUMBER
IF :GREATER? PRINT SENTENCE
    :GUESS [IS GREATER THAN THE
    NUMBER.] ELSE PRINT
    SENTENCE :GUESS [IS LESS
    THAN THE NUMBER.]
MARK.GUESS :GUESS :GREATER?
GUESS.NUMBER.2
END


TO GOT.IT
SETY :NUMBER
RT 90
FD 30
BK 60
PRINT " PRINT SENTENCE :NUMBER
    [IS IT EXACTLY!]
END


TO MARK.GUESS :GUESS :GREATER?
SETY :GUESS
IF :GREATER? THEN RT 90 ELSE LT 90
FD 15
BK 15
IF :GREATER? THEN LT 90 ELSE RT 90
END
```

PRIME.FACTORIZATION
LCSI version

```
TO PRIME.FACTORIZATION :NUMBER
LOCAL [PRIMES FACTOR.LIST]
MAKE "PRIMES [2 3 5 7 11 13 17 19 23
    29 31 37 41 43 47 53 59 61 67 71 73
    79 83 89 97]
IF EQUALP :NUMBER 1 [PRINT [1 IS
    NOT PRIME OR COMPOSITE]
    STOP]
IF LESSP :NUMBER 1 [PRINT [PLEASE
    GIVE A NUMBER GREATER THAN
    1] STOP]
MAKE "FACTOR.LIST []
```

```
    GET.PRIME.FACTORS :NUMBER
        :PRIMES
    IF (COUNT :FACTOR.LIST) > 1
        [OUTPUT :FACTOR.LIST] [OUTPUT
        [PRIME]]
    END


TO GET.PRIME.FACTORS :NUMBER
        :PRIMES
    IF EMPTYP :PRIMES [CHECK.SIZE
        STOP]
    IF MEMBERP :NUMBER :PRIMES
        [MAKE "FACTOR.LIST LPUT INT
        :NUMBER :FACTOR.LIST STOP]
    TEST EQUALP REMAINDER :NUMBER
        FIRST :PRIMES 0
    IFT [MAKE "FACTOR.LIST LPUT FIRST
        :PRIMES :FACTOR.LIST]
    IFT [GET.PRIME.FACTORS ( :NUMBER
        / FIRST :PRIMES ) :PRIMES]
    IFF [GET.PRIME.FACTORS :NUMBER
        BUTFIRST :PRIMES]
    END


TO CHECK.SIZE
    IF (SQRT :NUMBER) > 100 [PRINT
        [NUMBER TOO LARGE] THROW
        "TOPLEVEL] [MAKE "FACTOR.LIST
        LPUT INT :NUMBER
        :FACTOR.LIST]
    END
```

```
PRIME.FACTORIZATION
                      Terrapin version
```

```
TO PRIME.FACTORIZATION :NUMBER
    LOCAL "PRIMES
    LOCAL "FACTOR.LIST
    MAKE "PRIMES [2 3 5 7 11 13 17 19 23
        29 31 37 41 43 47 53 59 61 67 71 73
        79 83 89 97]
    IF :NUMBER = 1 PRINT [1 IS NOT
        PRIME OR COMPOSITE] STOP
    IF :NUMBER < 1 PRINT [PLEASE GIVE
        A NUMBER GREATER THAN 1.]
        STOP
    MAKE "FACTOR.LIST []
    GET.PRIME.FACTORS :NUMBER
        :PRIMES
    IF COUNT :FACTOR.LIST > 1 OUTPUT
        :FACTOR.LIST ELSE OUTPUT
        [PRIME]
    END
```

```
TO GET.PRIME.FACTORS :NUMBER
        :PRIMES
    IF EMPTY? :PRIMES CHECK.SIZE
        STOP
    IF MEMBER? :NUMBER :PRIMES
        MAKE "FACTOR.LIST LPUT
        :NUMBER :FACTOR.LIST STOP
    TEST REMAINDER :NUMBER FIRST
        :PRIMES = 0
    IFTRUE MAKE "FACTOR.LIST LPUT
        FIRST :PRIMES :FACTOR.LIST
    IFTRUE GET.PRIME.FACTORS (
        :NUMBER / FIRST :PRIMES )
        :PRIMES
    IFFALSE GET.PRIME.FACTORS
        :NUMBER BUTFIRST :PRIMES
    END


TO CHECK.SIZE
    IF SQRT :NUMBER > 100 PRINT
        [NUMBER TOO LARGE] TOPLEVEL
        ELSE MAKE "FACTOR.LIST LPUT
        :NUMBER :FACTOR.LIST
    END
```

```
GCD                      LCSI version
```

```
TO GCD.SETS :NUMBER.1 :NUMBER.2
    OUTPUT LAST INTERSECT
        ( GET.DIVISORS 1 :NUMBER.1 [])
        ( GET.DIVISORS 1 :NUMBER.2 [])
    END


TO INTERSECT :L1 :L2
    IF EMPTYP :L1 [OUTPUT []]
    TEST MEMBERP FIRST :L1 :L2
    IFT [OUTPUT FPUT FIRST :L1
        INTERSECT BUTFIRST :L1 :L2]
    IFF [OUTPUT INTERSECT BUTFIRST
        :L1 :L2]
    END


TO GET.DIVISORS :DIV :NUMBER.1
        :DIV.LIST
    IF :DIV > :NUMBER.1 [OP :DIV.LIST]
    IF (REMAINDER :NUMBER.1 :DIV) = 0
        [MAKE "DIV.LIST LPUT :DIV
        :DIV.LIST]
    OP GET.DIVISORS (:DIV + 1)
        :NUMBER.1 :DIV.LIST
    END
```

```
TO GCD.EUCLID :NUMBER.1
    :NUMBER.2
IF NOT GREATERP :NUMBER.2 0
    [OUTPUT :NUMBER.1]
OUTPUT GCD.EUCLID :NUMBER.2
    REMAINDER :NUMBER.1
    :NUMBER.2
END
```

GCD	Terrapin version

```
TO GCD.SETS :NUMBER.1 :NUMBER.2
OUTPUT LAST INTERSECT
    ( GET.DIVISORS 1 :NUMBER.1 [])
    ( GET.DIVISORS 1 :NUMBER.2 [])
END


TO INTERSECT :L1 :L2
IF EMPTY? :L1 THEN OUTPUT []
TEST MEMBER? FIRST :L1 :L2
IFTRUE OUTPUT FPUT FIRST :L1
    INTERSECT BUTFIRST :L1 :L2
IFFALSE OUTPUT INTERSECT
    BUTFIRST :L1 :L2
END


TO GET.DIVISORS :DIV :NUMBER.1
    :DIV.LIST
IF :DIV > :NUMBER.1 OP :DIV.LIST
IF (REMAINDER :NUMBER.1 :DIV) = 0
    MAKE "DIV.LIST LPUT :DIV
    :DIV.LIST
OUTPUT GET.DIVISORS (:DIV + 1)
    :NUMBER.1 :DIV.LIST
END


TO GCD.EUCLID :NUMBER.1
    :NUMBER.2
IF NOT :NUMBER.2 > 0 OUTPUT
    :NUMBER.1
OUTPUT GCD.EUCLID :NUMBER.2
    REMAINDER :NUMBER.1
    :NUMBER.2
END
```

LCM	LCSI version

```
TO LCM :NUMBER.1 :NUMBER.2
LOCAL "MULTIPLE
MAKE "MULTIPLE :NUMBER.2
IF OR :NUMBER.1 < 1 :NUMBER.2 < 1
    [PRINT [USE NUMBERS GREATER
    THAN 0] STOP]
```

```
OUTPUT GET.LCM :MULTIPLE
END


TO GET.LCM :MULTIPLE
IF EQUALP REMAINDER :MULTIPLE
    :NUMBER.1 0 [OUTPUT
    :MULTIPLE]
OUTPUT GET.LCM :MULTIPLE +
    :NUMBER.2
END
```

LCM	Terrapin version

```
TO LCM :NUMBER.1 :NUMBER.2
LOCAL "MULTIPLE
MAKE "MULTIPLE :NUMBER.2
IF ANYOF :NUMBER.1 < 1 :NUMBER.2
    < 1 PRINT [USE NUMBERS
    GREATER THAN 0] STOP
OUTPUT GET.LCM :MULTIPLE
END


TO GET.LCM :MULTIPLE
IF REMAINDER :MULTIPLE :NUMBER.1
    = 0 THEN OUTPUT :MULTIPLE
OUTPUT GET.LCM :MULTIPLE +
    :NUMBER.2
END
```

DIVISORS (Fig. 6.9)	Terrapin version

```
TO DIVISORS :NUMBER.1 :NUMBER.2
IF :NUMBER.1 > :NUMBER.2 STOP
IF :NUMBER.1 < 0 PRINT [USE
    NUMBERS GREATER THAN 0.]
    STOP
PRINT1 ( SENTENCE [DIVISORS OF]
    :NUMBER.1 [ARE:] ) PRINT1 CHAR
    32
PRINT GET.DIVISORS 1 :NUMBER.1 []
DIVISORS :NUMBER.1 + 1 :NUMBER.2
END


TO GET.DIVISORS :DIV :NUMBER.1
    :DIV.LIST
IF :DIV > :NUMBER.1 OP :DIV.LIST
IF (REMAINDER :NUMBER.1 :DIV) = 0
    MAKE "DIV.LIST LPUT :DIV
    :DIV.LIST
OUTPUT GET.DIVISORS (:DIV + 1)
    :NUMBER.1 :DIV.LIST
END
```

```
┌──────────────────────────────────────┐
│ MULTI.REPEAT              LCSI version │
└──────────────────────────────────────┘
```

```
TO START
LOCAL [HIGHEST LOWEST GOAL
    COM POSITION OLDPOSITION
    ANSWER NUMBER NUM
    DISTANCE]
MAKE "HIGHEST 13
MAKE "LOWEST 2
MAKE "GOAL ( :LOWEST + RANDOM
    :HIGHEST ) * ( :LOWEST +
    RANDOM :HIGHEST )
MAKE "COM []
MAKE "POSITION 0
CS
SETPC 1
AXIS
PU
COMMAND
END
```

```
TO AXIS
HT
PU
SETPOS LIST -120 ( -12 )
SETHEADING 90
PD
LINE 10
REPEAT QUOTIENT :GOAL 10 [FD 10
    LINE 6]
FD REMAINDER :GOAL 10
LINE 12
PU
END
```

```
TO LINE :LENGTH
RT 90
FD :LENGTH / 2
BK :LENGTH
FD :LENGTH / 2
LT 90
END
```

```
TO COMMAND
START.POS
SETHEADING 90
MAKE "POSITION 0
ST
PRINTALL
GETINPUT
RUN.IT :NUMBER :DISTANCE
END
```

```
TO START.POS
SETPOS LIST -120 0
END
```

```
TO PRINTALL
CLEARTEXT
PRINTLINE
IF NOT EMPTYP :COM [SETCURSOR [0
    21] PRINT SE [LAST TRY WAS:]
    :COM SETCURSOR [5 22] TYPE
    [NEW TRY:] SPACES 1]
END
```

```
TO PRINTLINE
SETCURSOR [10 20] PRINT SE "GOAL:
    :GOAL
SETCURSOR [20 20] TYPE "POSITION:
PRINTPOS
END
```

```
TO PRINTPOS
SETCURSOR [30 20] PRINT :POSITION
END
```

```
TO GETINPUT
MAKE "COM READLIST
IF EMPTYP :COM [GETINPUT STOP]
IF (OR NOT LISTP (LAST :COM)
    EMPTYP (BF :COM) NOT (FIRST
    :COM) = "REPEAT ) [PRINT [TYPE
    REPEAT, THEN A NUMBER, THEN
    A LIST WITH FD AND A NUMBER.]
    WAIT 120 CLEARTEXT PRINTLINE
    GETINPUT STOP]
IF OR NOT MEMBERP (FIRST LAST
    :COM) [FD FORWARD] NOT
    NUMBERP (LAST LAST :COM)
    [PRINT [JUST REPEAT FD'S] WAIT
    120 CLEARTEXT PRINTLINE
    GETINPUT STOP]
MAKE "NUMBER FIRST BF :COM
MAKE "DISTANCE LAST LAST :COM
END
```

```
TO RUN.IT :NUMBER :DISTANCE
IF :NUMBER * :DISTANCE > 240 [MAKE
    "POSITION :NUMBER * :DISTANCE
    PRINT [TOO FAR!]] [REPEAT
    :NUMBER [MAKE "POSITION
    :POSITION + :DISTANCE
    PRINTPOS FD :DISTANCE WAIT
    30]]
CHECKPOSITION
END
```

```
TO CHECKPOSITION
 IF :GOAL = :POSITION [SUCCESS] [IF
   NOT :POSITION = 0 [PRINT [TRY
   AGAIN.] WAIT 120 COMMAND]]
END


TO SUCCESS
 SETCURSOR [0 22]
 PRINT [THAT WORKS! CAN YOU THINK
   OF ANY]
 TYPE [OTHERS THAT WOULD WORK
   AS WELL?] SPACES 2
 IF ANSWERP = "YES [PRINT [TRY!]
   COMMAND] [CLEARTEXT TYPE
   [DO YOU WANT TO TRY ANOTHER
   GOAL?] SPACES 2]
 IF ANSWERP = "YES [START] [PRINT
   [GOODBYE!] THROW "TOPLEVEL]
END


TO ANSWERP
 MAKE "ANSWER READLIST
 IF EMPTYP :ANSWER [PRINT OP
   ANSWERP STOP]
 MAKE "ANSWER FIRST :ANSWER
 IF MEMBERP :ANSWER [YES NO] [OP
   :ANSWER]
 PRINT [PLEASE TYPE YES OR NO.]
 OP ANSWERP
END


TO SPACES :SPACES
 REPEAT :SPACES [TYPE CHAR 32]
END


MAKE "STARTUP [START]
```

```
+-----------------------------------+
| MULTI.REPEAT      Terrapin version |
+-----------------------------------+
```

```
TO START
 LOCAL "HIGHEST
 LOCAL "LOWEST
 LOCAL "GOAL
 LOCAL "COM
 LOCAL "POSITION
 LOCAL "OLDPOSITION
 LOCAL "ANSWER
 LOCAL "NUMBER
 LOCAL "NUM
 LOCAL "DISTANCE
 MAKE "HIGHEST 13
 MAKE "LOWEST 2
```

```
 MAKE "GOAL ( :LOWEST + RANDOM
   :HIGHEST ) * ( :LOWEST +
   RANDOM :HIGHEST )
 MAKE "COM []
 MAKE "POSITION 0
 DRAW
 PC 1
 AXIS
 .GCOLL
 PU
 COMMAND
END


TO AXIS
 HT
 PU
 SETXY - 120 ( - 12 )
 SETHEADING 90
 PD
 LINE 10
 REPEAT QUOTIENT :GOAL 10 [FD 10
   LINE 6]
 FD REMAINDER :GOAL 10
 LINE 12
 PU
END


TO LINE :LENGTH
 RT 90
 FD :LENGTH / 2
 BK :LENGTH
 FD :LENGTH / 2
 LT 90
END


TO COMMAND
 START.POS
 SETHEADING 90
 MAKE "POSITION 0
 ST
 PRINTALL
 GETINPUT
 RUN.IT :NUMBER :DISTANCE
END


TO START.POS
 SETXY - 120 0
END


TO PRINTALL
 CLEARTEXT
 PRINTLINE
 IF NOT EMPTY? :COM CURSOR 0 21
   PRINT SE [LAST TRY WAS:] :COM
```

```
   CURSOR 5 22 PRINT1 [NEW TRY:]
   SPACES 1
END

TO PRINTLINE
 CURSOR 10 20 PRINT SE "GOAL:
   :GOAL
 CURSOR 20 20 PRINT1 "POSITION:
 PRINTPOS
END

TO PRINTPOS
 CURSOR 30 20 PRINT :POSITION
END

TO GETINPUT
 MAKE "COM REQUEST
 IF EMPTY? :COM GETINPUT STOP
 IF (ANYOF EMPTY? BF :COM NOT
     FIRST :COM = "REPEAT NOT LIST?
     LAST :COM) PRINT [TYPE
     REPEAT, THEN A NUMBER, THEN
     A LIST WITH FD AND A NUMBER.]
     WAIT 2 CLEARTEXT PRINTLINE
     GETINPUT STOP
 IF ANYOF NOT MEMBER? FIRST LAST
     :COM [FD FORWARD] NOT
     NUMBER? LAST LAST :COM PRINT
     [JUST REPEAT FD'S] WAIT 2
     CLEARTEXT PRINTLINE
     GETINPUT STOP
 MAKE "NUMBER FIRST BF :COM
 MAKE "DISTANCE LAST LAST :COM
END

TO RUN.IT :NUMBER :DISTANCE
 IF :NUMBER * :DISTANCE > 240 MAKE
     "POSITION :NUMBER * :DISTANCE
     PRINT [TOO FAR!] ELSE REPEAT
     :NUMBER [MAKE "POSITION
     :POSITION + :DISTANCE
     PRINTPOS FD :DISTANCE WAIT
     0.5]
 CHECKPOSITION
END

TO CHECKPOSITION
 IF :GOAL = :POSITION SUCCESS
     ELSE IF NOT :POSITION = 0 PRINT
     [TRY AGAIN.] WAIT 2 COMMAND
END

TO SUCCESS
 CURSOR 0 22
```

```
 PRINT [THAT WORKS! CAN YOU THINK
     OF ANY]
 PRINT1 [OTHERS THAT WOULD WORK
     AS WELL?] SPACES 2
 IF ANSWER? = "YES PRINT [TRY!]
     COMMAND ELSE CLEARTEXT
     PRINT1 [DO YOU WANT TO TRY
     ANOTHER GOAL?] SPACES 2
 IF ANSWER? = "YES START ELSE
     PRINT [GOODBYE!] TOPLEVEL
END

TO ANSWER?
 MAKE "ANSWER REQUEST
 IF EMPTY? :ANSWER PRINT OP
     ANSWER? STOP
 MAKE "ANSWER FIRST :ANSWER
 IF MEMBER? :ANSWER [YES NO] OP
     :ANSWER
 PRINT [PLEASE TYPE YES OR NO.]
 OP ANSWER?
END

TO SPACES :SPACES
 REPEAT :SPACES [PRINT1 CHAR 32]
END

TO WAIT :SECONDS
 REPEAT 1000 * :SECONDS []
END

MAKE "STARTUP [START]
```

```
┌─────────────────────────────────┐
│ FRACTIONS (Fig. 8-12)           │
│               Terrapin version  │
└─────────────────────────────────┘

TO NUMERATOR :FRACTION
     OUTPUT FIRST :FRACTION
END

TO DENOMINATOR :FRACTION
 OUTPUT LAST :FRACTION
END

TO FRACTION :NUMERATOR
     :DENOMINATOR
 OUTPUT LIST :NUMERATOR
     :DENOMINATOR
END

TO PR.FRACTION :FRACTION
 PRINT1 NUMERATOR :FRACTION
 SPACES 1
 PRINT1 CHAR 47
```

```
SPACES 1
PRINT1 DENOMINATOR :FRACTION
PRINT "
END

TO SPACES :NUMBER
 REPEAT :NUMBER [PRINT1 CHAR 32 ]
END

TO REDUCE :FRACTION
 LOCAL "DIVISOR
 MAKE "DIVISOR GCD NUMERATOR
   :FRACTION DENOMINATOR
   :FRACTION
 OUTPUT FRACTION ( NUMERATOR
   :FRACTION ) / :DIVISOR (
   DENOMINATOR :FRACTION ) /
   :DIVISOR
END

TO GCD :NUMBER1 :NUMBER2
 IF NOT :NUMBER2 > 0 OUTPUT
   :NUMBER1
 OUTPUT GCD :NUMBER2 REMAINDER
   :NUMBER1 :NUMBER2
END

TO MULTIPLY.FRACTIONS :FR.1 :FR.2
 LOCAL "NUM LOCAL "DEN
 MAKE "NUM ( NUMERATOR :FR.1 ) *
   ( NUMERATOR :FR.2 )
 MAKE "DEN ( DENOMINATOR :FR.1 ) *
   ( DENOMINATOR :FR.2 )
 OUTPUT REDUCE FRACTION :NUM
   :DEN
END

TO ADD.FRACTIONS :FR.1 :FR.2
 LOCAL "NUM LOCAL "DEN
 MAKE "NUM (NUMERATOR :FR.1) *
   (DENOMINATOR :FR.2 ) +
   (DENOMINATOR :FR.1) *
   (NUMERATOR :FR.2 )
 MAKE "DEN (DENOMINATOR :FR.1) *
   (DENOMINATOR :FR.2 )
 OUTPUT REDUCE FRACTION :NUM
   :DEN
END
```

STRING (Fig. 9-4)
                              Terrapin version

```
TO STRING :X1 :Y1 :X2 :Y2
 IF :Y1 < :Y2 STOP
```

```
 SETXY :X1 :Y1
 PD
 SETXY :X2 :Y2
 PU
 STRING :X1 ( :Y1 - 10 ) ( :X2 + 10 ) :Y2
END
```

EXPLORE.CIRCLE (Fig. 9-11)
                              Terrapin version

```
TO EXPLORE.CIRCLE
 REPEAT 12 [FD 30 RT 30]
 REPEAT 6 [FD 30 RT 30]
 PRINT [THE ESTIMATES ARE]
 PRINT SE [CURCUMFERENCE] 12 * 30
 PRINT SE [DIAMETER] XCOR
 PRINT SE [PI] 12 * 30 / XCOR
END
```

SURVEY.CATEGORICAL
                              LCSI version

```
TO COLLECT.DATA
 TS CLEARTEXT
 MAKE "QUESTION []
 PRINT [WHAT IS THE DATA'S NAME?
   (ONE WORD)]
 TYPE [>]
 MAKE "DATA.NAME FIRST READLIST
 PRINT "
 MAKE WORD :DATA.NAME
   ".QUESTION []
 PRINT [WHAT ARE THE
   CATEGORIES?]
 PRINT [IF ORDER IS IMPORTANT,
   TYPE THEM IN]
 PRINT [ORDER. USE SINGLE WORDS
   FOR EACH, WITH]
 PRINT [SPACES IN BETWEEN. PRESS
   \<RETURN\> WHEN]
 TYPE [FINISHED. >]
 MAKE :DATA.NAME READLIST
 PRINT "
 PRINT [ARE YOU GOING TO ENTER
   THE NUMBERS]
 PRINT [\(D\)IRECTLY OR HAVE THE
   PROGRAM DO A]
 TYPE [\(S\)URVEY? >]
 IF EQUALP GET.ANSWER [D S] "D
   [DIRECT.ENTER :DATA.NAME]
   [SURVEY :DATA.NAME]
END
```

```
TO GET.ANSWER :ANSWERS
LOCAL "ANSWER
MAKE "ANSWER READLIST
IF EMPTYP :ANSWER [OUTPUT
    GET.ANSWER.2 :ANSWERS]
IF MEMBERP UPPERCASE FIRST
    :ANSWER [STOP QUIT DONE
    FINISHED] [THROW "TOPLEVEL]
IF NOT MEMBERP UPPERCASE FIRST
    :ANSWER :ANSWERS [OUTPUT
    GET.ANSWER.2 :ANSWERS]
OUTPUT UPPERCASE FIRST
    :ANSWER
END


TO GET.ANSWER.2 :ANSWERS
PRINT [PLEASE TYPE ONE OF THE
    FOLLOWING:]
PRINT :ANSWERS
PRINT [OR "STOP" TO QUIT.]
OUTPUT GET.ANSWER :ANSWERS
END


TO DIRECT.ENTER :DATA.NAME
TS CLEARTEXT
PRINT [TYPE IN A NUMBER FOR EACH
    CATEGORY.]
DIRECT.ENTER.2 THING :DATA.NAME
END


TO DIRECT.ENTER.2 :DATA
PR "
IF EMPTYP :DATA [STOP]
TYPE ( WORD FIRST :DATA "? )
SPACE 1
MAKE ( WORD :DATA.NAME FIRST
    :DATA ) GET.NUMBER
DIRECT.ENTER.2 BUTFIRST :DATA
END


TO GET.NUMBER
LOCAL [NUM MESSAGE]
MAKE "MESSAGE [PLEASE TYPE A
    NUMBER.]
MAKE "NUM READLIST
IF :NUM = [] [PRINT :MESSAGE
    OUTPUT GET.NUMBER]
IF NOT NUMBERP (FIRST :NUM)
    [PRINT :MESSAGE OUTPUT
    GET.NUMBER]
OUTPUT FIRST :NUM
END
```

```
TO SURVEY :DATA.NAME
TS CLEARTEXT
PRINT "
PRINT [WHAT IS THE QUESTION YOU
    WISH TO ASK?]
PRINT "
MAKE WORD :DATA.NAME
    ".QUESTION READLIST
INITIALIZE.VALUES THING
    :DATA.NAME
ASK :DATA.NAME
END


TO SPACE :NUM
REPEAT :NUM [TYPE CHAR 32]
END


TO INITIALIZE.VALUES :DATA
IF EMPTYP :DATA [STOP]
MAKE WORD :DATA.NAME FIRST
    :DATA 0
INITIALIZE.VALUES BUTFIRST :DATA
END


TO ASK :DATA.NAME
LOCAL "ANSWER
TS CLEARTEXT
PRINT "
PRINT ( SENTENCE "THE :DATA.NAME
    "SURVEY... )
REPEAT 39 [TYPE "-]
PRINT "
PRINT THING WORD :DATA.NAME
    ".QUESTION
PRINT "
SPACE 2
PRINT [CHOOSE ONE OF THESE:]
PRINT "
SPACE 2
PRINT THING :DATA.NAME
PRINT "
SPACE 6
PRINT [...OR TYPE "STOP" TO QUIT]
PRINT "
MAKE "ANSWER GET.ANSWER THING
    :DATA.NAME
MAKE WORD :DATA.NAME :ANSWER
    ( THING WORD :DATA.NAME
    :ANSWER ) + 1
ASK :DATA.NAME
END
```

```
TO REPORT :DATA.NAME
LOCAL "DRIBBLE
TYPE [SEND REPORT: \(S\)CREEN OR
    \(P\)RINTER? >]
IF EQUALP GET.ANSWER [S P] "P
    [DRIBBLE 1 MAKE "DRIBBLE
    "TRUE] [NODRIBBLE MAKE
    "DRIBBLE "FALSE]
TS CLEARTEXT
PRINT SENTENCE [REPORT ON
    DATA:] :DATA.NAME
PRINT "
FIND.GREATEST.AND.LEAST
    :DATA.NAME
CONT
MAKE "TOT 0
MAKE "TOT TOTAL THING
    :DATA.NAME
TS CLEARTEXT
TYPE [NAME NUMBER] SPACE 2 TYPE
    "% SPACE 4 PRINT [GRAPH (EACH
    * = 4%)]
REPEAT 39 [TYPE "-]
PRINT "
PRINT.DATA THING :DATA.NAME
PRINT "
NODRIBBLE MAKE "DRIBBLE "FALSE
END


TO CONT
LOCAL "FAKE
IF NOT :DRIBBLE [TYPE [PRESS ANY
    KEY TO CONTINUE...] MAKE
    "FAKE READCHAR]
END


TO FIND.GREATEST.AND.LEAST
    :DATA.NAME
LOCAL [GREATEST.VALUE
    GREATEST.CATEGORY
    LEAST.VALUE
    LEAST.CATEGORY]
MAKE "GREATEST.VALUE ( -99999 )
    MAKE "GREATEST.CATEGORY []
MAKE "LEAST.VALUE 99999 MAKE
    "LEAST.CATEGORY []
FIND.GREATEST.AND.LEAST.2 THING
    :DATA.NAME
PRINT "
PRINT [THE CATEGORY\(IES\) WITH
    THE GREATEST]
```

```
PRINT SENTENCE [FREQUENCY WAS
    \(WERE\):]
    :GREATEST.CATEGORY
PRINT SENTENCE [WITH A
    FREQUENCY OF:]
    :GREATEST.VALUE
PRINT "
PRINT [THE CATEGORY\(IES\) WITH
    THE LEAST]
PRINT SENTENCE [FREQUENCY WAS
    \(WERE\):] :LEAST.CATEGORY
PRINT SENTENCE [WITH A
    FREQUENCY OF:] :LEAST.VALUE
PRINT "
PRINT SE [THE RANGE IS:] RANGE
PRINT "
END


TO FIND.GREATEST.AND.LEAST.2
    :DATA
LOCAL "FREQ.NAME
IF EMPTYP :DATA [STOP]
MAKE "FREQ.NAME WORD
    :DATA.NAME FIRST :DATA
IF EQUALP THING :FREQ.NAME
    :GREATEST.VALUE [MAKE
    "GREATEST.CATEGORY LPUT
    FIRST :DATA
    :GREATEST.CATEGORY]
IF GREATERP THING :FREQ.NAME
    :GREATEST.VALUE [MAKE
    "GREATEST.CATEGORY ( LIST
    FIRST :DATA ) MAKE
    "GREATEST.VALUE THING
    :FREQ.NAME]
IF EQUALP THING :FREQ.NAME
    :LEAST.VALUE [MAKE
    "LEAST.CATEGORY LPUT FIRST
    :DATA :LEAST.CATEGORY]
IF LESSP THING :FREQ.NAME
    :LEAST.VALUE [MAKE
    "LEAST.CATEGORY ( LIST FIRST
    :DATA ) MAKE "LEAST.VALUE
    THING :FREQ.NAME]
FIND.GREATEST.AND.LEAST.2
    BUTFIRST :DATA
END


TO TOTAL :DATA
IF EMPTYP :DATA [OUTPUT :TOT]
MAKE "TOT :TOT + THING WORD
    :DATA.NAME FIRST :DATA
```

```
OUTPUT TOTAL BUTFIRST :DATA
END


TO PRINT.DATA :DATA
LOCAL "FREQ.NAME
IF EMPTYP :DATA [STOP]
PRINT.NUM FIRST :DATA 5 0
MAKE "FREQ.NAME WORD
   :DATA.NAME FIRST :DATA
SPACE ( 5 - COUNT THING
   :FREQ.NAME )
TYPE THING :FREQ.NAME
MAKE "PERCENT ROUND ( ( THING
   :FREQ.NAME ) / :TOT * 100 )
SPACE ( 4 - COUNT :PERCENT )
TYPE :PERCENT
SPACE 1
REPEAT QUOTIENT :PERCENT 4
   [TYPE "*]
IF NOT (EQUALP REMAINDER
   :PERCENT 4 0 ) [TYPE ".]
PRINT "
PRINT.DATA BUTFIRST :DATA
END


TO RANGE
OUTPUT :GREATEST.VALUE -
   :LEAST.VALUE
END


TO PRINT.NUM :NAME :NUM :COUNT
IF EMPTYP :NAME [SPACE ( :NUM -
   :COUNT ) STOP]
IF EQUALP :COUNT :NUM [STOP]
TYPE FIRST :NAME
PRINT.NUM BUTFIRST :NAME :NUM
   :COUNT + 1
END
```

SURVEY.CATEGORICAL
                        Terrapin version

```
TO COLLECT.DATA
NODRAW
MAKE "QUESTION []
PRINT [WHAT IS THE DATA'S NAME?
   (ONE WORD)]
PRINT1 [>]
MAKE "DATA.NAME FIRST REQUEST
PRINT "
MAKE WORD :DATA.NAME
   ".QUESTION []
```

```
PRINT [WHAT ARE THE
   CATEGORIES?]
PRINT [IF ORDER IS IMPORTANT,
   TYPE THEM IN]
PRINT [ORDER. USE SINGLE WORDS
   FOR EACH, WITH]
PRINT [SPACES IN BETWEEN. PRESS
   <RETURN> WHEN]
PRINT1 [FINISHED. >]
MAKE :DATA.NAME REQUEST
PRINT "
PRINT [ARE YOU GOING TO ENTER
   THE NUMBERS]
PRINT [(D)IRECTLY OR HAVE THE
   PROGRAM DO A]
PRINT1 [(S)URVEY? >]
IF GET.ANSWER [D S] = "D
   DIRECT.ENTER :DATA.NAME
   ELSE SURVEY :DATA.NAME
END


TO GET.ANSWER :ANSWERS
LOCAL "ANSWER
MAKE "ANSWER REQUEST
IF EMPTY? :ANSWER OUTPUT
   GET.ANSWER.2 :ANSWERS
IF MEMBER? FIRST :ANSWER [STOP
   QUIT DONE FINISHED] TOPLEVEL
IF NOT MEMBER? FIRST :ANSWER
   :ANSWERS OUTPUT
   GET.ANSWER.2 :ANSWERS
OUTPUT FIRST :ANSWER
END


TO GET.ANSWER.2 :ANSWERS
PRINT [PLEASE TYPE ONE OF THE
   FOLLOWING:]
PRINT :ANSWERS
PRINT [OR "STOP" TO QUIT.]
OUTPUT GET.ANSWER :ANSWERS
END


TO DIRECT.ENTER :DATA.NAME
NODRAW
PRINT [TYPE IN A NUMBER FOR EACH
   CATEGORY.]
DIRECT.ENTER.2 THING :DATA.NAME
END


TO DIRECT.ENTER.2 :DATA
PR "
IF EMPTY? :DATA STOP
PRINT1 ( WORD FIRST :DATA "? )
SPACE 1
```

```
MAKE ( WORD :DATA.NAME FIRST
    :DATA ) GET.NUMBER
DIRECT.ENTER.2 BUTFIRST :DATA
END


TO GET.NUMBER
LOCAL "NUM
LOCAL "MESSAGE
MAKE "MESSAGE [PLEASE TYPE A
    NUMBER.]
MAKE "NUM REQUEST
IF :NUM = [] PRINT :MESSAGE
    OUTPUT GET.NUMBER
IF NOT NUMBER? FIRST :NUM PRINT
    :MESSAGE OUTPUT GET.NUMBER
OUTPUT FIRST :NUM
END


TO SURVEY :DATA.NAME
NODRAW
PRINT "
PRINT [WHAT IS THE QUESTION YOU
    WISH TO ASK?]
PRINT "
MAKE WORD :DATA.NAME
    ".QUESTION REQUEST
INITIALIZE.VALUES THING
    :DATA.NAME
ASK :DATA.NAME
END


TO SPACE :NUM
REPEAT :NUM [PRINT1 CHAR 32]
END


TO INITIALIZE.VALUES :DATA
IF EMPTY? :DATA STOP
MAKE WORD :DATA.NAME FIRST
    :DATA 0
INITIALIZE.VALUES BUTFIRST :DATA
END


TO ASK :DATA.NAME
LOCAL "ANSWER
NODRAW
PRINT "
PRINT ( SENTENCE "THE :DATA.NAME
    "SURVEY... )
REPEAT 40 [PRINT1 "-]
PRINT "
PRINT THING WORD :DATA.NAME
    ".QUESTION
PRINT "
SPACE 2
```

```
PRINT [CHOOSE ONE OF THESE:]
PRINT "
SPACE 2
PRINT THING :DATA.NAME
PRINT "
SPACE 6
PRINT [...OR TYPE "STOP" TO QUIT]
PRINT "
MAKE "ANSWER GET.ANSWER THING
    :DATA.NAME
MAKE WORD :DATA.NAME :ANSWER
    ( THING WORD :DATA.NAME
    :ANSWER ) + 1
ASK :DATA.NAME
END


TO REPORT :DATA.NAME
PRINT1 [SEND REPORT: (S)CREEN OR
    (P)RINTER? >]
IF GET.ANSWER [S P] = "P MAKE
    "DEVICE 1 ELSE MAKE "DEVICE 0
OUTDEV :DEVICE
NODRAW
PRINT SENTENCE [REPORT ON
    DATA:] :DATA.NAME
PRINT "
FIND.GREATEST.AND.LEAST
    :DATA.NAME
CONT
MAKE "TOT 0
MAKE "TOT TOTAL THING
    :DATA.NAME
NODRAW
PRINT1 [NAME NUMBER] SPACE 2
    PRINT1 "% SPACE 4 PRINT
    [GRAPH (EACH * = 4%)]
REPEAT 40 [PRINT1 "-]
PRINT "
PRINT.DATA THING :DATA.NAME
PRINT "
OUTDEV 0
END


TO CONT
LOCAL "FAKE
IF :DEVICE = 0 PRINT1 [PRESS ANY
    KEY TO CONTINUE...] MAKE
    "FAKE READCHARACTER
END


TO FIND.GREATEST.AND.LEAST
    :DATA.NAME
LOCAL "GREATEST.VALUE
LOCAL "GREATEST.CATEGORY
```

```
LOCAL "LEAST.VALUE
LOCAL "LEAST.CATEGORY
MAKE "GREATEST.VALUE ( - 99999 )
    MAKE "GREATEST.CATEGORY []
MAKE "LEAST.VALUE 99999 MAKE
    "LEAST.CATEGORY []
FIND.GREATEST.AND.LEAST.2 THING
    :DATA.NAME
PRINT "
PRINT [THE CATEGORY(IES) WITH
    THE GREATEST]
PRINT SENTENCE [FREQUENCY WAS
    (WERE):] :GREATEST.CATEGORY
PRINT SENTENCE [WITH A
    FREQUENCY OF:]
    :GREATEST.VALUE
PRINT "
PRINT [THE CATEGORY(IES) WITH
    THE LEAST]
PRINT SENTENCE [FREQUENCY WAS
    (WERE):] :LEAST.CATEGORY
PRINT SENTENCE [WITH A
    FREQUENCY OF:] :LEAST.VALUE
PRINT "
PRINT SE [THE RANGE IS:] RANGE
PRINT "
END


TO FIND.GREATEST.AND.LEAST.2
    :DATA
LOCAL "FREQ.NAME
IF EMPTY? :DATA THEN STOP
MAKE "FREQ.NAME WORD
    :DATA.NAME FIRST :DATA
IF THING :FREQ.NAME =
    :GREATEST.VALUE THEN MAKE
    "GREATEST.CATEGORY LPUT
    FIRST :DATA
    :GREATEST.CATEGORY
IF THING :FREQ.NAME >
    :GREATEST.VALUE THEN MAKE
    "GREATEST.CATEGORY ( LIST
    FIRST :DATA ) MAKE
    "GREATEST.VALUE THING
    :FREQ.NAME
IF THING :FREQ.NAME =
    :LEAST.VALUE THEN MAKE
    "LEAST.CATEGORY LPUT FIRST
    :DATA :LEAST.CATEGORY
IF THING :FREQ.NAME <
    :LEAST.VALUE THEN MAKE
    "LEAST.CATEGORY          ( LIST
    FIRST :DATA ) MAKE
```

```
    "LEAST.VALUE THING
    :FREQ.NAME
FIND.GREATEST.AND.LEAST.2
    BUTFIRST :DATA
END

TO TOTAL :DATA
IF EMPTY? :DATA OUTPUT :TOT
MAKE "TOT :TOT + THING WORD
    :DATA.NAME FIRST :DATA
OUTPUT TOTAL BUTFIRST :DATA
END

TO PRINT.DATA :DATA
LOCAL "FREQ.NAME
IF EMPTY? :DATA STOP
PRINT.NUM FIRST :DATA 5 0
MAKE "FREQ.NAME WORD
    :DATA.NAME FIRST :DATA
SPACE ( 5 - COUNT THING
    :FREQ.NAME )
PRINT1 THING :FREQ.NAME
MAKE "PERCENT ROUND ( ( THING
    :FREQ.NAME ) / :TOT * 100 )
SPACE ( 4 - COUNT :PERCENT )
PRINT1 :PERCENT
SPACE 1
REPEAT QUOTIENT :PERCENT 4
    [PRINT1 "*]
IF NOT ( REMAINDER :PERCENT 4 = 0 )
    PRINT1 ".
PRINT "
PRINT.DATA BUTFIRST :DATA
END

TO RANGE
OUTPUT :GREATEST.VALUE -
    :LEAST.VALUE
END

TO PRINT.NUM :NAME :NUM :COUNT
IF EMPTY? :NAME SPACE ( :NUM -
    :COUNT ) STOP
IF :COUNT = :NUM STOP
PRINT1 FIRST :NAME
PRINT.NUM BUTFIRST :NAME :NUM
    :COUNT + 1
END

TO SAVE.DATA
NODRAW
PRINT1 [WHAT FILE NAME? >]
( SAVE FIRST REQUEST [NAMES] )
END
```

```
SURVEY.NUMERICAL        LCSI version

TO COLLECT.DATA
 TS CLEARTEXT
 MAKE "QUESTION []
 PRINT [WHAT IS THE DATA'S NAME?
   (ONE WORD)]
 TYPE [>]
 MAKE "DATA.NAME FIRST READLIST
 PRINT "
 PRINT [ARE YOU GOING TO ENTER
   THE NUMBERS]
 PRINT [\(D\)IRECTLY OR HAVE THE
   PROGRAM DO A]
 TYPE [\(S\)URVEY? >]
 IF EQUALP GET.ANSWER [D S] "D
   [DIRECT.ENTER :DATA.NAME]
   [SURVEY :DATA.NAME]
END

TO GET.ANSWER :ANSWERS
 LOCAL "ANSWER
 MAKE "ANSWER READLIST
 IF EMPTYP :ANSWER [OUTPUT
   GET.ANSWER.2 :ANSWERS]
 IF MEMBERP UPPERCASE FIRST
   :ANSWER [STOP QUIT DONE
   FINISHED] [THROW "TOPLEVEL]
 IF NOT MEMBERP UPPERCASE FIRST
   :ANSWER :ANSWERS [OUTPUT
   GET.ANSWER.2 :ANSWERS]
 OUTPUT UPPERCASE FIRST
   :ANSWER
END

TO GET.ANSWER.2 :ANSWERS
 PRINT [PLEASE TYPE ONE OF THE
   FOLLOWING:]
 PRINT :ANSWERS
 OUTPUT GET.ANSWER :ANSWERS
END

TO DIRECT.ENTER :DATA.NAME
 TS CLEARTEXT
 PRINT [TYPE NUMBERS. PRESS
   \<RETURN\> AFTER EACH]
 PRINT [ONE. TYPE "STOP" WHEN
   FINISHED.]
 MAKE :DATA.NAME []
 DIRECT.ENTER.2
END

TO DIRECT.ENTER.2
 LOCAL "ANSWER

 MAKE "ANSWER GET.NUMBER
 IF EQUALP :ANSWER "STOP [STOP]
 MAKE :DATA.NAME LPUT :ANSWER
   THING :DATA.NAME
 DIRECT.ENTER.2
END

TO GET.NUMBER
 LOCAL [NUM MESSAGE]
 MAKE "MESSAGE [PLEASE TYPE
   JUST ONE NUMBER OR "STOP"]
 MAKE "NUM READLIST
 IF OR EMPTYP :NUM GREATERP
   COUNT :NUM 1 [PRINT :MESSAGE
   OUTPUT GET.NUMBER]
 IF MEMBERP UPPERCASE FIRST
   :NUM [STOP QUIT END FINISHED]
   [OUTPUT "STOP]
 IF NOT NUMBERP UPPERCASE FIRST
   :NUM [PRINT :MESSAGE OUTPUT
   GET.NUMBER]
 OUTPUT FIRST :NUM
END

TO SURVEY :DATA.NAME
 TS CLEARTEXT
 PRINT "
 PRINT [WHAT IS THE QUESTION YOU
   WISH TO ASK?]
 MAKE WORD :DATA.NAME
   ".QUESTION READLIST
 MAKE :DATA.NAME []
 ASK :DATA.NAME
END

TO SPACE :NUM
 REPEAT :NUM [TYPE CHAR 32]
END

TO ASK :DATA.NAME
 LOCAL "ANSWER
 TS CLEARTEXT
 PRINT "
 PRINT ( SENTENCE "THE :DATA.NAME
   "SURVEY... )
 REPEAT 39 [TYPE "-]
 PRINT "
 PRINT THING WORD :DATA.NAME
   ".QUESTION
 PRINT "
 PRINT [(TYPE "STOP" TO QUIT)]
 PRINT "
 MAKE "ANSWER GET.NUMBER
 IF :ANSWER = "STOP [STOP]
```

```
MAKE :DATA.NAME LPUT :ANSWER
    THING :DATA.NAME
ASK :DATA.NAME
END


TO REPORT :DATA.NAME
LOCAL "DRIBBLE
TYPE [SEND REPORT: \(S\)CREEN OR
    \(P\)RINTER? >]
IF EQUALP GET.ANSWER [S P] "P
    [DRIBBLE 1 MAKE "DRIBBLE
    "TRUE] [NODRIBBLE MAKE
    "DRIBBLE "FALSE]
TS CLEARTEXT
PRINT [SORTING...]
MAKE :DATA.NAME SORT THING
    :DATA.NAME
REPORT.SORT :DATA.NAME
MAKE "DATA.LIST.NAME WORD
    :DATA.NAME ".LIST
MAKE :DATA.LIST.NAME []
COUNT.DATA :DATA.NAME THING
    :DATA.NAME :DATA.LIST.NAME
REPORT.FREQS :DATA.NAME
IF LESSP COUNT THING
    :DATA.LIST.NAME 11 [PR " ] [CONT
    TS CLEARTEXT]
REPORT.STATISTICS :DATA.NAME
NODRIBBLE MAKE "DRIBBLE "FALSE
END


TO SORT :LIST
IF LESSP COUNT :LIST 2 [OUTPUT
    :LIST]
OUTPUT INSERT FIRST :LIST SORT
    BUTFIRST :LIST
END


TO INSERT :NUMBER :LIST
IF NOT GREATER.THAN :NUMBER
    FIRST :LIST [OUTPUT FPUT
    :NUMBER :LIST]
IF GREATER.THAN :NUMBER LAST
    :LIST [OUTPUT LPUT :NUMBER
    :LIST]
OUTPUT FPUT FIRST :LIST INSERT
    :NUMBER BUTFIRST :LIST
END


TO GREATER.THAN :FIRST :SECOND
IF EMPTYP :FIRST [OUTPUT "FALSE]
IF EMPTYP :SECOND [OUTPUT "TRUE]
```

```
IF GREATERP :FIRST :SECOND
    [OUTPUT "TRUE] [OUTPUT
    "FALSE]
END


TO REPORT.SORT :DATA.NAME
TS CLEARTEXT
PRINT ( SENTENCE [THE SORTED
    DATA FOR] :DATA.NAME [ARE:] )
PR "
PRINT THING :DATA.NAME
PR "
END


TO COUNT.DATA :DATA.NAME :DATA
    :DATA.LIST.NAME
LOCAL "NUM
IF EMPTYP :DATA [STOP]
MAKE "NUM FIRST :DATA
MAKE :DATA.LIST.NAME LPUT :NUM
    THING :DATA.LIST.NAME
COUNT.DATA.2 BUTFIRST :DATA :NUM
    1
END


TO COUNT.DATA.2 :DATA :NUM
    :COUNT
IF EMPTYP :DATA [MAKE WORD
    :DATA.NAME :NUM :COUNT STOP]
TEST :NUM = FIRST :DATA
IFF [MAKE WORD :DATA.NAME :NUM
    :COUNT]
IFF [COUNT.DATA :DATA.NAME :DATA
    :DATA.LIST.NAME]
IFT [COUNT.DATA.2 BUTFIRST :DATA
    :NUM :COUNT + 1]
END


TO REPORT.FREQS :DATA.NAME
LOCAL "COUNT.LIST
MAKE "DATA.LIST.NAME WORD
    :DATA.NAME ".LIST
FIND.GREATEST.AND.LEAST
    :DATA.NAME :DATA.LIST.NAME
CONT
TS CLEARTEXT
TYPE "NUM. SPACE 2
TYPE "FREQ. SPACE 2
TYPE "% SPACE 4 PRINT [GRAPH
    (EACH * = 4%)]
REPEAT 40 [TYPE "-]
PRINT "
```

```
MAKE "COUNT.LIST COUNT THING
   :DATA.NAME
PRINT.DATA :DATA.NAME THING
   :DATA.LIST.NAME
PRINT "
END

TO CONT
LOCAL "FAKE
IF NOT :DRIBBLE [TYPE [PRESS ANY
   KEY TO CONTINUE...] MAKE
   "FAKE READCHAR]
END

TO FIND.GREATEST.AND.LEAST
   :DATA.NAME :DATA.LIST.NAME
LOCAL [GREATEST.CATEGORY
   GREATEST.VALUE
   LEAST.CATEGORY
   LEAST.VALUE]
MAKE "GREATEST.VALUE ( - 99999 )
   MAKE "GREATEST.CATEGORY []
MAKE "LEAST.VALUE 99999 MAKE
   "LEAST.CATEGORY []
FIND.GREATEST.AND.LEAST.2
   :DATA.NAME THING
   :DATA.LIST.NAME
PRINT "
PRINT [THE NUMBER\(S\) WITH THE
   GREATEST]
PRINT SENTENCE [FREQUENCY \(THE
   MODE\) WAS \(WERE\):]
   :GREATEST.CATEGORY
PRINT SENTENCE [WITH A
   FREQUENCY OF:]
   :GREATEST.VALUE
PRINT "
PRINT [THE NUMBER\(S\) WITH THE
   LEAST]
PRINT SENTENCE [FREQUENCY WAS
   \(WERE\):] :LEAST.CATEGORY
PRINT SENTENCE [WITH A
   FREQUENCY OF:] :LEAST.VALUE
PRINT "
PRINT SE [THE RANGE OF THE
   FREQUENCIES IS:] RANGE
   :GREATEST.VALUE
   :LEAST.VALUE
PRINT "
END

TO FIND.GREATEST.AND.LEAST.2
   :DATA.NAME :DATA
```

```
LOCAL "FREQ.NAME
IF EMPTYP :DATA [STOP]
MAKE "FREQ.NAME WORD
   :DATA.NAME FIRST :DATA
IF AND EQUALP THING :FREQ.NAME
   :GREATEST.VALUE NOT
   MEMBERP FIRST :DATA
   :GREATEST.CATEGORY [MAKE
   "GREATEST.CATEGORY LPUT
   FIRST :DATA
   :GREATEST.CATEGORY]
IF GREATERP THING :FREQ.NAME
   :GREATEST.VALUE [MAKE
   "GREATEST.CATEGORY ( LIST
   FIRST :DATA ) MAKE
   "GREATEST.VALUE THING
   :FREQ.NAME]
IF AND EQUALP THING :FREQ.NAME
   :LEAST.VALUE NOT MEMBERP
   FIRST :DATA :LEAST.CATEGORY
   [MAKE "LEAST.CATEGORY LPUT
   FIRST :DATA :LEAST.CATEGORY]
IF LESSP THING :FREQ.NAME
   :LEAST.VALUE [MAKE
   "LEAST.CATEGORY ( LIST FIRST
   :DATA ) MAKE "LEAST.VALUE
   THING :FREQ.NAME]
FIND.GREATEST.AND.LEAST.2
   :DATA.NAME BUTFIRST :DATA
END

TO PRINT.DATA :DATA.NAME
   :DATA.LIST
LOCAL [FREQ.NAME PERCENT]
IF EMPTYP :DATA.LIST [STOP]
TYPE FIRST :DATA.LIST
SPACE ( 5 - COUNT FIRST :DATA.LIST
   )
MAKE "FREQ.NAME WORD
   :DATA.NAME FIRST :DATA.LIST
SPACE ( 4 - COUNT THING
   :FREQ.NAME )
TYPE THING :FREQ.NAME
MAKE "PERCENT ROUND ( ( THING
   :FREQ.NAME ) / ( :COUNT.LIST ) *
   100 )
SPACE ( 5 - COUNT :PERCENT )
TYPE :PERCENT
SPACE 1
REPEAT QUOTIENT :PERCENT 4
   [TYPE "*]
IF NOT (EQUALP REMAINDER
   :PERCENT 4 0 ) [TYPE ". ]
```

```
PRINT "
PRINT.DATA :DATA.NAME BUTFIRST
    :DATA.LIST
END


TO REPORT.STATISTICS :DATA.NAME
PRINT SENTENCE [THE RANGE OF
    THE DATA IS:] RANGE LAST
    THING :DATA.NAME FIRST THING
    :DATA.NAME
PR "
PRINT SENTENCE [THE MEDIAN IS:]
    MEDIAN THING :DATA.NAME
PR "
PRINT SENTENCE [THE MEAN IS:]
    MEAN THING :DATA.NAME
PR "
PRINT SENTENCE [THE STANDARD
    DEVIATION IS:] STAND.DEV
    THING :DATA.NAME
PR "
END


TO RANGE :GREATEST :LEAST
OUTPUT :GREATEST - :LEAST
END


TO MEDIAN :DATA
LOCAL "NUM
MAKE "NUM QUOTIENT COUNT :DATA
    2
TEST EVENP COUNT :DATA
IFFALSE [OUTPUT ITEM :NUM + 1
    :DATA]
IFTRUE [OUTPUT MEAN LIST ITEM
    :NUM :DATA ITEM :NUM + 1 :DATA]
END


TO EVENP :NUMBER
IF EQUALP REMAINDER :NUMBER 2 0
    [OUTPUT "TRUE] [OUTPUT
    "FALSE]
END


TO MEAN :LIST
OUTPUT ( TOTAL :LIST 0 ) / COUNT
    :LIST
END


TO TOTAL :LIST :TOT
IF EMPTYP :LIST [OUTPUT :TOT]
OUTPUT TOTAL BUTFIRST :LIST :TOT
    + FIRST :LIST
END
```

```
TO STAND.DEV :LIST
OUTPUT SQRT VARIANCE :LIST MEAN
    :LIST COUNT :LIST 0
END


TO VARIANCE :LIST :MEAN :COUNT
    :SUMDIFFSQ
IF EMPTYP :LIST [OUTPUT
    :SUMDIFFSQ /      ( :COUNT - 1 )]
OUTPUT VARIANCE BUTFIRST :LIST
    :MEAN :COUNT :SUMDIFFSQ + ( (
    FIRST :LIST ) - :MEAN ) * ( ( FIRST
    :LIST ) - :MEAN )
END
```

```
┌────────────────────────────────────┐
│ SURVEY.NUMERICAL                     │
│                    Terrapin version  │
└────────────────────────────────────┘
```

```
TO COLLECT.DATA
.GCOLL
NODRAW
PRINT [WHAT IS THE DATA'S NAME?
    (ONE WORD)]
PRINT1 [>]
MAKE "DATA.NAME FIRST REQUEST
MAKE WORD :DATA.NAME
    ".QUESTION []
PRINT "
PRINT [ARE YOU GOING TO ENTER
    THE NUMBERS]
PRINT [(D)IRECTLY OR HAVE THE
    PROGRAM DO A]
PRINT1 [(S)URVEY? >]
IF GET.ANSWER [D S] = "D
    DIRECT.ENTER :DATA.NAME
    ELSE SURVEY :DATA.NAME
END


TO GET.ANSWER :ANSWERS
LOCAL "ANSWER
MAKE "ANSWER REQUEST
IF EMPTY? :ANSWER OUTPUT
    GET.ANSWER.2 :ANSWERS
IF NOT MEMBER? FIRST :ANSWER
    :ANSWERS OUTPUT
    GET.ANSWER.2 :ANSWERS
OUTPUT FIRST :ANSWER
END


TO GET.ANSWER.2 :ANSWERS
PRINT [PLEASE TYPE ONE OF THE
    FOLLOWING:]
PRINT :ANSWERS
```

```
OUTPUT GET.ANSWER :ANSWERS
END


TO DIRECT.ENTER :DATA.NAME
NODRAW
PRINT [TYPE NUMBERS. PRESS
    <RETURN> AFTER EACH]
PRINT [ONE. TYPE "STOP" WHEN
    FINISHED.]
MAKE :DATA.NAME []
DIRECT.ENTER.2
END


TO DIRECT.ENTER.2
LOCAL "ANSWER
MAKE "ANSWER GET.NUMBER
IF :ANSWER = "STOP STOP
MAKE :DATA.NAME LPUT :ANSWER
    THING :DATA.NAME
DIRECT.ENTER.2
END


TO GET.NUMBER
LOCAL "NUM
LOCAL "MESSAGE
MAKE "MESSAGE [PLEASE TYPE
    JUST ONE NUMBER OR "STOP"]
MAKE "NUM REQUEST
IF ANYOF :NUM = [] COUNT :NUM > 1
    PRINT :MESSAGE OUTPUT
    GET.NUMBER
IF MEMBER? FIRST :NUM [STOP QUIT
    END FINISHED] OUTPUT "STOP
IF NOT NUMBER? FIRST :NUM PRINT
    :MESSAGE OUTPUT GET.NUMBER
OUTPUT FIRST :NUM
END


TO SURVEY :DATA.NAME
NODRAW
PRINT "
PRINT [WHAT IS THE QUESTION YOU
    WISH TO ASK?]
MAKE WORD :DATA.NAME
    ".QUESTION REQUEST
MAKE :DATA.NAME []
ASK :DATA.NAME
END


TO SPACE :NUM
 REPEAT :NUM [PRINT1 CHAR 32]
END
```

```
TO ASK :DATA.NAME
LOCAL "ANSWER
NODRAW
PRINT "
PRINT ( SENTENCE "THE :DATA.NAME
    "SURVEY... )
REPEAT 40 [PRINT1 "-]
PRINT "
PRINT THING WORD :DATA.NAME
    ".QUESTION
PRINT "
PRINT [(TYPE "STOP" TO QUIT)]
PRINT "
MAKE "ANSWER GET.NUMBER
IF :ANSWER = "STOP STOP
MAKE :DATA.NAME LPUT :ANSWER
    THING :DATA.NAME
ASK :DATA.NAME
END


TO REPORT :DATA.NAME
.GCOLL
PRINT1 [SEND REPORT: (S)CREEN OR
    (P)RINTER? >]
IF GET.ANSWER [S P] = "P MAKE
    "DEVICE 1 ELSE MAKE "DEVICE 0
OUTDEV :DEVICE
NODRAW
PRINT [SORTING...]
MAKE :DATA.NAME SORT THING
    :DATA.NAME
REPORT.SORT :DATA.NAME
MAKE "DATA.LIST.NAME WORD
    :DATA.NAME ".LIST
MAKE :DATA.LIST.NAME []
COUNT.DATA :DATA.NAME THING
    :DATA.NAME :DATA.LIST.NAME
REPORT.FREQS :DATA.NAME
IF COUNT THING :DATA.LIST.NAME <
    11 PR " ELSE CONT NODRAW
REPORT.STATISTICS :DATA.NAME
OUTDEV 0
END


TO SORT :LIST
IF COUNT :LIST < 2 OUTPUT :LIST
OUTPUT INSERT FIRST :LIST SORT
    BUTFIRST :LIST
END


TO INSERT :NUMBER :LIST
IF NOT GREATER.THAN :NUMBER
    FIRST :LIST THEN OUTPUT FPUT
    :NUMBER :LIST
```

```
IF GREATER.THAN :NUMBER LAST
    :LIST THEN OUTPUT LPUT
    :NUMBER :LIST
OUTPUT FPUT FIRST :LIST INSERT
    :NUMBER BUTFIRST :LIST
END


TO GREATER.THAN :FIRST :SECOND
IF EMPTY? :FIRST OUTPUT "FALSE
IF EMPTY? :SECOND OUTPUT "TRUE
IF :FIRST > :SECOND OUTPUT "TRUE
    ELSE OUTPUT "FALSE
END


TO REPORT.SORT :DATA.NAME
NODRAW
PRINT ( SENTENCE [THE SORTED
    DATA FOR] :DATA.NAME [ARE:] )
PR "
PRINT THING :DATA.NAME
PR "
END


TO COUNT.DATA :DATA.NAME :DATA
    :DATA.LIST.NAME
LOCAL "NUM
IF EMPTY? :DATA STOP
MAKE "NUM FIRST :DATA
MAKE :DATA.LIST.NAME LPUT :NUM
    THING :DATA.LIST.NAME
COUNT.DATA.2 BUTFIRST :DATA :NUM
    1
END


TO COUNT.DATA.2 :DATA :NUM
    :COUNT
IF EMPTY? :DATA MAKE WORD
    :DATA.NAME :NUM :COUNT STOP
TEST :NUM = FIRST :DATA
IFFALSE MAKE WORD :DATA.NAME
    :NUM :COUNT
IFFALSE COUNT.DATA :DATA.NAME
    :DATA :DATA.LIST.NAME
IFTRUE COUNT.DATA.2 BUTFIRST
    :DATA :NUM :COUNT + 1
END


TO REPORT.FREQS :DATA.NAME
LOCAL "COUNT.LIST
MAKE "DATA.LIST.NAME WORD
    :DATA.NAME ".LIST
FIND.GREATEST.AND.LEAST
    :DATA.NAME :DATA.LIST.NAME
```

```
CONT
NODRAW
PRINT1 "NUM. SPACE 2
PRINT1 "FREQ. SPACE 2
PRINT1 "% SPACE 4 PRINT [GRAPH
    (EACH * = 4%)]
REPEAT 40 [PRINT1 "-]
PRINT "
MAKE "COUNT.LIST COUNT THING
    :DATA.NAME
PRINT.DATA :DATA.NAME THING
    :DATA.LIST.NAME
PRINT "
END


TO CONT
LOCAL "FAKE
IF :DEVICE = 0 PRINT1 [PRESS ANY
    KEY TO CONTINUE...] MAKE
    "FAKE READCHARACTER
END


TO FIND.GREATEST.AND.LEAST
    :DATA.NAME :DATA.LIST.NAME
LOCAL "GREATEST.CATEGORY
LOCAL "GREATEST.VALUE
LOCAL "LEAST.CATEGORY
LOCAL "LEAST.VALUE
MAKE "GREATEST.VALUE ( - 99999 )
    MAKE "GREATEST.CATEGORY []
MAKE "LEAST.VALUE 99999 MAKE
    "LEAST.CATEGORY []
FIND.GREATEST.AND.LEAST.2
    :DATA.NAME THING
    :DATA.LIST.NAME
PRINT "
PRINT [THE NUMBER(S) WITH THE
    GREATEST]
PRINT SENTENCE [FREQUENCY (THE
    MODE) WAS (WERE):]
    :GREATEST.CATEGORY
PRINT SENTENCE [WITH A
    FREQUENCY OF:]
    :GREATEST.VALUE
PRINT "
PRINT [THE NUMBER(S) WITH THE
    LEAST]
PRINT SENTENCE [FREQUENCY WAS
    (WERE):] :LEAST.CATEGORY
PRINT SENTENCE [WITH A
    FREQUENCY OF:] :LEAST.VALUE
PRINT "
```

```
PRINT SE [THE RANGE OF THE
   FREQUENCIES IS:] RANGE
   :GREATEST.VALUE
   :LEAST.VALUE
PRINT "
END


TO FIND.GREATEST.AND.LEAST.2
   :DATA.NAME :DATA
LOCAL "FREQ.NAME
IF EMPTY? :DATA THEN STOP
MAKE "FREQ.NAME WORD
   :DATA.NAME FIRST :DATA
IF ALLOF THING :FREQ.NAME =
   :GREATEST.VALUE NOT
   MEMBER? FIRST :DATA
   :GREATEST.CATEGORY THEN
   MAKE "GREATEST.CATEGORY
   LPUT FIRST :DATA
   :GREATEST.CATEGORY
IF THING :FREQ.NAME >
   :GREATEST.VALUE THEN MAKE
   "GREATEST.CATEGORY ( LIST
   FIRST :DATA ) MAKE
   "GREATEST.VALUE THING
   :FREQ.NAME
IF ALLOF THING :FREQ.NAME =
   :LEAST.VALUE NOT MEMBER?
   FIRST :DATA :LEAST.CATEGORY
   THEN MAKE "LEAST.CATEGORY
   LPUT FIRST :DATA
   :LEAST.CATEGORY
IF THING :FREQ.NAME <
   :LEAST.VALUE THEN MAKE
   "LEAST.CATEGORY        ( LIST
   FIRST :DATA ) MAKE
   "LEAST.VALUE THING
   :FREQ.NAME
FIND.GREATEST.AND.LEAST.2
   :DATA.NAME BUTFIRST :DATA
END


TO PRINT.DATA :DATA.NAME
   :DATA.LIST
LOCAL "FREQ.NAME
LOCAL "PERCENT
IF EMPTY? :DATA.LIST STOP
PRINT1 FIRST :DATA.LIST
SPACE ( 5 - COUNT FIRST :DATA.LIST
   )
MAKE "FREQ.NAME WORD
   :DATA.NAME FIRST :DATA.LIST
SPACE ( 4 - COUNT THING
   :FREQ.NAME )
```

```
PRINT1 THING :FREQ.NAME
MAKE "PERCENT ROUND ( ( THING
   :FREQ.NAME ) / ( :COUNT.LIST ) *
   100 )
SPACE ( 5 - COUNT :PERCENT )
PRINT1 :PERCENT
SPACE 1
REPEAT QUOTIENT :PERCENT 4
   [PRINT1 "*"]
IF NOT ( REMAINDER :PERCENT 4 = 0 )
   PRINT1 ".
PRINT "
PRINT.DATA :DATA.NAME BUTFIRST
   :DATA.LIST
END


TO REPORT.STATISTICS :DATA.NAME
PRINT SENTENCE [THE RANGE OF
   THE DATA IS:] RANGE LAST
   THING :DATA.NAME FIRST THING
   :DATA.NAME
PR "
PRINT SENTENCE [THE MEDIAN IS:]
   MEDIAN THING :DATA.NAME
PR "
PRINT SENTENCE [THE MEAN IS:]
   MEAN THING :DATA.NAME
PR "
PRINT SENTENCE [THE STANDARD
   DEVIATION IS:] STAND.DEV
   THING :DATA.NAME
PR "
END


TO RANGE :GREATEST :LEAST
OUTPUT :GREATEST - :LEAST
END


TO MEDIAN :DATA
LOCAL "NUM
MAKE "NUM QUOTIENT COUNT :DATA
   2
TEST EVEN? COUNT :DATA
IFFALSE OUTPUT ITEM :NUM + 1
   :DATA
IFTRUE OUTPUT MEAN LIST ITEM
   :NUM :DATA ITEM :NUM + 1 :DATA
END


TO EVEN? :NUMBER
IF REMAINDER :NUMBER 2 = 0
   OUTPUT "TRUE ELSE OUTPUT
   "FALSE
END
```

```
TO MEAN :LIST
 OUTPUT ( TOTAL :LIST 0 ) / COUNT
    :LIST
END

TO TOTAL :LIST :TOT
 IF EMPTY? :LIST OUTPUT :TOT
 OUTPUT TOTAL BUTFIRST :LIST :TOT
    + FIRST :LIST
END

TO STAND.DEV :LIST
 OUTPUT SQRT VARIANCE :LIST MEAN
    :LIST COUNT :LIST 0
END

TO VARIANCE :LIST :MEAN :COUNT
    :SUMDIFFSQ
 IF EMPTY? :LIST OUTPUT
    :SUMDIFFSQ /        ( :COUNT - 1 )
 OUTPUT VARIANCE BUTFIRST :LIST
    :MEAN :COUNT :SUMDIFFSQ + ( (
    FIRST :LIST ) - :MEAN ) * ( ( FIRST
    :LIST ) - :MEAN )
END

TO SAVE.DATA
 NODRAW
 PRINT1 [WHAT FILE NAME? >]
 ( SAVE FIRST REQUEST [NAMES] )
END
```

TOSS.COIN	Terrapin version

```
TO TOSS.COIN :NUMBER.TOSSES
 RANDOMIZE
 MAKE "HEADS 0
 MAKE "TAILS 0
 REPEAT :NUMBER.TOSSES [IF
    RANDOM 2 = 1 THEN MAKE
    "HEADS :HEADS + 1 ELSE MAKE
    "TAILS :TAILS + 1]
 PRINT (SENTENCE [AFTER]
    :NUMBER.TOSSES [TOSSES, THE
    RESULTS ARE:] )
 PRINT (SENTENCE :HEADS [HEADS
    AND] :TAILS [TAILS.] )
END
```

WALK (Fig. 10-11)	Terrapin version

```
TO WALK :NUM.STEPS
 PU HOME PD
```

```
 REPEAT :NUM.STEPS [TAKE.STEP]
 WALK :NUM.STEPS
END

TO TAKE.STEP
 IF ( RANDOM 2 ) = 1 THEN LT 30 ELSE
    RT 30
 FD 10
END
```

ESTIMATE	LCSI version

```
TO ESTIMATE
 LOCAL [NUMBER1 NUMBER2
    NUMBER3 EST]
 TS CLEARTEXT
 MAKE "NUMBER1 RANDOM 100
 MAKE "NUMBER2 RANDOM 100
 MAKE "NUMBER3 :NUMBER1 *
    :NUMBER2
 ESTIMATE.2
END

TO ESTIMATE.2
 PRINT "
 PRINT ( SENTENCE :NUMBER1 [* N =]
    :NUMBER3 )
 PRINT "
 TYPE [WHAT IS YOUR ESTIMATE? >]
 MAKE "EST FIRST READLIST
 PRINT "
 PRINT ( SENTENCE :NUMBER1 "* :EST
    "= :NUMBER1 * :EST )
 IF EQUALP :EST :NUMBER2 [PRINT "
    PRINT [THAT'S IT EXACTLY!]
    STOP]
 ESTIMATE.2
END
```

ESTIMATE	Terrapin version

```
TO ESTIMATE
 RANDOMIZE
 NODRAW
 MAKE "NUMBER1 RANDOM 100
 MAKE "NUMBER2 RANDOM 100
 MAKE "NUMBER3 :NUMBER1 *
    :NUMBER2
 ESTIMATE.2
END

TO ESTIMATE.2
 PRINT "
```

```
PRINT ( SENTENCE :NUMBER1 [* N =]
    :NUMBER3 )
PRINT "
PRINT1 [WHAT IS YOUR ESTIMATE? >]
MAKE "EST FIRST REQUEST
PRINT "
PRINT ( SENTENCE :NUMBER1 "* :EST
    "= :NUMBER1 * :EST )
IF :EST = :NUMBER2 THEN PRINT "
    PRINT [THAT'S IT EXACTLY!]
    STOP
ESTIMATE.2
END
```

REFERENCES

ALDERMAN, D. L., SWINTON, S. S., & BRAS-
WELL, J. S. (1979). Assessing basic arithmetic skills and understanding across
curricula: Computer-assisted instruction
and compensatory education. *Journal of
Children's Mathematical Behavior, 2,* 3–28.

ARGANBRIGHT, D. E. (1985). *Mathematical application of electronic spreadsheets.* New
York: McGraw-Hill.

ATKINSON, M. L. (1984). Computer-assisted
instruction: Current state of the art. *Computers in the Schools, 1*(1), 91–99.

ATTISHA, M., & YAZDANI, M. (1983). A microcomputer based tutor for teaching arithmetic skills. *Instructional Science, 12,* 333–
342.

BAKER, E. L., HERMAN, J. L., & YEH, J. P.
(1981). Fun and games: Their contribution to basic skills instruction in elementary school. *American Educational Research
Journal, 18,* 83–92.

BAKER, F. B. (1978). *Computer managed instruction: Theory and practice.* Englewood Cliffs,
NJ: Educational Technology Publications.

BEHR, M. J., WACHSMUTH, I., POST, T. R., &
LESH, R. (1985). Order and equivalence
of rational numbers: A clinical teaching
experiment. *Journal for Research in Mathematics Education, 15,* 323–341.

BEHR, M. J., & WHEELER, M. M. (1981). The
calculator for concept formation: A clinical status study. *Journal for Research in
Mathematics Education, 12,* 323–338.

BEJAR, I. I., & SWINTON, S. S. (1984). *Videodiscs in elementary mathematics education: A
final report.* Princeton, NJ: Educational
Testing Service.

BILLSTEIN, R., LIBESKIND, S., & LOTT, J. W.
(1986). *Apple Logo: Programming and problem solving.* Menlo Park, CA: Benjamin-
Cummings.

BORK, A. (1982). Computers and learning:
Don't teach BASIC. *Educational Technology, 22*(4), 33–34.

BOZEMAN, W. C. (1978). Human factors considerations in the design of systems of
computer managed instruction. *AEDS
Journal, 11,* 89–96.

BRANSFORD, J., SHERWOOD, R., & HASSEL-
BRING, T. (1986). *Computers, videodiscs and
the teaching of thinking* (Learning Technology Center Technical Report No. 86.1.1).
Nashville, TN: Vanderbilt University.

BRIGHT, G. W. (1984a). Teaching estimation
of measurement through a microcomputer instructional game. *Proceedings of
the 25th International ADCIS Conference*
(pp. 71–74). Bellingham, WA: Association for the Development of Computer-
Based Systems.

BRIGHT, G. W. (1984b, April). *Use of microcomputer games to teach mathematics concepts.*
Paper presented at the meeting of the
National Council of Teachers of Mathematics, San Francisco.

BROWN, J. M. (1986–87). Spreadsheets in the
classroom. *The Computing Teacher,* pp.
8–12.

BROWN, J. S. (1983). Learning by doing revis-
ited for electronic learning environments. In M. A. White (Ed.), *The future of*

electronic learning (pp. 13–32). Hillsdale, NJ: Lawrence Erlbaum.

BRUNER, J. (1985). Models of the learner. *Educational Researcher, 14,* 5–8.

BURCH, F., & AARONSON, T. (1985, November/December). The rocky road to logical thinking. *Classroom Computer Learning,* pp. 41–45.

BURKHARDT, H., FRASER, R., & RIDGWAY, J. (1986). *The dynamics of curriculum change.* Unpublished paper, Shell Centre for Mathematical Education.

BURNS, P. K., & BOZEMAN, W. C. (1981). Computer-assisted instruction and mathematics achievement: Is there a relationship? *Educational Technology, 21,* 32–39.

CARMICHAEL, H. W., BURNETT, J. D., HIGGINSON, W. C., MOORE, B. G., & POLLARD, P. J. (1985). *Computers, children and classrooms: A multisite evaluation of the creative use of microcomputers by elementary school children.* Toronto, Ontario, Canada: Ministry of Education.

CARPENTER, T., et al. (1980). National assessment. In E. Fennema (Ed.), *Mathematics education research: Implications for the 80s.* Alexandria, VA: Association for Supervision and Curriculum Development.

CARTWRIGHT, G. F., & DEREVENSKY, J. L. (1976). An attitudinal research study of computer-assisted testing as a learning method. *Psychology in the Schools, 13,* 317–321.

CARVER, S. M., & KLAHR, D. (1986). Assessing children's Logo debugging skills with a formal model. *The Journal of Educational Computing Research, 2,* 487–525.

CHAMBERS, J. A., & SPRECHER, J. W. (1983). *Computer-assisted instruction.* Englewood Cliffs, NJ: Prentice-Hall.

CHANOINE, J. R. (1977). Learning of elementary students in an individualized mathematics program with a computer assisted management system. *Dissertation Abstracts International, 38,* 2626A.

CHARLES, R. I., & LESTER, F. K. (1984). An evaluation of a process-oriented instructional program in mathematical problem solving in grades 5 and 7. *Journal for Research in Mathematics Education, 15,* 15–34.

CLEMENTS, D. H. (1983). Programming, problem solving, and practice. *The Arithmetic Teacher, 31*(4), 32–35.

CLEMENTS, D. H. (1983–84). Supporting young children's Logo programming. *The Computing Teacher, 11*(5), 24–30.

CLEMENTS, D. H. (1984). Training effects on the development and generalization of Piagetian logical operations and knowl-edge of number. *Journal of Educational Psychology, 76,* 766–776.

CLEMENTS, D. H. (1985a). *Computers in early and primary education.* Englewood Cliffs, NJ: Prentice-Hall.

CLEMENTS, D. H. (1985b). Technological advances and the young child: Television and computers. In C. S. McLoughlin & D. F. Gullo (Eds.), *Young children in context: Impact of self, family, and society on development* (pp. 218–253). Springfield, IL: Charles C Thomas.

CLEMENTS, D. H. (1986a). Effects of Logo and CAI environments on cognition and creativity. *Journal of Educational Psychology, 78,* 309–318.

CLEMENTS, D. H. (1986b). Logo and the nature of learning. *Educational Horizons, 64,* 172–176.

CLEMENTS, D. H. (1986–87). Testudinal testimony. [Logo research column.] *Logo Exchange.*

CLEMENTS, D. H. (1987). Longitudinal study of the effects of Logo programming on cognitive abilities and achievement. *Journal of Educational Computing Research, 3,* 73–94.

CLEMENTS, D. H., & BATTISTA, M. T. (1986). Geometry and geometric measurement. *The Arithmetic Teacher, 33*(6), 29–32.

CLEMENTS, D. H., & BATTISTA, M. T. (1988). *Progress Report: The development of a logo-based elementary school geometry curriculum.* Project funded by the National Science Foundation. Buffalo, NY/Kent, OH. (NSF Grant No. MDR-8651668).

CLEMENTS, D. H., & MERRIMAN, S. L. (in press). Componential developments in Logo programming environments. In R. Mayer (Ed.), *Teaching and learning computer programming: Multiple research perspectives.*

COLLINS, A., & STEVENS, A. L. (1983). A cognitive theory of inquiry teaching. In C. M. Reigeluth (Ed.), *Instructional-design theories and models: An overview of their current status* (pp. 247–278). Hillsdale, NJ: Lawrence Erlbaum.

DAVIS, R. B. (1984). *Learning mathematics: The cognitive science approach to mathematics education.* Norwood, NJ: Ablex.

DEVAULT, M. V. (1981). Computers. In E. Fennema (Ed.), *Mathematics education research: Implications for the 80's.* Alexandria, VA: Association for Supervision and Curriculum Development.

DUGDALE, S. (1983, March). There's a green glob in your classroom. *Classroom Computer News,* pp. 40–43.

EDWARDS, J., NORTON, S., TAYLOR, S., WEISS,

M., & DUSSELDORP, R. (1975). How effective is CAI? A review of the research. *Educational Leadership, 33*, 147–153.

EPIE INSTITUTE. (1985). *T.E.S.S. the educational software selector.* New York: Teachers College Press.

FEURZEIG, W. (1987). Algebra slaves and agents in a Logo-based mathematics curriculum. In R. W. Lawler & M. Yazdani (Eds.), *Artificial intelligence and education:* Volume One (pp. 27–54). Norwood, NJ: Ablex.

FEURZEIG, W., & LUKAS, G. (1972). LOGO— A programming language for teaching mathematics. *Educational Technology, 12,* 39–46.

FLETCHER, J. D., SUPPES, P., & JAMISON, D. T. (1972). *A note on the effectiveness of computer-assisted instruction.* Stanford, CA: Stanford University. (ERIC Document Reproduction Service No. ED 071 450)

FORMAN, D. (1982, January). Search of the literature. *The Computing Teacher,* pp. 37–51.

FORMAN, G. (1986). Observations of young children solving problems with computers and robots. *Journal of Research in Childhood Education, 1,* 60–74.

GAGNE, R. M., WAGER, W., & ROJAS, A. (1981, September). Planning and authoring computer-assisted instruction lessons. *Educational Technology,* pp. 17–26.

GELMAN, R., & GALLISTEL, C. R. (1978). *The child's understanding of number.* Cambridge, MA: Harvard University Press.

GROEN, G., & RESNICK, L. B. (1977). Can preschool children invent addition algorithms? *Journal of Educational Psychology, 69,* 645–652.

HANSEN, V. P., & ZWENG, M. J. (Eds.). (1984). *Computers in mathematics education* (1984 Yearbook). Reston, VA: National Council of Teachers of Mathematics.

HARTLEY, S. S. (1978). Meta-analysis of the effects of individually paced instruction in mathematics (Doctoral dissertation, University of Colorado, 1977). *Dissertation Abstracts International, 38,* 4003A. (University Microfilms No. 77–29, 926)

HARVEY, G. (1985). *Computer science Logo style: Vol. 1.* Cambridge, MA: MIT Press.

HASTINGS, D. (1980, April). Pre-school math. *Microcomputing,* pp. 77–78.

HATIVA, N. (1984). Designing flexible software for the "electronic board." *AEDS Journal, 18*(1), 51–62.

HEDGES, W. D. (1980–81). Teaching first graders how a computer can sort. *The Computing Teacher, 8*(5), 24–25.

INHELDER, B., & PIAGET, J. (1969). *The early growth of logic in the child: Classification and seriation.* New York: W. W. Norton.

JANKE, R. (1984, October). *Microcomputer diagnosis for effective classroom applications.* Paper presented at the Educational Computer Consortium of Ohio Annual Conference.

KEARSLEY, G., HUNTER, B., & SEIDEL, R. J. (1983). Two decades of computer based instruction projects: What have we learned. *T.H.E. Journal, 10*(4), 88–96.

KELMAN, P., BARDIGE, A., CHOATE, J., HANIFY, G., RICHARDS, J., ROBERTS, N., WALTERS, J., & TORNROSE, M. K. (1983). *Computers in teaching mathematics.* Reading, MA: Addison-Wesley.

KNIGHT, C. W., & DUNKLEBERGER, G. E. (1977). The influence of computer-managed self-paced instruction on science attitudes of students. *Journal of Research in Science Teaching, 14,* 551–555.

KRAUS, W. H. (1981). Using a computer game to reinforce skills in addition basic facts in second grade. *Journal for Research in Mathematics Education, 12,* 152–155.

KULIK, C. C., KULIK, J., & BANGERT-DROWNS, R. L. (1984). *Effects of computer-based education of elementary school pupils.* Paper presented at the meeting of the American Educational Research Association, New Orleans.

KULL, J. A. (1986). Learning and Logo. In P. F. Campbell and G. G. Fein (Eds.), *Young children and microcomputers* (pp. 103–130). Englewood Cliffs, NJ: Prentice-Hall.

KULL, J. A., & COHEN, B. (n.d.). *Pre-Logo games.* Unpublished manuscript, University of New Hampshire, Durham, NH.

LERON, U. (1985, February). Logo today: Vision and reality. *The Computing Teacher, 12*(5), 26–32.

LIPSON, J. I. (1976, January). Hidden strengths of conventional instruction. *Arithmetic Teacher, 27*(5), 11–15.

LUEHRMANN, A. (1982, September). Don't feel bad about teaching BASIC. *Electronic Learning,* pp. 23–24.

LUEHRMANN, A. (1986, April). Spreadsheets: More than just finance. *The Computing Teacher, 13*(7), 24–28.

MALONE, T. W. (1981). Toward a theory of intrinsically motivating instruction. *Cognitive Science, 4,* 333–369.

MARTIN, K., & BEARDEN, D. (1985). *Mathematics and Logo.* Reston, VA: Reston.

MCCONNELL, B. B. (1983). *Evaluation of computer instruction in math. Pasco School Dis-*

trict (Final Report). Pasco, WA: Pasco School District 1. (ERIC Document Reproduction Service No. ED 235 959)

MCKINLEY, R. L., & RECKASE, M. D. (1980). Computer applications to ability testing. *AEDS Journal, 13,* 193–203.

MEVARECH, Z. R., & RICH, Y. (1985). Effects of computer-assisted mathematics instruction on disadvantaged pupils' cognitive and affective development. *Journal of Educational Research, 79*(1), 5–11.

MOISE, E. E. (1984). Mathematics, computation, and psychic intelligence. In V. P. Hansen & M. J. Zweng (Eds.). *Computers in mathematics education* (1984 Yearbook). Reston, VA: National Council of Teachers of Mathematics.

MOORE, M. (1984). *Geometry problems for Logo discoveries.* Palo Alto, CA: Creative Publications.

NATIONAL COUNCIL OF SUPERVISORS OF MATHEMATICS. (1977). National Council of Supervisors of Mathematics position paper on basic skills. *Arithmetic Teacher, 25*(1), 19–22.

NATIONAL COUNCIL OF TEACHERS OF MATHEMATICS. (1980). *An agenda for action: Recommendations for school mathematics of the 1980's.* Reston, VA: Author.

NIEMIEC, R. P., & WALBERG, H. J. (1984). Computers and achievement in the elementary schools. *Journal of Educational Computing Research, 1,* 435–440.

NITKO, A. J., & HSU, T. (1984). A comprehensive microcomputer system for classroom testing. *Journal of Educational Measurement, 21,* 377–390.

NOSS, R. (1984). *Children learning Logo programming* (Interim Report No. 2 of the Chiltern Logo Project). Hatfield, U.K.: Advisory Unit for Computer Based Education.

PAPERT, S. (1980). *Mindstorms: Children, computers, and powerful ideas.* New York: Basic Books.

PERKINS, D. N., & MARTIN, F. (1986). Fragile knowledge and neglected strategies in novice programmers. In E. Soloway & S. Iyengar (Eds), *Empirical studies of programmers.* Norwood, NJ: Ablex.

PIAGET J. (1970). *Science of education and the psychology of the child.* New York: Orion.

POGROW, S. (1986). *Pedagogical and curricular techniques for using computers to develop cognitive and social skills: An overview of the HOTS program.* Tucson, AZ: Thinking With Computers.

PRESSLEY, M. (1986). The relevance of the good strategy user model to the teaching of mathematics. *Educational Psychologist, 21,* 139–161.

REYS, R. E., RYBOLT, J. F., BESTGEN, B. J., & WYATT, J. W. (1982). Processes used by good computational estimators. *Journal for Research in Mathematics Education, 13,* 183–201.

RIEDESEL, C. A., & CLEMENTS, D. H. (1985). *Coping with computers in the elementary and middle schools.* Englewood Cliffs, NJ: Prentice-Hall.

RIORDON, T. (1982). Creating a Logo environment. *The Computing Teacher, 10*(3), 46–50.

ROBERTS, N., ANDERSEN, D. F., DEAL, R. M., GARET, M. S., & SHAFFER, W. A. (1983). *Introduction to computer simulation: The system dynamics approach.* Reading, MA: Addison-Wesley.

ROSS, S. M. (1984). *Matching the lesson to the student: Alternative adaptive designs for individualized learning systems.* Paper presented at the annual meeting of the American Educational Research Association, New Orleans.

ROWE, M. B. (1978). *Teaching science as a continuous inquiry* (2nd ed.). New York: McGraw-Hill.

SCANDURA, J. M., LOWERE, G. F., SCANDURA, A. M., & VENESKI, J. (1978). Using electronic calculators with children ages 5–7, four mini-experiments. *School Science and Mathematics, 78,* 545–552.

SCHOEN, H. L., FRIESEN, C. D., JARRETT, J. A., & URBATSCH, T. D. (1981). Instruction in estimating solutions of whole number computations. *Journal for Research in Mathematics Education, 12,* 165–178.

SHOENFELD, A. H. (1985). Metacognitive and epistemological issues in mathematical understanding. In E. A. Silver (Ed.), *Teaching and learning mathematical problem solving: Multiple research perspectives* (pp. 361–379). Hillsdale, NJ: Lawrence Erlbaum.

SHUELL, T. J., & LEE, C. Z. (1976). *Learning and instruction.* Monterey, CA: Brooks/Cole.

SHULT, D. L. (1981). Appendix C: A review of research of calculator effects on mathematical abilities. In D. Moursund, *Calculators in the classroom: With applications for elementary and middle school teachers.* New York: Wiley.

SHUMWAY, R. J., WHITE, A. L., WHEATLEY, G. H., REYS, R. E., COBURN, T. G., & SCHOEN, H. L. (1981). Initial effect of calculators in elementary school mathematics. *Journal for Research in Mathematics Education, 12,* 119–141.

SIEGEL, M. A., & MISSELT, A. L. (1984). Adaptive feedback and review paradigm for computer-based drills. *Journal of Educational Psychology, 76,* 310–317.

SKEMP, R. (1976). Relational understanding and instrumental understanding. *Mathematics Teaching, 77,* 20–26.

SLAVIN, R. E., & KARWEIT, N. L. (1984). Mastery learning and student teams: A factorial experiment in urban general mathematics classes. *Americal Educational Research Journal, 21,* 725–736.

SPUCK, D. W., & BOZEMAN, W. C. (1980). A design for the evaluation of management information systems. *AEDS Journal, 14,* 30–44.

STERNBERG, R. (1985). *Beyond IQ.* Cambridge: Cambridge University Press.

STERNS, P. H. (1986). Problem solving and the learning disabled: Looking for answers with computers. *Journal of Learning Disabilities, 19*(2), 116–120.

SUYDAM, M. N. (1982). Update on research on problem solving: Implication for classroom teaching. *Arithmetic Teacher, 29*(6), 56–60.

TAYLOR, R. (1980). *The computer in the school: Tutor, tool, tutee.* New York: Teachers College Press.

TENNYSON, R. D., CHRISTENSEN, D. L., & PARK, S. I. (1984). The Minnesota Adaptive Instructional System: An intelligent CBI system. *Journal of Computer-Based Instruction, 11,* 2–13.

THOMPSON, C. S., & VAN DE WALLE, J. (1985). Patterns and geometry with Logo. *Arithmetic Teacher, 32*(7), 6–13.

THOMPSON, P. W., & DREYFUS, T. (1988). Integers as transformations. *Journal for Research in Mathematics Education, 19,* 115–133.

THORNBURG, D. D. (1983). *Discovering Apple Logo.* Reading, MA: Addison-Wesley.

USISKIN, Z. (1983). One point of view: Arithematic in a calculator age. *Arithmetic Teacher, 30*(9), 2.

VANLEHN, K. (1981). *Bugs are not enough: Empirical studies of bugs, impasses and repairs in procedural skills.* Palo Alto, CA: Xerox Palo Alto Research Center.

VISONHALER, J. F., & BASS, R. K. (1972). A summary of ten major studies on CAI drill and practice. *Educational Technology, 12,* 29–32.

VON STEIN, J. H. (1982). An evaluation of the microcomputer as a facilitator of indirect learning for the kindergarten child. *Dissertation Abstract International, 43,* 72A. (University Microfilms No. DA8214463)

WATT, D. (1983). *Learning with Logo.* New York: Byte/McGraw-Hill.

WILKINS, P. W. (1975). The effects of computer assisted classroom management on the achievement and attitudes of eighth grade mathematics students. *Dissertation Abstracts International, 36,* 3379A.

INDEX